ISBN 978-1-332-80106-0
PIBN 10455727

Publications of the Prince Society

COLONIAL CURRENCY REPRINTS

VOLUME III

𝔓𝔲𝔟𝔩𝔦𝔠𝔞𝔱𝔦𝔬𝔫𝔰 𝔬𝔣 𝔱𝔥𝔢 𝔓𝔯𝔦𝔫𝔠𝔢 𝔖𝔬𝔠𝔦𝔢𝔱𝔶 ᴸᵛ

Eſtabliſhed May 25th, 1858

COLONIAL CURRENCY REPRINTS

𝕭𝖔𝖘𝖙𝖔𝖓

PRINTED FOR THE SOCIETY

BY JOHN WILSON AND SON

1911

TWO HUNDRED AND FIFTY COPIES

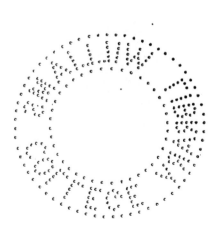

COLONIAL CURRENCY
REPRINTS

1682–1751

WITH AN INTRODUCTION AND NOTES

BY

ANDREW McFARLAND DAVIS, A. M.

VOL. III

𝔅𝔬𝔰𝔱𝔬𝔫

PUBLISHED BY THE PRINCE SOCIETY

1911

PREFATORY NOTE

HE following variations from the chronological list in Volume I are to be noted in the contents of this volume and in their arrangement: 1. The seventh newspaper extract in the group relating to the Merchants' Notes is ascribed in the chronological list to the New England Weekly Journal of March 11, 1734. The copy was actually taken from the Boston News Letter of March 7, the communication being the same in the two papers, and the differences being merely typographical. 2. The tenth of the newspaper extracts given at the beginning of this volume, that from the New England Weekly Journal of April 1, 1734, is an insertion which does not appear in the chronological list in Volume I, and which increases the total number of newspapers in this group from which quotations are taken, to eleven. 3. The two extracts from the New England Weekly Journal of January 1, 1740, which are inserted after the " Scheme for a paper currency," are also intruders, not to be found in the original list. 4. The " Discourse concerning the currencies," etc., the " Letter relating to a medium of trade," etc., the " Letter from a country gentleman at Boston," etc., and " An inquiry into thé nature and uses of money," etc., succeed each other in the foregoing order in the chronological list in Volume I. The " Letter relating to a medium of trade,"

etc., should have preceded the " Discourse " in that list, and
the " Inquiry," etc., should have preceded the " Letter from
a country gentleman," etc. The " Inquiry " is a lengthy
pamphlet, and the exigencies of the make up of the volumes
compelled its inclusion in Volume III, at the expense of
displacing the " Letter relating to a medium of trade," etc.,
from its proper chronological order. This, however, is un-
important as all of these pamphlets came out in rapid suc-
cession in the early part of the year 1740, so that a displace-
ment amounts to but little. As a compensation for this
violation of the chronological sequence it may be added that
it brings the " Inquiry " into its proper place in the discussion between the two authors, in direct touch with the
" Discourse." This will prove satisfactory to those who are
especially interested in the polemical contest of which these
pamphlets form a part.

My attention has been called by Mr. Worthington C.
Ford to a publication which he recently ran across in the
library of the Massachusetts Historical Society. It is
anonymous and has no imprint, but is dated March 1, 1733.
This must be accepted as Old Style since the pamphlet,
which is in the nature of a proposed act for the emission of
bills of public credit of a new form on loan, provides that the
first annual payment on the loans shall be made in 1735, thus
leaving it a fair inference that the bill was under consideration in 1734. The interest which attaches to this publication compels its reproduction. Since it is purely a legislative
document, being entirely without polemical character, it is
perhaps as well suited for this prefatory note as for a position in the pages of the volume. The following is the text
of the pamphlet:

PROPOSALS
Offered to Confideration,
WHEREIN
The Good of this Province is aimed at.

IT is Proposed, That an Act of this Government be Made and Pass'd in order to Ascertain and Establish the Value of Gold and Silver Money within this Province; That is to say, Silver Coin after the Rate of *Six Shillings* and *Eight Pence* per Ounce, Gold Coin after the Rate of *Five Pounds* per Ounce *Troy Weight*; And that all Debts, contracted from and after the time when said Act takes place, shall be understood to be payable in Silver or Gold Coin at the Rates aforesaid, or in Bills of Credit on this Province, of a New Form and Tenor at their Value therein express'd, (the making whereof to be Provided for by this Act) or in Bills of Credit of the Old Form and Tenor, *Twenty Shillings* thereof to be received as One Ounce of Silver, or *Six Shillings* and *Eight Pence* of the New Bills; But that all Debts, contracted before said Act commenceth, shall be understood to be Payable in Bills of Credit of the Old Form and Tenor according to their respective Denominations or express Value; or in Silver Coin after the Rate of *Twenty Shillings* per Ounce, or Gold Coin after the Rate of *Fifteen Pounds* per Ounce; or in Bills of Credit of the New Form and Tenor, *Six Shillings* and *Eight Pence* thereof to be received as in Value equal to *Twenty Shillings* of the Bills of the Old Form and Tenor.

It is then Proposed, That *One Hundred Thousand Pounds* in Bills of Credit be Made of a New Form and Tenor, and in Value equal to Silver at *Six Shillings* and *Eight Pence* per Ounce, or Gold after the Rate of *Five Pounds* per Ounce, to be redeemed by Silver or Gold at the same Rates at the Expiration of Ten Years: and that in the mean time, by an Act of the Government, said Bills be made fully sufficient to Pay all Debts whatsoever within this Province, contracted after the time when such Act shall take Place; excepting what the Borrowers hereafter mention'd shall oblige themselves from time to time to pay in Silver or Gold Money at the Rates before-mention'd for carrying on this Affair; And that *Six Shillings* and *Eight Pence* in Bills of Credit of the New Tenor, and *Twenty Shillings* in Bills of Credit of the Old Tenor, shall each of them be in Value equal to One Ounce of Silver, or One penny weight and eight Grains of Gold, and shall be so received for the Discharging of all Debts contracted before such Act shall take place.

One Hundred Thousand Pounds being Made of the Bills aforesaid; It is Proposed, That *Fifty Thousand Pounds* of it be delivered by the Makers to the Treasurer, and that by him they be distributed to the several Towns in the Province in proportion to their last Tax; and that Trustees be chosen by each Town respectively, to let it out on Interest at *Six* per Cent: The Income and Profit, arising by the Interest of the several Towns Parts and Proportions of the said Bills, may be as followeth, *viz. Four* per Cent thereof to be annually paid into the Publick Treasury for and towards discharging the publick Debts of the Province; the rest may be for the Use and Benefit of each Town respectively towards defreying any Charge, especially that which may arise in letting out of the said Bills.

The Funds for drawing in the said Bills for *Fifty Thousand Pounds* and the Interest, may be in the Years and manner following, *viz.*

Principal.   Interest.

l. 5000, Being One Tenth thereof, *Anno* 1735, with the Interest of *l.* 50,000, *l.* 2000.
l. 5000, Being One Tenth thereof, *Anno* 1736, with the Interest of *l.* 45,000, *l.* 1800.
l. 5000, Being One Tenth thereof, *Anno* 1737, with the Interest of *l.* 40,000, *l.* 1600.
l. 5000, Being One Tenth thereof, *Anno* 1738, with the Interest of *l.* 35,000, *l.* 1400.

l. 5000, Being One Tenth thereof, *Anno* 1739, with the Interest of *l.* 30,000, *l.* 1200.
l. 5000, Being One Tenth thereof, *Anno* 1740, with the Interest of *l.* 25,000, *l.* 1000.
l. 5000, Being One Tenth thereof, *Anno* 1741, with the Interest of *l.* 20,000, *l.* 800.
l. 5000, Being One Tenth thereof, *Anno* 1742, with the Interest of *l.* 15,000, *l.* 600.
l. 10000, Being Two Tenths thereof, *Anno* 1743, with the Interest of *l.* 10,000, *l.* 400.
_____
l. 50000.   The Sum arising for Interest, will be Gain to the Province,   *l.* 10,800.

The other *Fifty Thousand Pounds* may be deposited in the hands of Commissioners appointed by the Government, and by them let out to such Gentlemen in Trade, as will appear to borrow the same and oblige themselves to pay annually *One Hundred and Twenty Pounds* in Silver or Gold Money after the Rates aforesaid for each *Thousand Pounds* which they borrow for the Term of Ten Years; in which Time not only *Fifty Thousand Pounds*, the Sum first paid out in Bills, will be paid in Silver and Gold Money, but the *Twenty Pounds* annually paid by the borrowers over and above the tenth part of the Sum they first receiv'd, will amount to *Ten Thousand Pounds*; which Sum will also be gain to the Province.

As the publick Funds now stand there are to be brought in by Taxes *Twenty five Thousand Pounds* per annum, which in the term of Four Years will lessen the old Bills *One Hundred Thousand Pounds*; There being also *Five Thousand Pounds* per annum (parts of the Fifty Thousand lent to the Towns) to be paid into the Treasury, the first Four Years will amount to *Twenty Thousand Pounds*; and the Interest of the said four Years Payments to *Six Thousand and Eight Hundred Pounds*; the Sum Total of which will be *Twenty six Thousand and Eight Hundred Pounds*, and will lessen the Bills of the new Tenor that Sum; by which means the Bills that were passing in Trade of both the old and new Tenor will be so far diminished.

It is then proposed, that *One Hundred Thousand Pounds*, more in Bills of Credit of the same Tenor be made, redeemable as before at the Expiration of the aforesaid Ten Years: *Fifty Thousand Pounds*, one Moiety thereof may be distributed to the Towns in proportion and manner as the former: The Funds, to be laid for drawing in the same with Interest, may be in the Years and manner following, *viz.*

Principal.		Interest.
l. 10000, Being One Fifth thereof, *Anno* 1739, with the Interest of *l.* 50,000	*l.* 2000.
l. 10000, Being One Fifth thereof, *Anno* 1740, with the Interest of *l.* 40,000	*l.* 1600.
l. 10000, Being One Fifth thereof, *Anno* 1741, with the Interest of *l.* 30,000	*l.* 1200.
l. 10000, Being One Fifth thereof, *Anno* 1742, with the Interest of *l.* 20,000	*l.* 800.
l. 10000, Being One Fifth thereof, *Anno,* 1743, with the Interest of *l.* 10,000	*l.* 400.
l. 50000	Gain'd to the Province	*l.* 6000.

The other *Fifty Thousand Pounds*, or Moiety of the said Hundred Thousand Pounds, may also be deposited in the hands of the before-mentioned Commissioners, and be by them let out to such Gentlemen in Trade, as will appear to borrow the same, and oblige themselves to pay annually in Silver or Gold Money at the before-mentioned rates, *Two Hundred and twenty Pounds* per annum for each *Thousand Pounds* they borrow for the term of five years; in which Time not only the *Fifty Thousand Pounds* first let out in Bills of Credit will be paid in again in Silver and Gold Money, but the *Twenty Pounds*, annually paid by the Borrowers over and above the fifth part of the principal Sum they first receiv'd, will amount to *Five Thousand Pounds*; which Sum will also be gain to the Province.

If the foregoing Proposal be prosecuted, by the Year 1743, the two *Fifty Thousand Pounds* distributed to the several Towns will be wholly paid into the Treasury, and may then be consumed to Ashes: There will also be paid into the Treasury, for Interest of the two *Fifty Thousand Pounds* aforesaid, *Sixteen Thousand Eight Hundred Pounds*, which will belong to the Province: There will moreover by the Year 1743 be paid to the Commissioners in Silver and Gold Money by the Borrowers of the two Sums of *Fifty Thousand Pounds* the Sum of *One Hundred and fifteen Thousand Pounds*; which will be sufficient to redeem from the Possessors the Bills which were first of all let out: And there will be likewise a surplusage of Silver and Gold Money to the value of *Fifteen Thousand Pounds*, which Sum will also belong to the Province.

So that it appears, that in the space of Ten Years the Province may gain by the Towns for the two *Fifty Thousand Pounds* distributed to them, *Sixteen Thousand Eight Hundred Pounds* in Bills of Credit of the new Tenor; and also by the Borrowers of the two *Fifty Thousand Pounds* lent them the Sum of *Fifteen Thousand Pounds* in Silver and Gold Money, making in the whole *Thirty one Thousand Eight Hundred Pounds*, arising as here underneath, *viz.*

From the first *Fifty Thousand Pounds* Distributed to the Towns,   *l.* 10,800.
From the first *Fifty Thousand Pounds* Let out to Borrowers,   *l.* 10,000.
From the second *Fifty Thousand Pounds*, Distributed to the Towns, *l.* 6,000.
From the second *Fifty Thousand Pounds*, Let out to Borrowers,   *l.* 5,000.

l. 31,800.

Now this Sum of *Thirty one Thousand Eight Hundred Pounds* may be applied towards discharging the Debts of the Province; and that according to the difference between *Six Shillings & Eight pence* per Ounce the value of the new Bills, and *Twenty Shillings* per Ounce the value of the old Bills.

The said Sum of *Thirty one Thousand Eight Hundred Pounds* in new Bills, and in Silver and Gold Money, will be equal to *Ninety five Thousand Four Hundred Pounds*; and, being apply'd to that particular Use, may sink the Sum of *Ninety five Thousand Four Hundred Pounds* of the old Bills, and so discharge the Province of so much of its Debts.

There will then remain in the hands of the Commissioners *One Hundred Thousand Pounds* in Gold and Silver Money, which may be deliver'd out to the Possessors of the Bills; whereby the whole of the Bills will be drawn in, and there will remain extant in Lieu thereof *One Hundred Thousand Pounds* of Gold and Silver Money, after the rate of *Six Shillings and eight* pence per Ounce in Silver or Gold in proportion.

Boston, March 1*st.*
1733.

This " Proposal " is obviously one of a series of plans submitted about this time, the purpose of which was to secure relief from the depreciation of the bills of public credit. It was supposed that the trouble with the bills was that the statement on their face that they were in value equal to money was not explicit enough. It was therefore proposed to insert a price per ounce for silver, in which the bills were to be valued. These efforts to retrieve the currency, as they were generally termed, find record as early as 1724, crop out in 1728 and 1729, leave traces behind them in 1731 and 1732, and, as we see by this " Proposal," claim attention again in 1734. They also turn up in 1738 and 1739, after the adoption of the new tenor bill in 1737. Some of the proposed schemes are lost, but several of them have been preserved, and in these there is combined with the " fixed value in silver," the idea of giving the new bills circulation through loans to merchants who would agree to repay their borrowings in silver or gold. This would furnish the province treasury with coin, and if the process should be continued, resumption of specie payments might come. So also it was provided in most of them that the bills to be emitted should, like the bills in this " Proposal," be practically legal tenders. It will be observed that in addition to this the circulation of the bills proposed to be emitted in this scheme was provided for, simultaneously with those of the old tenor, by the establishment of a fixed ratio at which they should be received in trade, a feature which was also common.

In proposing a fixed rate for the silver in which the bills should be valued there were two methods which naturally suggested themselves, — one was to take the then current value of silver in province bills and merely hold the market steady at that stage of depreciation; the other was to take, either actually or approximately, the value of silver in the London market as the basis, in which case there would have to be provided a ratio at which the new bills and the old should circulate. The Jacob Wendell proposition in 1731 accepted the depreciation and proposed to emit bills valued in silver at seventeen shillings an ounce. In January, 1732, a scheme was submitted in which the interest on loans of bills of public credit was to be paid in silver at 8 *s* an ounce. This was reverting to the early part of the century, when silver was quotable for several years at this rate, during which time Governor Dudley wrote to the Lords of Trade that the assembly sought to rate silver at eight shillings an ounce, scarce fifteen pennyweight for six shillings.

The proclamation of Queen Anne, to which allusion is not infrequently made in these pamphlets, fixed the weight of the Spanish dollar which was to pass at 6 *s*, at 17½ dwt. The assembly of the province had, however, made the standard weight of the dollar which was at the basis of their currency 17 dwt. The rate per ounce for silver to be obtained from the proclamation was 6 *s* 10⅔ *d*, while that from the lawful money of the province was 7 *s* 0 *d* 3 *f*. The values for silver deducible from these different moneys, proclamation and lawful, are referred to by Vance in his "Inquiry," etc., page 44. Both of these values were based upon a London price of 5 *s* 2 *d* per ounce, the different results being caused by the different weights assigned the standard dollar.

The rate for silver in the new tenor notes was 6 *s* 8 *d* per ounce, while the proportionate value assigned to gold in those notes was £4 18 *s* per ounce. Besides the proposal which is printed in full in this note, there was another submitted in the fall of 1734, in which the price of silver was the same, but the proportionate rate for gold was given at £4 16 *s* per ounce. Turning to the proposal given herein, we find that with the same silver rate, the gold price is put at

£5 per ounce. The author of "Some observations on the scheme," etc., alludes to the fact that the gold was undervalued in the bills of the scheme which he was discussing in 1738, and comments on the same on the 22d page as follows: "Besides the other Things mentioned, The Proportion between Silver and Gold is not equal; for the Rate in the *Mother Country* (and Europe in general) ought to be ours; *i. e.* the pound *Troy* of *Silver* is made into 62 s. Sterling, and the pound *Troy* of *Gold* into 44 and a Half Guineas, which at 21 s *per Guinea* is 46 l. 14 s. 6. So that where Silver is put at 6 s. 8 d. Gold should be at 5 l. o s. 6 d. *per Oz.*" This value is so near that given in our proposal that it may be assumed that the author of the scheme regarded the 6 *d* as negligible and was merely trying to furnish a correct and practicable proportion.

The leaves of the "Proposal," etc., measure $10\frac{1}{2}$ by $7\frac{1}{4}$ inches. The general appearance of it leads to the suspicion that it was a government document. This opinion is strengthened by the fact that if the pamphlet be folded, as one would fold for filing away in a pigeon hole, there will be found on the back, printed across the upper end of the file, the words "Proposals for the good of the province."

The ownership of this particular copy is designated in these words: "Capt. Hutchinson's." This probably means Capt. Edward Hutchinson, a well known Boston citizen, a subscriber to the Merchants' Notes, and later the sponsor for the Silver Bank. Thomas Hutchinson, the father of the governor, was then in the council, and was on a committee that year, to which was referred the several schemes of this sort submitted for consideration, and reported a bill in November which failed of passage.

In "New news from Robinson Cruso's Island," etc., there is an allusion to "News from the North," the meaning of which is not clear. Mr. Albert Matthews came across a reference to the "North" in a contemporary Boston paper and kindly called my attention to it. I quote from his letter: "It [the reference] is in a letter printed in the issue "of March 26, 1722, which letter begins as follows:

To the Author of the New-England Courant.
Halt's Coffee-House, March 19.

SIR,

As we were reading over the Gazette this Morning we found a sublime Piece towards the Fag-End, which we were at first a little puzzel'd to understand; but when we observ'd it was tack'd to the Account of the Select-Men (and other Officers) newly chosen, we perceiv'd the Design of it, and concluded it came out of the *North.* No doubt the Author was very angry to find himself disappointed, after the great Pains he has taken to get in Select Men that would dance after his Pipe. However, we think he is very modest in comparing them, and the whole Town, to a Parcel of *Monkeys*, seeing it is not long since (in his Letter to his Friend at Portsmouth) he was pleased to call them *Dogs*, and *worse than the Monsters of Africa.* . . .

"Now 'New News' was written 'in a Letter to a Gentle-"man at Portsmouth,' and at II. 134 [of this series] we find "its author saying that the writer of 'a *venomous Epistle*' "has 'represented a *loyal* and *peaceable* People, as *Factious*, "and worse than the *Savage Monsters of Africa.*'"

We are unable to secure the contributory information which the article in the Gazette might furnish, since there is no copy of the Gazette of March 19, 1722, extant.

A. McF. D.

CAMBRIDGE, January, 1911.

TABLE OF CONTENTS

Contents

ILLUSTRATIONS

REPRINTS

H

THE

New-England *Weekly* JOURNAL.

NUMB. CCCL'VI.

Containing the moſt Remarkable Occurrences Foreign & Domeſtick.

MONDAY January 14. 1734.

Extract of a LETTER
To a GENTLEMAN
In a Neighbouring Government,
Concerning the New Notes of Hand.

SIR,

S to your Doubts about the Bills, called *the Merchants Notes of Hand,* I am ready to think they would in a great measure vanish, if you was fully appriz'd of the Circumstances of that Affair: and because I have a great Esteem for your Judgment, I will give you the best Account of it, I can.

You very well know, that for many Years past, Men of Tho't and Consideration, have been much concerned at the & miserable declining State of the Bills of Credit that have been the Currency among us; they knew, these were the Measures and Balances, by which Men dealt one with another, and that if they were uncertain and false, there must be Iniquity: Divers Weights and a false Balance have ever been an Abomination.

Accordingly, about Six Years ago, the General Court of this Province endeavoured to remedy this Evil, and to ascertain our Bills, by putting them upon a Foundation of intrinsic Value; but after much pains, the Scheme fell

through for want of Undertakers to import the Silver and
Gold. Something of this nature was revived in the Court
about two Years ago, and continued to be agitated till the
last Summer; but nothing was ever brought to perfection, -
or like to be so, at lest, not till after some considerable time ;
partly, because it was difficult to find particular Men that
were able and willing to take out the Bills and pay in Silver
and Gold in their stead, and partly by reason of an Instruction
from the Crown to the Governour, forbidding His Consent
to any Emission of Bills of Credit, unless for defreying the
charge of the Government, and then not for more than *l.*
30000.

While the *Massachusetts* were thus sensible of the common Calamity, and endeavouring some Relief, the Colony
of *Rhode-Island*, not only took no care to establish the Value
of the Bills they had before emitted, but went on, to put
forth new ones in great numbers, without giving the Possessors any satisfying account or assurance that they should
yield them what they took them for. This aggravated our
Misery, and vastly increas'd the discount upon our Bills:
For this Reason it was that several considerable Men for
some time refus'd to take the *Rhode-Island* Bills of the
l. 60000 Emission, that came out a little more than a Year
past; but hoping the *Massachusetts* would provide some
Remedy against this Evil for the future (for there was an
Act then depending in the General Court for establishing
the value of our Bills) and that *Rhode-Island* would take
warning by the Difficulties their Bills then met with, how
they Emitted more without putting them upon a good
footing, these Gentlemen accepted of them in common
Payment over a while. But instead of being more cautious,

contrary to the expectation of prudent Men, in about a Year
and half *Rhode-Island* agreed to Emit a much larger Sum,
the Sum of *l.* 104000, without taking any proper care to
ascertain their Value: As this was judged very unreasonable by many tho'tful & considerate Men in that Colony, so
it was very generally in the *Massachusetts*, for, beside the
want of proper care to keep them from sinking in their
Value, it was found upon the best inquiry that could be
made, that this small Colony had then out, more Bills, than
the *Massachusetts, New-Hampshire, Connecticut* and *New-
York*, all put together: This gave occasion to sundry Principal Merchants and others in *Boston*, sometime in *August*
last, to meet together and consider what might be proper to
be done to prevent so great and threatning a Mischief, as
such a large and sudden depreciation of our Money, would be,
which must necessarily follow upon this exorbitant Emission,
if it obtained Currency in common with other Bills. And
altho' I was not with them, yet from my knowledge of the
Men, their Sentiments, Circumstances & Interest, as well as
what I have often heard them say since, I verily believe this
was truly their Motive, and very generally their sole 'Aim;
that is, to agree upon something that might prevent the
Bills of Credit further sinking in their value ; to attain this
End, it was concluded absolutely necessary to prevent *Rhode-
Island's* multiplying their Bills upon us, or at lest their
Currency among us, it was judged very difficult, if not impossible to do this, unless the People were supplied with
some other and better Currency, at the same time that they
were told of the danger & loss of taking the *Rhode-Island*
Bills, for the *Rhode-Island l.* 104000 was just coming out,
and unwary People had order'd their Affairs so, as to

depend upon these Bills, poor as they were like to be, and the disappointment they would have been under, if there had been no Money of real value provided in their stead, would have made them warm Advocates for the *Rhode-Island l.* 104000, & paved the way for *Rhode-Island's* Emitting another *l.* 100,000 next Year, which was the Sum they intended annually to make, as was reported.

The State of the Case, the Company saw, was plainly this, either *Rhode-Island* must go on imposing their Bills upon us, especially the *l.* 104,000 just ready to rush in upon us like a torrent, or else there must be a quantity of other and better Bills provided for People immediately: Their choice and desire was very universally, that the Government should do it, but this they knew was impossible, at least, so soon as to stop *Rhode-Island* Bills Currency, before they got into this Province, and to stop them afterwards, would have been a great loss to our own People, more or less in proportion to what were got amongst us: The Government could do nothing, till the General Court got together; that was not to be till the latter end of *October;* when they were got together, it must take them some considerable time to digest such an Affair as this, and be in the several parts of the Legislature of a mind, and after this, there must be time to get particular Gentlemen to undertake to import the Silver and Gold to pay for the Bills they might take of the Government; this was like to be a Work of great difficulty and length of time, and if they might judge by two former Trials, hardly practicable at all: But after all this had been gone thro, if it could now have been got through, which it never could before; Application must have been made to His Majesty for liberty to the Governour to Consent to it, (for tho' such a Scheme for Emitting Bills of Credit would have been agreable to the spirit and end of the KING's Instruction to the Governour, which is to fix and ascertain the value of our Bills, yet it is directly against the words of the Instruction for the Governour to give his Consent so as to Ratify the Bill or Act without liberty from His Majesty) this would have raised a Dispute; and if we may judge of what will be, by what has been, the Act would have drop'd upon it; but supposing the Governour had been so good as to have sought for liberty himself, or that the Council and Representatives had agreed to pray for such a liberty, every body must be sensible it would have taken a considerable time, so long, that the *Rhode-Island* late Bills would have got into the Hands of the Inhabitants of this Province, and all thoughts been over of stopping their Currency, without making them a loss to our own People, insomuch that these Gentlemen had no choice, but to suffer themselves and others to be impos'd upon by *Rhode-Island* Bills, or give out their Notes of Hand as they did.

The Company therefore at their Meeting concluded upon these *Notes of Hand*, and that they should be Redeem'd with Silver or Gold, and appointed a Committee to draw up and methodize what they had discours'd of, against a further Meeting ordered to be a few days after, at which Meeting and sundry others following, they agreed that ten Men should sign the Notes, and be oblig'd to the Possessors for the Silver and Gold, and that the other Undertakers should be joyntly and severally bound to indemnify the Committee, & enable them punctually to pay the Notes according to their tenor; soon after this the Signers proceeded to prepare the *Notes of Hand*; but while they were in the midst of them the General Court thought proper to inquire into this Affair; and the Committee and Company chearfully laid before the General Court's Committee their Scheme, Securities, and whole Proceedings, who after considerable Deliberation, judg'd some alterations necessary in the Form of the Notes, and Reported accordingly; to which the Company agreed to conform their Notes, and thereupon directed all the Notes that were then sign'd, to be consum'd to Ashes, and that there should be new ones prepared exactly agreable to the Report of the Committee which was accepted by both Houses of the General Court, and these are the *Notes of Hand* you now see abroad.

This is a true and impartial Account of the Proceedings of the Gentlemen concerned in this Affair; and if the Event should be according to their sincere and main Design, to give us a more stable Medium, it must be a public Good. I know there are some very worthy Gentlemen, that have had Objections to this Undertaking, as

1. *That it is an Affair that should have been manag'd by the Government.* To this I answer,

That it must be granted, That if the Government could have done it, it had been best and as acceptable to the Gentlemen of this Company, as any others whatsoever; but as has been observed before, the Government have been upon it now for six Years, and nothing done; and in that time the Bills have fallen more than 20 *per Cent* and there was not any prospect of their doing it yet, for a considerable time at least; and long before the Government could have done it the *Rhode-Island* Bills would have obtained a Currency, and thereby have depreciated our Bills still a great deal more, so that Men of Interest in the Publick Bills, were driven into it, either to suffer *Rhode-Island* to pour *One Hundred Thousand Pounds* after another upon us, and thereby not only get from us our Substance for what cost them nothing but Pen Ink and Paper, but also lose from six to ten *per Cent.* per Annum in all the Money they had in Hand or due to them, or else they must themselves endeavour to withstand those *Rhode-Island* Bills, which they judg'd impractable without providing People with a better and more establish'd Currency: And Experience proves they were right in their Judgment, for with these *Notes of Hand* they are but just able to keep unwary People from being impos'd upon by the artifices used to put off these late *Rhode-Island* Bills, much less could they, if there had been no good Bills to have supply'd their Place: *Hungry Persons will be tempted to eat Trash, if they can't get wholesome Food.*

2. It is by some objected, *That perhaps these Bills or Merchants Notes will be multiplied upon us? What Security have we against it?* To this I would say,

If they are well and punctually paid, the Country can't be much injured, for the more Bills there are, the more Silver and Gold must be bro't into the Country and paid to the Possessors, and if they are not well paid the Signers of the Bills must go to Jail, and if they should put forth Bills there, few People will be tempted to take them, but there is all the certainty that there can be in humane Affairs, that they will be well paid; none who know the Circumstances of the Company can scruple their Ability to pay ten times the Sum, and it will be the Interest & Safety as well as Duty of the Ten Signers to compel them to it, which they have power also to do, or otherwise the Signers must pay all themselves, which if there should be necessity, they doubtless can do: But besides, it may be further observed, that as the Signers are Men of some considerable Substance, it will be their Interest, as well as other Men of Estates, not to increase Bills in such a manner as to depreciate them. But beyond all this, the precise Sum of *l.* 110,000 is to be Emitted, and no more, by the fundamental & unalterable Articles of the SCHEME, and all the Instruments and Securities are built upon it; nor can there be *one Shilling* more Emitted without contradicting them, and breach of the most solemn Agreement and Covenant under Hand & Seal, between the Signers of the Notes, and each individual Undertakers.

3. It is further objected, *that the Profit will be very large to the Undertakers.* To this I Reply.

This is no matter, if the Publick is profited at the same time, as, if our Medium become more fixt and stable, it will. But I am in great doubt their Profit is not like to be so large; and I am not alone in my Sentiments: One of my Neighbours I heard was desirous of some of these Notes, as I knew he was a Man likely to pay the Silver or Gold, I proposed to him to become an Undertaker; he told me he had considered the matter, and thought it would be more for his Interest to take it at *l* 6 *per Cent.* and pay in the same Bills, than to be obliged to pay the Silver with the addition the Scheme required to defrey the Charge of this Undertaking; for though the Possessor Receives but once in Three Years, yet the undertaker must pay in Silver or Gold, a tenth part of the Principal with an Addition of *Ten per Cent.* every Year, besides an extraordinary Penalty for neglect of Payment though but for a few days. But to come a little closer to the matter; the greater or less profit or loss of the Undertakers in this Scheme will turn upon their being able or unable to fix or retrieve the Credit of the Publick Bills: if, as some seem to think, the Publick Bills should notwithstanding sink to 23 *s* per Ounce for Silver, 't is evident the Undertakers must pay more than Six *per Cent.* Interest for what Bills they take out, for they pass from them now in common with other Bills, and other Men of equal Estates will be equally likely to possess these Notes, and get the Silver and Gold payable to redeem them, with the Undertakers; but if it be supposed that this Scheme should prevent the Province Bills sinking (which is the great design of it) yet when the Charge of this Undertaking is subducted, (which is far greater than Men not particularly acquainted, can imagine) their Profit will be little or nothing, so trifling, that the Scheme had never gone on, had it not been that this Company had considerable Sums due in the Publick Bills, which they were desirous to keep from sinking without bounds or end. And here I cannot omit observing how much it is the Interest, as well as profess'd Design of the Undertakers, to keep the Province Bills from sinking, and at par with these Notes; for besides, that they are generally considerable Creditors, and so for the sake of what is due to them, their Interest obliges them in common with other Men that have Province Bills due, to keep up their Credit, that their Estates may n't grow worse: I say, besides this, their Interest as Undertakers calls upon them also, for they pass these Notes in common with Province Bills, and must with these Notes and Province Bills, purchase Silver and Gold, or something that they must send abroad for the Silver & Gold, and for ten Years successively must pay in the Silver & Gold for them at the Price they are now set at; if therefore the Province Bills which they now máke equal with these Notes, they don't keep so, they will be as Undertakers, just so much losers, as the Province Bills fall below them, which loss they will save, if they can keep the Province Bills equal with them, which they trust they can and shall, if nothing extraordinary shall happen: 't is plain, it will be their great Interest and Endeavour to do so.

4. It is objected by some, *That the Indorsement of Mr. Clarke's Name on the back of the Bills, is unnecessary, if not dangerous to the Possessor.*

To this I would only say, that it was done peculiarly to secure to the Possessor, upon the Advice of the best & ablest Gentlemen of the Law, & he was more particularly described as to his Residence & Occupation, upon the judgment of both Houses of the General Court, and it is according to the common course of Negotiable Notes of Hand: the Possessors may arrest Mr. *Clarke*, or all, or any one of the Signers at their own choice, if they are not punctually paid according to the Tenour of every Note they have, and accordingly the Signers have given Bond to Mr. *Clarke* for his Indemnification.

5. Some object, *That the Possessors have no assurance of the Security the Signers Receive from the other Undertakers, as to the Bills they take out.* To this, I Reply,

It is not material whether the Possessors know this or not *Provided*, they have good assurance, that the Signers themselves, are able to pay these Notes, and that the Possessors can at their own pleasure compel them in the Law to make them good; now as to the Ability of the Signers, their Circumstances are so well known, that there can be no doubt made, but that if they were put upon it, they could pay them; and as to the Power of the Possessors to force them to it, I am so well acquainted with the Signers, that I dare say, if any body could tell them, how they could make these *Notes of Hand* more Authentick and Obligatory upon themselves, they would readily come into; for it has been their great and constant care to make them as certain and unfailing to the Possessors as possible; but to answer directly, they have the best of Security, either Real or Personal from the Undertakers, where it is Real, the Signers have viewed it themselves, and have taken it at but half the Value exclusive of Buildings, or whatever is subject to Destruction by Fire: where it is Personal it has been a Principal, with two Suretys well known to the Signers, as to their Circumstances; and the nature of the Obligations is such, That if the Undertakers should be negligent, there are enough will readily pay what is due from them, to the Committee or Company, and here it may not be amiss to observe, That as the Signers are by the Notes obliged to make them good to the Possessors, it has been their interest as well as duty to take the utmost care that the Security be as unfailing as possible, and besides the Bonds or Mortgages from each Undertaker, there is a Covenant also Interchangeably Sign'd, whereby each Undertaker is bound to make good all deficiencies, and to give better and further security if demanded.

6. But it is further objected by some, *That it is manifest this Emission tends to depreciate our Bills, because Goods are risen upon it already, and Silver is got to 22 s. per Ounce.* To this I would say,

I have enquir'd of the most knowing in these Affairs, and they tell me, that it is a mistake, and that Goods are not Risen since these Bills came out, they say, that some sorts of Goods, particularly Garlicks, Muslins, and some few others are high, but that they have been so, by reason of their great scarcity, for good part of the Summer, and that they gave as dear for them, before these Bills were Emitted or thought of, as they have since; and that some sorts of Goods, particularly *Yorkshire* Broadcloths are considerably cheaper, Shalloons full as Cheap or rather Cheaper than they have been these two Years; as to the Price of Silver there were a great many Ships Loading for *London* this Fall, and Oyl and Bone, the great Returns falling very short, Men that were under Obligation to make Returns, must make them in something, upon this Silver has Risen this Fall *six pence* or *twelve pence* an Ounce, but in this too, the New *Rhode-Island* Bills had a great hand, for as there came in considerable Silver there, Men that had Debts owing there, were glad to take them in Silver at this Price rather than to take or keep their new Bills : but after all, upon supposition, That so many Bills coming out at once, should have some such influence for a little while, it is manifest they cannot go on to do, this as other Bills have, because they can never grow worse, but must grow better, the longer they are kept; which cannot be said of the Bills that have generally pass'd among us, and we shall have the interest of this Company, who have a great share in our Trade and Commerce, to keep our Province Bills with them; I will say no more upon this head, but only pray every. Man that is at all acquainted with the Circumstances of this Country, to ask himself this plain Question, *Whether, if these* Notes of

Hand for Silver and Gold, *had not been put out, but the* Rhode-Island One Hundred and Four Thousand Pounds *had pass'd Currantly, and they had gone on putting forth such Bills, Goods and Silver and every thing else had not Risen vastly more?*

Thus I have truly and faithfully given you my Thoughts upon this extraordinary Affair, so far as I am acquainted with it, and I have taken all the pains I well could to understand it, as much as my Leisure and Capacity would allow me, and I don't at all wonder, that there are some, not well satisfied about it, that was my Case at first, but the Circumstances of it are such, that the longer I have tho't of it, the more I have seen it's necessity, and can't but hope, that we shall all feel the benefit thereof: I would not flatter or complement the Men concerned in it, and therefore tho' it has been much in my mind, I have said nothing about their Character; but as they are generally Men of Interest in this Country, Lovers of Peace, and Encouragers of good Order, and disposed to submit to Government, and to strengthen the Hands of those that are in Government, it has had great weight with me, and so I believe it will with you, and therefore I thought I was bound in justice to say it, as you are personally acquainted with but very few of them.

I am SIR, *&c.*

P. S You will see several particulars I have mention'd and Referr'd to, more fully, when the Scheme or Fundamentals of this Affair, are Printed, which I understand is design'd very speedily.

NOTE TO "EXTRACT OF A LETTER TO A GENTLEMAN IN A NEIGHBOURING GOVERNMENT, CONCERNING THE NEW NOTES OF HAND" PUBLISHED IN THE NEW ENGLAND WEEKLY JOURNAL OF JANUARY 14, 1734.

There are three copies of this number of the New England Weekly Journal known to have been preserved. One is in the Boston Public Library, one in the possession of the Bostonian Society, and one in the library of the Massachusetts Historical Society. The copy made use of for this reprint is that of the Massachusetts Historical Society, although it was found necessary to supplement certain defects by comparison with the number in the Boston Public Library.

The communication was published for the purpose of justifying the Boston merchants in their action in organizing a company and emitting the notes known as Merchants' Notes, in 1733. The object of the merchants was to prevent the circulation of an emission of Rhode Island bills, which had been put forth to fill the vacancy in the circulating medium of Massachusetts Bay, caused by the enforcement of the royal instruction ordering all the outstanding Massachusetts bills to be called in according to the terms of their emission, and limiting new bills to emissions for current expenses, £30,000 being the maximum amount authorized to be in circulation at any one time. To a certain extent the merchants were working along the same line as the Rhode Island assembly. Both thought that there must be some provision made to fill the impending reduction in the circulating medium of the province, and both realized that the limit of province bills permitted to be in circulation was utterly inadequate. The merchants distrusted the Rhode Island bills of which there was then in circulation an amount stated by the author of this communication to have been greater than the bills of Massachusetts, New Hampshire, Connecticut and New York all put together. There were inherent difficulties in the scheme of the merchants which would have prevented it from accomplishing all that the undertakers were after, but these weaknesses were never put to a test. The success of the experiment was absolutely dependent upon the maintenance of the boycott of the Rhode Island bills, to which signers of the merchants' scheme had agreed. The free circulation of these bills among the people of the province made the situation too difficult for the merchants; the boycott was violated and the scheme collapsed.

The writer of the " Letter to a Gentleman " refers to an effort on the part of the general court of the province "to ascertain our Bills, by putting them upon a Foundation of intrinsic Value," which he says " fell through for want of Undertakers to import the Silver and Gold." There was a committee of the general court appointed in February, 1728,[1] " to receive and consider in the recess of the court any scheme for retrieving the value of the bills of credit or for making a suitable provision for a medium of trade, and this committee was authorized to take subscriptions of any persons for the fulfilment of such scheme or schemes, and make report therein." A bill of the same import as the indicated functions of the committee was introduced in the assembly, December 20, 1729.[2] What the scheme then proposed may have been is not known, but taking the language of the writer of this communication to the Weekly Journal into consideration, it may well be believed that it corresponded with the plan proposed by the author of " A letter to a member of the honourable house of representatives," etc., a pamphlet published in 1736.[3] This was in effect that the province should emit bills, the value of which should be expressed in a fixed rate of silver, which bills were to be loaned to merchants who should repay the loans in gold and silver. Attempts were actually made to secure subscriptions to loans of this description in 1738 and again in 1739. The one in 1738 came near success, but not enough subscriptions could be secured to make a trial of the plan.

The reference to "something of this nature " which was "revived in the court about two years ago" which follows that to the proceedings of six years ago, can only relate to the petition of Jacob

---

[1] Massachusetts Court Records, Vol. XIV, pp. 47, 48.
[2] Currency and Banking in Massachusetts Bay, Vol. I, pp. 84–85.
[3] Reprinted in a " Search for a pamphlet by Governor Hutchinson." Proceedings Massachusetts Historical Society, February, 1899.

Wendell and others, merchants of Boston, originally presented to the general court, March 15, 1730–31, in which they asked the court to emit fifty thousand pounds, in bills of a new form to be loaned to merchants and others, on real security at fifty per cent of the valuation, the loan to be repaid to the province treasury one fifth part each year for five years, the silver rate being fixed in the proposed transaction at seventeen shillings per ounce. A bill was prepared to carry out the wish of the petitioners and was duly passed, but it is certain that it never became a law, and it probably may be identified with a bill to which the governor refused his assent in July, 1731.[1] Apparently the same process was gone through with in the following January and February.

Certain details are given in this communication to the Journal, concerning the organization of the Boston merchants in 1733, for the purpose of emitting the Merchants' Notes. The full story of this transaction is told in the Proceedings of the Massachusetts Historical Society for April, 1903.

It will be noted that, at the date of this letter, January 14, 1733–34, the scheme of the merchants had not yet been printed. It was, however, printed in the Journal just one week thereafter. A word may perhaps be properly said in this connection in regard to certain peculiarities of the notes which were emitted by the merchants in 1733. The intention of the promoters was to furnish a more stable currency, and this was accomplished by making the notes payable in given weights of silver and gold, the values being stated on the basis of the then current prices of those metals. It was further hoped that the furnishing of this large amount of the precious metals by way of redemption of the notes might facilitate a return to specie payments. It was evident that the gathering in at one time of so large a sum of coin as was represented by the total amount of notes emitted might create serious complications. To avoid this the prudence of the promoters of the scheme led them to propose that the redemptions should take place at three periods. The agreement was to run for ten years. The notes were also for ten years, but they were payable in three instalments,

[1] Currency and Banking in Massachusetts Bay, Vol. I, pp. 117, 118.

three tenths in three years, three tenths in six years, and the balance in ten years. Each note was drawn with the payments on the instalment plan expressed on its face, and it is evident that reissues were contemplated when the first and second instalments should be paid. The instalment feature of the notes has proved to be a stumbling block for writers in their attempts at describing them. In the Weekly Journal of September 17, 1733, and in the News Letter of September 20, 1733, they were described as payable "three tenths at the end of the first three years, three sevenths at the end of the first six years and the rest at the end of ten years." The intention was to say "three sevenths of the remainder at the end of the first six years," and this language was actually used in some of the contemporary accounts. Hutchinson described them as payable one tenth annually.[1] In the "Essay concerning silver and paper currencies" etc., Douglass says, in speaking of the value of the notes in 1739, "3 7ths of them paid off." With the full knowledge of the fact that these errors had been committed, I myself described them in the introduction to "A scheme for a paper currency," etc.,[2] as payable "three sevenths at the end of three years, three sevenths at the end of six years and the balance at the end of ten years," and these absurd fractions escaped the notice of all those who supervised the proofs of that volume.

[1] History of Massachusetts (1798), Vol. II, p. 341. A somewhat similar error was made in a communication to the Weekly News Letter, March 7, 1734, where the Merchants' Notes are described as payable to the possessors in ten years, at three short periods, "by one third Part at the End of each Period." See *post*, p. 82.

[2] Fifth Publication, Club for Colonial Reprints, of Providence, Rhode Island, p. xxviii.

THE   NUMB. CCCLVIII.

New-England *Weekly* JOURNAL.

Containing the moſt Remarkable Occurrences Foreign & Domeſtick.

MONDAY February 4. 1734.

To the Publisher of the WEEKLY JOURNAL.

SIR,

IF you will please to give the Public a few Tho'ts that I now send you referring to its Money and Trade, *I cannot but think that the Sentiments of many concerning them will be rectified.*

F the *Weights and Measures* of a Government were liable to Change and uncertain, endless Disorders and Confusion would arise in it. But, alas! these Disorders, which however all Wise Governments have taken effectual Care to prevent by the best Regulations, are not to be compared with those *greater ones*, arising from the Want of the good and only Measure of other Things, that is to say, from the Want of Money *well regulated and established.*

Money well regulated and established is the Measure of all other Things: If therefore *this*, which is the Measure of all other Things, be lost, it is no wonder at all if *the Price & Value of Things* be confounded: For how indeed, when Money is uncertain & consequently unlawful, as the present current Money of this Government is; how, I say, can we talk and judge aright of the Price and Value of Things in reference to regular and lawful Money, which is adjusted and kept to an unvarying Standard?

Every one knows, that *Money* is necessary for the carrying on of Trade : And common Experience has convinced us of this Government that where *Money* fails we cannot well buy. 'T is true *Credit* may supply the Defect of it to some small Degree for a little while. But what is *Credit?* It is only *the Expectation of Money* within some certain limited time : If therefore the Money is not to be had at the end of the term prefixed, What must become of the *Credit?* It must necessarily and inevitably sink : Nor will ever so many Acts at all avail to Support it.

The judicious Mr. LOCKE has irresistably prov'd, that *Silver is the Measure of Commerce by its Quantity,* by which its intrinsic Value is to be measured; and that *this Quantity is the Measure of the Value of all other Things*.

Many indeed, and it may be said most Men, think, that *this Measure of Commerce is entirely Arbitrary*: So that, according to the Pleasure of any Government, the *Names* belonging to this Measure may be varied ; as for Example, a *Shilling* may be called a *Crown*: But this is a very great Mistake: For this is the Instrument and Measure of Commerce in other Things; and it passes from Buyer to Seller, as being *in Quantity* equal to the Things that are Sold: So that it not only *Measures the Value* of the Commodities which it purchases, but is *given in Exchange* for them, as being of *equal Value with respect to its Quantity*: And therefore it is, that every one, who proposes to get as much as he can by the Goods that he vends, *Measures the Value of the said Goods by the Quantity of Silver* which he gets in Exchange for them, and by nothing else, as the aforesaid Author wisely Observes: For Men do not bargain for *Denominations and Sounds*, but for *intrinsic Value* or a *warranted Quantity of Silver*: And it is only by *having a greater Quantity of Silver* that Men grow rich: They may value themselves as much as they please upon their Estates; but, unless there be that *real Quantity of Silver* to be found which they imagine themselves to be worth, they will be greatly deceiv'd when they have Occasion of their Money; for, instead of *Substance*, they will only find *an Unmeaning Denomination*.

It belongs to the Government only, *to ascertain the Quantity of Money* by a public Mark: And, whereas, as was hinted before, it is confidently asserted by some, that the Publick by its Mark may declare a *Shilling* to be a *Crown*, it must be confessed that so the Public may: But still this Declaration, *not adding any intrinsic Worth to the Silver or Paper* in Lieu of it, is only *an Imposition upon the Subject*: For, while the Subject expects *a real Quantity of Silver*, or what is in Reality equal to it, he *receives only a nominal, not an intrinsic, Value*.

The Quantity of Silver being ascertain'd and the Standard settled by the Government, as it undoubtedly ought to be, there should *never be any Alteration of it*, until there be an absolute Necessity of such a Change; which there never can be, if it be *properly regulated and establish'd*, as the celebrated Author above-mention'd is of Opinion: And the Reason is, as I remember he gives it; because the Public is *Guarantee for the Performance of all legal Contracts; but Men are absolved from the Performance of all legal Contracts, if the Quantity of Money or Silver be under settled and the legal Denominations be altered.*

The *Raising of Coin and the Making of Money* in any Government ignorant & inconsiderate People are very fond of. But who is there that considers, that it is only *the*

Quantity of Silver in any Coin or Bill which is and eternally will be the Measure of its Value. For we may with as much Reason hope to lengthen a *Foot* by dividing it into *twenty four Parts* instead of *twelve* & calling them *Inches*; as *encrease the Value of Silver in a Shilling* by splitting the same into twenty four instead of twelve Parts & calling them so many Pence: This therefore may firmly be depended on, that if there be *any Variation from the Quantity of Silver* in any Emission of Money, it may *serve some present Occasion, but will prove a mere Trick in the Issue, and that always with Loss to the Country where the Trick is play'd.*

It is by this Means, that this Government is fallen into its Present unhappy Circumstances: Our worthy Predecessors, with proper Deference to their Names and Merits be it spoken, were very much to blame, that, when they assured the Subjects of this Government of a *certain Quantity if Silver* to be given and received under fix'd Denominations, they *did not lay a sure Foundation for the Payment of that Quantity of Silver;* the not laying of which has been the fruitful Source of our Mis-fortunes.

The fatal Effects of the *Depreciation of our present nominal Money*; Which I call *nominal*, in order to distinguish it from *such* as has a solid Foundation, even *an invariable Quantity of Silver*; The fatal Effects of this are many: These are some of them, that *the Prices of Things* are by means of this at the utmost Disorder & Confusion; that the *Landlord and Creditor* are defrauded of what they contracted for and is their just Due, because their *Tenants and Debtors* Pay considerably less Silver than what was at the time of Bargaining agreed for; that many *Widows and*

Orphans, whose Revenues were competent and equal to their Support, can now scarcely subsist with them; that the poor *Country Ministers* have not the Salaries which by Contract is their Due; that the *Day Labourer* has not his full Wages; and, in fine, that many *Officers* in the Service of the Government have scanty and miserable Allowances in Comparison with what they had formerly: These are a few of the innumerable Mischiefs, which have fallen out in this Government *thro' the Want of a good Regulation and an invariable Establishment of Money*; Or, in one Word, because we have *no lawful Money* among us.

But, as by these means we are now fal'n into such deplorable Circumstances, it must surely belong to the Government to bring us out of them and set us to Rights again: Private Gentlemen may, associate and form themselves into a *Bank*, emit Bills of their own and ascertain the Value of their Bills and the Rate at which they shall be taken in the Government: But such a Method of Proceeding, will be far from redressing our Grievances.

Would it not therefore be much better, if a Scheme were put in Execution by the Government, whereby the *Value of the Bills of Credit may be ascertain'd and establish'd*, and full Provision be made for their being duely paid off in Gold and Silver Money at a certain Rate and Time prefix'd; and likewise *a large Proportion of the public Debts of the Province may be discharged*, and in Consequence of this its *Inhabitants may be relieved* from the Burthen of so great a Proportion of Taxes; and, not only so, but *the Value of Money within this Province may be fix'd for Futurity*, at a Rate in no wise disagreeing from the Act of Parliament made and pass'd in the *Sixth* Year of Queen *Anne*, ascertaining the

Rates of Foreign Coin in her Majesty's Plantations in
America, which is to be found in our *Law-Book*, p. 194. &c.
and, in a Word, by which all this may be *done in a just and
legal Manner under the wise Conduct and Authority of His
Majesty's Government*: I say, would it not be much better
if *such a Scheme were put in Practice?* And must not such
a Scheme be *esteemed of much greater Advantage to the
Province*, than any other Scheme whatsoever?

*Si quid novisti rectius istis,
Candidus imperti: si non, his utere mecum.*

NOTE TO COMMUNICATION ADDRESSED "TO THE PUB-
LISHER OF THE WEEKLY JOURNAL" OF FEBRUARY 4, 1734.

Mr. E. M. Barton, librarian emeritus of the American Antiquarian
Society, informs me that a manuscript copy of this communication
in possession of that society is apparently in the handwriting of
Samuel Mather. It is endorsed in the handwriting of Isaiah Thomas,
"Essay on Money and Trade, written for the Rehearsal, a weekly
journal published in Boston, 1733 to 1735." To this C. C. Baldwin,
a former librarian of the Society, has added "by Rev. Sam. Mather."
Reference to the manuscript was made in the Council Report of
the Antiquarian Society in April, 1903, and it is stated that a careful but unsuccessful search was made in the file of the Rehearsal
in possession of that Society for the published paper. This file of
the Rehearsal is not complete, but about the time of this publication and for some time before and after there is no number missing.
It may be assumed that it was not published in the Rehearsal. It
was doubtless sent to both papers, was accepted by the Journal
and rejected by the Rehearsal. A few verbal changes from the
manuscript were made as it passed through the press and one or
two superfluous paragraphs were suppressed, but in the main the
published copy agrees with the manuscript at Worcester. The
copy was procured from the Massachusetts Historical Society.

It will be noticed that the number of this copy of the Journal is CCCLVIII while that of January 14 was CCCLVI. An inspection of the files shows that the copy issued January 21 was numbered CCCLVII. In the issue of January 28 this number was repeated. This will account for the number of the copy issued February 4, which obviously would have been three hundred and fifty-nine had the regular sequence of the numbers been applied to these issues.

B · THE NUMB. CCCLX.

New-England *Weekly* JOURNAL.

Containing the moſt Remarkable Occurrences Foreign & Domeſtick.

M O N D A Y February 18. 1 7 3 4.

A LETTER

From a Gentleman to his Friend.

SYR,

Since you have been pleas'd in a late Letter to signify to me, that you were at a stand whether to take or refuse the Merchants Notes in Payments; and at the same time to desire my Sentiments concerning them; and also Promise to govern your self by my Advice: I shall give it to you with the utmost Candour; but, lest you should think I determine rashly, I will *First* acquaint you with the Nature and profess'd Design of this Bank, and give you a short History of it from its very beginning, and *then* shew how much it comes short of answering the End propos'd.

The miserable Condition of our Province Bills, which have been gradually Sinking for several Years past, has been the cause of great Concern to many true Friends to their Country; every Man's Estate has been affected by it, and the number of those who have receiv'd benefit bears no proportion to those that have been injur'd. This has put several Persons upon Projecting Schemes from one time to another, which they thought might give us relief under our unhappy Circumstances; but, by some means or other, none of them were ever Prosecuted, until News was bro't us that our Neighbours at *Rhode-Island*, had Pass'd an Act *For the*

Emitting One Hundred *&* Four · Thousand Pounds *in Bills of Credit*, of the same Tenour with those which were before Current among us. This surpriz'd us all; and some of our Principal Merchants thought it high time to bestir themselves, and endeavour some way or other to prevent the inconveniencies that might thereby arise to us; for it has always been found, that upon a large Emission of Bills, the Credit of our Money has at once sunk very considerably. These Gentlemen met several times for this purpose, and at length each of them oblig'd himself to refuse the New *Rhode-Island* Bills in all Payments whatever; and, seeing we had not Current among us, Bills sufficient for a Medium in Trade; and it was not in the Power of the Government to make any more; they agreed to Emit the Sum of *One Hundred* and *Ten Thousand Pounds* in *Notes of Hand*, to be Exchang'd for Silver and Gold; the whole in Ten Years, but at Three several Periods. Most if not all of these Notes now pass current among us. I will not here, as some have done, Reflect upon the Gentlemen, and Charge them with having a regard to their own particular Interest, without any to that of the Publick, for I know you have no Pleasure from Ill-natur'd Reflections upon any Person or Parties; besides there is no scruple, that many of them sincerely aim'd at the Publick Good, and still think that this SCHEME will be a means of Promoting it; but, when I have shewn to you the various Defects in it, and they have seen the Event of it, I make no doubt we shall all have a different Opinion concerning it.

In the *First* place then I apprehend, that this Company has assum'd a Power that no ways belongs to it; it being indisputably the Government's right, and theirs only, to

Emit and Regulate the Money. This is allowed by some of the Bankers themselves; but, say they, we have several times apply'd to the Government for relief, and have not been able to procure any; *Must we therefore for ever continue under these miserable Circumstances?* I Answer, It would have been better to have continu'd as we were, than to have taken so indirect and unwarrantable a Method, in order to relieve us: The Disease was bad; but the Remedy, I think, is worse. It is besides very probable, that, if these Gentlemen had offer'd to Subscribe to the carrying on a Scheme somewhat of the Nature of this, to have been under the Direction and Management of the Government, it would have been engag'd in; and there is no doubt, that leave might have been obtain'd for his Excellency's Consenting to an Act for Emitting the Bills; for His Majesty's Instruction seems to have been occasion'd by the ill Effects which our making Money and suffering it to pass current, with only an imaginary value, has produc'd. Some object here, that, while this had been doing, *Rhode-Island* would have pour'd in a flood of Bills upon us; and, when they had once obtain'd a Currency, it would be difficult, if not impossible, to have stop'd them: But this Objection is of no validity; for the Merchants Notes have no tendency to put a stop to the New more than the Old *Rhode-Island* Bills, or those of the other Governments; and the only reason, why so few of the New Bills are now passing among us, is because so great a number of Men of Business have refus'd to receive them; and this their refusal would have had just the same Effect, if not one of their Notes had ever been extant.

But then,

Secondly, These Notes, passing at the same rate with the Bills which were before Current, have produc'd just the same ill Effect; as the multiplying those Bills would have done.   I observ'd to you before, that always, when a large quantity of Bills has been Emitted, the Credit of the whole has sunk, and the Price of all Commodities risen; and, that this has been the case with the present Emission, is plain from Experience; for the difference of Exchange between Sterling and our Currency, before the talk of this Bank, was ·but Two Hundred and Seventy *per Cent.* whereas it is now Three Hundred and Upwards, and the price of every thing is following it.   But this, they say, proceeds from the present difficulty of making returns to *England*, which Factors are oblig'd to do at any rate, or lose their Business; but I am certain, that, not only Factors, but those who Trade on their own Accompt, have given this Price for Bills of Exchange; which they would never have done, unless they knew the Price of the Goods they send for, must follow it, let Returns be ever so plenty when they arrive.   Others of the Bankers say, that, tho' their Notes now pass at the same rate with the Publick Bills, it can never hold so long; there must quickly be a difference made between them, and; if they continue Current, I am apt to think there will.

Then,

Thirdly, In the *third* place, What difficulty and con-fusion must it produce in our Trade to have two sorts of Money, of a different and uncertain value, Current at one and the same time?   How shall Bargains be made, or any kind of Business transacted?   All Debts, that by agreement are to be discharg'd by these Notes, must have some special Obligation for their Payment;   The difference between the two Currency's will be daily encreasing, and no body will be able to determine exactly what it is.

Fourthly, The last thing I shall take notice of is, That this Emission, instead of ascertaining and fixing the real Value of every just Debt, which ought to be the Principal End of a SCHEME of this Nature, has a tendency still further to sink the Value of them; for, while we have two sorts of Money of a different value, *one* with a real and intrinsick, the *other* only an imaginary one, People will daily esteem and be more fond of the one, and more convinc'd of the fallacy of the other, till it sinks almost to its primitive nothing.

These are some of the defects which appear to me in this SCHEME; and, in Friendship to you, I must advice you to be cautious of receiving any large Sum in these Notes, without a certainty of passing them to others immediately; for I have no scruple, that either our Legislature, or, if they neglect it, a Superior Power will quickly put a stop to their Currency.

It is meer trifling to say with some Gentlemen, that these are only *Notes of Hand*, and no Power upon Earth can hinder one Man from giving his Note to another: I will not differ with them about Words; nor do I think it signifies, Whether they call them *Money* or *Notes of Hand*: The Name does not change the Nature of the thing: They pass from one man to another, as a Medium of Trade, and this is the only intent and use that I know of Money; and, if these Persons may Emit *One Hundred Thousand Pounds*, another Sett may Emit another, till we have enough of this sort of Money to carry on the Business of the Province, or accomplish any other Design which the Emitters may engage in.

Thus, SYR, I have let you know my Opinion of this BANK, which has made so much noise in this part of the World. I wish all the ill Effects of it, with which our Dear Country seems to be threaten'd, may be diverted.

I *am*, &c.

NOTE TO " A LETTER FROM A GENTLEMAN TO HIS FRIEND," IN THE NEW ENGLAND WEEKLY JOURNAL OF FEBRUARY 18, 1734.

This is an attack on the Merchants' Notes, moderate in tone and well founded in the objections stated. The writer gives but little consideration to the other side of the question, the hopes and the expectations of the merchants who entered into the scheme, but perhaps this is just as well, since these hopes were not realized and the expectations were frustrated. His proposition that an increase of the currency raised prices was incontestable and his assertion that the Merchants' Notes were contributory causes for the rise at this period is undeniable.

The copy was procured from the Massachusetts Historical Society, certain defects in this number being cured through examination of the copy of the paper in the Boston Public Library.

THE
Weekly Rehearſal.

Numb. 125.

Monday, February 18. 1734.

A Letter from a Gentleman in Rhode-Island to his Friend in Boston.

SIR,

According to your Request, I shall now give you my Thoughts on the Value and Tendency of your Merchants' Notes of Hand, and satisfy your Doubts of the real Worth of our last Bank.

When the Reasons which influenced this Colony to make so large an Emission of Bills at this Juncture, their Usefulness and Advantage to the Country in general, and the sure Foundation they are emitted upon, are duly considered, it will, I doubt not, appear very Extraordinary to you, that any Persons in your Province, except the few professed Usurers, should at all hesitate about their Currency.

The whole Country complained loudly of the Difficulties we laboured under, for want of a sufficient Medium of Exchange; for the vast and swift Growth of the Country, the prodigious Increase of Trade, the annual Sinking of some of the first Banks in the several Governments, and the stopping of above Seventy Thousand Pounds in the Treasury at *Boston*, which ought to have been circulating among the People, had all of them together occasioned so great a Scarcity of the only Medium of Trade we had, that *That* was generally accounted the greatest Calamity of the Country.

The *Massachusetts* and *New-Hampshire* were forbid by the Royal Instructions to their Governour, to emit any more Bills, except to a trifling Sum. All the bold and repeated Attempts of the Assembly at *Boston*, for seven Years together, to evade those Instructions, or have them recalled and emit a sufficient Quantity of Bills, had been defeated and frustrated. *Connecticut* had in vain tried a private Bank, the Legislature there not suffering particular Men, tho' incorporate by Charter for Trade and Commerce, to emit their Negotiable Notes of Hand; which Projection a Gentleman of Eminence in the Legislature of the *Massachusetts* was Reported to have had a great Hand in putting an End to, as unsafe, and dangerous to the Liberties and Properties of the whole Country; so that every Body was ready to despond under this Melancholy Prospect.

It appeared then to *Persons of Thought and Consideration*, that the only Method to uphold the Trade and Business of the *whole Country*, was for some of the Governments not yet restrained from Home, to emit a sufficient Sum, that might pass among the People, while they were paying in and burning their old Bills, and till Silver and Gold could gradually fix among us. Our Government had no more Occasion or Need of such an Emission, than the neighboring Governments, nor did our Landed Men take greater Pleasure in involving and mortgaging their Estates, than others: But what was there elso to be done? *Connecticut* was all in Confusion, the *Massachusetts & New Hampshire* were restrained from Home, contrary to their *general Desire and Inclination* (which by the way proves, they judged a New Emission both *Necessary and Expedient* for the Good of the whole) It therefore remained only for this Colony to make this Emission. When this was agreed upon, our Assembly took all due Care to ascertain the Value of the Bills, as much as 'tis possible for a Paper Currency to be ascertained. They are lent as the Loans in the other Governments, on the best Land Security of double the Value, all Buildings excluded, and over and above as a collateral Security, there are Bonds taken for both Principal and Interest; so that it can be for no Body's Advantage to deceive the Country in the Value of the Estates mortgaged; and the whole Sum is to be paid in a shorter Period by three Years, than the first Banks; the Profits are appropriated to the Support of the Government, to the encouraging such Manufactures as are at Home allowed; and especially the furnishing with Cannon and Stores of War this Island, which in the last War was a Barrier to your Province, and the Safe-guard of your Coasting Trade, which it is to be feared will soon want the like Protection.

From this plain State of the Case, you can't but see how little Reason there is for the Aspersions so freely cast on the Legislature of this Colony, by the Author of the Letter in the Gazette of *January* the 14th past; you see how false and injurious it is to assert our New Bank cost us nothing but *Pen Ink* and *Paper*; you see also how trifling and delusory it is to assert, that we *had then out more Bills than the Massachusetts, New Hampshire, Connecticut and New York all put together.* Were the Assertion as true, as I doubt not it is groundless, yet it cou'd be no Damage to the Country in general, since we have pledged our Lands, and must purchase those Bills wherever they are lodged to redeem them. If it be suspected our Colony will make any *peculiar Advantage* by this (*which yet I doubt all Things*

considered is not like to be so great) I answer in the Words
of that Gentleman himself, *This is no Matter, if the Publick
is profited at the same Time.*   But whatever will be the
Effect of this Emission on us, who must procure and pay
it in, certainly it's Usefulness and Advantage to the Country
in general, is obvious to Persons of the meanest Capacity,
for thereby at our Risque and Venture, the Inhabitants of
your and the other Governments are furnished with a
proper Medium, and enabled to carry on Trade and Business, and keep it in a flourishing Condition, which must
otherwise decline and wither away.   And this Medium
supplying the Place of your Province Bills, you may the
more easily pay them in as they become due.

If it be further objected, that this Emission tends to
depreciate the former Bills, *because Goods are risen already,
and Silver is got to Twenty two Shillings per Oz. or more.*
I answer in the Words of the Writer above-mentioned, vindi-
cating their private Notes from the same Objection, to wit,
*In general it is a Mistake to affirm that Goods are risen, as the
most knowing in those Affairs* (who he doubtless thinks
are the Undertakers themselves) *do declare.*   As to the
Silver rising, this Gentleman unwarily blabs a great Truth,
which well considered, discovers to us the true Instrument
of all Misfortune from the Fall of the Publick Bills, and
does at once clear our Emissions.   *Persons*, says he, *that
are under obligation to make Returns* MUST *make them in
something* (hinc illae lacrymae) *and Bone and Oyl falling
very short this Fall, upon this Silver has risen six Pence or
twelve Pence an Ounce.*   By this we see that the original
and continued Means of the depreciating the Publick Bills,
is the Conduct of those Gentlemen, that are most clamorous

against us: For they have continually in their pressing Necessities for Returns, *out-bid one another*, for the Silver imported here from Time to Time; and the next Year *advanced* upon their Goods to the general Hurt of the whole Country. The Reason why any of the *Boston* Merchants have this Fall bid higher than others, and why *a certain Signer of the Private Notes out-bids the Rest*, is not to draw in the Debts from this Colony, for they have been and are still ready to give fresh Credit to those Traders they draw upon, but the true Reason is, *they must make Returns*, and as they pass with you their own Notes of Hand for three, six and ten Years Credit, they can really *afford* to give more for Silver than any other Persons.

The Fact is notorious, let them disguise it as they will, that notwithstanding our Emission of Sixty Thousand Pounds in 1731. our Bills have been for five Years near at Par, with as little Fluctuation almost as Silver and Gold suffer in Europe, and so had continued, but for the Reasons they have furnished us with; they do not indeed carry the specious Words, *Silver of Sterling Alloy, or Standard Gold*, yet are on the best Foundation possible; and being sanctioned by the Publick Faith, are better secured than by any Private Contracts whatever.

In Fine, we apprehend our selves doing a *Publick Service* to the whole Country, and tho' some *few Persons* had made a small Stick about taking our Sixty Thousand Pounds Emission, we tho't they had grown wiser by Experience, and that none would refuse these Bills, but such as were *waiting for what they esteemed the happy Advantage of Forty One.* And we judged that the Body of the Country would the sooner give them a Currency, out of a just Indignation of the unrighteous Designs of those Persons: Nor are we wholly deceived in our Expectations of the Event; and you Sir, I doubt not, and such as you, who have not by any *inconsiderate* Promise to *designing Men* shut your Hands, will follow the Example of such Gentlemen as gladly take our *New Bills*, finding they will *here*, which is the *Market*, purchase pure Silver and Gold at the same Rate with your *old Bills*, whilst the *Merchants Notes* won't purchase it at *any Rate at all*.

Let me now, Sir, consider the plausible and artificial Encomiums on the Private Notes, that are so industriously spread about the Country, and shew their *small and uncertain Value*; the almost *incredible Damage* they will do the *Body of the People* in your Province, and the vast and unequal Profit the Undertakers are like to make of them, if they are allowed to pass current throughout the whole Country.

Here then first of all pray observe, That the Gentlemen, who have appeared to defend and recommend this Scheme in the Prints, have declared upon *different and inconsistent Motives*: For the Gentleman who appeared in the Gazette *December* the 3d insinuates, that these Notes were designed to promote the Publick Good, by *preventing* the *Oppression* that is expected at the Year Forty One; which every Body knows must be by the RISE *of the Province Bills*: The Gentleman who writes *January* 14th, says, their Design was to serve the Publick, by *preventing the* FALL *of the Province Bills, and their being depreciated*. This Difference gives just Reason to suspect, that neither of them has told the true Aim and Design of the Scheme: And what makes this Suspicion the more just is, That as to the first, the Oppression feared, will be, as I shall presently shew, *infinitely increased* by this pernicious and destructive Scheme: And the last Pretence is a *mere Imposition on Common Sense, and evidently ridiculous.* For there was no Likelihood or even Possibility of the Province Bills falling in Value Now, but only by the Artifice of these pretended Upholders, but on the contrary, as the Periods at which the Funds are fixed, are now begun, or drawing very near, they must of Necessity soon begin to rise very fast in their intrinsick Value, and cease to be a Medium of Trade. And if I may be indulged so obvious a Conjecture, I should assign *this* as their *true* and *sole* Motive and View. For if these Undertakers, in Lieu of their private Notes, which can *never be worth more* than Silver at Nineteen Shillings *per* Ounce, but in Fact now are and ever will be, worth *much less*, can get into their Hands the *old Bills*, which will *soon be worth Silver at Eight Shillings per Ounce*, who sees not that they design, and certainly will make, an immense Gain, to the Ruin of Thousands whose Estates are Mortgaged for the Publick Bills, and can't be redeemed by these Notes of Hand, but by purchasing said publick Bills at almost *One Hundred and Fifty per Cent.* advance by the Year Forty One, of those very Men from whom they now receive these Notes of Hand *at Par.* Let the World now judge of these *Pretences* to a publick Spirit; and for further Light therein, if it were Necessary, I would observe with the Writer last mentioned, That after *much Pains the Scheme and Endeavours of your General Court have twice fell thro', within these Seven Years, for want of Undertakers* (of a publick Spirit) *to import Silver and Gold.* I would ask also, whether the Leaders of a certain Society have not for many

Years opposed the Emitting any more Publick Bills, and whether they have not got vast Estates by the Fluctuation of those Bills, of which Fluctuation they were the only Instruments. And is not this enough to alarm the Traders and Landholders of the Country, who must be *infatuated* to a strange Degree, to give any Currency to those Notes which are plainly designed for, and necessarily tend to, the Enriching the Undertakers, at the Expence and Ruin of the Rest of the Country?

It ought, I say, to *alarm* every *Landholder and Trader* in the Country, to see about Eighty *private Persons* at such a Conjuncture, making themselves Owners at once, *at no other Expence than Pen, Ink and Paper*, of One Hundred and ten Thousand Pounds, and thereby possess themselves of so much in the Publick Bills, by which they will gain so much at least as 110,000 of the Publick Bills will be worth more at Forty One, than they now pass at. This is so apparent already, that the only Method to prevent it, is for *other Persons* jointly or singly to emit such or more plausible Notes in their own Defence. And this the Writer *January* the 14th insinuates there can be *no Damage from hence, since every one's Notes will pass only as their Credit is*: Yet it is self-evident, that the *bare Attempt* to multiply such private Banks, will fling the whole Country into Convulsions and Ruin. It wou'd set up and promote that destructive and accursed Practice of *Stock-jobbing*, whereby all honest Industry wou'd be discouraged, and our Estates rendered wholly precarious, and at the Mercy of a *few Jobbers* of a greater Magnitude and Dexterity than others.

What Judgment shall we think the Gentleman so often mentioned forms of our Understanding, and what shall we form of his, who would smile in our Faces with an Insinuation, *That the Design, the Interest and the Labour of the Undertakers will be to keep the Province Bills from Sinking, and at Par with their Notes?* when he well knew Publick Bills are vastly better now, and in their own Nature must rise still higher without their Help; and that their apparent Interest and Design, as Undertakers, is to hurry on, and increase their Rise as soon and as high as possible, when their Notes are once *shoved out.*

But what surprises me still more, is the Effrontery of this Gentleman, who brings *The abominable Charge of divers Weights and a false Ballance* against the *Legislature* of our Colony and yours also, when he knew there was a Falsehood implied, and an absolute Deception in the very Face of the Notes he would recommend to the Publick. For who can imagine one Ounce of Silver to be paid Three, Six and Ten Years hence, can be worth *Nineteen Shillings* now in Hand in publick Bills, even abating their Necessary Rise? For admitting their Scheme meets with no overthrow from the *Royal Authority* or your *Legislature* (which I dare say this Gentleman himself hardly expects) and even supposing all the Undertakers perform their Obligations, the real Value of one of those Notes they would palm upon us for *Twenty Shillings,* can be but little more than *Twelve Shillings* in Publick Bills, if you allow for the Times of Payment, and that they are not a Tender in Law: So that one hundred of their Ten Pound Notes are really now worth but about Six Hundred Pounds in Silver at their own Standard, and at the Price to which these Notes have helped to advance Silver, they can be now worth but about *Seven Hundred and Twenty Pounds* in Publick Bills. And yet this is what that Gentleman pretends *will save the Country from being imposed upon by the Colony of Rhode-Island.*

Besides all this, I might have observed how bold and daring it is for *private Persons* to attempt what they know the King has expressly forbid the *Legislature,* and when they themselves own *it would have been better for the Legislature to have done it.* I might have added, how vainly these Notes are pretended to be a Stable Medium of Trade, when the very Nature of them is utterly inconsistent with such a Pretence; for granting they are worth the Silver they promise, at the Periods it becomes due, yet in the intermediate Spaces they must of necessity fluctuate, and their Fluctuation will be quick and short, like a broken chopping Sea, which puts all in Confusion, while the publick Bills fall and rise slow and gradually. I might have added also, that the Notes are now passed on the Credit of the Present Signers, when by the Twelfth Article of their Scheme, *the Company may, if they find it for* THEIR INTEREST, *chuse a new Committee upon the Arrival of the first and second Periods, that is at the close of the Third and Sixth Years.* And further I might have taken Notice, that supposing what is yet very unlikely, the Undertakers do actually give out Twenty or Thirty Thousand Pounds at a Period, it can have no more Influence to give Silver a Currency, than a like Sum lately imported here in one Ship had, if that fatal Necesity of *Returns remains.* But I have not Time to enlarge upon, or enforce these and several other material Points.

I hope nothing I have said will be construed as an Imputation on the *personal* Character or Credit of the Undertakers, which I allow in the general to be unspotted and clear, and am as willing to do them Justice as their own *Apologist*, with all his affected and ill placed Compliments, with one of which I could be very merry, were we not upon too serious an Argument. But *miserable is the Fate* of that Country, which must trust and depend upon the *meer Honesty* and *Integrity* of any Set of Men whatever, and have it in their Power at Pleasure to make their Market of them. We have heard, Sir, and we have not forgot what we heard of the *fatal South-Sea Scheme*, by which Thousands of Families, that were even Creditors to the Publick, and others were ruined and undone by the Intrigues of a *few Directors*, in whose *Integrity* and *Capacity*, those Creditors and the Publick did implicitly confide.

We have a later Instance in the *Charitable Corporation*, who by giving such great and needless Opportunities to their *Managers*, corrupted some Gentlemen of Superiour Credit for Integrity and Capacity, and of Superiour Fortune and Circumstances in Life to any Gentleman in *New England*. Shall we then put it in the Power of a few Merchants and Traders, whose professed Aim, as such, is Gain, to enrich themselves at the Ruin of others, and fondly trust to their Ability and Conscience, because they have hitherto maintained a fair Character in the World? forgetting the *homely Proverb*, That Opportunity makes the Thief; and that the Love of Money is the Root of all Evil.

On the whole, I apprehend it appears evident to you, that if our Bills are by some undervalued at present, thro' the Artifice or Self-interested Management of any Number of Traders, who impose on their Credulity, yet they must and will rise in Value to their true Heighth, let any Number of Men do what they will to hinder it. And in the mean Time the refusing to take them is falling into the Snare so artfully prepared for you. It will oblige you to give their private Notes an exclusive Currency, when I have demonstrated they are not worth what they are passed at; that they must necessarily be always fluctuating; that they will ruin all the midling Traders, Shop-keepers and Land-holders, if they obtain such a general Currency; that the true Design and natural Tendency of this selfish and narrow spirited Scheme, is the Enriching the few Undertakers, by making them the Possessors of the Province Bills against the Year *Forty One*, and engrossing the whole Trade of *New-England*, and the best part of the Land too.

I am, Sir, &c.

Newport, February, 4th 1733,–4.

NOTE TO "A LETTER FROM A GENTLEMAN IN RHODE ISLAND TO HIS FRIEND IN BOSTON," PUBLISHED IN THE WEEKLY REHEARSAL OF FEBRUARY 18, 1734.

This letter, which was also published in the Boston Gazette of the same date, purports to have been written at Newport, for the purpose of satisfying the doubts of a friend in Boston as to the real worth of one of the so-called Rhode-Island Banks. The spirited defence of the Rhode Island emissions gives foundation for the belief that it must actually have come from the pen of a Rhode Islander. It may not be superfluous to remind the reader that the banks referred to were emissions of bills of public credit for purposes of loans. The fateful year of 1741 which finds frequent mention in this discussion was important because the royal instruction curtailing the emission of bills of public credit would then be in full force. The reference to a communication to the Boston Gazette of December 3, 1733, may be accepted as correct, but we have no means of testing its accuracy. No copy of the issue of this particular number of the Gazette has been preserved, so far as known. The large balance in the public treasury alluded to in the beginning of the paper was doubtless due to the contest which occurred at the beginning of Belcher's term between himself and the assembly, during which appropriations were withheld. The statement that the attempts of the assembly at Boston, to evade royal instructions or have them recalled and then to emit a sufficient quantity of bills had been defeated, may perhaps require explanation. The bills of public credit were originally emitted through authority acquired from acts passed by the assembly. All acts were submitted to the privy council for approval but it made little difference whether acts authorizing emissions were approved or not since the action of the council would not be known in the province till after the bills had been put in circulation. In 1721, orders were given to submit for approval all acts authorizing emissions, before emitting the bills. Following this came the emission of bills by the assembly, by the mere passage of resolves without the formality of acts. This was prohibited by royal order in 1730.

The attack upon the Merchants' Notes is vigorous and in parts well founded. The writer, however, bears testimony to the personal character or credit of the undertakers. He intimates that the closing up of the "New London Society for Trade & Commerce" was largely due to the exertions of an eminent member of the Massachusetts legislature, but gives no clue to his personality. He also asks, "Whether the Leaders of a Certain Society have not for many years opposed the Emitting any more Publick Bills, and whether they have not got vast estates by the Fluctuations of those Bills, of which Fluctuations they were the only Instruments?" It would be interesting to know what was referred to by the above.

The reference to the "South Sea Scheme" requires no explanation, but the "Charitable Corporation" is not so well known. An account of that corporation will be found in the note to the communication to the Weekly Rehearsal, dated March 25th, 1734.

The copy was procured from the American Antiquarian Society.

NEW-ENGLAND   Numb. 738

The Bofton *Gazette.*

Publifhed by Authority.

From *MONDAY* FEBRUARY 18, to *MONDAY* FEBRUARY 25. 1734.

To the Author of the Letter from Rhode-Island in the Boston Gazette of the 18*th Current.*

SIR,

IN yours dated *Newport, Feb.* 14. 1733 4. in our *Boston* Gazette of the 18th of *Feb.* you tell us you will give us your thoughts on the Value of our Merchants Notes, and Satisfy our Doubts of the real worth of your last Bank.

You say, that the whole Country complain'd loudly of the difficulties they labour'd under for want of a sufficient medium of *Exchange,* and that the *Massachusetts* and *New-Hampshire* were forbid by the Royal Instructions to their Governours to Emitt any more Bills, except a Triffling Sum; so that every body was ready to Dispond under this melancholy prospect, and you therefore insinuate that your Government out of a generous Concern for the Neighbouring Governments, without any selfish Views for your own (for the Landed Men took no greater pleasure in *Involving* and *Mortgaging* their Estates than other) have determined to furnish all your Neighbouring Governments with a medium sufficient to carry on the Trade of them all, which is such a noble and generous Undertaking as is not to be met with in History: I dont hear any body blame your Generosity in *Mortgaging* your own Estates, in order to furnish a Medium for His Majesty's good Subjects in this Part of the World;

VOL. III — 4

but they blame the Generosity of the easy good natur'd People, who takes them as pay for any thing they have to Sell, when there is really no Value in them but that which they put upon them who take them. You say notwithstanding your Emission of 60000 in 1732, your Bills have been for five Years near at Par with as little Fluctuation, as Silver and Gold suffer in *Europe*, but you dont say what, neither can I Imagine what you mean they are at Par with, except it be with themselves, they have not been at Par with Silver and Gold, at any certain Rate for these five Years, and as to their Fluctuating, I never heard of their rising but ever of their falling in Value, which I think is improperly called Fluctuating, for that supposes, sometimes a rising and sometimes a falling, but truly they are of no real Value, your saying your Government took all due Care to ascertain their Value without telling us in what manner, proves nothing, but it is very likely you Imagine that the Easy good Natur'd People who take them without Knowing what Foundation they are upon, will be well enough satisfied with the method you take in making out their certain Value, which is by saying, your Assembly took all due Care to ascertain it, but I can assure you we have some People among us who are not so easily deluded and will not be persuaded to believe that your saying a thing is so, proves it to be so; you say they are Let out on Land Security, and the whole Sum is to be paid in a shorter Period by three Years than the first Bank's, but you dont tell the World, That this short Period is twenty Years and that when this twenty Years is out there is not so much as the promise of paying the Possessors of them one single Farthing for them, either in Silver or Gold, or any thing else, but that they shall be equal in Value to

Money in all publick Payments and shall be accordingly accepted by the Treasurer and Receivers Subordinate to him and for any Stock at any time in the Treasury. We are very well informed that the Interest you receive for the Bills your Government Lets out, amounts to Considerable more than the Charge of your Government, so that you have no great matter of Publick Payments to be made, and what Stock you have at any time in your Treasury, you better know than I can tell you. We allow your Government to be a very Wise, or rather Cunning Government, to make a parcel of Paper Bills which you call Money, which really cost you little more than Pen, Ink, and Paper, and let it out, the Interest whereof amounts to not only enough to Support the Charge of it, but to encourage the setting up of Manufactures, and giving Bountys, &c. but what must we call the People of the other Governments who assist you in doing so, not only by taking them in Trade, and by paying Interest, for them but by puting in your Power to be very considerable rivals to them in Trade, and lessening the Value of their own Paper Credit, I wish I could call them Wise too. You also say we may see how false Injurious it is to assert your New Bank cost you nothing but Pen, Ink and Paper, and how Triffling and Delutory it is to assert that you had then out more Bills than the *Massachusetts, New-Hampshire, Connecticut* and *New-York* all put together, you say we may see it, but you dont tell us where we must look for it. I cant find it proved any where in your said Letter, neither do I find that you even so much as say you are Injured in that regard, by any thing in said Gazette of the 14th of *Jan.* you only say, that were that Assertion true as you doubt not it is groundless, yet it can be no damage to the Country in Generall I suppose you mean *Rhode-Island*, since you Pledge your Lands and must purchase those Bills wherever they are lodged to Redeem them which I think is fairly giving up what you would prove to be false, viz. *That the Bills Cost little else but Pen, Ink and Paper*, and certainly that Money that cost nothing is worth nothing. We are very much obliged to you for the warning you give us against what some call (I suppose you mean the Usurers) the happy Advantage of Forty One, I am really of Opinion that we have a sort of Men among us, who hope to make a considerable Advantage on the necessitys of their Neighbours who shall about that time want Province Bills to pay their Bonds and Taxes by making pay what they will be mercifully pleas'd to ask for them, but I am under as dismal Apprehensions from the *Rhode-Island* Usurers as our own on that Account for its well known, that there are very considerable Sums let out there, and it is as well known, that the Gentlemen of that Place have made considerable if not all their Bonds payable in Bills of Credit on this Province (which is a very sufficient argument with me, that they reckon our Bills of more Value than those of their Colony) so that they seem to have an Eye to Forty One, as well as the Usurers of this Province, and which will be the most mercifull I know not, I fear both their Mercy's will be Cruelty, but I hope the Wisdom of this Government will find out righteous Ways and Means to deliver us out of both their Hands and not suffer the poor honest Debtor to be squees'd to Death by either of them, and yet do equall Justice to the Poor and the Rich, which I conceive will not be difficult, when you come to consider the small and uncertain Value (as you are pleas'd to term it) of the Merchant's

Notes, which you say can never be Worth more than Silver at Nineteen Shillings per Ounce, but in Fact now are and ever will be worth much less; you say the Undertakers will get into their Hands the old Province Bills which will soon be worth Silver at Eight Shillings per Ounce, and make Immence gain of them to the ruin of Thousands, whose Estates are Mortgaged for the Province Bills; in answer to which I would only say, that I hope the Legislature of this Province will take the same Care to prevent their Oppressing their Neighbours (if there be any danger from them as I apprehend their is none, for what they · Let out upon Interest, is to be paid in the Notes, or Silver Money of equal value with them, and not in Province Bills) as they will to prevent Oppression by *Rhode-Island* as well as our own Usurers, who are most likely to Hoard up Province Bills against that good time.

And how you calculate Twenty Shillings of thes Notes to be but about equal to Twelve Shillings Prooince Bills, I can't see, except you value Province Bills eight Shillings of them to be equal to an Ounce of Silver, when we all know that Twenty two Shillings of them is daily given, when it is to be purchased, But supposing as you say, that our Province Bills are equal Eight Shillings of them to an Ounce of Silver, I wou'd fain know what makes Eight Shillings of yuur Bills to be of the same Value; you make the reason of ours being so, because the Period for their being called in draws nigh; but you don't give one single Argument why yours should be of that value, for the Time of your Bills being to be Call'd in is not till about Twenty Years hence; And I think you say the Undertakers of the Merchants Notes can afford to give more for Silver Money than other

Persons, when they pass their own Notes of Hand, and have Three, Six and Ten years Credit, but you don't say they are obliged to pay in one tenth Part in Silver or Gold every year, as a sure Fund to pay their Notes to whoever possesses them when they become due, which is fact. and if you can't imagine an Ounce of Silver to be paid at Three, Six and Ten Years hence, to be worth Nineteen Shillings now in hand, in public Bills, what do you imagine Twenty Shillings of your Bills to be paid Twenty Years hence can be now worth in the same Bills, and what it will be paid in then, no Mortal knows. Upon the whole, there is nothing more uncertain than the Value of your Bills, and every one knows, or may know, the now certain Value of the Merchants Notes, and may make a Bargain for what he has to sell for them, accordingly, and as I am humbly of Opinion that no paper Credit can be very valuable without the promise of Silver or Gold for it, at some certain Time, and at some certain rate or other, and I leave you and all Mankind to judge which are most Valuable, your Bills, or these Merchants Notes, and I really believe the main and true Design of the Merchants in Emitting these Notes was to prevent our Province Bills being run down to almost nothing, on the one hand or be raised more than the Value the Government was pleased to put upon them on the other, and to introduce a Currency of some certainty, which show'd very much a public Spirit.

I am &c

Boston, Feb 22, 1733, 4.

N. B *A fuller and more particular Answer to the Letter from* Rhode Island, *came so late, that we cannot Insert it now, but the Publick may depend upon it next Week.*

REMARKS concerning a late large Emission of Paper-Credit in *Boston,* called *Merchants Notes.*

THE *pretended good Intenitons of those* Notes, *were, to lower the* price of Silver, *an addition to our* Medium of Trade, *and to bring more* Silver into the Province.

Silver *before this Emission was* 20 *s per Ounce, upon that large addition to our* Paper Currency, *it immediately did rise to* 23 *s.*

The Undertakers *did not Employ it in Trade and Manufactures, but made a* Snare *of it for those who wanted Money,* and *did generally let it out upon Interest to the deluded* Countrymen *who refuse Money of no kind* Our Administration *have found by experience, that Publick* Loan Money *was of* pernicious *Consequence, in affording the unthinking part of the People an opportunity of Morgaging their Lands, and thereby rendring themselves* Miserable, *or at best* Tenants *instead of Freeholders*: *those* Notes *have the same* Malignity, *but to a greater Degree*; *the* Province *can and hath shown* Mercy *in such a Case, which is not to be expected here.*

The Company *oblige themselves for ten Years,* to lodge *every Year one tenth Value of the whole Sum,* in pledges (*if they please*) *to be redeemed at the several* Periods *of three six and ten Years*; *which may be done by bringing in of their own* Notes to the Value; *that is, instead of* importing Silver, *they only oblige themselves to gather in and* cancel *their own Notes at certain Periods.*

The private Profit to the Undertakers will be unreasonably great. *I only mention one Article of their Profit. If a Person receives a Bond bearing Interest upon good Security, if he pays a Debt, or if he brings it into Trade; it is equivalent, and answers to him as so much ready Money:* the Company therefore in issuing these Bills have received *One hundred and ten thousand Pounds* ready Money, *to pay* Thirty three thousand Pound *after three Years,* Thirty three thousand Pound *after six Years and* Forty four thousand Pound *after ten Years; Whereas those several Sums payable as above, are worth in ready Money (allowing for simple Interest) only* Twenty eight thousand eight hundred & thirteen Pound, Twenty four thousand two hundred & sixty four Pound, *and* Twenty seven thousand five hundred Pound, *in all* Eighty thousand five hundred & seventy seven Pound, *that is,* the Company gets Twenty nine thousand four hundred and twenty three Pound, *and they who take and circulate these Notes are so much imposed upon. The Government only ought to have a* Credit to lay such Impositions upon the People, *in lieu of a Tax towards defraying the publick Charges, for the Protection of the Community:* this is therefore only a* Bubble for the Benefit of some private Men.

Instead of One hundred and ten thousand Pound, *they may from the same Plates,* emit any large Quantity of Notes; *it is not without precedent, that* Directors, *Men of Good Estates (if we may compare small things with* great) *have been tempted by opportunities to impose upon the publick for* private Gain.

Any Companies of Men in Credit, may make more such Emissions, *to the utter Confusion of all Currency.*

Any large new Emission of Paper Money occasions a great Import of superfluous Foreign Goods. *If I am well informed, Some concerned have wrote to Merchants in* London, *that by this Emission Money will be plenty and Silver cheaper, to encourage them to send quantities of Goods.*

These Notes are not strictly a Tenour to the Emitters *Themselves in currency of Trade by the Tenour of the Bills.*

They endeavour to depretiate the Province Bills, *by their speciality.*

The Endorsers variation in writing his Name, *is such that by comparing, no Man can swear or be positive to his Hand*; *which, if he should die or be out of the Province, might occasion* disputes in Law.

There is a fallacy on the pretended main Support of the Credit of these Notes. *That* Nineteen Shillings *worth of these Notes will purchase* (*one Ounce of Silver*) *as much as* Twenty three Shillings *of our Province Bills. The Notes are payable at remote Periods*; *while by our* Governours steady adherence to his Instructions, *and the* laudable Discretion *of the Administration in* Connecticut, *in emitting of Paper Money*; *some Years before the expiration of those Periods, the* Massachusett, Connecticut *and* New Hampshire *publick Bills, growing yearly scarcer, will be all come in, and* Nineteen Shillings *of these Notes* (*one Ounce of Silver*) *will be worth only* Eight Shillings *our Currency.*

The wild unbounded Emission of *Rhode Island* Bills, I take to be out of the Question. *Our Merchants* (*with reluctancy*) *did in* 1731 *continue to circulate a* Sixty thousand Pound *more new Emission of their Bills, therefore* they vainly imagine *that* One hundred and ten thousand Pound, *or perhaps a Million more, will have the same good fate*: *but the great Quantity already issued in that small Colony, the cancelling of them* by that *Government put off for many Years, and their* breach of public Faith *in postponing them further beyond the Times limited by the original Acts* (*thus from* 1715 *they have emitted at Times on loan* Two hundred and eighty thousand Pounds, *whereof only the small Sum of* Twenty thousand Pounds *is all that time cancell'd*) *considered, with that of the other* New England *Province Bills growing yearly scarcer and consequently more valuable, must soon bring a* discount on the *Rhode Island* Bills, and length a none Currency.

NOTE TO THE COMMUNICATION IN THE BOSTON GAZETTE OF FEBRUARY 25, 1734, ADDRESSED "TO THE AUTHOR OF THE LETTER FROM RHODE ISLAND IN THE BOSTON GAZETTE OF THE 18TH CURRENT."

The communication to which this is a reply was in the nature of an attack on the Merchants' Notes and a defence of the Rhode Island emissions. As would naturally be inferred, this answer to the letter from Rhode Island is just the reverse. The writer repudiates the arguments in the former letter in favor of the Rhode Island bills, applauds the purpose and intentions of the Boston merchants, and endeavors to overthrow the various arguments brought forward by the previous writer. In view of what was said in the note to that letter, which was appended to the copy taken from the Weekly Rehearsal of the 18th of February, there is nothing that calls especially for explanation, except the allusion to the impending scarcity of bills of public credit in 1741. Had the royal instructions been enforced and the circulating medium of the province reduced to £30,000, the impossibility of the adjustment of debts which is foreshadowed in this reference would inevitably have resulted from the situation unless silver had been artificially introduced.

The copy was procured from the Boston Public Library.

NOTE TO "REMARKS CONCERNING A LATE LARGE EMIS-
SION OF PAPER-CREDIT IN BOSTON CALLED MERCHANTS
NOTES," IN THE BOSTON GAZETTE OF FEBRUARY 25, 1734.

The writer is not a believer in the scheme of the Boston merchants for relieving the financial situation by the emission of their
notes. He regards the notes as contributory to the rise' of silver
and he thinks that under pretence of relief the merchants sought
profit. He distrusts the notes and has no faith in those who
emitted them. He does not, however, believe in the Rhode Island
bills. On the contrary he abuses them with pretty much the same
vigor as that in which he attacks the Merchants' Notes.

The assertion that the Merchants' Notes "are not strictly a
Tenour to the Emitters *Themselves in currency of Trade* by *the
Tenour of the Bills*" is not on its face intelligible. The word Tenor
came into use in connection with the bills very shortly after this,
when a bill having a new phraseology was emitted and was at once
christened "new-tenor." The bills already in circulation were thereafter called "old tenor." The phraseology of the Merchants' Notes
was peculiar. The signers promised to pay Richard Clarke or order,
so much silver or the equivalent gold, in three payments, three-
tenths by December 30, 1736, three-tenths more by December 30,
1739, and the other four-tenths by December 30, 1743; and on each
of the first two payments to renew their bills accordingly. This
was not only a note but a contract, and that too of a somewhat com-
plicated character. Perhaps the writer was endeavoring in the involved and unintelligible sentence quoted above, to bring out the
fact that this feature of the bills unfitted them for currency.

The copy was procured from the Boston Public Library.

THE   𝔑umb. 127.

Weekly Rehearſal.

𝔐onday, March 4. 1734.

To the Author of the Weekly Rhearsal.

SIR,

THE Letter you published in your last Paper from a Gentleman in *Rhode-Island* has so misrepresented the Subject he wrote upon, that in Friendship and Justice to the Publick, I thought it necessary some Remarks should be made upon it, and lest it should not be done by sóme other and better Hand I send you the following Lines:

To begin then, I observe he enters upon the Matter, with a very unfair suggestion, *That none but a few professed Usurers can have any reason to hesitate about their late Emission;* as though they were the only Men that could be hurt by large Emissions of Bills of Credit, of the Nature of those put out by *Rhode-Island*, and the discount that has ever ensued thereon; whereas he must know, that all Men trading upon their own Stock, that give Credit, must suffer according to the Sum and length of Time they give such Credit, and so must all Men that have settled Stipends, whether from the Publick, subòrdinate Societies, or from particular Persons; and in like manner must Widows and Orphans, who have their Legacies in such Bills or Debts, as well as many others: It is therefore a plain and unjust piece of Art to confine the Dislike of their Bills to a few professed

Usurers; which Reflection on Usurers by the way, must come very ungracefully from an Advocate for *Rhode-Island*, where they allow such an Exorbitant Interest to be taken, which nothing can give Colour for, but their Consciousness of the ill Foundation their Bills are upon, and the Expectation of a Discount necessarily following, which this excessive Interest gives some Relief against.

This Gentleman goes on with the same or greater Unfairness, in his Account of the late *Rhode-Island* Emission; he tells us the Assembly there took all due care to ascertain the Value of their Bills, as much as 'tis possible for a Paper Currency. He makes it out, by telling us they are let out upon the best Land Security of Double the Value, *&c.* Let us now consider how secure the Possessor of the Bills is by this, tho' the Mortgage was worth ten times more. We must observe the Bills are not payable (in this shorter or quciker Bank) till twenty Years, the possessor then must stay till that time before he can get the Value of his Bill, and when that Time comes, for all the Credit he has given, and loss by Discount he has suffered, he gets another Bill of the same Denomination, to be paid in the same Manner Twenty Years after; and so from Term to Term, the possessor may be as well led on to an Hundred or a Thousand Years. Nor is this a bare Suggestion or Possibility, but plain Fact and the true State of the Case, and the very Method and Practice of the Government in *Rhode-Island*, or in one of their Emissions, I think the 60000 *l.* they give. this as the Reason of it, in the Preamble of the Act, *To Enable those that had given their Mortgages for Bills in a former Bank, to redeem their Lands.* Now supposing you or I had any of the Bills of the first Bank, and came to the

Government for the Value of them, what can the Government give us but a New piece of Paper to be redeem'd in like manner An. 1753. instead of the Old one they promised to redeem in 1733? The first Bill perhaps we took for two Ounces and half of Silver, the present Bill we shall be glad to part with for less than one Ounce, or else wait Twenty Years longer, when probably twice as many will not purchase so much. I don't pretend I have seen this Act, nor can I expect it, to see their Acts for emitting money, especially their last Act, is a Favour they would not grant, when requested by the Government of this Province, and therefore not to be expected by a private Person; but I had the Account of this Act from a Gentleman that was a Member of the General Assembly of the Colony of *Rhode-Island*, who merrily added, *That this was the only true Thing in it.* The Nature therefore and Manner of these Bills is plainly thus, I promise to pay you *Five Pounds* Twenty Years hence, or else then to give you another Note for *Five Pounds* to be paid at such further Time as I think proper, at which Time I will also have the Liberty to pay you, or put you off as I please, and as a Security and Pledge that I will then pay you or not, as I please, and when I please, I Bind over my House and Land which I will likewise improve all the while to my own Use and Benefit. Now I pray you to tell me what this *Five Pound* Note is worth, for which I have given you a *Thousand Pounds* Security, exclusive of Buildings, just so much and no more Security have you and every Man for a *Rhode-Island Five Pound* Bill; nor is it possible to shew from the Tenour of their Bills, or their Practice in redeeming them, that there is any better Security than this to the Possessor, that is the best landed Security to pay him nothing, nor can any possible Reason be given, why as they have already gotten to *twenty two Shillings* an Ounce for Silver, they should not go to *twenty two Pounds* an Ounce, and from thence to nothing : This is what there is double Security for; *and now they are come to their true heighth.* But besides, as the Mortgages really secures nothing, so according to the practice in *Rhode-Island,* the Mortgages are over a while like to come to little or nothing themselves; the Method is this, A Man that has forty Acres of Land, puts it into the Bank for *two hundred Pounds,* but growing weary of so large an Encumbrance, he goes to his Friend when a New Emission is made, & borrows a couple of hundred Pounds, and pays it, and now his Land is at liberty, immediately he Banks the one half of it again, that is twenty Acres for another 200 *l.* upon the third Emission he takes the same Method, and gets another 200 *l.* for ten Acres, and so by the same Progression his Mortgage will quickly get near the value of the Bills, and then the Security and Bills will be pretty much of a Piece, and very much *at their true heighth,* no Security for paying nothing.　The Account of this I had from a Gentleman born in that Government, and Owner of an Estate in Lands of several Hundreds a Year there; and there is no doubt but many Instances may be given of it.

　　And now is it a melancholy Reflection, that honest inconsiderate Men of this and a neighbouring Government should be impos'd on at such a strange Rate as they are, not only to take these Bills, but to hire them at ten and some at *fifteen per Cent.* and give Security to pay the whole in our Province Bills, which (as this Gentleman tells us) will be soon worth *Eight Shillings* an Ounce, which in ten

Years will be to pay above *five hundred Pounds* for one? and what a dismal prospect have the People of this Province, when they consider what they have parted with, and have nothing to shew but these miserable Bills, by which they are secured of nothing, and for which (if *Rhode-Island* go on hereafter as they have hitherto, which the Messenger sent by this Government to obtain a Copy of their last Act to Emit Bills, was told by a great Man there, they would) the People here will in the End certainly get little or nothing.

By this time, I hope I may take some Notice of this Gentleman's hard words, on the saying, that the *Rhode-Island* Bills cost nothing but *Pen, Ink and Paper*: he says this is false and injurious, I am sure it is true as to the Bills of the last Bank; by this Expression, every Body knows, is meant the Charge of making and Emitting, did the Bills of the Old Bank when put out, cost any thing but this, that is, *Pen, Ink and Paper*, or the charge of making and Emitting? and did the Possessors of those Old Bills, when called in, Receive any thing but New Bills? Did the Government give One Shilling or Shillings worth in Silver or Gold, or any thing else than New Bills, and were not the New Bills made with *Pen, Ink and Paper*, or did they cost any thing, or have they cost any thing yet, but the charge of making and Emitting? And if they wind up this Bank as they did the other, will they cost any thing else? and have the Government promised in the Bills, that they will redeem them any other way? The Gentleman knows the Case to be as I now Represent it, and therefore neither he nor his Friend could possibly see that Charge to be false and injurious; I spoke of what was past and is present;

these have as yet certainly cost nothing else: As to what is to come, neither he nor I can certainly tell, but in all Probability they will do as they have done, and if they should, what I have said will be true of the Bills for the Future, tho' I did not assert any thing concerning them, and the contrary he cannot see, for the Government have not promised it. I cannot tell who this Gentleman is, but I am sure he should be careful to consider Matters thoroughly before he makes so heavy a Charge.

As to what this Gentleman says upon the Observation, that *Rhode-Island* had more Bills out than four other Governments, whatever his Friend may see, I am sure I cannot see how it is either Trifling and Delusory, it is no trifling matter to carry Two or Three Hundred Thousand Pounds in valuable Commodities, out of other Governments, to that small Colony for such sort of Bills as *Rhode Island* have Emitted. As to the delusory part, I know, and heard it my self discoursed of, and finally so said in the Presence of Gentlemen of great Note and Publick and Honourable Stations in the three largest of the four Governments mentioned, and there were present also several Gentlemen of Publick and Honourable Stations in the Government of *Rhode-Island*, who could not or at least did not say and make out the contrary, and I suppose it was by them universally concluded to be so.

I cannot forbear taking Notice of the Observation this Gentleman makes in the close of this Section, in order to encourage us to take the New *Rhode-Island* Bills, that they will supply the place of the Province Bills, and enable People more easily to pay the Province Bills in, as they become due; turn over to the next Page, and there he tells

us, that the true and sole Motive and View of the Undertakers in the Notes of Hand, is to get the Province Bills in
Lieu of them against Forty One. Now can any possible
Reason be assigned for these contrary Effects, that the Currency of the New *Rhode Island* Bills will make the Province
Bills more easy for People to come at, and the Currency
of the Notes of Hand more difficult? Will People part
with Province Bills more easily for *Rhode-Island* Bills, that
Promise and have always paid nothing but a New Bill of a
farther Period, for an Old Bill of a nearer, than for these
Notes that must bring at their Periods Silver and Gold, or
else the Signers and Company too must resign their Estates?
But allow them both to be Current, which this Gentleman
supposes, will not the *Rhode Island* Men have an equal
Advantage of hoarding up the Province Bills with the
Undertakers? Nay, is there not greater Reason to fear it
from them than the others, from their frequent Practices
afore mentioned of insisting on Bonds for our Province
Bills, when they lent out their own? Is there one Instance,
where the Undertakers have thus insisted? If they have
taken such Bonds, has it not always been at the Choice and
Desire of the Borrower? I observe this Gentleman takes
notice of what he calls an Inconsistency between two Papers, written by different Men, on *December* 3d. and *January* 14. it must be much more Inexcusable for the same
Paper to contradict itself; and especially if what he calls an
Inconsistency appear to be none, as I think is very evident,
for these Notes of Hand will prevent the Oppression which
almost ever accompanies a Trade by Barter, which must
necessarily arise upon a scarcity of a Medium, even tho' the
Bills did not rise, which we did not find in the greatest

Scarcity of our Province Bills, but even last Spring, when *Seventy Thousand Pounds* was lock'd up in the Treasury, Province Bills instead of rising any thing at all, fell *twelve Pence* in *Twenty Shillings* in their Value, from Silver at *Twenty Shillings* to *Twenty One Shillings* per Ounce. It is difficult to account for it, but so it has been, that tho' the Plenty of these imaginary Bills has made them fall, their Scarcity has not made them rise, and many Times could not keep them at a Stand. And now I am on this Head, I cannot but express my Wonder at this Gentleman's Declaration, That it is notorious, that the *Rhode-Island* Bills have been for five Years near *at Par*, with as little Fluctuation as Silver and Gold suffer in *Europe*; when in that Time, they have been *at Eighteen* and *Twenty two Shillings* per Ounce, above Twenty *per Cent.* odds. Can this Gentleman pretend this is the State of Silver and Gold in *Europe?* Nor is this Gentleman fair in what he says, that their New Bills will purchase pure Silver and Gold, while these Notes of Hand will not purchase it at any Rate at all; when it is notorious, that one of their own People in *Newport* (their Capital) refus'd to take any of their new Bills for Silver, and as notorious, that Quantities of Silver and Gold have been purchased by these Notes of Hand. *Shifting and Evasion is of no Service to a Cause, not even to a bad one.*

As for the Charge of Impudence, which this Gentleman so freely bestows upon me, if he had abounded with the contrary Virtue, I believe he would have been more sparing especially if he had acquainted himself with the Authority I had for what I said, both with relation to the Bills of this Government and that too, I mean that of our General Court, who allow'd and declar'd as the Foundation and Cause of

their Endeavours now six Years ago to put their Bills on
a Foundation of Silver and Gold, that Injustice and Wrong
had been done by their uncertain Value; and if they had
not had as bad or worse Apprehensions of *Rhode-Island*
Bills, they had not taken the Pains to have sent up for a
Copy of their Act; but I have the Authority of that Government likewise, who many Years ago, when their Bills
were much more valu'd than now, joyn'd with other Governments to stop the Injustice that was then begun by
them. Will he pretend to say, that Bills have not been
the Rule and Measure in Commerce? or will he say they
have been stable and certain? or will he say, that an uncertain and changeable measure has not always been accounted an Abomination? I did not make a direct Charge,
but only observ'd what all Mankind allow, and left every
one to apply those general Rules, as their best Judgment
should direct them. It is beyond all dispute that great
Injustice has been done, tho' I hope not intentionally in
those who have conducted those Affairs: And now I am
upon the Nature and Value of these *Rhode-Island* Bills,
I would take occasion to pray and urge this Advocate for
them, to go thorough with this Matter, and give us in Print
the several Acts, whereby their Bills have been Emitted,
and how they have been discharged and paid. I shall be
glad to be mistaken, and find that the many Bills this Province are possess'd of, Emitted by *Rhode-Island*, may appear to give Security for something, at present I do
seriously think they give Security for nothing, and that
finally the Possessor can recover nothing. Be sure hitherto
it has been so with the Possessor; and if there be any more
Security given now than before, we shall see it when we

have the Acts printed, which I again beg and urge, for the sake of the Publick and of Truth, and to confute me if I am mistaken. Truth and Justice will bear Examination. It is judg'd the Notes of Hand are founded upon them, and therefore the Scheme is printed, together with the Occasion of the Undertaking; if the *Rhode-Island* Bills are founded on the same solid Bottom of Truth and Justice, it is pity but it was known; nothing will give us this, but printing an Account of their Emissions, and the Method of discharging them, and the several Acts for those Purposes.

And now we have done with the *Rhode-Island* Bills, till we have a more particular Account of them publish'd: Let us consider the Notes of Hand this Gentleman exclaims so much against. And here I cannot pass by his ridiculing the design of the Undertakers of these Notes, to prevent the fall of the Province Bills, which he calls an Imposition on *Common Sense*, because it is impossible they should fall by reason of the King's Instruction, and the Arrival of their Periods; whereas nothing is more certain than this, that within these Eighteen Months the Province Bills have fallen *Ten per Cent.* notwithstandidg the King's Instruction, and the Arrival or nearness of the Periods too.

I am at a loss what this Gentleman means by calling upon the Land-holder as he is pleas'd to name him; how this sort of Men should be hurt I cannot see; surely for them to sell their Produce this Year for such a Currency as will be as good next Year, as it is this, cannot hurt them, but on the contrary save them from a loss in the Sinking of the Money, which they have not been free from these Twenty Years. The same may be said of the Trader that has any Stock; the only Man that has any Colour to complain, is the Man that has little or no Stock, that runs largely into Debt, and depends upon paying *One Hundred Pounds* with *Seventy five*; and if this unjust Trade was bro't to an End, it must be very well for the Publick, as it would prevent great Injustice.

This Gentleman seems so fond of using several of my Expressions, that he has not taken Time to find out whether they are applicable or not; as particularly, that of no other expence than *Pen, Ink and Paper*; as if because the *Rhode-Island* Bills are made of *Pen, Ink and Paper*, and paid with *Pen, Ink and Paper*, that is, with a New Bill, instead of an old one, that therefore these Notes of Hand payable in Silver and Gold cost nothing else. I dare say when the Period comes for paying the Silver and Gold, if this Gentleman be a Possessor, he will not accept of a New Note instead of the Silver or Gold promis'd. It is as improper to say, these Notes cost nothing but *Pen, Ink and Paper*, as it is to say, that a Farm I give my Bond, and must pay a Thousand Ounces of Silver for, at a certain Period, costs me nothing but *Pen, Ink and Paper*, nor could it be so said of the *Rhode-Island* Bills, if they promis'd Gold or Silver, or any other Thing whatsoever of value.

As for what this Gentleman says farther, of the vast Profit by getting the Province Bills into the Undertaker's Hands, there is ten times more hazard by *Rhode-Island* Bills, which may be made by Wholesale, as they promise nothing, but the Notes of Hand promise, and must bring Silver and Gold; and it is difficult to get Undertakers, which this Government hath found more than once, and nothing but the vast Mischief coming on us by the *Rhode-Island* Bills, could have prevailed upon this Number of Men to have engaged in this Affair : For notwithstanding all that is said of the Profit to be made by the Undertakers, it is hardly possible but that the Undertakers in general will be losers; for they pass these Bills in common Payments as other Bills which are now *Twenty two Shillings* per Ounce, and must pay these Notes at *Nineteen Shillings* per Ounce. The Undertakers must loose above Six *per Cent.* It is therefore very unjust Treatment to charge the Company with wicked and pernicious Designs, and the Bills carrying Deceit in their Face, and that they are not worth *Nineteen Shillings* in Publick Bills; whereas he knows the Notes plainly declare how much Silver or Gold, and at what Times they shall be paid, and that none of the *Rhode-Island* Bills promise an Ounce of Silver, or any other Thing of Value at any Period whatsoever: And as a further Encouragement to the Possessor, they have that for *Nineteen Shillings* at the Periods, that is now worth about *Twenty two Shillings*, and he uses the Money all the while besides. Let *Rhode-Island* do so by their Bills, and give as good Security for performance as the Undertakers, and they will be in much better Esteem among all Judicious Men.

I cannot but observe how unlucky this Gentleman is in his Objections against these Notes, and particularly in the Charge he makes upon the Undertakers of being *bold* and *daring*, in giving out these Notes of Hand, because of the King's Instruction. If that Instruction be examined, together with the Original Occasion of it, as it will be found that not one Word forbids Notes of Hand or Bills, or any thing else from private Persons; so that the Nature and Tendency of these Notes is agreeable to the real Design and Spirit of it; and had such Bills as these and no other been always Emitted, we had had no such Instruction, but some of the Plantations had got into a Method of Issuing Bills, without a good Foundation, and therefore it was thought time to stop them; but such Bills as these cannot sink in such an unbounded Manner, so much Silver and Gold as they Promise, according to the distance of the Payment, they are really worth, besides the Advantage of using them the mean while, and as they will not grow worse, which other Bills ever have, they so far answer the true intent of the Instruction; whereas, if we consider the *Rhode-Island* Bills, they are as much against the Words of the Instruction, as these Notes, and directly against the De-sign of the Instruction, both as to the Nature of their Bills, which have nothing to stop their sinking, as likewise on ac-count of the Place where the Bulk of them pass, which is this Province; and every one knows passing such Bills in this Province, is directly contrary to the Design of the Instruc-tion, and renders it so far intirely ineffectual, and should not that Government take notice of the Instruction, especially so far at least, as to prevent their Bills Sinking, which we know by sad Experience, *Rhode-Island* has not?

As to what this Gentleman says of the Fluctuation of these Notes of Hand, the Alteration or Change there will be in their Value, is very improperly called a Fluctuation because it may be known before Hand and every Body can agree accordingly: Could the same Thing be done by the *Rhode-Island* Bills, the great Mischief might be prevented, of Men's receiving worse Money than they sold for; but no Man can tell what Price their Bills will be at, at any certain Period. This Gentleman indeed, tells us once and again, that they are coming and will come *to their true height*; but he does not say when, and that is the only thing I am at a loss about, *their true height* I am well satisfied about, it is what they promise, which is nothing; but when they will come to that, that is, the exact time when People will universally be convinc'd of this, and treat them accordingly, I cannot certainly say, tho' I believe it will not be a great while first, and but a very short Time before there will be a considerable Discount between all the *Rhode-Island* Bills and other Bills, and especially if this Advocate can be perswaded to go on in their defence, and shew us their Foundation, as I hope he will.

As to what this Gentleman says upon the Character of the Undertakers, (or *affected and ill plac'd Complement*, as he is pleas'd to call it) I would only say, that the Extract. printed the 14th of *January* last, was truly a private Letter design'd for a Gentleman of my Acquaintance in a neighbouring Government, who was a Stranger to most of the Company, and so much I thought I would say to him of them : It was printed at the desire of some, to whose Judgment I readily submit my own; and now it is publish'd I readily appeal to those best acquainted with the Company, if I have in the least Measure exceeded or flatter'd them: But this is not to the Argument, much less is it for me to take Notice of this Gentleman's Mode of Expression, *Blabbing*, *Effrontery*, his three Latin Words, his Disposition to Tears or to Mirth. I have endeavour'd to keep as close as I could to the main Business, and to treat this Gentleman (who he is I cannot tell, nor do I want to know) with Decency, and the Subject with that Gravity an affair so deeply affecting my Country requires; and in the Name of ' my injured suffering Country, I beseech this Gentleman to shew us how we shall be reimburs'd the Loss we have sustain'd by taking *Two or three Hundred Thousand Pounds* at *ten*, *twelve*, and *sixteen Shillings* per Ounce, which are already got to *twenty two* or *twenty three Shillings* per Ounce, and what Course we shall take, that these Bills may not fall to *twenty two* or *twenty three Pounds* an Ounce for Silver, and from thence to nothing and so lose the small Remainder; for near about two thirds are lost already. Perhaps he may say our Province Bills have been as bad. If they have been bad, it has been occasion'd by taking *Rhode-Island* Bills with them, and what one in the Province has lost, another has got, and the Province has it; but in the Case of *Rhode-Island* Bills, we gave them the Money, that is, we gave it the Value and Currency, and without our Favour, it would at first have been *at its true heighth*, worth nothing, and the Reward for this mighty Favour, is for them to take no Care of their Bills, and thereby carry away two Thirds from us already, and to continue in the way to defeat us in a little while of all the rest.

I thought to have said nothing about this Gentleman's Reflections upon the Undertakers in these Notes, from the ill Conduct of the Directors in the *South Sea Scheme*, and the Managers in the *Charitable Corporation*, when the Affairs are almost as different as possible. It is certain these Bills can be worth no more than *Nineteen Shillings* per Ounce, there is therefore no Room for bidding upon them, and making a Bubble; and there is plain and full Security that they shall be worth so much, and when, and in what manner they shall be paid; there can be no Imposition here: If these Undertakers had a Design of hoarding the

Province Bills, could they not much easier have done it, by *Rhode-Island* Bills, which they could have had without promising Silver at *Nineteen Shillings* per Ounce, being already possess'd of a great part of them, and more than they can tell what well to do with, unless they were better; which by the way, is the Reason why Men have bid one upon another: It will ever be so, while there are such Bills passing of *Rhode-Island's*, which have only an imaginary Value, and being founded on a Fallacy it is discovered more and more every Day, and so they daily sink, and yet are still higher than they really ought to be, because they have no Reality in them at all. And now to look back upon the melancholy Subject we have been considering, must it not fill every lover of his Country with Sorrow, to see the Province (I can hardly help saying) *Robbed* of so much of its Substance, by such a strange Delusion? If it had been foretold by the wisest Man on Earth Thirty Years ago, that we should have suffer'd .our selves to be thus bubbled by *Rhode-Island*, he would not have been believed.

And should not every Freeholder, and indeed the meanest Inhabitant in this and the Neighbouring Governments, be moved with a just Zeal and Indignation in behalf of his Country, Family and Estate, be it either small or great, to see what they have their Sweat and Toil, and the Inheritance of their Ancestors made a Prey and Property of by the *Rhode-Island* Bills, that in the End are like to be little better than blank bits of Paper?

I must beg Excuse, that I have not been more full and particular on this important Subject: It happens to be at a Season when I can call but very little Time my own; but I hope the Publick will hear further from this Gentleman, when he prints the Acts about the *Rhode Island* Bills, when, I promise to recant my Opinion in these Matters, or give a particular Account of my Reasons to the contrary.

NOTE TO COMMUNICATION ADDRESSED "TO THE AUTHOR OF THE WEEKLY REHEARSAL" OF MARCH 4, 1734.

The writer of this communication is obviously the person who addressed "A Letter to a gentleman in a neighboring government concerning the new notes of hand," which letter was published in the New England Weekly Journal on the 14th of January. It is probable, also, that this is the "more particular answer to the letter from Rhode Island" which was promised to be given to the public "next week" in the postscript to the communication in the Boston Gazette of February 25th.

The exposition of the effect of the decline in the value of the Rhode Island Bills loaned upon mortgages was strong, and the argument that the process of paying off the loans when due and effecting new mortgages for the same nominal amounts, the security required for which would each renewal be smaller, would if continued long enough result practically in the borrower obtaining his original loan for nothing, was ingenious and convincing.

The allegation that the Massachusetts people were borrowing the Rhode Island bills at ten and fifteen per cent interest, and at the same time agreeing to pay their loans off in Massachusetts bills seems incredible, but there can be no doubt as to what the writer says. This statement also would lead us to recur to the charges made by both sides in this controversy that usurers were hoarding the Massachusetts bills with a view of taking advantage of debtors having obligations to meet, specifically payable in such bills, after the bills should have become scarce in consequence of the enforcement of the royal instruction.

The call for the printing of the legislative acts establishing the Rhode Island "banks" and the statement that a messenger had been sent by the Massachusetts government for a copy of their last act of emission, reveals a condition of affairs that seems incredible. Although most of the laws passed by the Rhode Island Assembly were printed, yet they were not put in type promptly after their passage, but were from time to time collated and published in volumes. As a result of this method of proceeding not all the acts were printed and many temporary acts, the date of whose application had expired, were only referred to in these publications by title, so that to-day it is not possible to review the legislation relative to these Rhode Island banks without consulting laws still in manuscript.[1]

The references to the South-Sea Scheme and the Charitable Corporation are repeated in this communication. More particulars concerning these references are given in the note to the article from the Weekly Rehearsal of March 25, and to that note the reader is referred for an account of the latter of these two enterprises.

The copy was obtained from the American Antiquarian Society.

[1] See Currency and Banking in Massachusetts Bay, Vol. I, p. 336.

New-England.   Numb. 1570

The Boſton Weekly News Letter.

From Thurſday February 28, to Thurſday March 7. 1734.

To the Publisher of the Weekly News Letter.

SIR,

If you have room for the following Lines in your next Paper, be pleas'd to insert 'em and you will oblige,

Yours, &c.

Argenteis pugna telis, ac omnia Vinces.

 F the old proverbial saying is true, that *Riches are War's Ground*, then the last *Rhode Island* Emission, and the Notes of the *Massachusett* Merchants, have at least one property of Wealth in them; for they have already begot a *Paper War*.

I am a Neuter, Sir, in the Dispute, as to my private Interest, but am led into the Consideration of the Merits of it, by the perusal of a piece which entered the publick Lists in the Gazette of the 18th instant, on the part of the *Rhode Island* Emission, which is, I perceive, a performance much in Vogue with the Partizans of the Bills of that Colony, and Opposers of the Merchants Notes: and to do the Author of it Justice, his Letter is smoothly and plausibly Pen'd, but his Arguments when brought to the Touchstone, seem to be no more of Sterling Alloy than the Money, in Defence of which he employs his Pen.

Among the Reasons that influenced the Colony to make this last Emission, their Apologist assigns this as the chief, viz. *The want of a sufficient Medium of Exchange for the prodigious Increase of Trade*, Wherefore *it appeared to Persons of Thought and Consideration that the only Method to uphold the Trade and Business of the whole Country, was for some of the Governments not yet restrained from Home, to Emit a sufficient Sum, that might pass among the People, while they were paying in and burning their old Bills; and till Silver and Gold could gradually fix among us.*

I must confess Sir, that I look upon *this prodigious Increase of Trade*, for the Support of which these *Rhode Island* Bills (if you will take this Writer's Word for it) are calculated, to be the real Source of our present Difficulties, and that this boasted Blessing, supposed to be produced by their new Emission, is one of the most pernicious Evils, that can befal the Country; for is it not notorious that the Ballance of Trade (I mean the European Trade, wherein this prodigious Increase chiefly consists) has been for several Years vastly against us; and that *the prodigious Increase* of it must therefore as inevitably bring Poverty upon the Country, as the Increase of a losing Trade would Bankruptcy upon a private Merchant? and can any Person of the least *Thought or Consideration* imagine, that such Emissions as serve to uphold this *prodigious Increase of Trade*, can possibly tend to *fix Silver and Gold among us*; which must necessarily be exported every Year at any rate to make up the Deficiency of our other Returns?

This losing Trade, Sir, is a Monster, that can't be supported upon the natural Produce & Industry of our Colonies, but must be fed with Silver and Gold: It devours every Year what might serve for the Subsistence of many Families of our Province, and requires the Skill and Fortitude of some *Perseus* to destroy it; in order to preserve the remainder of our Substance.

It was *this Increase* of Trade, which at first Introduced into our Province the fatal Necessity of paper Money; which has ever since tended to depreciate, and render it a Cheat upon the British Merchant, the publick Officer, and honest Creditor, and has quite confounded our Notions of a just Payment of our Debts; which by unprofitably employing a Number of Hands in its Service; prevents the Growth of Agriculture and Manufactures among us, and introduces Extravagance, Vanity and Luxury into our private Families.

Now is it not evident that the most effectual Remedy of this growing Evil would be to cut off the Means of it's Support? To restore the Use of Silver and Gold among us, by requiring it in all publick Payments, and making it once more the Medium of Trade within our Province; by this means to *fix* it among us; and thereby reduce this extravagant, spendthrift Trade within the Bounds of our Income; that so we may Traffick for no more foreign Commodities, than what the natural Produce of our Country, our Fisheries and Industry will pay for; and not prodigally consume every Farthing of our Money in the Importation of unnecessary Merchandizes.

This Limitation of our Trade would serve to keep us from growing Poorer; but if we would be a rich, wise and flourishing People; we should still proceed further, and Manufacture at home for our selves (as far as our Country & Number of Hands will afford) whatever Commodities we now purchase with our Silver & Gold from other Countries; and instead of profusely squandering that away abroad, circulate it within our selves in the Improvement of Agriculture and Manufactures, in fortifying and adorning our Country with Defencible and other publick and private Buildings, in the Incouragement of all kinds of Industry, & promoting Arts and Sciences; This, Sir, would effectually produce a Golden Age; and banish this Dishonest Trash, this Imaginary Wealth, and real Poverty from among us.

But I am sensible that such a Jubilee Year is not to be expected under half a Century at least, and that it will require time to regain a Silver and Gold Currency, which must *gradually fix* among us; but in the mean while, Which is the most likely Expedient to prepare the way for it, the *Rhode Island* Emission, or Notes of the Merchants?

It is certain that that paper Currency approaches nearest to Silver Money, which is the least Subject to *fall*: And let any Person impartially determine this point between these two Currencies: The whole of the *Rhode Island* Emission is to be paid in to the *Government* in Twenty Years: The Merchants Notes are payable to the *Possessors* in Ten Years, at three short Periods, by one third Part at the End of each Period. The Author of the *Rhode Island* Letter seems sensible of this Difference, and thereupon observes, *That the fluctuation of the Merchants Notes will be quick and short like a broken, chopping Sea, which puts all in Confusion, while the publick Bills fall and rise slow and gradually.*

That the fluctuation of the Merchants Notes must be quick and short, is certain, because at the End of the two first three Years, and the last four, they must be at least at par: And their fluctuation within the time of each Period, in all probability must be very inconsiderable, the fall of our old Bills is near Two hundred *per Cent.* and I don't perceive that they yet begin to rise: Now it seems in this Writer's Apprehension, this small fluctuation of the Merchants Notes will be *a broken, chopping Sea, that will put all things in Confusion,* but *the slow gradual fall of the publick Bills,* 200 *per Cent* will be attended with no ill Consequence: I must confess, Sir, that on the contrary this fall of the publick Bills seems to me to have produced such Mountain Billows, as threaten to overwhelm the unhappy Adventurers in the public Loans with much greater Ruin, than the gentle fluctuation of the Merchants Notes can possibly bring on the Borrowers in their Scheme.

But in another part of the *Rhode Island* Letter, the Writer acknowledges *that the fall of the publick Bills will prove a Ruin to Thousands*; but imputes it intirely to the Merchants Notes, by means of which *the Merchants* (he says) *will get into their hands the old Bills at par, & sell 'em out again to those who have Mortgag'd their Estates for them, and must redeem them at* 150 *per Cent. advance.* How contradictory to himself is he in this acknowledment! How trifling the Reason, he assigns for this Ruin! I would feign know whether these poor Mortgagors will be in a better Case, if the *Rhode Islanders* should purchase our old province Bills with their new Emission, which I dare promise will not be equal to Silver at *Nineteen Shillings* per Ounce, by the Year 1741, *even tho' they are Sanctioned with the publick Faith of their Government.* Can any thing be more groundless & frivolous than this Charge against the Notes? Would not any new *public Bills* be liable to the same Exception? And is it not in the Power of the *rich Men* of the Province to ingross into their hands these old Bills, tho' the Merchants Notes had never been Emitted?

Another Advantage of the *Rhode Island* Bills, insisted upon by this Writer, is, that they have *the Sanction of the publick Faith:* This is a Pledge of inestimable Value in his Eyes: But for what is their publick Faith given? Why, that *these Bills shall be equal in Value to Money in all publick Payments, and shall be acoordingly accepted by the Treasurer and Receivers subordinate to him,* &c. Now would not any honest well meaning Man be apt to imagine from the Tenour of their Bills, that the publick Payments into their Treasury were equal to their Emissions, and would consequently take in and satisfy their publick Bills to the Possessors? And does not the Tenour of them imply as much? For who would think that they should propose their publick Payments as a security for the Satisfaction of these Bills to the Possessors, unless those Payments were equal to the Bills? But the Fact, Sir, is really otherwise; the Charge of their Government amounts to but a Trifling Sum in Comparison of their Emissions, and may be defray'd with the *Interest only* of their Loan Bills: And now what a wonderful Satisfaction and Security must *the Sanction of their public Faith* be to the Possessors of these Bills, after giving such a notable Instance of it upon the very Face of them.

But I suppose it will be answer'd, that if their publick Payments are not equal to the Quantity of their Bills; yet the whole of the Bills being to be paid within the Space of Twenty Years, by the Borrowers of the several Loans, who have Mortgaged their Lands, to double the Value of the Bills for the Payment of 'em; the Possessors of the Bills will be secure of being paid, at the end of Twenty

Years, because the Mortgagors must purchase 'em to redeem their Lands, at the end of that Period at farthest :
But who will be bound for *the Publick Faith* in this Case ?
that the Government will not postpone the calling in the
Bills to a further Day; they have once violated the *Publick
Faith* in this Point already : And what great *Sanction* does
their *broken Faith* give to this last Emission; is it not surprizing in this Gentleman to talk *of the Sanction of their
Publick Faith*, in this Case, to Persons who have experienc'd so late a Breach of it ?

But we will suppose the Bills punctually called in, the
Bonds and Mortgages of the several Borrowers, who prove
deficient in their Payments, put in suit: Yet what legal
Demand have the Possessors of the Bills to be paid out
of the Lands or Silver when recover'd by the Publick ?
None in the least ? they must in such Case become humble
Suitors, and stand to the Courtesy of the Government :
But I am much afraid that such a Suit would at the best
prove long and tedious; and would not any Person who
depends upon a punctual Payment, choose to have his
Remedy in his own Hands; and prefer the *Sanction of
a Writ, Judgment, and Execution*, against the Persons, and
Estates of the ten Signers of the Merchant's Notes, for the
Payment of his Debt in Silver or Gold, at three short Periods, then *the Sanction of this boasted Publick Faith*,
for a distant Payment, no Body knows when, nor how ?

But to resume the *Motto* at the Head of my Paper, which
is a Translation of an old Greek Line, that was grown into
an Adage among the Ancients, the English of which, when
apply'd to our present Purpose, may be thus render'd viz.
A Silver Currency is the best means for us to surmount all

our Difficulties. I declare, Sir, for Silver against general Paper Currencies of all kinds.

Paper Money is the Reproach and Scandal of our Province; *First*, for that whereas we had originally a Silver Currency among us; we have Extravagantly squander'd it away in purchasing foreign Commodities, which we ought either *industriously* to have produc'd and manufactur'd our selves; or (if that was not to be done) frugally to have liv'd without 'em. *Secondly*, for that it has made us dishonest in the Payment of our Debts, both at Home and abroad, to the great Dishonour and Infamy of our Country: Have we not therefore, more need of Sumptuary Laws to restrain our Vanity and Extravigance than of new Emissions of Paper to incourage it?

But since under our present Circumstances, a Paper Currency of some kind is necessary: Ought we not to choose that, which has a natural Tendency to redress our Grievances, before that which tends to increase 'em? And after all the Objections, Cavils and Surmizes, that have been made against the Merchant's Notes, we must own that their *Scheme* is better calculated to answer the great Purposes, of fixing the Price of Silver; bringing a greater Quantity of it into our Province, and retrenching that Bane of the Country, the excessive Importation of *European* Goods, not only than the *Rhode-Island* Emissions, which I look upon to have no Intrinsick Value in 'em, but even than the usual Emissions of our own Government, *First*, because the Merchants Notes must at the End of each of their Periods, be equal to Silver at *Nineteen Shillings* per Ounce, and consequently fix the Price of it, as far as 110,000 *l.* in these Notes will go; And the Fluctuation in the mean time must be inconsiderable. *Secondly*, if this Scheme is faithfully executed, it must bring a Quantity of Silver into the Province, to answer the Notes, and fix it there; and *Thirdly*, lessen the Importation of *European* Goods, by hindering so much Silver from being exported by way of Returns, to the *European* Merchants, for such Goods; the natural Consequences of which, are the restoring by degrees a Silver Currency among us, and Improvement of our own Manufactures.

Whereas on the contrary every Publick Emission has been found by Experience to increase our *European* Trade; by that means to carry our Silver out of the Province for Returns to *Europe*; consequently to raise it's Price every Year, thereby to depreciate the former Emissions, and make your whole Paper Currency become a general Cheat upon *our foreign Correspondents*, in that they are not honestly paid the Price agreed upon for their Goods upon *our selves*; in that it impoverishes our Province more and more every Year.

These are the known, acknowledg'd ill Effects of the Publick Emissions; whilst on the other hand the Merchant's Notes have all the *sterling Properties* in 'em, that Paper can have; that is, there is a Bank or Stack of Silver or Gold to answer 'em; they are payable at a certain Day, which is not to be protracted by the Emitters, without the Possessors Consent; and may be demanded and recovered by the Possessor in an ordinary Course of Law: These are the very *Properties*, which give the Bank Notes and Bonds of our Companies in *England*, the same Currency with Silver all over *Europe*.

For these Reasons, Sir, the Merchant's Scheme seems to me to promise fairer for retrieving our Circumstances, than any other Scheme yet offer'd to the Publick: Whether it is arriv'd to perfection, is another Question; if it has any Defects in it, let it be amended & improv'd: But what folly! to vote it's Dststruction (if it is in the main for the Service of the Publick) either because of the Clamour of the Self-interested designing *Rhode Islanders*, or of the little Cavils of some of our Province, who perhaps are disappointed of an Exorbitant Interest, which they exacted before the Circulation of these Notes, or of others who perhaps are deep in Debt, which they hope to pay more easily by the depreciating of our Paper Money, still more and more every Year.

NOTE TO COMMUNICATION ADDRESSED "TO THE PUB-
  LISHER OF THE BOSTON WEEKLY NEWS LETTER" OF
  MARCH 7, 1734.

The writer of this communication was stimulated to action by the voluminous defence of the Rhode Island bills which appeared in the Boston Gazette of February 18th. He believes that paper money is responsible for the increase of imports which the writer in the Gazette claimed to be the cause for the Rhode Island emissions, and if this were the case then more Rhode Island bills would cause more imports, and other emissions would be needed to meet the situation. Paper money he thinks prevents the growth of agriculture and manufactures, and fosters extravagance, vanity and luxury.

He analyzes the promises of the Rhode Island government to receive their bills at the treasury in all public payments and points out that the annual public payments would not absorb the interest on the loans. As for the bills being called in at the end of the loans, he calls attention to the fact that the colony has once violated that promise and believes that it will be done again.

His argument in favor of the stability of the value of the Merchants' Notes is sound, but he does not seem to appreciate the fact that even if these notes were better than the Rhode Island bills, the emission of £110,000 had the same effect on the financial situation as the emission of the same amount of any other bills which could circulate for the same value would have done.

The copy was obtained from the Boston Public Library. The same communication was published in the New England Weekly Journal, March 11, 1734.

A Modest Apology for PAPER MONEY,

In A LETTER to a Friend.

SIR,

I Do the more readily comply with your Request, in giving you my Thoughts in the Nature and Consequence of *Paper Money*, because I imagine 'tis altogether a Mistake to say, " it is of no real Value, and prejudicial to the Country, and the Interest of *Great Britain*," as you are pleased to express your self.

I shall readily allow, that the Worth of *Silver* depends in a great Measure on its Scarcity; but it don't follow thence, that the Quantity of *Silver* is an invariable Measure of the Value of other Things, because other Things do also vary their Value according to the Scarcity, let *Silver* it self be Plenty and Scarce. There is no Intrinsick Value in any Thing, but the *Necessaries of Life*, and and what is immediately necessary to produce them, as *Land* and *Labour*. Mankind may put an imaginary Value on *Silver* and *Gold*, to facilitate 'Commerce, which is the Exchange of the Produce of their *Land* and *Labour*, and so *Gold* and *Silver* may be a common Measure between that Produce; but so may any Thing else, if Men will, and they often have agreed in it. There is from hence no more intrinsick Value in them, than in the Weights and Measures by which Men

buy and sell. The Reason why *Silver* is better than
Wampumpeag, is only that more People are, or have agreed
to pass it; and tho' for that Reason *Silver* and *Gold* are
better for exporting, or for foreign Payments, yet in all
rich trading Countries, *Paper Money*, or Bank Bills are best
esteemed for large Payments and Inland Trade. You will
object perhaps, that they are valued so high, because they
will always command *Gold* and *Silver* at the Banks: But
I answer, 'tis because they will command the Things for the
sake of which alone the *Gold* and *Silver* is so highly valued.
It is a grand Mistake to think the running Cash gives the
Credit to such Bills; the Bills of *Venice* are 20 *per Cent.*
above *Silver*, when there is not a *Ducket* in their Treasury.
'Tis the *Land Security* which supports them and gives
them a Currency; and that is the very best Security.
They are *coined Land*, and actually worth the Land which
is pledged for them; and that has most certainly an intrinsick Value in it. You will object the Fate of our *Paper
Bills*, and think perhaps *that* effectually confutes whatever
can be said in their Favour. But there are several Things
to be considered before you pass your *definitive Sentence.*
1. The Money which passes in the Plantations and Colonies,
must always be worse, that is of more nominal Value than
in the Mother Country, except where *Silver* is the natural
Produce of the Country. 2. 'T is in the Power of Traders
to advance or depreciate any Currency in spight of the Government, and they always will do that which Interest directs.
3. Our Bills not passing or being designed to pass in
England, our Necessities and our Improvements have forced
us to submit to the depreciating our Bills. But as they are
on *Double Land Security* in a growing Country, I fear we

shall all be sadly convinced, they have all along been worth more than they have ever passed at, or were designed to pass at. And I apprehend had a small Premium been added to them in all publick Payments, they had never fell below what they were first passed at, whatever had become of *Silver* and *Gold.* So that 'tis not the Nature of *Paper Money* which has occasioned the Fall of our Bills, but other Causes obvious to every Man who is acquainted with the State and Circumstances of the Country.

I was sorry to hear you say, *Paper Money had impoverished the Country*; for tis most certain the richest Trading Countries have the most *Paper Money*; they cannot carry on so great Trade without it, and have got part at least of their Riches by it. It has facilitated their own Commerce among themselves at Home, and that is for ever the true Way to have a large and gainful Trade abroad. I own I have heard a dismal Complaint of the declining State of the Province, and the deplorable Condition of this Town, ever since I can remember; but what is there in such Complaints, but only the Impatience and Vanity of Humane Minds? Is not this Cry universal, and as old as *Solomon?* Was it not the Cry in *England* for 100 Years together after Queen *Elizabeth*, while the Nation increased so prodigiously in Riches? Let us compare the present Condition of this Province, with what it was 30 Years ago; Tell the new Towns and Parishes; observe the Buildings, the Furniture, the Habit and Diet of the People in general, but especially take Notice of this Town, tell the New Buildings the Rope-walks, Ship-yards, Still-houses, Sugar-houses, and the other Trades Depending upon these; the Number of Ships and Vessels of all Sorts, but especially, tell the

Merchants and Traders, consider our Expence in Tea, Cloths, Velvets, Silks, Lace, Jewels, Plate and Chaises, the Country Seats, and many other Things not to be numbr'd, increasing Daily. I am far from ascribing all these Alterations to *Paper Money*, but can you seriously think we shou'd have grown faster if we had had none at all? In my Opinion, we owe more to *Paper Money* than any People on Earth, except the Dutch. It is true, Bills have unhappily fallen in their Value, but what Harm has this really done the Country in general? For *what one in the Province has lost, another has got, and the Province has it*, as a very ingenious, 'tho' otherwise mistaken Gentleman has observed: And certainly it is very hard to be reproached with the Fall of our Bills or our Luxury, by such as were the immediate Instruments and greatest Gainers by both.

Most certainly the Emission of *Paper Money* to pay the Publick Debts, was so just and necessary, that no Body can with any shew of Reason object against that. If I owe any Man, and can't pay him directly, he expects my Bond or Note. This was the Case of the Country, and therefore was honest, just and prudent, and had the Bills run in the Tenour of those emitted in 1690. I know no Inconvenience wou'd have happened. And as to the *Banks of Loan*, the Circumstance of the Province made them necessary and prudent. For our *Silver* being gone when, or before we emitted the first Bills, we cou'd not carry on our Trade and spare the Bills in our Taxes. And our Climate and Soil necessitate us to live by Trading, more than any other of the Plantations, who have some Staple Commodity to send Home for the Manufacturers they consume, while we have none, and that is the Foundation of our Difficulties.

I suppose that it will be allowed me, that the more we consume and pay for of the *English* Manufactures, the more beneficial we are to our Mother Country: The more Hands we employ then in Fishery, in Husbandry, and such Manufactures as don't interfere with *Great Britain*, the more we consume of their Manufactures; and as we live in a cold Climate, the more numerous we are, and the better we affect and can afford to go, the more we consume of that Manufacture the *Woollen*, which is the proper Staple of *England*. The Question then is, How can we best pay for so much as we want, and wou'd have if we cou'd pay for it? Now our Soil is so like that of *England*, that we naturally raise nothing they want, in Exchange for their Woollen and other Manufactures which we must always want from them, except Lumber, and Masts and Fur. Much of the Fur Trade was lost by the Settling the Country, and other Means, but we hope the prudent Conduct of his Excellency and the General Assembly, will recover part at least of that valuable Trade to us again. Ships and other Vessels are rather a Manufacture, than the Produce of our Land; but the Returns herewith made, and by Fish and Oil which we catch in our own and distant Coasts, will not near pay for what we must be necessarily supplied with from *Great Britain*. And we have powerful Rivals in the Fur and Fishery, not only from our Own but other Nations; so that we are forced to be industrious to Trade on an equal Foot with them, and make Remittances to *Great Britain*. This gives Rise to our Plantation Trade; we send our Refuse Fish, Lumber, Horses, &c. to purchase what is necessary to the Fishery, or such other Commodities as will answer in *England*. But for the carrying on this Trade among ourselves, we want the

Assistance of *Paper Money*. The whole Country may be compared to a Man on a New Farm; there he must work diligently to bring his Land to, and besides that must work abroad at Day-Labour, or at some Trade to support his Family, and provide Clothing and Utensils in the mean Time. If Money be scarce, the Difficulty of exchanging the Produce of his Labour will keep him low and back; but if there be a reasonable Plenty of any Currency (be it *Silver* or *Paper*, and the nominal Value what you please) he could the more easily support himself by his Labour in a comfortable Manner, as having more Work and more Ease in procuring his Pay: So I say, we can't carry on the Fishery and other Business without some Currency, and Silver being gone, *Paper Money* was necessarily and consequently Beneficial to *England*, as enabling us on the whole, to buy more of their Manufactures. Had we no *Paper*, some *Silver* wou'd have doubtless stopped with us, but not enough to carry on our Trade, and it is by *that* we live, at least, so well as we do live. And *Silver* I believe wou'd have been higher than now it is with us; for 'tis no Absurdity to say, that *Silver* is even 25 Shillings *per Ounce* in some parts of *Great Britain* now, tho' called by the same Name and Denomination as at *London*. We must without *Paper Money*, have all lived poorer, and sent less Fish and other Things abroad, and *Silver* to *England*, and received less of their Woollen and other Manufactures which we shou'd feel the Want of. For whatever People may think, who are unacquainted with the Country, or have never made a Calculation, we have scarce Wool of our own for each Person a pair of Stockings once a Year, and the Linen Manufacture wou'd interfere with *Ireland*, and as for Hemp, we see excessive Bounties do not prevail with the People to raise it; and this it is to be feared is in some measure owing to the Nature of our Soil. Considering our necessary Subjection to, and Dependance on our Mother Country, we are as much obliged to be a Trading People, if we wou'd be beneficial to *England*, as the *Dutch* are for their own Subsistance. We have no Staple as the other Plantations have to remit to *England* for what we want; and as we consume vastly more of the Woollen Manufacture than any other Plantation, & as that is the Staple of *England*, 'tis certainly their Interest to encourage us in our Plantation Trade, that we may pay them for what we can consume, and for that End to suffer or rather to necessitate us, to have chiefly a *Paper Currency* among our selves. This has made me wonder at the Policy of forbiding our Emitting any Bills, and the Duty lately laid on Molasses and Rum, which amounts to more than a Prohibition of our Trade with the Foreign Plantations, while our own can't consume half what we have to spare. For thereby we shall be forced sore against our Wills, and the Interest of *England*, to contract our Trade and our manner of Living, to raise more Wooll, or go much meaner clad, or leave the Country for a warmer Climate.

If it be objected, that some Merchants have lost in their Trade with us, it can't be justly imputed to *Paper Money*, more than Silver is chargeable with the Losses in any Voyage to Spain or elsewhere. If the Merchants in *London* over-stock any Country with the *English* Manufactures, they must and always will lose whether their Money be *Paper* or *Silver*; such Country will always advance on their own Produce, or lower the Value of the Good so imported. But the Market will find it self, and such Loss is only the Merchant's, the poor People were paid for their Labour before-hand. And if it was constantly a losing Trade, no Merchant wou'd be concern'd with it. I own I am concerned at the melancholy Prospect that is now before us, since our Trade is crampt, but I hope a kind Providence will find some Way, yet unthought of, for our support, or else I comfort my self with hoping, that the Poverty of our outward Circumstances will bring us back to our pristine Simplicity, Frugality, Sincerity, and other Virtues which always thrive most in the poorest, thinest and least polite Countries. But as all Men seem to think Riches the true Happiness of every Country, I can't but hope, if not for our own, yet for the Sake of *England* it self, we shall find Favour at Home, so far as to have equal Liberty with other Governments, of supplying our selves with a proper Medium of Exchange, suitable to our Necessities; which besides the vast Advantage it wou'd be to the Trade of the Country in General, and consequently to our Mother Country, wou'd prevent the ill Effects of *private Contracts*, and the *groundless Objections* daily raised against our Neighbours, for using that Liberty we shou'd rejoice to have the Advantage of. But why may we not hope for it? We have the Merit of the most expensive Loyalty of any of the Plantations to boast of: 'Twas our vast Expence in our Attempts to enlarge the *British* Dominions, which first forced us into *Paper Money*: And by the Way, should there be a War, notwithstanding our ill success for want of supplies at one Time, and thro' Treachery at another, instead of being discouraged or terrified with a *French* Invasion, I hope I shou'd still see one more Visit paid to our Neighbours at *Canada*. And certainly the Reduction of that Place wou'd be of more Service to the Crown of *Great Britain*, than even *Gibraltar* and *Port-Mahon* can possibly be.

I am Yours, &c.

Boston, March 8th. 1734.

NOTE TO "A MODEST APOLOGY FOR PAPER MONEY, IN A LETTER TO A FRIEND," PUBLISHED IN THE WEEKLY REHEARSAL OF MARCH 18, 1734.

This defence of paper money is well written, temperate in tone, and whether one accepts the inferences drawn by the writer or not, he may still turn to it for a clear and concise exposition of the trade relations which then existed between England and the New England colonies. The writer calls attention to the fact that New England had nothing to offer the mother country in exchange for her manufactures except things which she produced herself. Other colonies were able to furnish products which England could not successfully raise, but the similarity of the New England country, and the limitations imposed by the seasons cut off the New England colonies from any special resources which could be made use of by way of exchange in dealing with Great Britain. The fur trade had been ruined as the country was settled. The fisheries remained, but the fishermen were compelled to go farther and farther afield for their catches, and at best England had fisheries of her own. Moreover, the Molasses Act, which he termed "prohibitory," threatened the colonial fisheries, and if enforced would reduce the field to the supply of the local demand, since it cut off our dealers from a market for their low grade products, or, as the writer termed them, their refuse fish.

The writer says that no inconvenience would have happened in Massachusetts from the bills of public credit, had they "run in the Tenour of those emitted in 1690." What is the meaning of this? The bills emitted in 1690 were in the form of certificates of indebtedness on the part of the "Colony," as it was then termed, and were declared to be equal in value to money. They were in terms receivable by the treasurer and his subordinates for all public dues and for any stock in the treasury. The bills of public credit in circulation in 1734 were replicas of the " Colony" bills with the exception that the word " Province " was substituted for "Colony." The writer makes still another statement which requires some sort of explanation in order that it shall become credible. "'Tis no absurdity to say," he remarks, " that *Silver* is even 25 shillings *per Ounce* in some parts of *Great Britain* now, tho' called by the same Name and Denomination as at *London.*" The price of silver in Boston at the date of the emission of the Merchants' Notes was 19 *s.* an ounce, and the value of those notes was expressed in weights of silver based upon that price. What currency was there in circulation in any part of Great Britain which was so much more degraded than that of Massachusetts? Does he mean to include the colonies under that term?

At any rate these statements, which are probably capable of some sort of explanation, are suggestive and interesting.

The copy was procured from the American Antiquarian Society.

THE   Numb. 130.

Weekly Rehearsal.

Monday, March 25. 1734.

To the Author of the Weekly Rehearsal.

SIR,

As I think my self obliged to detect the Fallacy, and shew the Weakness of the Letter you published *March* the 4th. 'tis but common Justice to give me the Opportunity of your Paper: And I must desire you to correct the Errors of the Press.

However Shifting and Evasion, and a Multiplicity of Words are always used in a bad Cause, and however his good Judges in private may applaud his Artifice; yet the Author of that Letter can never excuse to the Publick, his being so tediously Prolix, so positive, and so Pathetical in an Affair, he confesses himself to know little or nothing of, with any Certainty; when he so lightly passes over what he is well acquainted with, *viz.* the small and uncertain Value of the private Notes, the vast Gain of the Undertakers, and the bare-faced Imposition on the Publick. We don't wonder he so misrepresents our Banks, since he pretends not to have seen our Acts of Assembly; but we admire he would amuse the Publick with the meer Inventions of his own Fancy. We were so far from making a *Secret* of our Acts of Assembly, (as 'tis well known a certain Society long refused to shew their Scheme to the Publick) that all but the very last have been printed above two Years in our Colony Law-

Book, by which the Gentleman might have better informed himself, than by inquiring of any particular disaffected Persons, altho' Natives and Proprietors of the Colony. And I have Authority to say, the Messenger sent for a Copy of the last Act, (which by the Way, I did before shew wherein it differed from the former) was so far from being denied, that it was by Order drawn for him, but he refused to pay the Clerk, and left it upon his Hands, in whose Office it still lies, and this Gentleman or any Body else may have it for the Fee. On the Perusal of our Acts, this Gentleman will see the Account he gives of the Preamble of our *Sixty Thousand Pound* Emission, is inconsistent both with the Spirit and Letter of that Preamble; that Emission was not designed to enable our Mortgagers, more than yours, to redeem their Land, but to promote and encourage Trade and Industry, while the former Bills were sinking. And the Account he gives of the Method of banking Land, is the very reverse of the Case: Our Law requires not only double Land Security, which their Scheme supposes sufficient, but Bonds over and above. But I must needs ask the Gentleman where is the Injustice, if some Lands are mortgaged for more now than formerly, when every Body knows they have risen by Improvements and the Growth of the Country, more than half in their intrinsick Value, since our first Bills were emitted? But the Gentleman shews he is entirely misinformed of the Nature of our last Emission, and the Security taken for it, as well as of our Law respecting the Interest of Money, which allows of no exorbitant Interest, but the very same with the Law of *England*.

But is it excusable, or even credible, that this Gentleman can be so entirely mistaken in the Nature, the Tenour and

Design of the Publick Loan Bills in general, or that he should wilfully so misrepresent them? He says, "*our Bills don't promise one Ounce of* Silver, *and therefore are worth nothing.*" I might say, neither doth their own private Scheme secure the lodging one Ounce of coined *Silver* in their Bank or Treasury, to redeem their Notes with, notwithstanding all their high Pretences, and the Tenour of their Notes; which therefore by his own Logick, are *nothing*, and worth *nothing*, and will fetch *nothing*. And what inexpressible Confusion will there be at their Periods, if Law-Suits be found necessary! For it was very unjust to say, as he did at first, that no Body who knew the Company, could doubt their Ability to pay Ten Times the Sum of their Notes, which is more than all *New-England* can advance. He talks of a Man's "waiting Twenty Years for the Value of his Bill, and then for all the Credit he has given, and Loss by Discount he has suffered, he gets another Bill, &c." Surely this Gentleman thought he was speaking of his own Notes of Hand, and not of the Publick Bills, which are established for a Medium of Exchange. How absurd are all his suppositions! Do Men keep their Bills lock'd up Twenty Years, and not use them in Trade? or doth or can any Man carry the Bills to the Government, but in Publick Payments, in which they are in Value equal to Money, or by way of redeeming their Land, and then they are cancelled? Neither do your Province Bills, which he acknowledges have a real Value in them, promise more *Silver* than ours, nor does any Man expect they will be changed by the Government. So that all that long and empty Flourish, and affected Repetition of the Word *Nothing*, proves *nothing*, but that he knows *nothing*, or can say *nothing* against our Bills, but what militates as much against yours, but indeed affects neither, as being nothing to the purpose. And besides all this, the Gentleman in the Account he has given, doubled the Time our Bills are emitted for and set at.

I could put Cases not so different from the Truth and Fact, and more probable, in Order to shew the *true Heighth their Notes may come to*, if I would suffer my Fears, or other Passions to work on my Imagination. I could sup_pose, that the Undertakers of the private Notes, finding the Sweet and Benefit of Minting and Coining, without telling the World, or that their Committee without telling the rest or all of their own Company, should strike *two or three hundred thousand Pounds* more off the same Plates, and that when the Secret began to take Air, and the Cheat to be discovered, the Indorser, having taken due Care to vary his Hand writing, should for a valuable Consideration, go and live abroad with KNIGHT and THOMPSON. I don't say this will be the Case, I hope it will not; but if it should, where would be the odds between this *Bubble* and the *South-Sea*, or *Charitable Corporation*, but only that the last robbed the Public of the largest Sum? And I would ask what Security the Publick has, that this will not be the Case, except the meer Honesty of the Committee against an immense Gain? This Gentleman well knows, the Fraud in the *South-Sea* arose from the People's Fault, in implicitly taking Stock at the imaginary Value, the Company or Directors put upon it; and that the first Step to the Ruin of the *Charitable Corporation*, was the Managers Contrivance to enlarge their Capital Stock beyond their Charter or first Scheme.

The Pretence to find an Inconsistency in my Letter, is

too plain a Piece of Art, to palliate the Contradiction between himself and the other Advocate, which is farther widened by their last Letter; and 'tis very odd to see this Gentleman observing on some of my Words; were he not conscious those Words were properly used and rightly applied, (except the Latin Words, which it is plain he misunderstood,) he wou'd never so resent their Use. But in good earnest, what Right has an Anonymous Writer, that has insulted our whole Colony, without any Regard to Truth or Decency, to complain of hard Words, or to expect Bows and Cringes? Had he designed his Letter should pass, as the Merchant's Notes, on the bare Credit of the Signer, and an implicit Confidence in his Judgment and Fidelity, he should have signed his Name at Length, and then we should have treated him with all due Deference: But as it is, in point of Civility, we owe nothing to him, who has done his utmost, tho' ineffectually, to injure the Colony in the highest Degree. I seé therefore no Reason to recede from any of my Expressions; it does yet appear to me false and injurious to say, our New Bank costs us nothing, but *Pen, Ink and Paper*; nor will his mean Evasion clear him of that Charge: For would any Man think him so intolerably impertinent, as by that Expression to mean only the Charge of Emitting or making our Bills? And don't he himself plainly shew, that that was not his meaning, or at least that he did not design to be so understood? It is no wonder he is ashamed of this Expression, when it is plain and self-evident that our Bills are actually equivalent to the Mortgages of our Land, transferred from one Person to another; and their own Scheme supposes Land Security the best. I must also repeat it, that twas trifling and delusory to say, we had more Bills out than the *Massachusetts, New-Hampshire, Connecticut* and *New-York*, all put together; for by the best Information I am assured, and can easily make it appear, that the *Massachusetts* alone have more Bills out than we; and did New-York Bills ever pass among us here, any more than the Bank Bills of *Amsterdam*? or did we ever emit any Bills but upon the same good Security? Unless therefore he will say and demonstrate, there was no need of a new Supply of a Medium of Exchange, to support the Trade of the Country in general; unless he will prove there was any other Way for a reasonable Supply, by denying *Connecticut* was in an Uproar about the ill Effects of their private Bank, and that your Province had made before at least one Bank, partly to prevent such pernicious Contrivances of private Men, and is now unhappily restrained from Home; I say, unless he denies and disproves all this, 'tis trifling in the highest degree, to reckon how many Bills we have out, and a gross Delusion of the Country.

I admire he should persist in ascribing their Undertaking to a *publick Spirit*, when in his first Letter, he had assured his Friend, that the Design had not taken Effect, but for the sake of the private Interest of the Undertakers themselves. Indeed if the Undertakers really expect in general to lose Six *per Cent.* on their Notes, as the Gentleman roundly affirms, it furnishes a parallel to that Generosity and publick Spirit, which diverts my pleasant Correspondent in the Gazette of Feb. the 25th. But can any Man imagine how he makes such a Calculation? or what they do with the *Thirty thousand Pounds* at least, which they gain the first Day their Notes are emitted, supposing they obtain a general Currency; or the Six *per Cent.* they let them out at, and the immense Gain they will make other ways, as well as by having such a large Addition to the Currency at once? Tho' by the Way, we never supposed all the Undertakers would make a proportionable Profit.

It is no ways difficult to account for *Silver's* Rising *one Shilling* per Ounce last Spring; but 't is impossible to prove from that alone, that Bills really sell so much at the same Time: And it is a Fallacy to insinuate from thence, that Publick Bills will not rise as the Periods of the Funds draw near, as it is also to say, the Undertakers could have as easily engrossed or hoarded the Publick Bills, by the help of our new Emission, as by their own Notes; for our new Bills wou'd cost them as much as the other Bills, while their own Notes really cost them nothing at all: for their odd *Ten thousand Pound* is plainly designed to bear the Charge of *Pen, Ink* and *Paper*, and their Dividends generally let out at Interest to other Men,.if paid in publick Bills, those Bills will, when the Periods arrive, be vastly better than their private Notes, as has been shown; and if paid in the same Notes, they will be ready for cancelling, without the Undertakers advancing one Ounce of *Silver*, or putting themselves to one Penny charge, and gaining Twelve *per Cent.* at least from the Publick, they can certainly better afford to hoard up the Publick Bills. And it is as great a Fallacy to insinuate, that our Mortgagers could make such Advantages, since they have the Bills we emit only in small Quantities, and can have no Advantage in your Government, without exposing their real Estates as much in this by it. And as to the Usurers, of whom this Gentleman bespeaks a Favour, we suppose they are in all Governments on an equal Footing, and no one can any

more see the Reason than the Justice of their Views; but
'tis absurd to say, Fore-handed Men are peculiarly exposed
to any Losses by the Fall of Bills, as they above all Men
have it in their Power to help themselves, and we know are
never wanting to their own Interest: And every body sees
none are so hot against New Emissions, as those who have
raised the greatest Fortunes by the Old.

It is pleasant to hear this Gentleman gravely affirm their
Scheme is no Bubble, because the Notes can never be pretended to be worth more than *Silver* at *Nineteen Shillings*
per Ounce, while it is a Bubble to pretend they are worth
so much now, or even till the last Period is safely arrived,
thro' the many Dangers it is attended with, when there
will be only four Tenths to receive. Sometimes he encourages us to take their Notes, by saying, they will grow
better daily; at another time he says, they can never rise
above what they express. Does he not consequently allow,
that they are not worth so much now? And tho' he pretends People may agree before-hand accordingly, yet the
honest and inconsiderate People, he is so melancholy about,
and which make up the Bulk of his injured suffering
Country, are incapable of such a Calculation, and must
therefore of Necessity be imposed on by such as are, *to wit*,
the Undertakers themselves. All his Complaints against
our Emissions, for tending to sink the Value of Publick
Bills, come with the worst Grace imaginable from an Advocate for those Notes, which do actually depreciate the Bills
vastly more than any of our Emissions, undervaluing them
more than *Sixty per Cent.* at once, purely that the Undertakers may pass off their own Notes, which can never
rise to the true Height of the Bills, to the unavoidable

Damage of the Land-holders, and all others, except themselves.

The other Gentleman afore mentioned is very merry in the Use of the Word *Fluctuation*: Our Bills, *he says*, have only fell in Value, which is no Fluctuation; but as he makes *Silver* the Standard, 'tis his Mistake, for *Silver* rose and fell, and rose again within the Period I mentioned. And it is absurd for this Gentleman to say, the Alteration of the Value of their Notes can't be properly called a *Fluctuation*, because 'tis known before-hand; for I may safely say, the wisest Man on Earth cannot foretel how great the Necessities of some, or Artifice of other Persons may make that Alteration: And whoever is acquainted with the Course of Exchange in *Europe*, knows there is *almost* as great an Alteration, if I may not say Fluctuation, between the several Countries there, as in the Price of *Silver* in the Time I mentioned; which Fluctuation or Alteration by the way, is unfairly made *Ten per Cent.* more than the Truth.

But since I am not so happy as to please this Gentleman in my own Mode of Expression, nor in the Application of his, I shall take leave to use the Words of some other Persons, which being in Point, can't be misapplied by me, any more than they can be disproved by himself. 1 *The Company* (he is Advocate for) *has assumed a Power that no ways belongs to it.* I must add that as the Attorney-General's Opinion in this Case was published, they should have taken Warning by that; for no Jesuitical Distinction between Spirit and Letter can reconcile their Scheme to that Opinion. 2. *Instead of importing Silver, they only oblige themselves to gather in and cancel their own Notes at certain Periods*, after they have had double Interest on them, besides other Advantages the whole Term.   3. *Their Profit will be unreasonably great, and their Scheme is only a Bubble for the Benefit of some private Men. They depreciate the Publick Bills by their Speciality. There is a Fallacy on the pretended main Support of the Credit of those Notes, and they are not strictly a Tenour to the Emitters themselves.*

I would recommend these Things, and what I have now urged against the pernicious Consequences of their Scheme, to this Gentleman for a Satisfactory Answer, when he shall be more at leisure, or to *some other and better Hand*; reminding him, that he has not attempted to Answer several of those Objections I had urged before: Particularly let him shew if he can, what Reason we have to believe there will not be numberless *Bubbles* of this sort if this should take, as was the Case in *Lotteries*. Let him shew if he can, that their Necessity of making Returns, has not equally affected all Paper Currency. Let him shew if he can, that one Ounce of *Silver*, to be paid three, six, and ten Years hence is worth *Nineteen Shillings* in Hand in publick Bills; especially as we have no Security of being paid any *Silver* at all. It will be Time enough after that for him to see our Acts of Assembly, which he with such seeming Earnestness so often demands of me, after they have been published by Beat of Drum in our Capital, as he calls it, proclaimed in every Town in the Colony, and all but the last printed above two Years ago. And I appeal to the Judgment of the whole Country, whether this Advocate has defended their private Scheme, and justified the rash Conduct of the Company, in providing a Remedy for our Difficulties, which is already found much worse than the Disease, involving all Trade & Commerce in such Confusion & Uncertainty, as no Man can tell how or when we shall be extricated from; besides imposing so prodigiously on the whole Country, making the Publick pay them most exorbitant Interest for the Credit it gives them, for this Medium of Trade, which is of no certain Value, must constantly vary, and is without any Security to the Publick.

I am, Sir, Yours, &c.

Newport, March 13th, 1733 – – 4.

P. S. As to the Letter in the *News-Letter* March the 7th, I have only Room to Remark; The Author was unhappy in the Choice of his Motto, which was only Advice to gain the leading Men by Presents, and was always understood to be a Recommendation of Bribery. It is unfair in him to pretend he is a *Neuter*, since he prefers their larger Emission, which affords more Food to the Monster he is so afraid of. It is a Mistake to suppose, the Merchants Notes will have any Tendency to *fix*, or even *bring in* Silver among us. He says, *Silver* can't fix among us under half a Century; consequently it was prudent whilst we had Power, to provide for a Supply of Paper after Forty one. By the pretended Certainty of the Merchant's Notes, they render all Debts and Contracts much more uncertain than before.

The Defects of their Scheme, which he confesses, are essential, can never be amended, but by cancelling their Notes entirely, or grafting them on the Province, as *Connecticut* was forced to do by their private Bank last Year.

NOTE TO A COMMUNICATION FROM NEWPORT DATED MARCH
13, 1734, ADDRESSED "TO THE AUTHOR OF THE WEEKLY
REHEARSAL" AND PUBLISHED MARCH 25, 1734.

The writer of this letter suggests the possibility of an over issue of
the Merchants' Notes.   The committee which managed this Boston
enterprise was composed of ten of the most prominent merchants of
that place.   Each note that was emitted not only bore the personal
signatures of five of these committee men, but it was also endorsed
by Richard Clarke, in whose favor all of the notes ran.   Any over-
issue would have required the coöperation of five of the committee
men and the endorser.   This seemed to the writer of the letter not
beyond the range of possibility, and he even added that the endorser
might give his assistance to the commission of the fraud " by varying
his hand-writing."   Should such a conjectural conspiracy be actually
carried out, he thought that the endorser might be induced " for a
valuable consideration " to " go and live abroad with KNIGHT and
THOMPSON."   "I don't say," he then added, " this will be the case.
I hope it will not ; but if it should, where would be the odds between
this *Bubble* and the *South-Sea*, or *Charitable Corporation*, but only
that the last robbed the Public of the largest Sum?"   He attributed
the losses in both of the above-mentioned cases to stock dealing,
saying, in the case of the South-Sea affair, that they "arose from
the People's fault in implicitly taking Stock at the imaginary Value
the Company or Directors put upon it;   and that the first Step to the
Ruin of the *Charitable Corporation*, was the Managers Contrivance
to enlarge their Capital Stock beyond their Charter or first
Scheme."
There would be no occasion to annotate this paragraph if the
reference had been confined to the South Sea Company and its
cashier, for although the name of Knight may not suggest itself at
once to the reader on mention of the title of that company, still the
story of his prominent connection with the speculation in the stock
of the company and of his flight with the books has caused mention
of his name to be made by many encyclopædic writers upon this

topic, so that even if one were unfamiliar with the history of the
. period, very slight investigation would disclose the ignominious
flight of Knight.   Such, however, is not the case in connection with .
the career of Thompson.   Nor was the failure of the Charitable
Corporation so markedly impressed upon the history of the period
as to leave traces easily to be discovered by casual inspection.[1]   As
a matter of fact, writers of history of the class that one would ordinarily consult for information upon topics of this sort have neglected
the Charitable Corporation and have failed to exhibit Thompson in
the position of the awful example where he was pilloried by the
Boston writer in 1734.   The disturbance created by the failure of
the Corporation was confined to London; but its story has been
preserved in parliamentary documents connected with proceedings
directed against the company itself, and simultaneously, with hearings relating to the establishment of a lottery for the relief of the
creditors and of the proprietors of the Corporation.   The ingenious
and thoroughly up-to-date methods by which Thompson appropriated all and even more than all that there was of the Charitable Corporation are to be found in detail in committee reports made to the
House of Lords [2] and to the House of Commons.[3]

[1] I ought, under the circumstances, to acknowledge that I was set upon the
track which has enabled me to furnish the sources of authority for a history of
the Charitable Corporation by the kind assistance of Mr. Albert Matthews.
Once started in the right direction the resources proved to be abundant.   Quite
recently I found by chance in a bound volume of pamphlets in the Library of the
Massachusetts Historical Society, a pamphlet bearing the title " Five Speeches
as they were spoken in the House of Commons.   By W------ S--------, Esq;
[Price One Shilling] "   A second title-page read as follows: " Four Speeches
against Continuing the Army, &c.   As they were spoken on several occasions in
the House of Commons.   As also, A Speech for Relieving the Unhappy Sufferers in the Charitable Corporation ; as it was spoken in the House of Commons,
May 8. 1732.   By W ------ S ------, Esq. London.   1732."
    The speaker has apparently been identified by some person who has written
the word " William Shippen " on one of the leaves.   There was nothing of importance in the speech.
    [2] The Report of the Commissioners appointed for taking, stating and determin-
ing the claims of the Creditors and proprietors of the Charitable Corporation.
Printed by order of the House of Lords, London, 1732.
    [3] Details concerning the progress of legislation and investigation are scattered

In Strype's Stow's Survey it is stated that the incorporation of this company took place in the 6th of Queen Anne, December 22, 1708.[1] A committee appointed by the House of Commons to investigate the affairs of the Corporation reported that it was incorporated December 22, 1707. If the date of the year be changed to 1707, in the paragraph in Strype, the statement there made will be reconciled with the facts of the case. The assertion is also made in the report that until October 26th, 1725, the company did little business, the probability being that until that date its transactions were confined to the legitimate sphere of the work for which it was organized. The field of action was specifically set forth in the title of the company in the following words: The " Charitable Corporation for the relief of industrious poor, by assisting them with small sums upon pledges, at legal interest."

In 1719, the directors began a campaign for the enlargement of their operations. They issued a pamphlet entitled " Mons Pietatis Londinensis: A narrative or account of the Charitable Corporation,"[2] etc., in which they described in full the purposes of the corporation and pointed to the safeguards thrown around their business. After enumerating these the writer of the pamphlet goes on as follows: " Thus Sir, You will see there is no Danger, that *the Fund of the Corporation will ever be imbezled, or sunk* by Mismanagement. . ." The concluding sentence of the pamphlet proper is couched in these words: " And now, Sir; it is submitted not only to you, who by the generosity of Your Temper, are favorable to all Charitable Designs, but even to the most severely Critical Person to judge, whether this Undertaking does not answer its Title, and Merit the Encouragement of every Honest Gentleman." It is but

---

through Volume XXI of the Journals of the House of Commons. A partial Report of the Committee to which the petition relative to the affairs of the Charitable Corporation was referred is also to be found in this volume — A " Further Report" of the same Committee is to be found in " Reports from Committees of the House of Commons, Which have been printed by Order of the House, And are not inserted in the Journals." Reprinted by order of the House. Vol. I, p. 363.

[1] Strype's Stow's Survey of London, Vol. II, pp. 373, 374.

[2] Mons Pietatis Londinensis : A narrative or account of the Charitable Corporation, for relief of Industrious poor, by assisting them with small sums upon pledges at legal Interest, etc. Printed in the year 1719.

fair to say that the various checks and restraints imposed upon the servants of the Corporation as set forth in this pamphlet fully justified the use of this language. The author of "A short history of the Charitable Corporation,"[1] etc., published in 1732 says that in 1719, instructions for all the officers were settled, and then adds that efforts were begun by the proprietors to secure from Parliament authority for an increase of the capital, but that "government took a long time to consider the suggestions in this petition." These dates are significant. They show that the publication entitled "Mons Pietatis Londinensis" was in substance a prospectus issued presumably for the purpose of selling stock, and although the corporation was then confining its work to the field which it had appropriated to itself, it is not improbable that this attempt to reach the public was engineered by those who at a later date shipwrecked the corporation. The original capital of the company was £30,000. It was divided into three hundred shares. When the company sought to increase its activities, the secretary, at a general court in 1718, called attention to the size of the shares, and recommended that the number be increased by dividing the present capital, £30,000, into twelve hundred shares of £25 each, in place of the three hundred shares of £100 each, into which the capital of the company was divided at a general court held March 11, 1707, 8. This proposition was carried without opposition.

The application for the increase of the capital of the company was made at a time when the English government was about to attempt in England an experiment similar to that which was then in full swing in Paris under the management of John Law, namely, the conversion of a national debt into the shares of a trading company. In the summer of 1719, Law's scheme was on the verge of collapsing, the shares of the company having been raised to such high prices that the purchasers were beginning to sell out in order to realize the profit already gained by this rise. In England at that

---

[1] A short History of the Charitable Corporation from the date of their charter, to their late petition. In which is contain'd a succinct history of the frauds discovered in the Management of their affairs, which occasion'd the Proprietors application to Parliament; etc., London, MDCCXXXII.

time the sharp contest which had taken place between the Bank of England and the South Sea Company for the privilege of managing this similar English conversion, had resulted in the award of the prize to the South Sea Company at a price which was fraught with peril for the success of the enterprise. At such a time it was impossible for any small company to secure recognition or favor from Parliament. The prolonged delay in considering the petition of the corporation for an increase of capital is, therefore, easily to be accounted for.

On the 22d of June, 1722, however, the petition of the corporation for a license to increase its capital to £100,000 was granted by Parliament. In the petition submitted by the corporation, which was at the basis of the grant, the petitioners alleged that "their fund had never been stock-jobbed as other Funds had been."[1] Notwithstanding the fact that the reduction of the size of the shares had something of a stock-jobbing flair, it is quite likely that up to this time the philanthropic motives which led to the establishment of the company still prevailed in its management. When the writer of "Mons Pietatis Londinensis" appealed to "the most severely critical person to judge whether the undertaking does not answer its title," he must have been met with an affirmative answer, if the corporation was at that time actually managing, or intending to manage, its affairs along the lines set forth in that pamphlet. The increase of the capital to £100,000 came at a time when financial affairs were beginning to rally from the depression produced by the collapse of the South Sea bubble, and it would seem as though this was when the attention of the speculators was attracted to the possible use that could be made of the charter of this company.

The increase of the capital and the reduction of the size of the shares is not inconsistent with good intentions, but on the 2d of November, 1725, the par value of the shares was reduced to £20 a share; and power was given the officers to loan money on notes.

---

[1] 1732—Further report with the appendix from the Committee to whom the petition of the proprietors of the Charitable Corporation, etc., was referred, p. 365. This report is in a volume of Reports of Committees to the House of Commons in proper chronological sequence.

This is the date assigned for the commencement of actual work. October 25, 1726, the then par value of the shares was divided in two and the par value was fixed at £10 a share. March 28, 1727, the par value of the shares was again cut in two and the capital, which was then £100,000, was divided into 20,000 shares of £5 each.

The increase of the capital to £100,000 had been secured openly and no question seems to have been raised as to the propriety or the legality of the transaction. This increase was followed by another successful application to Parliament for an increase, and June 21, 1728, license was granted to the corporation to raise its capital to £300,000. July 31, 1730, by means of a similar proceeding, the capital was again raised to £600,000. The Investigating Committee of the House of Commons stigmatized these transactions in their report in the following terms: " Licences for augmenting to £300,000 and £600,000 were obtained upon false suggestions and representations, and were applied for to the Crown without any order of a General Court, or of a court of Committee of said Corporation, and in a private and clandestine manner, and kept secret for some months for the private advantage of some of the committee and assistants and their agents during which times great numbers of shares were bought by them." The Gentleman's Magazine is authority for the statement that the managers bought shares at £6 and sold them at £10.3s.[1]

In " Mons Pietatis " the author writing in behalf of the corporation had, in 1719, with a view of securing public confidence, published what he termed the instructions settled for the officers. These contained a set of checks and restraints imposed upon those having charge of the funds and pledges which would have made it practically impossible to rob the warehouses or to deplete the treasury of the corporation. All these checks were now set aside and power was concentrated in the hands of one or two individuals, the most prominent of whom was John Thompson the warehouse keeper. An ingenious device secured for the corporation a sort of Jekyll and Hyde method of doing business, through the establish-

[1] Vol. II, p. 766, 1732.

ment of two warehouses, each devoted to a special department of the business. One of these was in Spring Garden, near Charing Cross,[1] and here the philanthropic side of the work was performed; here small pledges alone were received. This building was apparently owned by the corporation and figured in its assets as being worth between eighteen and nineteen thousand pounds. The other warehouse was in Fenchurch Street, and was spoken of as on Lawrence Pountney's Hill. As it does not figure in the company's assets, the premises were probably hired.

By some means, not altogether easy to understand, the corporation put forth large numbers of notes on the market, which were supposed to be secured by the pledge of goods deposited in their Fenchurch Street warehouse. Thompson, the warehouse keeper, devised a regular system for the sale of these notes, his operations being carried on through certain brokers, with whom he had contracts for the handling of the corporation notes. Before the final collapse came, the notes were for a short time protected by the negotiation of corporation bonds. Ultimately it was discovered that the Fenchurch Street warehouse was practically empty, and if the alleged securities had ever existed, they were no longer there. Property valued at above £500,000 had disappeared.

May 15, 1731, the Lord mayor, aldermen and commons of the city of London presented a petition to the House of Commons, setting forth the condition of the affairs of the corporation and praying for relief. This was followed by a petition from the merchants, traders, shopkeepers, master workmen and manufacturers of the city of Westminster, which was favorable to the cause of the Charitable Corporation and set forth its great use to the people. A similar petition from the merchants and others in the city of London was presented the next day. Protracted proceedings took place in the House of Commons as well as in the House of Lords; committees were appointed and hearings were held. The reports of the committees and commissioners were in part separately printed and in part are to be found in the Journals.

---

[1] This is described as the " Capital House " of the company in an inscription in a copy of "Mons Pietatis " in the Harvard College Library.

A bill was matured for the restraint of the corporation in the transaction of business. During the parliamentary investigation a great number of witnesses was examined, some of whom were brought from the prison of the Court of King's Bench, some from the Fleet Prison, and some from the prison of the Poultry Compter. Thompson, who had fled the country, was by Act of Parliament required to surrender himself to the commissioners in a commission of bankruptcy awarded against him, under the pain of felony without benefit of clergy. In May, 1732, a letter was received from a banker in Rome, by the name of Belloni, who had caused Thompson to be arrested and who conveyed the information that the prisoner was at that time confined in the Castle of St. Angelo. Ultimately, through legislation which exempted him from arrest in England for a period and which rendered him immune from proceedings against him based solely upon his disclosures, Thompson was prevailed upon to appear.

Charges were made during the discussion of the affairs of the company that some of the funds appropriated by Thompson had been paid to the Pretender, thus bringing politics into this melange of philanthropy and crime.

Much sympathy was felt for those who suffered through the neglect of the directors of the company to supervise properly its business, and a lottery was established by Parliament for the benefit of the sufferers, among whom the stockholders were included. A list of the sufferers by the failure, giving the amount of their several claims and the allowance to each claimant, was published by the committee having in charge the distribution of the funds received from the lottery.[1]

The " Short History of the Charitable Corporation " was written in behalf of the proprietors of the corporation and was evidently intended to influence Parliament when the act for the establishment of a lottery in aid of the creditors and proprietors of the corporation was under consideration. It sets forth in plain language the iniquities of Thompson and fitly characterizes the delinquencies of the officials

---

[1] This is to be found in the Gentleman's Magazine, Vol. IV, 1734. The London Magazine contains information relating to the affairs of this corporation.

of the corporation whose neglect of their duties, or whose connivance at the frauds, rendered the transactions possible through which the wrecking of the company was accomplished.

The actions of the committee in permitting the concentration of power in Thompson's hands and in abolishing the checks, restraints, and protective devices which might have served to screen the public and the proprietors from harm, is thus epitomized in the history: "The Committee suffer him to certify for himself; there is no longer any Body to inspect the ware-house, J — n T — certifies for *John* Th———n, that he has left such a Pledge, worth so much, in the Ware-house; with himself. And this was allowed to the amount of Thousands at a time."

For some months after the disappearance of Thompson and his broker, the exact date of which is not given, but which obviously was in 1730, no steps were taken to examine critically the condition of the corporation. When this was done, it was found that its affairs were hopelessly embarrassed. Dividends had been declared and apparently paid out of the capital. Goods pledged by Thompson and his broker to the corporation to secure notes emitted on the pledges were not to be found in the warehouse. Others besides Thompson and his broker apparently participated in the profits derived from this system of wholesale robbery and fraud, the result of which was stated by the author of the "Short History" in these words: "Our Cash is gone, our debts large, our Accounts confused and our Reputation totally ruined."

This brief sketch of the career of the Charitable Corporation, winding up as it did with the flight of Thompson, shows such a parallelism with that of the South Sea Company and the sudden disappearance of Knight with the books of that company, that it is not astonishing to find them linked together as ignominious examples of what was to be avoided. The long-protracted parliamentary examination of the affairs of the Charitable Corporation and the frequent allusion to the progress of the investigations made in the pages of the Gentleman's Magazine and the London Magazine must have brought the subject before a wide circle of colonial readers, and must therefore have made familiar to a large public the name of

Thompson, and the gravity of the crime which had been committed in the name of philanthropy.

No paragraph has yet been found in the columns of the Boston press dealing with the subject of the Charitable Corporation, but the Boston Gazette of February 6, 1721, contains the following information concerning Knight and the South Sea Company:

"Last Monday night there was a General Council at St. James's in which a Proclamation was ordered to be forthwith printed and published, for apprehending Robert Knight Cashier, or Treasurer, of the South-Sea Company who after his Examination before the Committee, thought fit to fly from Justice. A Reward of Two Thousand Pound is offered by the Government for Apprehending him.

"It is Reported that Mr. Knight drove himself out of Town, on Saturday last, in a Calash; and that he was seen at Gravesend, on Sunday Morning, going on Board a small Vessel, which was towed down the River, he being in too much haste to wait for the Tide: But we hear Orders are sent to all the Ports, to stop more of those Gentlemen from getting off."

This is among the items of European news received by the paper. Possibly a careful examination of the European news in the Boston papers of the proper dates might furnish similar news of Thompson.

The copy of this letter to the Rehearsal was obtained through the courtesy of the American Antiquarian Society.

THE   NUMB. CCCLXVI.

New-England *Weekly* JOURNAL.

Containing the moſt Remarkable Occurrences Foreign & Domeſtick.

MONDAY April 1. 1734.

To the Publisher of the WEEKLY JOURNAL.
   SIR,

Hop'd when I first heard of the Letter from *Rhode-Island*, printed in the last Monday's *Gazette* and *Rehearsal*, to have seen the *Rhode-Island* Acts for Emitting their Bills, upon which their value must depend; which is the Matter in Controversy: Had these Acts given any better Security than I represented, I cannot think this Gentleman would have had so much Compassion on me as to have kept them from us on this Occasion, and till we do see them, we must suppose that they no ways secure the value of their Bills, but that they will still go on sinking, till they come to little or nothing. The Account this Gentleman gives of the Conduct of their Government, when the General Court here sent for the Act for their last Emission, is so strange that in favour to them, I would hope it is a mistake, they must surely be very fond of Money, that for the sake of a Shilling or two they should deny the Request of the whole General Assembly of this Province.

As for their Loan Bills or any other, (as I said before) they are worth no more than they promise or secure. The Notes of Hand promise Coin'd Silver and the Scheme secures it, for Plate at 17 *s.* per Ounce, will always fetch Coin'd Silver at 19 *s.* but their Bills, whether kept by one Man or by ten, neither promise nor secure any thing; for at the term, he that has any Bills cannot come at the Land Mortgaged, for the Government has always made them new Bills, whereby they have redeemed their Lands, which the Possessor must take for the old, or keep the old for nothing.

This Gentleman's discourse about *Knight* and *Thompson* is plainly nothing but an amusement; nor has he the Face to pretend he suspects any such thing in this Affair; nor can the Signers secure themselves from paying those Notes, any more than any other Note or Bond, whatsoever.

As to what is said about the meaning of Pen, Ink and Paper, that I did not mean as I said, the Charge of making and Emitting, I solemnly declare, that was what I truly intended, and I cannot conceive what other meaning can possibly be put upon it; and accordingly I ever supposed that a *Five Pound* Bill cost the Colony of *Rhode-Island* no more than a *Twelve penny* Bill, each consisting of much the same Ink and Paper, and each paid by such a new Bill for the old one, and nothing else.

This Gentleman's forbearing to make appear that the *Massachusetts* (as he says) have more Bills out, than *Rhode-Island,* is, upon the same Principle, that he avoids giving us the *Rhode-Island* Acts for Emitting their Bills; the Truth is against him, his Cause will not bear a strict Examination.

There is one thing this Gentleman seems to take for granted, (which is a great mistake) that these Notes of Hand are all or almost all, Let out to Interest by the Undertakers; whereas it is quite otherwise, the Sum put to Interest is very small; and as the Undertakers put the Notes away in common Payments, at 22 *s.* per Ounce, and must pay them in at 19 *s.* the Possessor must be benefited, as he will have 22 *s.* paid him for what costs him but 19 *s.*

His pleasantness upon what I give as a reason that the Scheme for the Notes is no Bubble, I cannot help; but I am sure, it is just and true; for as they are plain, both as to the Time and Specie they promise, there can be no room for an imaginary Value: As for the Bubble he mentions, of their being worth Silver at 19 *s.* per Ounce. now; no body pretends to it, there must doubtless be some allowance for the distance of Payment; tho' upon what this Writer says, there need be no allowance, because they may be used the mean while in Trade between Man & Man, for I need not inform the Public, they have a very ready Currency, notwithstanding what is suggested to the contrary in the Paper we are upon.

As to the Observations or Objections, this Gentleman borrows, I answer, to the first, *that the Company has assumed a Power that no ways belongs to it;* that there are far greater Sums in Bills circulated by private Men in our Mother Country: and this Proceeding was absolutely necessary, to preserve the Publick from being made a Prey of by *Rhode-Island.* To the second, *that they only oblige themselves to cancel their Notes,* and not *import,* by which he means *pay* Silver. I reply, it is a mistake, they promise Silver and Gold, and nothing else; and if they don't seasonably pay it, the Officer will take it from them; The Possessor may indeed before or after Payment give them the Silver or Gold, and so he may for any Bond, Mortgage or Specialty whatsoever; but no reasonable Man can suppose this a just Objection against such Securities. To the third, *that the*

Profit will be unreasonably great: I say, this is built upon the mistaken Supposition of their being all Let to Interest. In other Cases, it is plain, the Undertakers hurt their own Interest, otherwise than as they may serve themselves in common with other Men of Substance: the Fallacy I cannot understand. They were designed at first by the Undertakers, and afterwards by the Committee of the General Court, to be made as plain & certain as possible.

As to what I am desired to do, in answer to that which is said towards the close of the Paper, I say, there never was any pretence to hinder Men from giving their Notes or Bonds, and where the security is good, they will be valu'd, nor is it reasonable, this liberty should be taken away. The necessity of making returns has affected all Paper Money, but principally because we have heretofore Admitted *Rhode-Island* Bills to pass in common with others. As to the value of an Ounce of Silver at three, Six and ten years distance, I am firmly of Opinion, that it is of more worth than a *Rhode-Island* Bill of that Denomination, though the Note of Hand was not to be redeem'd in less than twenty years, because in that time it will bring the Silver and pass the mean while, whereas the *Rhode-Island* Bill if it should pass, would never bring any thing but a New Bill, and probably in that time would lose more than two thirds of it's present low value, which cannot be the case of the other.

As to what this Gentleman says of my being tediously prolix in what I wrote, perhaps that might arise from the uneasiness he met with in reading it, pain & perplexity will make that which is really short appear very long; as for my being positive, it was only where I was certain; and therefore about their Acts which I had not seen, but had only had an account of, I was not positive, but told my Authority, & I believe I was informed right, and if I am not, I still beg this Gentleman to Print their Acts & Convict me of my mistake, for at this distance we don't hear their beat of Drum, nor see their Law-book; as to my being pathetical, it is in an Affair that deeply concerns my Native Country, by which we have been greatly injur'd, and under which we are still suffering, and it becomes every lover of his Country to be moved and deeply affected in such a Case; and altho' I did not know their Acts, yet I knew the ill effects of the want of good Acts, that we had lost *two* or *three Hundred Thousand Pounds* by their unstable Bills, and they had un-justly gain'd so much from us, and it had been much more becoming if this Gentleman had shewn us (as I desir'd) how we should have been reimbursed this loss.

As for my not saying more about the Notes of Hand, they don't need it, all this Gentleman has said or can say about them, is so much against Truth & Reason, that without my saying more, he is dasht to pieces as a bubble that contends with a rock; they have as ready a Currancy as any Bills whatsoever.

I would say something of the coarse and ungentlemanly Expressions in this Paper, but that the Author seems to be too much out of temper to receive it, and yet I would not my self, and I am sorry others do, censure him so hard upon this head, it is but a common infirmity, I have often observed that Men (otherwise worthy) when unhappily engag'd in a bad Cause, and hard put to it for Reason and Argument, substitute Anger and hard Words, rough Usage and harsh Expressions in their place.

I *am*, SIR, *&c.*

NOTE TO COMMUNICATION "TO THE PUBLISHER OF THE
WEEKLY JOURNAL" OF APRIL 1, 1734.

This reply to the letter of March 25th published in the Weekly Rehearsal, is by the author of the letter which appeared in the Rehearsal
and the Journal, March 4th.   It requires no special annotation, except perhaps a word as to the expression of the writer in which he
says that " as the undertakers put the notes away in common payments at 22 s. per ounce, and must pay them in at 19 s. the Possessor
must be benefited, as he will have 22 s. paid him for what cost him
but 19 s."   The effect of the emission of the Merchants' Notes combined with the continued inflow of the Rhode Island bills, notwithstanding the boycott, was to send silver up.   The purchasing power
of the bills of public credit was steadily reduced by this rise, but the
Merchants' notes being drawn payable in silver at a fixed rate did
not participate in the decline of the bills of public credit.   It is to
this feature that the author refers.

The copy of the communication was obtained through the
courtesy of the Massachusetts Historical Society.

THE　　　　　**Numb. 131.**

Weekly Rehearfal.

Monday, April 1. 1734.

A few REMARKS *on the present Situation of Affairs respecting Silver and Paper Money.*

THERE has been much said of late, concerning a *Silver*, *Gold*, and *Paper* Currency; and it must be owned, that it is high Time this Country were determined which to have; for it is evident, in a few Years, there will be the utmost Confusion, unless something be absolutely fixed and determined in that Affair.

A *Silver* and *Gold* Currency or Medium of Trade, is esteemed by many to be best and most proper for us, because it will be of a more fixed and certain Value, and consequently keep the Prices of all Things more Uniform, and we should by Richer by having *Silver* and *Gold* among us, which has something of a substantial Value, or at least an imaginary one put upon it by all civilized Nations. And furthermore it is thought by some we have too much Trade, and this would be a sure Means of lessening it, in as much as there could never remain such a Quantity of it in the Country, as to make a sufficient Medium for so much Trade as is now carried on and consequently many Persons who now run into Trade and Shop-keeping, and Shipping, and Fishing, *&c.* must set themselves to improve the Land, which is judged will be more Advantageous to us, than the carrying on such a great deal of Traffick and Trade; tho' this seems

VOL. III — 9

to be a Thought different from all other People in the World: For what Encouragement or Advantage is there to improve Land, if Trade fails, which makes the Consumption of what the Land produces?

The *Proposals offered to Consideration, wherein the Good of the Province is aimed at,* are certainly well calculated, and must be approved of by all who think a *Silver* and *Gold* Medium absolutely Necessary: Only it may be doubted whether Gentlemen in Trade would take out these new Bills, and bind themselves to pay *Silver* and *Gold.* For tho' the Gentlemen of the Bank make such Promises in their Bills, yet it is thought, they design to make good that Promise by bringing in and sinking their own Bills; but those who should take these new Province Bills, must unavoidably procure the *Silver* and *Gold,* cost what it will.

It may be considered, whether the *Silver* when thus brought in, would remain and continue among us, at least such a Quantity of it, as to enable the Publick to pay the Charge of any considerable Undertaking, and so obstruct and hinder many Things that might be for the Good and Benefit of the Province.

It may be observed, That our *Silver* and *Gold* Currency being all gone, and an entire *Paper* Credit been in Use among us for so many Years; it seems plain, that the purchasing or procuring a *Silver* Medium must cost several Hundred Thousand Pounds; As for Example, if there is now 400,000 Pounds in Bills of Credit in the Four Provinces, which serves as a Medium in Trade, and we are resolved to have *Silver* and *Gold* in the Room thereof, to continue as a constant Medium; then these Provinces must be at the direct Charge and Cost in procuring 400,000

Ounces of *Silver* instead of the Bills; which Sum might be much better improved, than by being laid aside for a constant Currency; it will lessen our Trading Stock, and withhold so much Returns to *Great Britain*.

It cannot be made appear, but that a *Paper* Currency be so regulated, as to answer the End of a Medium of Trade: For these four Provinces who have been used to it for so long a Time, as well as *Holland* and *Venice*, and other Parts of *Europe*, who carry on their Trade by *Bank Notes*, which are never paid in Specie, and yet being under the Direction and Credit of the Government, they pass constantly for the Value they express, with an Advance of two or three *per Cent.* more than *Silver* or *Gold*, they being much more easy and convenient for carrying on of Commerce. And could the Bills of Credit here be kept to a steady Value, they must needs answer the End of a Cash Account in Trade, as well as *Silver* and *Gold*. And to keep them to a fixed Value, the only way is to keep the Quantity fixed and determined; and doubtless it will be in that as in all other Things where the Quantity is the same, and the Demand for it the same, the Price or Value will continue the same. And in this Particular, it's likely as the Country and Trade increases, the Demand for the Bills must increase, and consequently the Value of them; unless it were in Time thought Necessary both by the Government at Home and here, to Augment in Proportion to the Trade, the Quantity of Bills. It is worth observing, that for several Years when the Quantity of Bills was near about the same, the Value of them for all that Time was near about the same.

But is it not a vain Thing to talk at this Rate about a Paper Medium, when the Government at Home is so opposite to it? However, with great Submission, it may be proposed, that these Four Governments should humbly Address the Throne with a true State of their Circumstances with Relation to this Affair, and show a settled Paper Medium would be beneficial to the *British* Trade to these Provinces, and manifestly tend to the Encouragement of our Fishery, and other Branches of Trade, which as they are many, cannot be carried on without something to pass between Buyer and Seller: And then as Trade is encouraged, the Consumption of *British* Manufactures will be augmented, and the *Silver* and *Gold* as it comes in to us, will be sent Home for Returns, and our selves (having no *Gold* or *Silver* among us) left in less Danger of being invaded by a Foreign Enemy. These, with many such Reasons as the Wisdom of our Rulers cou'd suggest, might perhaps prevail with our most gracious Sovereign to appoint to each of these Four Governments, a certain, precise, fixed Quantity of *Paper Money* to be constantly kept out, and not to be diminished or increased without express Allowance. Furthermore, it may be easily shewn, that this is much better and safer, than to have a Paper Currency under the Direction and Management of private Persons, which may plainly be made appear, is both Disadvantageous and Dangerous to any Government.

If such a Proposal should ever be promoted, it is humbly judg'd, the Quantity of Bills that are now out, exclusive of the Bank-Bills, and the last Emission of *Rhode-Island*, would be a suitable Quantity for the Four Governments to have, being about the Quantity that has been out for a good many Years together. And if this takes Place, it would be Justice in these Provinces to make a reasonable Advance or Augmentation of all Salaries, Fees, &c.

The last *Remark* shall be upon the great Concern of Frugality and Industry, which above all Things (next to Religion) should be encouraged; particularly the promoting of those Products which will not interfere with the Manufactures of *Great Britain*, as the raising of Hemp and other Naval Stores, and making Sail-Cloth, *&c.* whereby very great Sums of Money would be sav'd yearly to the Country; and likewise the encouraging of the Cod and Whale Fishing, and building of Ships, whereby we are enabled in a great Measure to pay for what we absolutely need from Home. Now there is no Reason to think but a Paper Medium would answer as well for promoting of these as a *Silver* one; especially if we consider the inexpressible Difficulties and Hardships the Country in general will be brought to, before a *Silver* Medium can be brought about, which will obstruct their Improvements, and it may be put them to a Loss for a Market for what they want to sell. These Things are not like to befriend Industry, whatever some People may think of it: For it is a Maxim pretty generally received, *That what is encouraging to Trade, is so to Industry.*

These few *Remarks* are offered and submitted by a Lover of the Country.

NOTE TO "A FEW REMARKS ON THE PRESENT SITUATION OF AFFAIRS RESPECTING SILVER AND PAPER MONEY," PUBLISHED IN THE WEEKLY REHEARSAL OF APRIL 1, 1734.

The writer of this communication approaches the subject with some comprehension of the causes of the troubles of the currency question. He realizes that without some control over the emissions there can be no such thing as a fixed relation between the needs of the trade of the people in New England and the currency furnished by the four governments.   On the whole he is satisfied with a paper currency, prefers bills of public credit to private emissions, and believes that the co-operation of the four governments might secure from the crown a modification of the instructions for the withdrawal of the currency, and that a settlement might be agreed upon of certain fixed amounts which each of the governments might be permitted to keep in circulation.   If a fixed proportion of currency to trade were maintained, he believes the value of the bills would remain stationary.

He apparently considers the amount of bills of public credit in circulation in the four New England governments as being £400,000. The price of silver being then in the neighborhood of 20 s. an ounce in bills of public credit, the same number of ounces of silver might replace the £400,000 as a medium of trade.   The value of silver bullion in coin was approximately seven shillings an ounce. Hence it may be inferred that the writer thought that £140,000 in coin would suffice for the business of these four governments.   This was a low estimate.

The copy was obtained through the courtesy of the American Antiquarian Society.

THE

Melancholy State

OF THIS

PROVINCE

Confidered, in a

LETTER

From a Gentleman in *Bofton* to
his Friend in the Country.

———————————————————

Printed in the Year 1736.

the trade of the people in New England and the currency furnished by the four governments. On the whole he is satisfied with a paper currency, prefers bills of public credit to private emissions, and believes that the co-operation of the four governments might secure from the crown a modification of the instructions for the withdrawal of the currency, and that a settlement might be agreed upon of certain fixed amounts which each of the governments might be permitted to keep in circulation. If a fixed proportion of currency to trade were maintained, he believes the value of the bills would remain stationary.

He apparently considers the amount of bills of public credit in circulation in the four New England governments as being £400,000. The price of silver being then in the neighborhood of 20 s. an ounce in bills of public credit, the same number of ounces of silver might replace the £400,000 as a medium of trade. The value of silver bullion in coin was approximately seven shillings an ounce. Hence it may be inferred that the writer thought that £140,000 in coin would suffice for the business of these four governments. This was a low estimate.

The copy was obtained through the courtesy of the American Antiquarian Society.

THE
Melancholy State
OF THIS
PROVINCE
Confidered, in a
LETTER
From a Gentleman in *Bofton* to
his Friend in the Country.

Printed in the Year 1736.

THE

Melancholy State

OF THIS

PROVINCE

Confidered, in a

LETTER,

From a Gentleman in *Boſton* to
his Friend in the Country.

Printed in the Year 1736.

[2]

SIR,

YOUR'S of the 20th of *May*, I have received. in which you complain of the Extortion and Oppression which is breaking in upon this People, and admire that the Government does not by some sutable Laws prevent it, more especially you complain of the Gentlemen concerned in the Bank, and wonder how any Men can be so blind as not to foresee the fatal Consequences that would attend that Project.

In the first Place, I must inform you, That the Scheme these Bankers are come into is not the Scheme which was first proposed: The first Proposal was to make *One hundred thousand Pounds*, in Notes to be Paid in to the Trustees of the Bank in ten Years, in Silver at *twenty Shillings* per Ounce; the Silver to remain in the Bank until the ten Years were expired. By this Me-[3]thod we should have been sure of *One hundred thousand Pounds* passing amongst us to carry on our Trade, & at the End of the ten Years there would have been *One hundred thousand Pounds* in Silver to exchange for those Bills, for it would not have been worth any Man's while to have lock'd up these Notes in their Chests for ten Years, though it might answer their End to lock them up for three Years as they now do: I

must say it was surprizing to me to see the Gentlemen concerned in that Affair so easily imposed on and perswaded
to alter the Scheme, and agree to have the Silver drawn out
at three Periods, *viz.* three Tenths at the End of three
Years, and three Tenths more at the End of other three
Years, and the remaining four Tenths at the End of the
tenth Year; How doth this agree with their pretended
Design in erecting this Bank; they pretended that their
Design was to supply the People with a Medium of Exchange, and under that Notion refused letting in any to
subscribe who would not oblige themselves to refuse the
Rhode Island Bills emitted in 1733. Actions speak louder
than Words, and are more to be regarded: When they
first proposed this Alteration in their Scheme, they were
told it would ruin their Design, for that the Bills or Notes
would be hoarded up, and that it would raise the Price of
Silver and Gold, instead of lowering the Price thereof, as
they pretended it would do: I confess I was sick of the
Project when I heard that one Gentleman signed *ten thousand Pounds*, which was a tenth Part of the Stock, and that
he and others for him insisted on his having twenty Votes;
to suffer this I said [4] was Distraction in the Subscribers,
and contrary to the Policy of all Nations: Power is usually
Handmaid to Riches, therefore when Men of overgrown
Estates are grasping after Power, every where People have
a jealous Eye over 'em, least they be swallowed up by them
before they are aware: I suppose there never was the like
Instance in any Bank. In the Bank of England, South
Sea, or India Stocks, any Man who hath *One thousand
Pounds* original Stock hath two Votes, and he who hath
One hundred thousand Pounds hath but four Votes, and

these Banks are settled by Act of Parliament, so careful is the Government to prevent the Rich oppressing their poor Neighbours, and I shall always be of Opinion, that the Parliament of *England* which is composed of so many wise, able Statesmen, and so many ingenious Merchants, and have been in the Practice of these Things for Ages past, are better Judges in such Matters than we who are but of Yesterday.

It was easy to see what these Men were driving at who proposed drawing the Silver out at three Periods: But much the greatest Part of the Subscribers were drawn in by others before they considered the Consequences that would attend the Alteration, and now dearly repent and say they were imposed on, and all they have to say for themselves is, alas, who would have thought that Men who swim in abundance, and have as one would think more than Heart can wish, should shew themselves so unsatiably Avaricious, so Unconscionable and Unjust as to pay Men *Rhode Island* Bills and oblige them to [5] give Bonds to pay in Lieu thereof Merchants Notes, or on Failure of paying such Notes, to pay Silver at *nineteen Shillings* per Ounce, and at the same time these very Men are ingrossing the Notes, and give an Advance on them to get 'em all, if possible, into their own Hands, that so those who have mortgaged their Estates to them may never be able to redeem them, and so of Consequence such Estates must fall into their Hands for what they will be pleased to allow for them: I can't but pity those who are exposed to the Mercy of such Men.

But to these Things the Usurer will reply and say, That it is at the Borrower's Election whether he will take up their Money on such Terms or no, and perhaps he will pretend it was out of pure Friendship and to serve the Man that he lent him his Money, &c. But will not every impartial Man who hears him say so, laugh at all such idle Pretences; a Friend will rather abate of the common Interest than make any Advantage of his Friend's Necessity: A Man ought not to exact on a Stranger, much less on his Friend: But the Right of the Matter is this, The Law of the Land ought to be a Rule to the Usurer in this Case, that Man who can't be content with the common Interest, but will exact more than the Law hath set Interest at, is a Breaker of the Law and oppresses his Neighbor; but notwithstanding we have a good and wholesome Law to prevent Men's taking excessive Usury, many Men make no Scruple to exact *ten* per Cent for Loan of Money in Defiance of the Law; as I said before. the Law ought to [6] be kept strictly unto, for if Men swerve from the Law, and it is winked at by the Government, it is like breaking down the Hedge or Wall, and letting in the wild Creatures to devour the Vineyard; and as to the frivolous Pretence that it is at the Election of the Borrower to take the Money or leave it, it is Necessity that obliges Men to take up Money when they give more than the common Interest, and that the Lender knows very well, and no Man ought to make another Man's Necessity his Opportunity, and take Advantage thereof to squeeze and oppress him: Let us eat and drink to day, for tomorrow we die; rather than go into a Goal Men will comply with any Terms be they never so hard and unreasonable: And it is for this Reason that the Legislator makes Laws to restrain the Corruptions & vicious Inclinations of Men, without which

Laws Men would prey upon one another like Fish in the Sea, the greater would devour the less: But yet notwithstanding the good Laws we have to prevent this Evil from spreading amongst us, it is too much practised at this Day to the Ruin of many Families, and if some speedy Remedy be not found out to prevent it, a few Usurers will soon eat up the Substance which many industrious People have been many Years scraping together, in Hopes that their Children would reap the Benefit of it.

As to what you say about the Government's interposing their Authority to prevent the Destruction of so many Families as are in Danger of being ruined by this vile Bank, I am informed it was proposed in the Assembly to make our [7] Province Bills a lawful Tender for them; how that Matter came to be dropt I know not, it is great Pity it was not prosecuted to Effect, for such an Act would have been of great Service, not only to those who have mortgaged their Estates for these Bank Notes, or have borrowed Money on Bond, to pay in these Notes or in Silver, but to the greatest Part of the Bankers themselves, who groan under the Burthen when the Time comes to pay in their Silver, for it hath raised the Price of Silver to *twenty seven Shillings and six Pence* per Ounce; what dreadful Sufferers then are they like to be, who as soon as they received their Money out of this Bank, put it away immediately to pay their Debts, and never had the Advantage of making any profitable Improvement of it, it hath been a very unhappy Bank to such Men, their Case calls for Pity.

The Objections made by some in the Assembly against making the Province Bills a lawful Tender for these Notes are, First, They make a Matter of Conscience of it, to oblige

a Man to take any thing for his Bond, other than what is
mentioned in the Condition. And Secondly, They say it will
be a Means of having the Province Bills hoarded up; In
Answer to these Reasons, I must observe, That the Government have in their great Wisdom, with great Justice and in
Compassion to the Poor, as well becomes the Fathers of the
People, made the Bills of this Province a lawful Tender for
any Debt that should be contracted after the making that
Law, so that no Person may be imprisoned who ten-[8]ders
those Bills for Payment; and shall the same Government
see a few Men issue out their own Notes as a Bank, and call
nineteen Shillings of those Notes an Ounce of Silver and
take Bonds for them accordingly? Shall Usurers as they
come to be possest of these Notes, call in their Bonds and
Mortgages, and oblige their Debtors to give new Bonds and
Mortgages, payable in these Notes, or Silver at *nineteen
Shillings* per Ounce? Shall a few mercenary Men so prey
upon their necessitous Neighbours, as to pay them *Rhode
Island* Bills, & oblige them to give Bonds or Mortgages to
pay in Lieu thereof Bank Notes or an Ounce of Silver for
every *nineteen Shillings*, when an Ounce of Silver is worth
twenty-seven Shillings and six Pence, and rising, and will be at
thirty Shillings per Ounce before the Year comes about, if
this Bank continues as it is, I say will the Government
suffer such horrid Injustice? No surely. No Christian
can hear these Things and not be deeply affected at the
Thoughts of such monstrous Extortion and Oppression
breaking in like a Torrent upon the People, much less will
a Christian Government suffer it: But I have heard some of
these Bankers say, It is not in the Power of the Government
to do anything to relieve the People in this Matter: To

which I reply and say, When a Physicain finds his Patients
Case extremely hazardous, he will venture to go further than
in ordinary Cases, desperate Diseases call for extraordinary
Remedies, even so when the State is disordered and Extortion and Oppression comes rowling over a People like the
raging Sea, and all Things are running into Confusion;
whence can we expect [9] Relief but from the Government,
who are cloathed with Power for that very End, and GOD
expects it from them; that they be Eyes to the blind, and
Feet to the lame, and deliver the Poor out of the Hands of
their Oppressors: The Rich are always able to help themselves, and it is in their Power, very often, to oppress their
Neighbours, if the Government do not take care to prevent
it, and their Assistance was never more wanted than at this
Day to deliver this poor oppressed, and distressed People
out of the Hands of the Rich and Mighty: I believe every
disinterested Man in the Province will say, That he who
receives *Rhode Island* Bills, ought to pay in the same. and
all others ought to pay in Bills of this Province.   Shall any
Man's Note be better than the Money of the Government
established by the Law of the Land and confirmed by the
King?   Can there be any Injustice in making a Law to
oblige every Man who hath paid *Rhode Island* Bills to accept the same for any Specialties for which he paid no other
than those Bills, and to oblige all others to receive the Bills
of this Government in lieu of the Merchants Notes?   No, I
know it is the Opinion of many good Men and rich Men
too amongst us, That such a Law would do a great deal of
Good, and do no Injustice to any Man: Most certainly it
would do this Good, it would bring abroad the Merchants
Notes, we shou'd soon see them abroad circulating in Trade

and doing the Office for which it was pretended they were made, *viz.* pass from Man to Man to facilitate our Payments in our Commerce, and I am perswaded that nine Tenths of the Bankers were concerned with no other [10] Views, but that the whole People should reap that Benefit by the Circulation of the Notes; but when it was proposed to draw 'em in at three Periods, no Man that wou'd bestow a Thought on it, could think they ever would Circulate or do the least Good to the Trade, or to People in general, but quite the contrary: It was easy to see that some Men would build great Estates by them, and that many Families would be ruined by them. And can this be thought to be for the Good of the Publick? All Men know that the middling Sort of the People are the greatest Support to the common Wealth, they pay the greatest Part to support both Church and State. But we, in the Method we are in, shall in a little Time have no middling Sort, we shall have a few, and but a very few Lords, and all the rest Beggars: Some there are among us who say there is Money enough, and that there is no Want of Money with them to whom the Money belongs; as if Money was designed only for a few rich Men to lye in their Chests, until a lucky Opportunity offers it self for them to make their Market with on their poor Neighbours; I confess these Men's Notions concerning Money, vastly differs from mine: I think every Man is Intitled to Money, as much as the richest Man amongst us; I mean to so much as he Earns; the Tradesmen and Labourers ought to receive their Money as soon as their Work is done, and not be turned away to Shops, *or perhaps to a Shop for their Pay:* The Labourers at this Day will work for *Six Shillings* per Day in Money rather than for *Seven Shillings* in Goods, and

I believe it is their Interest so to do, I confess, I shall never
[11] think there is Money enough till poor Men can get
Money for their Labour, and have it in their Power to lay
it out where they can be best used, and not be obliged to go
to such a particular Shop for their Pay because their Im-
ployer deals with that Shop and no other, which is the Case
of many in this Town every Day, and it is to be feared, some
Shopkeepers use but little Conscience with such Customers,
but make 'em pay dearly for what they have.

The second Objection some make against the Province
Bills being made a lawful Tender for the Merchants Notes
is, That in lieu of hoarding up these Notes, they will then
hoard up the Province Bills : But I confess I can see no
weight at all in this Argument, for these Notes are mostly
in the Hands of the Merchants who made 'em, and now
keep 'em on Purpose to make a Market of 'em by letting 'em
out to receive Silver at *Nineteen Shillings* per Ounce in lieu
of them, and they never will come abroad until there be such
a Law made.   But admit it should have that Tendency as
they pretend, we shou'd be much better than we are now
with Respect to our Trade; for we should then as I said
before, have the Notes abroad Circulating in Payment, and
that would prevent hundreds of Law-suits which are brought
into the Courts only through the scarcity of Money.   This
Consideration alone methinks should induce the General
Court to make the Province Bills a lawful Tender for them.
But add to this the mighty Advantage it would be to many
poor Men whose pressing Necessities have obliged 'em to
Mortgage [12] their Estates for these Notes, who if something be not done for their Relief will be obliged to pay forty
per Cent for the Money they have so borrowed, over and

above the common Interest established by Law. But I can't believe the Province Bills will be hoarded up more than they now are, if there were such a Law; for every Man who keeps any Money by him, keeps our Province Bills as long as he can, it is the last Money he will part with. We see very few of 'em abroad, we have little else but *Rhode Island* Bills to go to Market with from Day to Day to buy our Provisions with. To speak plain, our Misfortune is, we have a few lucky Men among us who have had the good Fortune to raise considerable Estates from nothing within these twenty or thirty Years; these Men are for sinking all paper Mediums, and say, If the paper Bills were once gone we shou'd have Silver among us; but I confess I can't be of their Opinion, I rather think we must have a paper Medium or none at all: While the Ballance of our Trade with *Great-Britain* is so much in their Favour, all our Silver and Gold which we Import from other Places, will go to *England* to Ballance that Account, we shall have none of it stay with us until we can find a Way to live more Independent of them: And every Scheme that can be projected to bring in Silver, will most certainly be attended with the same Inconveniences which have attended the Merchant's Notes. I wish some Method could be found out to revive our dying Trade, for I see nothing but Poverty and Misery before us in the Way we are in; our Neighbours at *Rhode Island* Thrive and grow Rich while [13] we decline every Year; they sit easy, the Interest of their Money out on Loan pays the whole Charge of the Government, while we are loaded with Taxes, more especially this Town, we set at a very great Charge, more then the People will be able to pay, unless some way can be found out to enliven our Trade, which I am of opinion must

be by supplying the People with Money, or assisting them
in supplying themselves in a private Way.

It seems very strange, that Men who have raised themselves and Families from nothing by the Help of our Province Bills, should be such bitter Enemies to a Paper Medium; I am sure it is past the Art of Man to make Silver
pass as Money unless you can prevent the Silver which
comes in being ship'd off again: If some Way be not found
out to supply the Trade with some Medium or other, to buy
and sell with and pay our Debts with, our Trade will sink
and come to nothing, and Poverty will soon overspread the
whole Land, both Town and Country: We in this and the
other Sea Ports will be first affected with it, but the whole
Land will feel the sad Effect of it in a little Time: We may
speak as contemptibly as we please of the *Rhode Islanders*
emitting Bills, they have found the Sweet of it, for they have
eaten up half our Trade with it, and will soon eat us out of
all if we don't contrive some sort of Money to pass amongst
us: It is easy for us to have a better Medium than what we
now have, for we have nothing but *Rhode Island* Bills passing among us, whereas if we had a Medium of our own we
[14] might soon sink all their Bills. but to talk of refusing to
take them, before we can have some other Medium to
answer in Lieu of them, seems very strange, it is Necessity
alone which gives them a Currency: Did ever any trading
Place pretend to carry on their Trade without some sort of
Money; I believe every Nation under the Sun have something passing amongst them, which answers instead thereof.
It is evident that the Heathen in this Land had their Wam-
pum which passed amongst them, and no doubt, was in as
much Esteem with them as Silver is with us, and with it

they traded; the Inland Country supplied those who dwelt
on the Sea for Cloathing. and they who dwelt on the Sea
Coast supplied the Country Coast with Furs, &c. with Fish,
Fowl, &c. according to the different Seasons of the Year. I
have heard some Gentlemen cry up this Merchants Bank for
the best Paper Money that ever was made, but I think I
have plainly proved it to be just the Reverse; had they stuck
to the first Proposal it would have been of general Service
for eight or nine Years, but some Gentlemen had not
Patience to wait so long for the Silver, which proved the
Ruin of the Scheme. To Conclude, Happy should we be if
we always bore in mind those wise Sayings left us upon
Record; *Riches profit not in the Day of Wrath; a little that
a righteous Man hath is better than the Treasures of many
Wicked.*

I am, Sir,
Your assured Friend.

Boston, June 1.
1736.

NOTE TO "THE MELANCHOLY STATE OF THIS PROVINCE
  CONSIDERED IN A LETTER FROM A GENTLEMAN IN
  BOSTON TO HIS FRIEND IN THE COUNTRY."

The brief résumé of this pamphlet given in the Introduction practically includes all that there is of importance to say of its general
character and method. The writer was opposed to the Merchants'
Notes and notwithstanding the fact that he himself says that those
who emitted them were at that time paying a premium for them in
order to retire them from circulation, he feels called upon to attack
them. It is, indeed, their withdrawal from circulation which irritates
him. The feature of the notes which especially arouses his opposition is their redemption in three instalments. This, according to

him, was not the original proposition. " The first Proposal," he says, " was to make *One hundred thousand Pounds*, in Notes to be paid to the Trustees of the Bank in Ten Years, in Silver at *Twenty Shillings* per Ounce; this Silver to remain in the Bank until the ten Years was expired." He then adds that at the end of ten years there would have been one hundred thousand pounds in silver to exchange for the bills. The normal rate for silver measured by the price in Great Britain at this time when converted into the New England currency was about seven shillings an ounce. One hundred thousand pounds of notes the value of which was expressed in silver at the rate of twenty shillings an ounce would not therefore have furnished over thirty-five thousand pounds in silver coin. The boycott of the Rhode Island bills indicates that the Boston merchants proposed to make their attempt at resumption of specie payments in Massachusetts alone, and for this their total emission converted into silver, though inadequate to supply the entire circulating medium required for the province, might have served as a basis for an experiment. The author of a " Letter to a member of the honourable house of representatives," etc., a pamphlet printed in 1736, thought that with sixty thousand pounds in circulation of bills whose redemption in silver was promised in ten years, silver and gold might perhaps be furnished by merchants in sufficient quantity to meet the needs of the province, provided the circulation of bills of other governments were prohibited.

The one hundred and ten thousand pounds of Merchants' Notes valued in silver at nineteen shillings an ounce would have provided only about forty thousand pounds, and the probable efficacy of this amount was still further diminished by the plan to furnish the silver in three instalments. Against this plan of instalment redemption the writer of this letter inveighs, not because in his opinion it would interfere with specie resumption, but because it would reduce the amount of paper-money in circulation. People who wanted silver could not afford to lock up notes for eight or nine years in order to get the metal, but they could afford to hold them for three years. Hence the change of the scheme, in the writer's opinion, affected the amount of the circulating medium of the province.

We get a statement of what was considered an excessive charge for interest in those days, through the following: " Many Men make no Scruple to exact *ten* per Cent for Loan of Money in Defiance of the Law." The price of silver when the author wrote is given in the following: " for it hath raised the Price of Silver to *twenty seven Shillings and six Pence* per Ounce." The wages of daily labor are indicated in: " The Labourers at this Day will work for *Six Shillings* per Day in Money rather than for *Seven Shillings* in Goods." The new tenor bill was first emitted in February, 1737, so that the writer, if by his expression " in money " he was referring to bills of public credit, meant in old tenor bills. Six shillings in silver were worth one Spanish dollar, but six shillings in a currency that was based upon silver at twenty-seven shillings and sixpence an ounce were worth only about twenty-five cents.

The greater part of the letter is devoted to the advocacy of the passage of a law which should relieve those who had contracted to make payments in Merchants' Notes from the penalty which the rise in the price of silver imposed upon them. The proposed remedy was to legalize the payment of such contracts in the bills of public credit.

The only copy of this pamphlet that I have found is in possession of the American Antiquarian Society. Through the courtesy of that society we are enabled to produce the reprint and the facsimile of the title-page. The leaves measure 6 by 4 inches.

A

LETTER

TO A

Member of the Honourable House

OF

REPRESENTATIVES,

On the prefent State of the

Bills of Credit.

Jactabatur enim temporibus illis nummus, fic ut nemo poffet fcire quid haberet. Cicero.

BOSTON:

Printed in the Year, MDCCXXXVI.

A

LETTER

TO A

Member of the Honourable Houſe

OF

REPRESENTATIVES,

On the preſent State of the

Bills of Credit.

---

*Jactabatur enim temporibus illis nummus, ſic ut
nemo poſſet ſcire quid haberet.*　　　Cicero.

B O S T O N:
Printed in the Year, MDCCXXXVI.

SIR,

 HE Interest of any People depends so much on a proper regulation of their Money or Medium of Trade, that I am perswaded you will not be displeas'd at my freedom in sending you my Sentiments on the present fluctuating and unsettled Condition of our Money.

Every one is ready to acknowledge that the Bills of Credit, which are the only current Money of the Province, are far from answering the end propos'd at their first Emission; for without doubt the Legislature then in being expected they would keep their value, and serve for a Measure of Commerce, which ought always to be invariable: But instead of answering their expectation, they have been gradually sinking, till at length *Twenty Seven Shillings* of them, the price of an Ounce of Silver, is but equal to *Eight Shillings* at first.

The very great mischief that the thus sinking the Credit of our Bills has produc'd, is so plain & obvious, and has been felt by so many Persons, that one would think it need not be describ'd. The Widow with the Orphans, whose Money was under the management of their Guardians, and who could improve it only by letting it on Interest, have

not one third left of what they [2] possess'd Twenty
Years ago. The Clergy and most other Salary Men are
great Sufferers; and every Person who has debts out of a
long standing, has lost more by the falling of the Money,
than the ordinary profits in Trade will countervail. In
short, most of us have been deluded and carried away with
an empty sound, and the Man whose Estate was worth so
much last Year, is apt to imagine, if he can call it the same
this, it is not decreas'd, tho' perhaps it really is a fifth part;
and he governs his Expences accordingly.

But this is what you have often seen in Print, and it's
become Common-place Talk, and in the Mouths of all sorts
of People. What we are more divided about is, The cause
of the Bills being depreciated. Which plainly, I think,
appears to be this. They were Emitted on a meer imaginary bottom, and are never to be paid off. The Land
Security that is given for them, is a sufficient Surety to the
Province, that they shall be paid in again, but its no Security
to the Possessors or the Persons that give a Credit to them,
that they shall keep their value, and that *Twenty Shillings*
of them shall purchase as much Silver and Gold the next
Year, as it does the present; so that we may rather wonder
they have not fell to *Forty Shillings* per Ounce, or even
to their first nothing, than that they have sunk to what
they now are.

Now as the Government have brought us into all these
Difficulties, so it is they only that must extricate us; and
since the danger of our continuing to suffer is so apparent,
if they neglect all Remedies, and leave the Money of the
Province to continue under its present Circumstances, I
think they may be charg'd with as great Injustice, as if they

took the Estate of one Man and gave it to another, without any reason or pretence for so doing.

[3] But what Methods are proper to be taken in order to relieve us, we are too much divided in our Sentiments to determine. I can't find an Instance of any State's being brought into Circumstances exactly like ours. *Cicero* tells us, that the Money of the old Romans in the time of their Consuls, was so fluctuating, that it was not possible for any Man to know what he was worth: And this I think plainly appears to be the Case with us at this day. But then he says nothing of the cause of it, nor how at last it was settled, only that *C. Marius* by whose Wisdom and Prudence it was effected, had the greatest Honours confer'd upon him, Statues erected in every Street, and render'd himself very dear to the People. The clipping and debasing the Money of *England* in King WILLIAM's time, had the same influence on their Credit, as the sinking of our Currency has on our's. But it was easier to be remedy'd; for although the Coin was so far diminish'd or debas'd that *Five Pounds* in Silver Specie was scarce worth *Forty Shillings*, yet there was some intrinsick value left; and as it was Silver that was still current, the recoining of it according to the Standard, intirely retriev'd the value of it without any loss or inconvenience to the Possessor, who suffer'd only in denomination and sound, for his Half Crown in new Money would immediately purchase him more than a Crown of the old. But here we have no Silver or Gold to work upon, and instead of an intrinsick real value, the money we have left has only a meer imaginary one.

We have many Men among us who are for using no means to relieve us, only wait with Patience till the Bills that are now extant are all brought in, as in a few Years they must be : For, say they, as the Bills by multiplying have been depreciated, so consequently as they are diminished and the Periods for their be-[4]ing drawn in approach, they must rise in their value: And its true, that immediately after a large Emission, the currency has always fell, but then no consequence follows from thence, that upon the quantities being lessen'd, it must rise again; nay the contrary is evident from Experience as well as Reason : And we may instance in the late sudden stop put to the currency of the Merchants Notes, as they are called; for tho' the Emission of them, with other Bills·at the same time, sunk our Money at least twenty five *per Cent*, yet their ceasing has not reduc'd it in any degree.

But it's argued, that in a little time the Bills of the Province will fall into the Hands of a few Persons, and every one that has Taxes to pay must purchase them at what rates they'l please to demand. But surely, no Man in his senses can think the Government will ever suffer such Oppression as this, and it is our Happiness that they are already thinking of an expedient to prevent it.

However let us suppose, that our Bills may come to rights of themselves, and that as they have gradually fallen, so they will gradually rise again, yet it would never be just and reasonable that they should, for as much wrong and injustice would be occasion'd by their rising, as has already been by their falling. It is undoubtedly a great Injury to the Creditor, who contracted a Debt many Years ago, when Silver was at *Eight Shillings* the Ounce, that he is forc'd to receive it at *Sixteen* or *Twenty Shillings*, or may be now it is at *Twenty Seven Shillings ;* and will it not be equally injurious to a Man who borrows Money, or contracts a debt to day, when Silver is at *Twenty Seven Shillings* per Ounce, if he should pay it some time hence at *Twenty, Ten* or *Eight Shillings* per Ounce; for whether the Creditor be forc'd to receive less, or the Deb-[5]tor to pay more than he contracted, the Injury is the same, and some Body is defrauded of their due.

But I need say no more to convince you, that this method is neither expedient nor practicable. And I am satisfy'd that nothing will effectually serve for an Instrument of Commerce in any particular Kingdom or Government, but what Mankind by universal assent have plac'd a value on. Indeed if we had no Correspondence with the rest of the World, and all our Trade and Business was with one another, and within our selves, I don't see why Leather, Paper, or any thing that we agreed to and put a Stamp on, should not answer the end as well as Silver, provided it be durable, and we have but just a sufficient quantity of it. If this be true, then nothing can relieve us, but the putting a stop to our present Currency, that has only an imaginary value, and introducing Silver and Gold, which the World has given a real value to. The easiest and best way therefore of doing this is what we must pitch upon. It can't be done, as you have heard it propos'd, by a Tax on the People: For how is it possible at this day, for a Farmer or a Tradesman to find Silver or Gold to satisfy their Taxes. It must be the Merchant and Man in Trade, and he only can introduce it. And if any way can be found that this may be done with advantage both to the Undertakers and the Publick, that certainly is what we must come into.

The Scheme which has been several times before the

General Court, appears to me the best calculated for this purpose of any I have yet heard of. And that we may better examine it & judge of it, let us first see the Scheme itself; the substance of which I shall give you in as few words, and as comprehensive as may be. [6]

That the Sum of . . . . . be Emitted by the Government in New Bills of a different tenor from those already extant, to be let out to such Persons as will oblige themselves to pay for each Thousand Pounds annually, *One Hundred & Ten Pounds* for Ten Years, in Silver Coin after the rate of *Six Shillings & Ten Pence* per Ounce, or Gold Coin in proportion.

This will lay a sufficient Fund for the redeeming or exchanging of said Bills; and accordingly at the end of Five Years there shall be delivered to the Possessor of any and all of them one half of their value in Silver at *Six Shillings & Ten Pence* the Ounce, or Gold in proportion; and the other half in new Bills, which new Bills shall be paid off or exchanged at the end of other Five Years.

That these Bills in all Courts, shall be adjudg'd a legal tender and discharge for all Debts Contracts or Obligations whatever, and for all Specialties payable in Silver and Gold, the Bonds and Obligations of the Undertakers in this Scheme excepted.

That *Six Shillings & Ten Pence* of these Bills shall be receiv'd in all Payments, and made equal to one Ounce of Silver, and to . . . of the old Bills, and so of consequence shall discharge . . . of all Debts that are already contracted.

That the Currency of the Bills of the other Governments be
forbidden, and that all Persons who tender or receive
the same, be liable to a severe penalty.

There can be but two Objections against this Scheme.
The principal is, that the Bills will not always purchase so
much Silver as they are to be exchang'd for, but that there
will be a discount proportionable to the distance of the
Periods when they are paid off; for [7] certainly a Note payable five or ten Years hence, is not so good as one payable
on demand.

But I fancy you'l not find so much weight in this Objection as appears at first sight; for though a Note of Hand
payable at a distant Period, is not equal to one payable on
demand, yet a Bond which carries Interest where the Security is certain, is very little inferior and by many Persons
esteem'd equal to Money in Hand; and I think the Case the
same with these Bills as with a Bond with Interest; and any
Person may make the same advantage from them as from
such a Bond.   Please to suppose that you are possess'd of a
Thousand Pounds in these Bills, which are by Law the
Money of the Province, and in which, or in Silver and Gold
all Debts are to be paid, you let the same to your Neighbour, receive the annual Interest of *Six* per Cent. and at the
Periods when they are to be exchang'd receive the Principal,
what difference does it make to you the being possess'd of
these Bills or a Bond with Interest for Silver, or even of the
Silver and Gold it self.   And here lay the great defect of
the Merchants Notes, that they were not the Money of the
Province; for had there been an Act that all Debts should
be paid in those Notes, or in Silver or Gold at the rates ex-

press'd, every Person who had Debts outstanding, would have been as secure as those Gentlemen are who have taken Bonds to be paid in the said Notes, or in Silver at *Nineteen Shillings* per Ounce; and I am satisfy'd not one of those, provided their Bonds were good, would repent their bargain. Were *Sixty Thousand Pounds* of these Bills once current among us, the currency of the Bills of the other Governments entirely ceas'd, and to facilitate the affair, would most of our Merchants endeavour to introduce the currency of Silver and Gold, by passing it with the Bills, though but in a small proportion, I am perswaded that, as the Bills alone would not be suffi-[8]cient for the Trade of the Province, we should quickly see Silver and Gold current with them, and no better esteem'd than they. The Bills of our Neighbours at *New-York* are on no better foundation than our's that are already extant, only as they have but very few, and not enough to carry on their Trade, Gold and Silver passing current with them, and at the rates fix'd by the Government, in a great measure supports their Credit. But allowing there should be a discount on these Bills, it is impossible it should be any thing considerable, for then any Man by letting his Money to Interest without any risque, might make a greater advantage than can be had ordinarily in Trade, though attended with trouble as well as risque; I say, allowing there should be a small discount, surely it is better than to continue in our present Condition. If any other or better method can be propos'd to satisfy Men who will be content with nothing but perfect demonstration, I shall be glad we may come into it.

The other Objection which has a dependance on the former is, The Undertakers will be in such danger of suffering, that there will not be found Persons enough to engage in it: The Merchants have been hurt by their late Scheme, and therefore will not be fond of trying another, which their's was so much like.

But I am satisfied their own Scheme will convince them that this must be profitable, and they must know that the only thing they wanted was such an Act to support them, which destroys the Bills of the other Governments, and also makes all common Debts as good as their Bonds & Specialties, excepting the Interest they carry: And for my part, I am so convinc'd of the profit of it, that I should be willing to engage for as large a Sum as my Estate and Circumstances will admit of. But allowing there should be [9] any difficulty here, which I think cannot be, it is undoubtedly the Interest of the Province to give a still greater encouragement rather than continue as we are.

I think nothing need be said to that Objection, that Silver and Gold will never tarry among us, till by retrenching our Expences and improving our Trade, we bring the balance in our favour. The first and main thing that we stand in need of is the fixing and ascertaining the Money, and so the Debts of the Province, which has a tendency to lessen our Extravagance, and to improve our Trade, which has really been on the decay, ever since the depretiating our Money, and without this imaginary Wealth we should never had a supply for so much Luxury and Extravagance as there is among us.

I pray, Sir, you would consider that the Government is the Guarantee that all just & legal Contracts shall be perform'd; but with us they are daily broken, & necessarily will be so, whilst our Money continues in its present fluctuating

Circumstances. If a Cure be effected the benefit is so great, & on the contrary if nothing be done the extream Calamity is so evident, that I'm satisfy'd you'l chuse rather to run the hazard of some small inconveniencies in order to relieve us, than by a longer neglect to expose the Country to apparent ruin.

I am,

SIR,

Your Humble Servant,

Philopatriæ.

—— —— *Si quid novisti rectius istis Candidus imperti, si non his utere mecum.*

✳✳✳✳✳✳✳✳✳✳✳✳✳✳✳✳✳✳✳✳✳✳✳✳✳✳

NOTE TO "A LETTER TO A MEMBER OF THE HONOURABLE HOUSE OF REPRESENTATIVES," ETC.

In the "Diary and Letters of Thomas Hutchinson," P. O. Hutchinson, the editor, makes the statement that in 1736, Governor Hutchinson published a small pamphlet upon the subject of paper-money. There is but one among the pamphlets published that year which are to be found on the shelves of our libraries that can by any chance respond to the claim that it was from the pen of the governor, and that one is the " Letter to a member of the honourable house of representatives." In method of construction, mode of reasoning, literary style and financial opinions, it would answer all the demands which we should require for the identification of Hutchinson as the author. In 1898 I investigated the pamphlet literature of the period to see if I could find the Hutchinson pamphlet and came to the conclusion that this "Letter" must be accepted as his work. The result of my study was published in the Proceedings of the Massachusetts Historical Society, February, 1899, under title of " A search for a pamphlet by Governor Hutchinson."

The publication of this paper gave opportunity for the inclusion of a full account of the attempts of the hard-money men of Boston to resume specie payments along the line of Hutchinson's proposition. The author of the " Letter " says that he should be willing to invest as much of his property in such a venture as his circumstances would permit. The names of Governor Hutchinson and of his father appear among the subscribers for the proposed new currency, which was to be emitted to those who would pay it back to the province on certain terms in silver. The scheme failed for lack of adequate support, but the story is worth preserving.

The copy and the facsimile of the title-page were procured from the Massachusetts Historical Society. The leaves of the pamphlet measure 8⅛ by 5⅜ inches. Other copies of the " Letter," etc., may be found in the American Antiquarian Society, the Boston Public Library, the Harvard College Library, and the Library of Congress.

A
PROPOSAL

to supply the

TRADE

with a

Medium of Exchange,

and to sink

the Bills of the other Governments.

BOSTON:

Printed in the Year 17

The publication of this paper gave opportunity for the inclusion of a full account of the attempts of the hard-money men of Boston to resume specie payments along the line of Hutchinson's proposition. The author of the "Letter" says that he should be willing to invest as much of his property in such a venture as his circumstances would permit. The names of Governor Hutchinson and of his father appear among the subscribers for the proposed new currency, which was to be emitted to those who would pay it back to the province on certain terms in silver. The scheme failed for lack of adequate support, but the story is worth preserving.

The copy and the facsimile of the title-page were procured from the Massachusetts Historical Society. The leaves of the pamphlet measure 8¼ by 5⅛ inches. Other copies of the "Letter," etc., may be found in the American Antiquarian Society, the Boston Public Library, the Harvard College Library, and the Library of Congress.

A

PROPOSAL

to supply the

TRADE

with a

Medium of Exchange,

and to sink

the Bills of the other Governments.

BOSTON:

Printed in the Year 1737.

A

PROPOSAL

to supply the

TRADE

with a

Medium of Exchange,

and to sink

the Bills of the other Governments.

BOSTON:

Printed in the Year 1 7 3 7.

A
PROPOSAL

to supply the Trade with a

Medium of Exchange,

and to sink the Bills of the other Governments.

HAT Money is wanted, or some other Medium of Exchange, to pass from Man to Man to facilitate our Trade, is allowed by every Body: but how to fix on a Scheme which may be acceptable to all Sorts of Men, will be found very difficult. The People were in Expectation of something being done for their Relief by the General Court, but are from Session to Session disappointed; nothing is done to Revive and Encourage our dying Trade, or to supply the People with a Medium of Exchange to purchase the Necessaries of Life. The small Money, which passes daily for that Service, is so debased that it is a Scandal it should pass among us: and since there is no prospect of any Relief from the Government, and that we must expect no farther Emissions from them, there seems to be no way left us, to save our Selves and Posterity from Ruin, but by erecting a private *Bank*, founded on [2] our Lands, we having no Silver to put in for Security. This seems to be our last Refuge to fly to;

and therefore I would propose, That there be a sufficient Sum agreed on to manage the Trade of the Province, and to sink the Bills of the other Governments; that there may be but one Sort of Bills passing among us, that so every Man may Know what he receives; for as there are four Sorts now passing, it is all Guess-Work; and we know not but that half the Money we receive is Counterfeit. Could we agree on such a *Bank*, I am of Opinion we might, in a great Measure, recover our Trade again, and be yet the Head of these Provinces, as we have hitherto been: And without this or some other such Method it is to be feared, our Neighbours, who have of late got from us so great a Part of our Trade, will, in a little Time, *eat us out of the rest.* And as Banks are projected for the common Good of the Community, they ought not to be engross'd by a few rich Men; no Man ought to sign too largely: and good Housekeepers, who can sign but *Two hundred Pounds*, ought not to be excluded. They pay lot and scot as much, and more in Proportion, than their rich Neighbours, and therefore they ought not to be refused, if they can give Security. Every Scheme projected to bring in Silver will be attended with ill Consequences, unless the Silver could be prevented being exported; and that we are sure can never be effected. If ever we recover our former happy State, and have Silver pass among us, it must be by going on Manufactures here, and so lessning our Import; and that can't be done in a Day; it must be the Work of many Years to accomplish it, and can never be carried on without a further Supply of Money.

[3] I would propose, in order to supply the Trade with a Medium of Exchange, and to sink the Bills of the other

Governments, to erect a Land Bank of *Five hundred thousand Pounds.*

1. *Two hundred thousand Pounds* in Bank Notes to be printed and given out; the rest to be negociated by Transfer in the Books of the Bank, which I believe will suit the Merchants in this Town, as well as to have the Notes in their own Possession: but if this should not Answer as well as to have the Bills passing, that Inconveniency may be remedied by printing the Bills.

2. Every Man to give a real Security for his Subscription; and take out the Value in Notes, or have Credit in the Books, and so draw it out as his Occasions call for it, and pay Interest for it into the Bank *6 per Cent. per Ann.*

3. Two *per Cent.* of the whole Interest of the above Sum, to be paid by the Bank annually into the Town Treasury, to be improved in a Work-house, the Alms-house, and other good Uses which may be thought of for the good of the Town.

4. Every Partner to be obliged to accept no Bills of the other Governments, but at such a Discount as shall be agreed on by the Company. This will soon bring all their Bills into disrepute; and they will sink in Value in a little Time; and it will discourage their making any further Emissions.

5. The Interest Money to be improved at Interest at *6 per Cent. per Ann.* the Two *per Cent.* to [4] Town-Treasurer, and the Charge of managing the Affair, first to be deducted. This will prevent the Usurers preying upon their poor Neighbours. and exacting more than common Interest.

6. It shall be in the Power of any original Subscriber to

redeem the Estate he hath mortgaged into the Bank, at any time, by paying in so much as it is mortgaged for; which Money, so paid in, shall be improved for the Benefit of the Company, at Interest, or by discounting Bills of Exchange, or Notes of Hand, as is usual in the Bank of *England* and other Banks; and yet the first Subscriber shall continue a Partner, and be intituled to his Part of the Profits, by vertue of his first Subscription, until he see cause to sell or dispose of his Part of the Profits so arising, to any other Person. And any such Purchaser may and shall, from the Time of his Purchase, be intituled to the Profits.

7. Any such Purchaser may sell or dispose of his Profits so purchased to any other, and he to another, and so on.

8. The Books of the Bank shall be settled annually, and the neet Profits carried to every Subscribers Account; but if any have sold his Part of his Profits, then the Purchaser shall have Credit in the Books accordingly.

We find by Experience that Silver goes from us as fast as it is brought in, and so it is in all Places where the Necessity of their Trade requires its Export. Nothing can bring Silver amongst us but Trade; if that dont bring it in, no [5] Law can do it; nor can any Law be made which will effectually prevent its being shipp'd off, if the Necessity of our Trade calls for it to Balance our Accompts abroad, so that we must have a Paper Medium or none at all: And it is impossible for a Trading Place as this is, to carry on their Trade without some Sort of Money: And why a Silver Bank should be prefer'd to a Land Bank, seems to me very strange: For should the Management of a Land Bank happen to fall into bad Hands, they could never embezel any Part of the capital Stock, it being all Mortgages of Lands

upon Record; so that if the Company were cheated by ill
Managers, it could be only of Part of the growing Profits,
the Capital would not be diminished in the least; but on the
contrary, the Security will grow better as the Lands rise in
Value: whereas a Silver Bank may be embezled by ill Directors or Managers: A sad Instance whereof our Nation
experienc'd in the Year 1720, in the Affair of the *South Sea*
Company.   We have lately tryed an Experiment to bring in
Silver, and what good hath it done: A few Men of plentiful Estates have had the Opportunity to enrich themselves,
whilst many more have been Hurt by them.   All such
Schemes are unjust in their Nature, and will prove fatal in
their Consequences.   They seem calculated only to enrich
a few, and impoverish a great many.   By the Scheme here
proposed no Man can be hurt, neither can any Man be benefited more than in Proportion to his Subscription: It will
be a general good; Every Man will be eased in his Taxes,
Trade will be carried on with more Justice and Honour then
it is possible it should be by a Truck Trade, which naturally
puts [6] Men upon Tricking and Sharping one another.
The Usurer will be obliged to content himself with *6 per
Cent.* as the Law hath set Interest; and consequently the
Landed Man's Estate will rise in Value, for as Interest rises
Lands fall in Value; that is plain beyond all Contradiction.
No Man will buy Land to bring him in *5 per Cent.* if he can
let out his Money at *10 per Cent.* and have the same Land
made over to him for his Security.   It seems strange that
our General Court, who are all Landed Men, do not see this
ill Effect attending the want of Money amongst us.   All wise
States endeavour to lower Interest; and it is with this View,
to encourage Men to improve their Money in Trade and

Land. No Man can afford to give *10 per Cent.* for Money to Trade with; neither can the Farmer afford to give such an Interest for Money to stock and improve his Land with: such an Interest would soon eat out his Farm: but at a moderate Interest Men would be encouraged to stock and improve much more Land than now they do, which would advance their Families, and serve the Publick also. But it can never be expected that Interest will be low whilst Money is so scarce, and it will be a long Time before it will be so plenty as to lower Interest, if we expect to do it by a Silver Medium, which leaves us as fast as any Opportunity offers of a Ship to carry it away to *London.* I confess I can't see the Necessity of having Silver or Gold for a Medium to pass among us. *Romulus,* the Founder of the Roman Empire, made Leather pass as Money, and they had no other Medium until by their Trade with their Neighbours they grew rich and powerful; and yet from a mean beginning they arrived to [**7**] that height of Glory as to give Laws to the greatest Part of the World. But to come nearer our own Time, the *Hollanders* Money is what indeed they call Silver, but great Part of it is such a Mixture of base Metal, that it will pass no where but among themselves. What then is that Money better to them than our Paper Bills is to us; our Bills will answer all the Ends among our selves, which their Money will among themselves: Our Bills indeed will not do to send to *England* to pay our Debts, neither will that coarse Silver of theirs pay their Debts in *England;* but it serves among themselves to buy and sell with, and to manage their Trade with, which are the principal things Money is designed for. And how Rich & Powerful is that Nation grown by their Trade, in the last One hundred and fifty

Years, for they have very little Land to improve. But some
amongst us say, we have too much Trade, and that our over-
trading our selves runs us into our Difficulties, I confess
some particular Men may over-trade themselves, and may
Hurt themselves by so doing; but that such a Place as this,
whose whole Dependence is on Trade, should be Hurt by
it, I deny; it is just the contrary, for the more Goods is
imported the better it is; for this Reason, The Plenty of
Foreign Goods brings down their Prices, and so the People
are supplied at easy Rates; and at the same Time it keeps
up the Price of our own Produce, which is most certainly
an Advantage to the Farmer. The *Dutch*, who are allowed
by all Nations to understand these Things as well as any,
encourage every Body to come to them with their Commodities, and the Duties on all Foreign Commodities are
but a Trifle: They lay [8] their Excise or Duty on the
Consumption among themselves, and let Trade go in a
manner free. This they do to encourage every Body to
come to them, and say that they are sure of getting something by every Ship that comes to them, whether they who
send to them get any thing or no. And the People of this
Province are as much spirited for Trade as any People can
be, if there were Money to carry on their Projects; but, alas,
let Men be never so willing & industrious, they can't make
Brick without Straw. But now let us come even to our own
Doors; What have our Neighbours at *Rhode-Island* done
within these fifteen Years? or rather, What have we done
for 'em? They have I presume emitted within these fifteen
Years *Five hundred thousand Pounds*, which was so much
clear Gains the Day they were emitted. This Money we
have given a Credit to by accepting it in Payment equal

with the Bills of our own Province; by so doing we have
enabled them to cut us out of the most valuable Branches
of our Trade. And if we don't put a Check to their Bills
by making a Bank among our selves, they will soon eat us
out of every other Branch which they think worth their
having. Was ever any People so thoughtless of their own
Interest? We receive their ragged Bills, when we have all
the Reason in the World to believe they are many of them
Counterfeits. Nay we oftentimes find them to be such;
and the Loss falls on those who happen to receive them, for
they never make them good, not being obliged so to do:
Whereas had we a Bank of our own, the Office would be
kept in this Town, and whoever was suspicious of any Bill
might go to the Office and be satisfied whether it were good
[9] or no. But so great is the Want of Money among us,
that as bad as these *Rhode-Island* Bills are, I know some
who have considerable Sums due by Bond in Bills of our
Province, would gladly accept these *Rhode-Island* Bills in
Lieu of them, but can't get their Pay in any Sort of Bills.
From hence we may reasonably believe, That if we had a
private Bank, the Bank Notes would answer for these Bonds
as well as the *Rhode-Island* Bills; and if so, what a vast
Ease and Benefit would it be to poor Men who are involved
in Bonds and Mortgages? Again, if we had a private Bank
it would be a means to bring abroad our Province Bills; for
most certainly, the Hopes of seeing our Province Bills rise
in Value, is the sole Cause of their being hoarded up, Men
vainly imagining that *Twenty Shillings* of these Bills will
in Time fetch three Ounces of Silver: But if we had a
Medium of Exchange in any Proportion answerable to our
Trade, such Men would soon be of another Opinion: No

Man as yet ever got much by hoarding up the Province
Bills; and it is to be hoped that no Man ever will, since their
Design in so doing, cannot be founded on common Justice.
The *Rhode-Islanders* find the Want of Money, and are many
of them for making another *hundred thousand Pounds* in
Bills; which it is supposed will soon come here to pay their
Debts, and to purchase such Commodities as they want from
us to carry on their foreign Trade.   If their Government do
not oblige the trading Men in this Point, their next Step
will be, they will most certainly make a private Bank among
themselves; they will never suffer their Trade to languish
and die for Want of Money, as we do: And if ever they do
so, we in [10] this Province shall do by their Bank Bills as
we have done by their Province Bills, receive them in Payment for Goods and Debts; and why not?   Their Bank
Notes will be as good as their Province Bills.   Thus as we
have been, so we shall continue to be, bubbled by that People,
if we do not unite and come into a Bank among our selves.
The common saying among us is, that we must a bate of
our Extravagancies, and go more into Manufactures, that
our Import may be less, and our Export more; and no Man
will deny but that this is one good Way to help us out of
our Difficulties; but these things alone will not do it; encouraging of Trade is found the most effectual Way to help
any People: I confess it would save abundance of Money,
if People would abate of their Extravagancies in their Buildings, Furniture, Apparel and Tables: but this can never be
remedied until they who find most Fault with these Things
remedy them at home, and set their Inferiours a good Example.   But it is very certain that this Truck Trade, which
the Want of Money inevitably runs us into, leads many

People into such Extravagances. If Tradesmen were paid in Money they would not lay it out in such Ways. If Money were Plenty, many more People would go to work on the Mines, and on raising Hemp & Flax, so that in a few Years we should raise so much of those Commodities, that we should not want any supply of them from abroad: This would lessen our Import very considerably, and be a very great Advantage; but such Things can't be carried on without Money. It is impossible to project any Scheme which will make your Bank Notes equal, in the Esteem of People, with Silver, let the Price [11] you set Silver at be what it will; for if you could lay into your Bank *One hundred thousand Pounds* in Silver, and made but the same Sum in Bank Notes, the Circumstance of your Trade is such at present that the Merchants and Factors would, in a few Months, draw out all that Silver, and leave you the Notes in Lieu thereof; and then would want Silver to ship off as much as ever; and then what would those Bank Notes be worth; the Bank would be at an End, because there would be no manner of Security for them, neither Money, Lands or Bonds. But I will venture to say, the Bank of *England's* Notes are not equal in Value to Silver, and yet are among the trading Part of the Nation prefer'd before Silver for their Conveniency, being light of Carriage, &c. For if they were as valuable in the Opinion of the Possessor as Silver is, Men would not on every turn, when they apprehend any Danger of the Nation's being invaded by their Neighbours, run upon the Bank and carry in their Bank Notes, and draw out their Money: No surely, if they were in no Apprehensions of losing by a Turn of Affairs in the Government, they would be easy in letting their Money remain in the Bank: And this is a further Proof that a Money Bank is not so safe as a Land Bank, for the Lands cannot be carried away by Enemies, nor embezled by corrupt Managers. All the Things of this World are valued by Men, according to the good or bad Opinion they have of them, and that which is most solid and durable, and least exposed to Casualities & Accidents, we esteem most; then surely a Land Security is to be prefer'd before Silver, for we are told, *The Earth endures for ever.*

F I N I S.

NOTE TO "A PROPOSAL TO SUPPLY THE TRADE WITH A MEDIUM OF EXCHANGE," ETC.

Royal instructions at this time in force required the province to provide for the retirement of all bills of public credit then in circulation, according to the terms of the funds established in the acts of emission. Thirty thousand pounds was the limit of the amount of bill of public credit thereafter to be permitted in circulation. The fund having the longest time to run which was in existence when these instructions were issued expired in 1741. This pamphlet was published in 1737. The province had before it, therefore, the task of retiring by taxation within four years the sum of about £275,000 in province bills beside providing for the annual expenses of government. Under these circumstances men of all classes were speculating as to what provision could be made for the emergency. On the one hand there were those who submitted propositions which they hoped would, if adopted, lead to a resumption of specie payments. On the other, there were those who believed that it was better to continue on a paper-money basis, and if the province was to be prohibited from emitting bills of public credit, then it was desirable that the citizens of the province should take possession of that field and provide their own paper currency. Of this latter class was the writer of this pamphlet, and his proposition was to establish what he termed "a private *Bank*, founded on our Lands, we having no Silver to put in for Security." This bank was not to be an organization of stockholders. The profits of the enterprise were to be divided among the borrowers. Notes were to be printed, and those who were willing to patronize the scheme were to receive these notes or if they preferred it bank credit, upon furnishing satisfactory land security. They were further to agree to receive the notes in trade, and in addition to agree to receive in trade the bills of other governments only at the discount which should be settled by the bank. Having no capital behind it, the words in which the writer describes it as a "Land Bank of Five hundred thousand Pounds" must be interpreted that the sum mentioned was the limit of the total credit the bank would furnish to borrowers. Two hundred thousand pounds was the limit which he set for the emissions of the bank; the balance he thought would be available in the way of bank credit which could be used by transfers in bank. One third of the interest money to be received by the proposed bank was to be paid to town-treasurers for alms-houses and work-houses.

The arguments adduced by the writer in favor of his private bank are much the same as some that we have already met with in the pamphlets of advocates of similar institutions. He discusses the Rhode Island bills, and while he disapproves of their free circulation, he evidently regards their emission as a piece of financial sagacity.

The copy and the facsimile of the title-page were procured from the Boston Public Library. The leaves of the pamphlet measure 5¾ by 3⅝ inches. The Boston Athenæum is also the possessor of a copy of this pamphlet.

SOME
OBSERVATIONS
ON THE
SCHEME

projected for emitting 60000l.

in BILLS of a
New Tenour,

to be redeemed with

SILVER and GOLD.

Shewing the various *Operations* of these
Bills, and their Tendency to *hurt* the
Publick Interest.

In a LETTER from a Merchant in *Boston*, to his
Friend in the Country.

BOSTON:
Printed and Sold by S. KNEELAND and T. GREEN
in *Queen-street.* MDCCXXXVIII.

SOME

OBSERVATIONS

ON THE

SCHEME

projected for emitting 60000 *l*.

in 𝕭𝕴𝕷𝕷𝕾 of a

New Tenour,

to be redeemed with

SILVER and GOLD.

Shewing the various *Operations* of these
Bills, and their Tendency to *hurt* the
Publick Interest.

In a LETTER from a Merchant in *Boston,* to his
Friend in the Country.

BOSTON:
Printed and Sold by S. KNEELAND and T. GREEN
in *Queen-street.* MDCCXXXVIII.

OBSERVATIONS

ON THE

SCHEME

For 60000 l. in *Bills* of a

NEW TENOUR

SOME

OBSERVATIONS

ON THE

S C H E M E

projected for emitting 60000 *l.*

in 𝕭 𝕴 𝕷 𝕷 𝕾 of a

New Tenour,

to be redeemed with

SILVER and *GOLD.*

Shewing the various *Operations* of thefe
Bills, and their Tendency to *hurt* the
Publick Intereft.

In a LETTER from a Merchant in *Bofton*, to his
Friend in the Country.

B O S T O N:
Printed and Sold by S. KNEELAND and T. GREEN
in *Queen-ftreet.* MDCCXXXVIII.

A

Letter from a Merchant in *Boston*, to his Friend in the Country.

SIR,

Boston, Feb. 1. 1737, 8.

I N Conformity to your Desire, I send you a few Thoughts on the Scheme proposed for emitting Bills of a new Tenour. The Scheme, in brief, is as follows.

SCHEME.

That the Sum of 60000 l. be emitted in Bills *promising Silver at the Rate of* 6 s. 8 d, per Ounce, *or* Gold *at the Rate of* 4 l. 18 s. per Ounce, *to be paid, one Half at the End of* Five *Years, and the other Half at the End of* Ten *Years*; *upon Loan, to Undertakers.*

For every 1000 l. *borrowed, the Undertakers are to pay in Yearly* 105 l. *in* Silver *at* 6/8 *per Ounce, (or* Gold *as above) for* Ten *Years, which Sums are fully discharge their Bonds.*

The Bills are to pass at the Rate of 6/8 *for* 20 s. *of Bills of the old Tenour, or One for Three, as Bills of the new Tenour, which are already extant, do.*

Six Shillings *and* Eight Pence *of these Bills is to be received as a lawful* Tender, *where* One Ounce *of* Silver *is promised, or where* 6/8 *in* Bills *of the* new *Tenour, or* 20 s. *in Bills of the old Tenour are promised.*

[2] This is the Substance of the Scheme: And in order to form a Judgment upon it, I shall consider the *various Operations* of the Bills proposed therein.

However, before I proceed to this, it will be needful to consider the *Value* of the *other* Bills and Notes now passing, with which I shall have Occasion to compare these Bills, together with the *Value* of *these* Bills at their *first Emission:* And likewise for your Satisfaction, to propose the *Method* which I make Use of, in *computing the Value* of Bills or Notes that are paid off at *different* (or *partial*) Payments, by giving you an Example in the Computation of the late *Merchant's-Notes* at their *first Emission;* which, as they were the most difficult, so will give the greater ·Light to the Subject in Hand.

	Oz.	dw.	gr.
Principal	70	03	00
Intrest 3 Years	12	12	12
	82	15	12
1*st* Payment	30	00	00
	52	15	12
Interest 3 Years	09	10	00
	62	05	12
2*d* Payment	30	00	00
	32	05	12
Interest 4 Years	07	14	12
	40	00	00
Last Payment	40	00	00
	00	00	00

Compound Intr. at 27 s. 8d.

Thus 95 *l.* in *Merchants-Notes* promised 100 *Ounces* of *Silver;* 3 10ths thereof payable in three Years, 3 10ths in six Years, and 4 10ths in ten Years ; *without any Interest.* And therefore when *Allowance* of *Interest* is made for the *Distance* of Payments, it is found upon Trial that they are *only equal* to 70 Ounces and 3 P. wt. of Silver, *prompt* Payment: For that Sum (as in the Case of a *Bond*) requires 100 Ounces, paid after the Manner of the Promise of the Notes, to make up the *Principal* and *Interest* due upon it in Ten Years; as you have it wrought in the *Margin.* And thus, the Notes *promising* Silver at 19 s. *per Oz.* at distant Payments, were *only worth* Silver at 27 s. 1 d. *per Ounce* prompt Payment: For 70 *Ounces* and 3 *P. wt.* of Silver at 27 s. 1 d. *per Ounce,* amounts to 95 l. in *Notes* which promised 100 *Ounces* of Silver.

I allow *Interest,* because I suppose no Man will imagine that the best Note or Bill in the World, payable at a [3] *distant* Time, will be negotiated in Trade any otherwise than with a proper *Discount* for the *Time*, and daily Experience amongst ourselves confirms it.

Merchants Notes, according to the same Method of Computation, were, at the End of *December* 1737, or the Beginning of the fifth Year, equal to *Silver* at 23 s. 11 d. *Compound Interest at* 24 s: 1d. *Publick* Bills of the *new* Tenour, to be discharged after *December* 1742, being 5 Years, equal to *Silver* at 26 s. 3 d. *Compornd Intr. at* 26 s. 9d. *per Ounce.*

Bills of the *old* Tenour, if discharged at the same Time, 26 s. 3 d. *per Ounce.*

Bills proposed by *this Scheme*, at their *first* Emission, equal to *Silver* at 29 s. 6 d. *per Ounce*, or the promising *Compound Intr. at* 30 s. 6 d. for every 1000 l. *Three* Thousand Ounces of *Silver*, only equal to 2042 Ounces prompt Payment. Besides you'l observe, that in these Computations I have not (save *Comp.* 1959 *Oz.* by the Hints in the Margin) made any *Allowance* (or Compound) to the Possessor for *lying out of Interest* for Five Years at a Time, nor for the *natural* (or market) Rate of *Interest*, continually subsisting in all Countries, sometimes under, sometimes above the Rate of lawful Interest, whatever that natural Interest may be: Which brings me to the Consideration of the *various Operations* of the Bills.

1. As to the *Undertaker;*
2. The *Borrower* from him or other Persons;
3. The *Possessor;*
4. The Province.

1st. As to the *Undertaker.* Now if he takes up 1000 l. conditioned to pay in at Times 3150 Ounces of *Silver,* or 315 Ounces yearly, he then receives in *present Value* only 2042 Ounces, for which he must pay yearly 315 Ounces for Ten Years, *i. e.* to a Trifle at the Rate of 9 *per Cent.* Interest *per Annum.*

If he *Lends* his 1000 l. for the whole Ten Years, to *B. C.* and *D.* conditioned to pay 2042 Ounces of *Silver* (which Sum he ought not in Equity to exceed, nor to be allowed in the Practice of it if he should) at 6 *per Cent.* Interest, he then receives yearly for Interest 122 Ounces, to which he must add 193 Ounces, in order to make up his yearly Payment (to the Trustees) of 315 Ounces, his Account will stand thus, —

[4] He *advances* 193 Ounces of his own Silver for $\left.\right\}$ 1930
      Ten Years,

Interest on the same allowed him for 9 Years $\left.\right\}$ 521
      and downwards at 6 *per Cent.*

$\underline{ 2451}$

He *receives* his Principal at the End of 10 Years $\underline{2042}$

He loses Ounces — — — — — — — — 409

If he yearly calls in of his Principal sufficient to discharge his own yearly Payment, he will lose above 500 Ounces.

Again, if he lends his 1000 l. for a shorter Time, con-

2042 dition'd to pay in the *same* Bills again (which indeed

2293 has a plausible Appearance, but the *Borrowers*

251   will find a Sting in it) he then lends in Value

64   2042 Ounces of *Silver,* or Silver at 29 s. 6 d, *per*

315   *Ounce,* and receives of Interest and Principal at

the Year's End, Bills worth 2293 *Ounces* (or Silver at 27 s. 10 d. *per Ounce*) and above the Number of

Ounces lent 251, (*i. e.* near 12 and a Half *per Cent.*
Interest) which, if (continuing to lend at the same
640   lay) he advances yearly 64 *Ounces,* in order to
173   make up his own Payments, which costs him Prin-
813   cipal and Interest 813 *Ounces,* he then *saves* his
1229 *principal Sum* lent, excepting the said 813 *Ounces,*
2042 and has a *clear Gain* of 1229 *Ounces,* for advancing only 64 Ounces yearly upon Interest, and his
Trouble. I make no Doubt but you 'l readily observe that this extraordinary Increase is occasioned by the
Bills growing daily more valuable as approaching nearer
their Periods.

If he lends condition'd to pay in Bills of the old Tenour
(supposing them *fixt* to an assign'd Quantity of *Silver*) or
Bills of the new Tenour, he then lends *Silver* at 29 s. 6 d. *per
Ounce,* and receives Principal and Interest at the End of
the first Year, in *Bills* equal to 24 s. 9 d. *per Ounce.* If to
be paid in *Merchants-Notes,* he receives in Notes equal to
22 s. 7 d. *per Ounce,* and in both these Cases his Gains will
be very great.

Whereas he runs *only an equal Chance with the Borrower,*
if he lends condition'd to pay in the *natural Pound* of this
Province, *viz* in *Silver* and *Gold* at the current *market
Price,* or in *Bills* of the *old* Tenour (supposing them not
fixed by the late Act) or in Bills of the other *New England*
Colonies, which are all three of the same [5] Value; for
these Bills do, in effect, only promise *Silver* or *Gold* at the
current *Market-Price,* which will be higher or lower according to the *Changes* in the *trading* Circumstances of the
Province. For *these Changes* operate the same Way upon
the *Price* of *Silver* among us, as the Changes in the Stocks

in the Mother-Country do upon the *Purchase-Value* they bear in the *Market*. That is, A Man gives so many hundred Pounds for One hundred Pounds Share of a Stock, and runs all Risques of gaining or losing according to any Changes that may happen in the Circumstances of said Stock: Agreeably our *Lenders* and *Borrowers* run just the same Chance, with Regard to the *different* Rates of *Silver* our Bills may be worth, when *Lent*, and when *Repaid*.

But finally, if he follows the *main Design* of the *Scheme* (namely, to *fix* the *Bills* at once to *Silver* at 20 s. *per Ounce*, by making them a lawful Tender at that Rate) he must then lend his 1000 l. conditioned to pay 3000 *Ounces* of *Silver*, and *Interest*.

Thus he *lends Ounces* — — — — — —	3000
He *receives* yearly for *Interest* 180 *Ounces*, and advances 135, to make up *his own Payments* for Ten Years,	1350
Interest lost, for Nine Years and downwards, on that Sum, at 6 *per Cent*,	365
His *clear Gain*, for advancing 135 *Ounces* yearly upon Interest,	1285
	3000

Or if he advances nothing, but calls in yearly sufficient to make up his own Payments, his Gains may be about 1220 *Ounces*, or 1647 l. of the present Money.

2dly. As to the *Borrower*. Now certainly the *Lender's* Gain will be *his* Loss: He had need therefore take Care of himself. His best Way, in my Opinion, will be to borrow and pay in *common* Bills, and run his Chance: But if he must borrow in those proposed; or others of the same Kind, he had best give Bond for so many *Ounces* of *Silver* as they are worth *at the Time* he borrows them, and Interest in the same; for if he pays in the same *Bills*, or takes them at the Rate of 20 s. *per Ounce*, he may undergo very great Difficulties; for in the last Case he receives but 2042 *Ounces*, and pays, Principal and Interest, 4800 *Ounces*.

[6] *3dly*. As to the *Possessor*. Now if he be a *money'd* Man, these Bills must be of vast *Advantage* to him. For if he *lends* on Condition to pay in *Silver*, his Principal and Interest are fixed to a certain Quantity; and if he lends to be paid in the *same* Bills, his Principal and Interest will be daily growing *better*. Or if he *trades*, he will have the Advantage of giving Credit for Goods at the Rate of 6 *per Cent*. Interest, and his Capital secured from growing worse.

But if the Possessors be Men either of *middling*, or but *low* Circumstances, depending upon a reasonable Credit, in the industrious Pursuit of their Business, and a free Circulation of Money, they will both stand a *miserable Chance*, under the Operations of these Bills, and such as no trading or landed Interest can bear.

4thly. As to the *Province*. And here observe,

1st. These Bills are intended to lower *Silver* down to 20 s. *per-Ounce* at *once* This indeed may be done where Debts are sued for in the *Law* (but can never alter their natural Value in *Trade*) and if a Man may be allowed to pay a Debt of *Three* Ounces of Silver with but *Two*, it may be a vast Injury to many; tho' I hope and believe few Men would take any such Advantage in the *Law*. But at most it can only affect *Post Contracts*: For all Men will industriously avoid the Consequence, as having Demonstration before their Eyes, that there is no such Value in them at Market.

And since all Debts whatsoever, payable in *Silver* and

Gold, are to be subjected to *this Scheme,* consequently those due to the *Mother Country* must be included. Now as *their* Pound is fixed to a certain Quantity of *silver,* and as they would not take even the *Notes* of the Bank of *England,* payable at a *distant* Time, without a proper *Discount,* in proportion to the *natural Interest* of Money, it is highly probable that our Brethren in that Country will by no Means relish the present Projection.

2dly. It is at least expected, by the Scheme, that Silver should fall *by Degrees* to 20 s. *per Ounce*; But it is impossible that the mere Operation of the *Bills* should produce any such Effect, but the quite contrary. For the Price of *Silver,* in Trade, depends (as was hinted before) wholly on the trading Circumstances of the Province: And if we can export a greater Value in Produce, Shipping, Silver, *&c.* to all the World, than the Value of all other Things which we take off from them; in that Case, [7] there being a greater Value in the whole Exports, than the whole Demand requires, the Prices of Silver and all other Exports must *fall* in Proportion: as on the contrary, if the whole Value of Exports be *less* than the whole Demand, Silver and other Things must *rise* in the same Proportion. And this *Deficiency* in the *Exports* or *Imports,* I call the *Ballance of Debt,* against us, or for us. And thus, supposing *Silver* now at 27 s. *per Ounce,* and the whole Value of *Imports* this Year 100000 l. and the whole Value of *Exports* but 90000 l. Silver must undoubtedly rise to about 30 s. *per Ounce*; as contrariwise, suppose the *Exports* should as much *exceed* the *Imports,* Silver must undoubtedly fall to about 24 s. 6 d. *per Ounce;* and on the further Continuance of the Ballance of Debt *for* us, go on falling *ad infinitum.*

And from hence it is that I call a 20 s. *Bill* of the *old* Tenour (not fixt but left free to its Course in the Market) or 20 s. worth of *Silver* at the current Market-Price, the *natural Pound-Value* (or current Money) of this Province; which may many ways be made worse (and in a particular Manner by the *present Scheme*) but can never be made *better*, save by the Operation of the *Ballance of Debt* in *our* Favour, and that whether we have *Bills* of publick Credit in Being, or not: For the Bills of the *old* Tenour were only the Promise of Silver at the *Market-Price*, and (while left free) never could, nor now can, promise any otherwise in *Trade;* whatever some few special Bills (as those of the *new* Tenour, and these proposed) may do, but to the *Damage* of the *old* Ones, as we shall show presently.

To reduce this to common Observation, by a low and easy Comparison, let us suppose *N.* owes 20 l. in *Notes* of 20 s. each, promising Silver at 20 s. *per Ounce*, but when he comes to pay his Debts, he has wherewithal to discharge them only Six *Ounces of Silver* worth 20 s. *per Ounce*, Six Quintals of Fish worth 20 s. *per Quintal*, and Six Barrels of Tar worth 20 s. *per Barrel*, amounting in all but to 18 l. In that Case his Creditors must compound for 18 s in the Pound, or in other Words, take his Silver at the Rate of 22 s. 3d *per Ounce*, and his Fish and Tar at the same Rate, which is the same Thing as compounding for 18 s. in the Pound. Now in this Case *N's natural Pound* is 20 s. in Silver at the Rate of 22 s. 3 d. *per Ounce*; and his *Notes*, if negotiated in Trade, will pass for no more: Or if he had never given out any Notes, but only owed [8] by a Book-Debt, his *Pound* must still have been reckon'd after the same Manner, and if sold or transferr'd would fetch no more.

Again, Suppose *N.* for some particular Reasons, should lay by, and safely reserve *One* of these Ounces of Silver, which would help him to pay his Creditors, and for the present only pay them 17 l. but for that *Ounce* give them his *Notes*, promising *Silver*, one Half in Five, the other Half in Ten Years, at the Rate of 14 s. *per Oz*; in this Case his *present Notes* would be made *worse*, and only equal to *Silver* at 23 s. 6 d *per Oz.* and his *other* Notes equal to about 20 s. *per Oz* stript of Discounts, and when passing in Trade together, the latter be receiv'd with a *Premium* in Proportion to the former, *i. e.* 20 s. of the Latter pass for 23 s. 6 d. of the former: Or if his latter Notes promised Silver at 20 s *per Oz* at Five and Ten Years, they would only be worth present Silver at 29 s. 6 d. *per Oz.* or 29 s. 6 d. of them pass for 23 s. 6 d. of his former Notes. But by this Management his Creditors would be considerable Losers, he himself no Gainer, nor any Body else; except some particular Persons, who knowing that his future Pound was upon a Silver-Bottom, might at certain Times make an Advantage by keeping up his Notes till the Periods.

Furthermore, Supposing, after these Misfortunes *N.* should get into better Circumstances, and be enabled to pay his full Debt, his *old Notes* would then pass at the Rate of 20 s. *per Oz.* but his last Notes receive no Alteration by the Change in his Circumstances.

But supposing he should attain to be worth 1000 l. clear Estate, more than what he owes, if he did not then like his former Pound, *viz* Silver at 20 s *per Oz.* he might buy and sell upon the footing of the Sterling-Pound, *i. e.* Silver at 5 s. 2 d. *per Oz.* or at any other Rate he pleased: And his *Notes* must necessarily continue to pass current at whatever

Rates he should fix them at, so long as his Circumstances continued in that prosperous Condition.

This is the best Comparison of the present State of this Province that I can think of: And by using a very small Sum instead of a very great one, it is designed to demonstrate, that the *natural* or current *Market-Pound* (or Money) is founded upon the *trading* Circumstances of the Province, and wholly influenced by them; that, as they change for the better, or worse, so must the natural Pound, and whilst they continue at a stand, so [9] must the natural Pound; and that all *special, Bills* promising Silver at any Rate and Time whatsoever, when passing in *Trade*, must unavoidably be regulated by a *Premium* or *Discount*, in proportion to the then-present Value of the *natural Pound*, or *Market-Price* of Silver: That is, supposing the present Rate of Silver 27 s. *per Oz.* and that *Bills* should be emitted, promising *Silver*, (free of Discount) even at 1 s. *per Oz.* in that Case 1 s. of *these Bills* would pass for 27 s. *natural* or *current Money;* as contrariwise, supposing *Bills* were emitted, promising *Silver* (free of Discounts) but at 54 s. *per Oz.* in that Case 2 s. of *these Bills* would pass only for 1 s. *natural* or *current Money*, and so in proportion, and would be liable to *change* their Value every Day from any Change in *themselves*, or in the currant Money, or in both. And further, That upon a favourable *Turn*, begun and continuing, in the trading Circumstances of the Province, the *natural Pound* may either

1st. Be permitted to grow *better* (*i.e.* Silver to fall lower and lower) *ad infinitum :* For herein the Case of the *Province* differs somewhat from that of *N.* because *he* (upon his Change of Circumstances) is not obliged to pay *his Notes* any otherwise than at 20 s. *per Oz.*; but if the trading Circumstances of the *Province* grow better, the Estate of every Member must necessarily be affected by it, and as the *Province Bills* of the *old* Tenour were founded upon the Credit of its Circumstances, the Bills must, on the Continuance of such a favourable Turn, grow better, *ad infinitum:* And, to make *N*'s Case exactly *parallel*, we should suppose him giving out Notes promising *Silver* at such Rates as *his Circumstances* would admit of; which in his *best* Circumstances he would never do, as by that Means giving all his Gains to his Creditors: Therefore his Case cannot be reduced to private common Dealings, tho' perfectly agreeable to the Case of the *Province*.

But if we suppose *N*. emitting Notes, promising that he will receive the *same Notes*, in all Payments due to him, and for all Things which he may have to dispose of, equal to *Silver* or *Gold* at the current *Market Price;* and further that the said Notes of *N's*. be received as *current Money* amongst the Inhabitants of the Province. *N's*. Notes, as they are founded upon so they must necessarily change their Value according to the Changes in the *trading Circumstances* of the *Province;* and operate the very same Way as Bills of the *old* Tenour do, *i. e.* be worth Silver at *any* [**10**] Rate, agreeable to our varying Circumstances. Or,

2dly. Upon the Continuance of a favourable Turn in the trading Circumstances of the Province, the *Government* might stop at any Rate which Silver should fall to, and make that Rate the fixed *Silver Pound*, make it a *lawful Tender*, and the *common Consent* or Acceptance of the People compleat the Scheme of Silver Money: And thus the *Sterling Pound* is fixed to 3 *Oz* 17 *P. wt.* 10 *gr.* Silver of a certain fineness, or Silver at 5 s. 2 d. *per Oz*. But if that Kingdom were under *our* unhappy Circumstances, as not having a Sufficiency in Value, of Silver and all other *Exports*, to discharge the whole Demand in return for their *Imports*, it would then be next to a Miracle, if *Silver* did not rise above 5 s. 2 d. *per Oz.* in the *Market*, in proportion to the Ballance of Debt against them : and their trading Circumstances continuing to decline (as ours have) their Silver would be brought to 27 s. *per Oz.* (as ours is) and the *current Money* of *Great Britain* be at the Rate of Silver 27 s. *per Oz.* whatever the *lawful Money* might be.

This is evident from the Success of Queen *Ann's* Proclamation in the 3*d* Year of her Reign, and the Act of *Parliament* subsequent upon it, designed to fix the *Plantation Pound* to 2 *Oz.* 16 *p. wt.* 16 *gr.* or Silver of the fineness of common *Pieces of Eight* at 6 s. 10 d. Half-penny *per Oz.* which most certainly was well intended, but for the aforesaid Reasons could not take Effect; and there is but one Plantation that I know of, namely *Barbados*, where common Silver is received by *Weight* agreeable thereto : *Virginia* not so high, and all the others got beyond that Standard, in very different Degrees.

Nor would the *Prohibition* of the Export of *Silver* and *Gold*, hinder the Operation of the fatal *Ballance of Debt:* For the best Authors agree, and daily Experience shows, that this Treasure cannot be kept by the severest Means, where the Ballance requires it; nor would it be the Interest of any Country to attempt it by violent Means; for the Importers must sell their *Goods* dearer in proportion to the Charge or Risque in carrying off *Silver*. But there is no such Thing as a *Ballance of Debt* to be found amongst the States of *Europe*, and rather than such a Thing should be (if other Means failed) they would reduce their Subjects to the lowest Mode of *living*, and this perfectly consistent with publick Justice.

[**11**] But the Friends to the *present Scheme* will say, *That by Degrees so great a Quantity of* these *Bills might be emitted, as fully to supply the* Trade *of the Province, all* other *Bills by that Means shut out, and so* Silver *fall by Degrees in proportion to the Promise of such Bills.*

For Answer, I grant that a *sufficient Quantity* of *any* Bills, received in the Province, and having *free* and *full Circulation* (*i. e.* which may always be borrowed upon sufficient Security, and at a moderate Interest, as low or lower than in other Colonies) would in effect keep out all *other* Bills, and probably nothing less than that would accomplish it; but such a Circulation of *these* Bills can never be bro't about, whilst our present Circumstances continue, for the Reasons following.

1*st*. Whether *such* Bills be worth *Silver* at a higher or lower Rate than the *Market-Price*, they will have a *Premium* or *Discount*, in proportion to the Difference between them and the Market-Price; and by Means of the Premium or Discount, be always fixed to a certain *Rate of Silver* to the Possessor, with Interest till he is paid, and every Day he keeps them be growing better, like a rising Commodity.

2*dly*. All Bills of *that Kind* have an unavoidable Tendency to *raise* the *Market Price* of *Silver*, because of the much greater *Demand* for Silver (too great already) occasioned by their Means, both in publick and private Dealings: And as *Silver* rises in the Market, *they* will become comparatively more valuable.

The Expectations of *Silver* being brought in by their Means, in *greater* Plenty, and so of its growing *cheaper*, are not founded in Reason: For if the *Undertaker* imports it, he applies it to the Payment of his own Engagements, and this don't affect the *Market;* or if another Person imports, it must be where he has a Prospect of a *risiing Market,* or at least as having as much for it as for other Goods, and knowing that the *Demand* is greater than usual, he will be encouraged to *keep up* the Price as much as he can. But whether the *Silver* to be paid in publick and private Dealings, be taken out of the *current* Silver in the Province, or be *imported* in lieu of other *Goods,* which we take off, the Prices of Silver or other Goods must be *raised* by Means of this Demand: The raising of either must be hurtful to the Province, and the raising of one will contribute to raise the other.

[12] Again, Supposing that the *whole Returns* made to this Province, belonging to its Inhabitants, were in *Silver* and *Gold* only; still in that Case, altho' the Quantity would be much larger than common, yet probably *Silver* would rather *rise* than fall upon it: For this very Thing would give Encouragement for *other* People to import greater Quantities of *Goods* than at other Times, and consequently, in that Case, the *Demand* of Silver will be greater, and the Price higher in Proportion.

Besides, it might even be the *Interest* of many People to raise the Price of Silver, if *such* Bills should be introduced as the *only* Ones passing in Trade: For the *natural* Pound must still subsist, and it is most certain that *not all* Things in Use in the common Mode of living, but *only* those that are *imported* or *exported* (and these under some Exceptions) change their Value according to the Changes in the Rate of *Silver.* And with Regard to the publick Interest, it were better in all Contracts, particularly Salaries and the like, to

make Allowance for the Changes in the Mode or Circum-
stances of living, by a greater Quantity of *Bills* in proportion
thereto, than to promise in proportion to the Price of *Silver*.
For all Contracts to pay in or according to a fixed Rate of
Silver, have an unavoidable Tendency to raise the *Price* of it.
It appears to me, there is certainly more in this Case than
most are aware of: And under our present unhappy trading
Circumstances, such a Practice must be very hurtful to us.

3*dly*. Upon these Accounts, being kept up from the free
Course of Trade, the Bills will become *scarce* in the *Market*,
and bear a greater *Interest* (for that is always governed by
the Quantity of Money to be lent, in proportion to the Demand for that Quantity) and so not be brought out (and then
but in Part) without a large *Premium ;* and upon the sinking
of that, be laid up again, till a larger be given, and so on.

Indeed there have been, and still are Instances of something *like* these Bills in the Mother-Country, *e. g* the *East
India* Company have *Bonds* outstanding, promising Money
at a distant Time, and Interest till paid; and these are so
fa negotiated in Trade in *London* (especially in *Exchange-
Alley*) that some will take them in Payments: *i. e.* suppose
that they promise 6 *per Cent.* Interest, and that *M.* owes
106 l to *P.* & is possessed of one of those Bonds of 100 l.
which has one Year's Interest due upon it, *P.* may take that
Bond in full Discharge of his 106 l. and if he keeps it by
him [13] for a Year longer, may pay it to *R.* for about
112 l. . . . or if he keeps it but for a few Days, pay it away
at nearest a *Groat* a Day advance. But these *Bonds* are
never negotiated as *current Money in the Market*, because
of their own daily *changeable* State: And yet the Case is
vastly worse with us; for *our Bills* promise *no Interest*, for

which Reason their *Value* must be reduced by *Discounts*. The Change of Value is only in the *Bonds*, not in the current Money of *Great-Britain;* but with *us* it is both in the *Bills* and *current Money*.

Therefore such Bills can never answer the End of Money, *viz.* to have free Circulation in Trade, nor to lower the Price of Silver; but must on the one Hand greatly encourage all money'd Men, where the Bills are known, to purchase and keep them up, or make a *Stock Jobbing* Affair of them, let the Quantity be never so great: And on the other Hand equally discourage all Men, that have a Dependance on Money, to improve the landed and trading Advantages of the Province, from engaging in or favouring such Schemes.

Some think, That together with Endeavours to shut out all other Colony-Bills from passing among us, an Act to *shorten* the Time of *Credit* given for *Goods sold*, would be another great Means of reducing the Price of *Silver*.

I answer, Shortning of Credit for the *Imports* of the Province would doubtless be a vast Advantage, and a very large Sum would be saved Yearly thereby: For Men in Trade must have Profits equal to the length of Credit they give, and the Risque they run of being further put off beyond their Agreements. But *Credit* for Goods in Trade is wholly governed by the *Plenty* or *Scarcity* of *Money;* and where Money is exceeding scarce, Credit must be long, and Payments often delay'd and precarious, and the Prices of Goods sold upon Time proportionably high: And as the *Bills* proposed have no Tendency to promote a full and free *Circulation* of Money, but the contrary, no *Law* could possibly prevent the Consequence.

Before I leave this Head, I must take some further Notice

of the *Bills* of the *old Tenour*, and clear up some Difficulties
with Regard to them. For tho' I have demonstrated, That
neither the Government of this Province, nor any other upon
Earth, under our Circumstances, could nor now can promise
any otherwise for *Bills* that are to be received (equal to
Money) and to pass current in *Trade*, than *Silver* or *Gold* at
the current *Market Price;* [14] yet inasmuch as some People
think, that the *Government* have *obliged* themselves (by saying upon the Face of the *Bills*, that they shall be *equal to
Money*) to *discharge them* by paying *Silver* at the Rate of
17 *p wt.* for 6 s. or 7 s. 3 far. *per Oz* the then current *lawful*
Silver-Money (tho' I believe it was then higher in the *Market*) and that they have also been to blame in *postponing* the
calling in of the Bills according to the limited Funds, upon
which they were emitted; their Neglect in both these Respects, they think, has been in some Measure the Means of
the rise of *Silver:* I shall, in order to refute these Mistakes,
consider, (1.) the *Acts* upon which they were emitted: (2.)
the Promise of the *Bills* themselves: and (3.) the *postponing*
of the *Funds* for calling them in.

1. As to the *Acts.*

In the Year 1702, the Government first began to emit Bills
of the old Tenour; and the general Reasons assigned in the
Act then, and in the subsequent Acts for and relating to
the Emissions, were the *extream Scarcity of Money*, and *the
Want of other Media of Commerce:* And in 1704 they say,
*and the Impossibility that the Money, Plate, and Bullion
within this Province can support the Charge of the War:*
And in 1716, they say, *All the Silver-Money, which formerly
made Payments in Trade to be easy, being now sent into*
Great-Britain, *to make Return for Part of what is owing*

there; by Means of all which the Trade of the Province is greatly obstructed, and the Payments of the publick Debts and Taxes retarded, and in a great Measure rendred impracticable, &c. And in 1704 they add, *which Bills have been issued and obtained good Currency, and very much facilitated a Dispatch of the necessary Occasions of the War, and have also been of great Advantage to Trade.*

In 1712, by an Act entitled, *An Act to prevent the Oppression of Debtors,* in the Preamble of which they set forth, *That the Bills of Credit had by common Consent obtained universal Currency throughout the Province in all private Trade and Dealings, were found very beneficial and serviceable for facilitating the same; the whole Course of Trade from* 1705 *generally managed and regulated thereby, and all Debts since made and contracted (without any special Agreement) generally understood to be for the said Bills; and Merchants and Traders having made Application to the Court for further Encouragement to be given to the said Bills in the Way of private Dealings, and to prevent rigorous Exactions of Money (which is not to be had) for Debts, where the In-*[15]*tent of both Parties was to be paid in Bills, tho' not expressly mention'd:* Upon these Considerations it was Enacted, *That no Debtor who shall tender Bills of Credit for any Debt contracted from* 1705 *to* 1715 *(Specialties and express Contracts in Writing always excepted) shall be liable to have Execution levied on his Estate, or his Person imprisoned.*

Now from the general Scope of these Acts it is plain, that the great *Design* of the *Government* in emitting *Bills,* was, for Want of *Silver* Money, to supply the People with something in *Lieu* thereof (or with a *new* Kind of *Money* in Lieu of the *old* Sort) in order to enable them to pay their publick

Taxes, and to carry on the trading and landed *Improvements* of the Province; *hoping* (and very justly) that by Means thereof they might again introduce *Silver*, to pass current in *Trade*. The first Emissions had a more immediate View to the Supply of the *Treasury* (tho' the Trade was not excluded) But the *People* of the Province having *voluntarily* gone into the Use of them *as Money*, and after several Years Experience found them *very beneficial*, petitioning the *Government* for their Sanction or Encouragement in private Trade, and by the last cited Act being made a *lawful Tender*, and the People still continuing to take them, we must look upon the *Bills* as the *current Money* of the Province, both in publick and private Dealings; which brings me to consider,

2*dly.* The *Promise* of the *Bills* themselves. And from what has been said, namely, That the *Bills* must be understood as *respecting* both the Supply of the *Treasury* and the Accommodation of *Trade*, the *Government* and *People* both concurring in the Scheme, and promising to accept them *as Money*, the Meaning or Promise of the Bills is easy to be understood; and may be rendred thus.

This Indented BILL *of* Twenty Shillings *shall be received in all publick and private Payments within this Province, as the current Money thereof (Specialties and express Contracts in Writing always excepted) until such Time as the Province be in Circumstances to have* Silver *again pass current as Money, which is now carried off in Payment of our Debts to the Mother Country.*

It is plain, that the Government *only* promise to receive the *Bills* as Money, *without any Regard* to the Price of *Silver*, the Want of which was the Cause of their Emission: And for this Reason I believe they wisely avoided Emissions of Bills promising a *certain Quantity* of *Silver* at a *distant* Time; as knowing, according to the trading Cir-[16]cumstances of the Province, that such *Bills* must have been regulated by the *Market-Price* of *Silver*, and that by Means of their *distant Payment*, as well as the *greater Demand* they would have occasioned for *Silver*, the *Price* of it must have been *raised* in the Market, and so *their* Usefulness as *Money* (the End of their Emission) in a great Measure frustrated.

In this View, we must consider the *Bills* as a certain Instrument in Writing, introduced in the Province, and used *as Money*, by common Consent (which can give a comparative Value to Things, that had little or none before, according to the Extent of the Community) *at first* received *equal* to a certain Quantity of *Silver* and other Things, and *ever since* liable to *change* their *Value*, from a Change in the *Proportion* of *their own* Quantity and Demand, and to purchase more or less of *other Things*, according to the *Changes* in the *Proportion* in the Quantity and Demand of said Things.

In like Manner, *Silver*, at first valu'd as a *Metal*, was afterwards by some Community introduc'd into Use as *Money*, which Use of it in Time became general: 'Tis still receiv'd in both these Respects by *common Consent*, and *changes* it's *Value*, in the World in general and every Country in particular, by the very *same Causes*. All the Difference is, that *Silver* is a *general* Commodity, as *Wheat, Iron*, &c. and will be received to pay a Debt almost any where in the trading World: But *our Bills* (or *Money*) are only a *special* Commodity, having their Value chiefly within this Province, as *Lands, Houses*, and many Articles, which are not exportable or usually exported. But this is no just Objection against them: for tho' they will not (usually) in *Specie* be accepted to *satisfy* a Debt in other Countries, yet they will *purchase* (or are equal to) *Silver* and all other Things within the Province, that will be received in the trading World for the Payment of that Debt, and are the necessary Means of *bringing* these Things in Plenty to the *Market*.

And as to their *other Qualifications* for Money, they vastly exceed *Silver*. Thus, *They* may be fixed to an assigned *Interest*, and so be made a just Measure or Standard of the Value of all Things bought or sold, which *Silver* cannot, and it has been and may be greatly depreciated by the Excess of its Quantity. *Their* Demand is not only secured by common *Consent*, but in the Acts of *Government* by which they may be called in, and cannot want Demand [17] or go into Disuse; but *Silver* is *only* founded in common Consent, which may be withdrawn. Besides, *they* are much more easily transported, less liable to Counterfeits in Whole or in Part, more easily reducible to the lowest Species of Money, for the Conveniency of small Change, than *Silver:* And in all these Respects a better Instrument of Commerce. Indeed they are not so *durable;* but that may easily be remedied by renewing them.

3dly. As to the *postponing the Funds*, by which some of the Bills were to have been called in; I answer, If the *Bills* had been promised *Silver* at a *certain Time*, it would have been unjust to have postponed the Payment, at least without full *Allowance* for the Time: But when we consider the Bills as *Money*, the sole Question is, *Whether the* Quantities *that have been in free Circulation in the Province, have* exceeded *the* Demand? For in that Case they would have been *depreciated* by a *Change* in their natural Produce, or *Interest*, to the Damage of the *Possessor;* as Houses and

Lands change their Purchase-Value, by a Change in their yearly *Rent* or Produce. Whereas, no Man can say but that his Money will now bring him in as much Interest as ever, or that the Bills have ever fallen in Point of natural Produce. And therefore has no Cause to complain of postponing the Funds: and if *Silver* and other Things be risen by a *Change* in *their own* Circumstances, he must impute it to the unhappy State of the Province.

Therefore in this Case the *Funds* are only to be regarded as *Circumstantial* Things; and as there is so *little Money* at present in free Circulation, and natural *Interest* incredibly high. the *calling in* of the present Funds, without *emitting* a sufficient Quantity upon new Funds (or rather emitting upon a more regular Method) might have *woful Effects* with Regard to the Interest of this Province, and proportionably to that of the Mother Country.

Upon the whole, the *Wisdom* of the Government and People in agreeing upon so good an Expedient, as the Bills of the old Tenour, in order chiefly to the Improvement of the natural Advantages of the Province, is highly to be commended: And the *Success* was answerable to the Design; the Quantity of *Exports* were vastly encreased, and the *capital Stock* of the Province rendred vastly more valuable; and if the Quantity of *Produce, Shipping*, &c. which we have for a long Time been capable of *exporting*, did but now bring half the Value at *Market*, which they have done for many Years together since the first Emis-[18]sions of Bills, we should be able to pay for our most extravagant *Importations:* But it is otherwise, and almost all our Exports (a Case too common to all the other *British* Colonies) are become exceeding *low* at Market. Or if we had *continued* the Emissions of Bills in *proportion* to *Demand* (under good Regulation) and also *regulated* our *Trade*, we might have been in quite different Circumstances: But one of the greatest Misfortunes has been the extream *Scarcity* of *Money*, which has forced us to the Use of *Shop-Notes*, *Usury*, and many other hurtful Practices.

But you will perhaps *object* to what I have said in comparing the *Bills* of Credit to a *Commodity;* when it is plain that other Commodities as *Silver, Cloth, Iron*, &c have changed their Value, not really, but only in *Denomination*. For whereas in 1702 one *Ounce* of Silver was rated at about 7 s. and a *Yard* of Cloth at 7 s. and thus were equal in Value to each other; so at this Time, as the Silver is rated at 27 s *per Oz.* so is the Cloth at 27 s. *per Yard*, and are still equivalent: But 7 s. in *Bills*, which were then equal to 1 *Ounce* of Silver, will now purchase but about 5 *p wt.* of Silver, *&c.*

I answer, there is a great Difference between a *fixed* Measure and an *unfixed* One. The Measures of *Quantity*, as of a Pound-Weight, Yard, *&c.* are *fixed;* but the Measure of *Value*, or Money of this Province, *cannot be fixed*, but is changeable under our present Circumstances, as I have fully shown in the Case of *N.* and of this Province: And if there never had been any *Bills* emitted, and we had reckoned by the Rates of *Silver, Iron*, &c. our *Shilling* and our *Pound Value* would have contained just the *same* Quantity of those Metals, or other Commodities, that they now do. So that the Pound-Value is changed in *all Goods*, as well as in the *Bills*: And 20 s. in *them* is as good as 20 s. in any other Thing. Which shows the Reason why Seven *Shillings* in Bills, Silver, Iron, *&c.* are not now so valuable as an *Ounce* of Silver, *&c.* were in 1702, *viz.* that our

Shilling and *Pound Value* (or Money) entirely depends upon the *trading Circumstances* of the Province, but the *Ounce* and *Pound Weight* do not.

But to explain the *Bills* being a *Commodity*, I shall consider them under their different Views, in which that of a *Commodity* is included; and

1*st.* I consider them as *Bills promising* so much of every Thing to be sold, as the *Circumstances* of the *Province* will [19] *allow*, and changing their Value (not from their own natural Operations of Quantity and Demand, but) according to said Circumstances: And *this* is the most plain and obvious Light, in which they ought always to be put.

2*dly*. I consider them as *Money;* which I think may be properly defined to be any Matter or Thing whatsoever received by the common Consent of any Community, as the *Measure of Value* and *Instrument of Commerce:* And herein they differ from other Bills or Notes promising a *certain Quantity* of Silver or other Things, at a *distant* Time, which are either kept up, or pass but through a few Hands, until the Time of Payment.

3*dly*. I consider them as a *Commodity*. The judicious Mr. *Lock* (as I remember) observes to this Purpose, *That amongst all Commodities passing in Trade Money is truly one.* Our *Bills* are truly a Commodity, passing by common Consent in Exchange for any other Commodity, not as a Pledge given, but a Value paid. And daily Experience evinces, That they are indeed the *best* Commodity, as being most readily receiv'd in the Market. For he that is now possessed of **27** s. in *Bills*, one *Ounce* of *Silver*, and **32** lb. of *Iron* (all which may be nearly equivalent) finds by daily Experience, that the *Bills* are the *best* Commodity of the

Three, and will be *more readily* received for any Thing he wants than the others.

They are not indeed a Commodity that have their Value from the *usefulness* of their *Matter*, as *Iron*, *Lead*, &c. but are more fitly to be compared with *Silver* and *Gold*, which have *their* Value not so much from their *usefulness* as *Metals* (for that Value is inconsiderable, even less than that of *Iron*) but from the common *Consent* of Mankind, in chusing them for *Show* and Grandeur, and for a *general Commodity* or Treasure which will be most readily received every where, but chiefly for their usefulness as *Money*: Upon all these Accounts their Value is kept up; but would be lessened upon the withdrawing of any one of them, more especially that of *Money*. In like Manner our *Bills* have their Value from the *Demand* for them, by the *common Consent* of this Community, founded upon this solid Reason, *That they are a Commodity the best qualified for the Ends and Uses of Money*.

From what I have said you'l plainly perceive, that in *one Respect* the Bills *are changed* by the *Circumstances* of the *Province* (without any Operation of their own) which is best known by their *Purchase* of *Goods* in the Market; [20] and in *another* Respect they change their Value from a Change in the *proportion* of their *own* Quantity and Demand, which is infallibly known by the Changes of their yearly *natural Interest*: And in both these Respects they may fitly be called a *Commodity*.

3. Now to proceed to a further Operation of the *Bills proposed*: supposing that the extream *Scarcity* of Money should oblige many People to receive them, at their *first* Emission, upon the same footing as Bills of the *old* Tenour

without any *Discount;* yet even in that Case their Value being well known, we must expect that they will be the Means of *raising* the Price of Silver, at least near to their own Worth, *viz* 29 s. 6 d. *per Oz.*

The *Merchants-Notes* are an Evidence of this, which rose in a very short Time to the Value they were worth at their first Emission: For, tho' it must be allowed that the Operations of the *Ballance of Debt* might have occasioned that Rise, even *without* their Emission, and as just *before* that there was a long and great *Scarcity* of *Money*, by Means of which the Debts due to the Mother-Country were greatly postponed, and upon the *large* Sums then made and emitted in a very *short* Time, and the sudden and great *Demand* consequent upon it, the Prices of *Silver* and other *Returns* might have risen in a greater Degree than at other Times, as in all other the like Cases; yet inasmuch as the Value of the Merchants-Notes was pretty well known to some, and all Men would chuse to part with Bills passing at much more than their true Worth, I think the said Notes cannot be excused. And as this would most likely be the Fate of the *Bills now proposed,* the whole capital Stock of the Province, as well as the Debts due to the Mother-Country, would be sunk in Value by their Means, at least 8 and a Half *per Cent, viz.* the Difference between *Silver* at 27 s. and 29 s. 6 d. *per Oz.* But when they are got above *Par*, we may be assured they will not pass without a *Premium.*

4. Besides the raising of *Silver* by the *Distance* of their *Payments*, these *Bills* will also be the Means of raising it by the *greatness* of the *Quantity* emitted *at once*, as just hinted. For tho' this Province might require a much *greater Sum*, than is proposed, in order to enable it to improve its natural

Advantages, if emitted in such a *regular progressive* Way, as not to hurt the Trade by a sudden Flood; yet so great a Quantity emitted *at once* must have a Tendency to lower their Value, as in all other Cases [21] where Markets are at once glutted with a certain Commodity. And this is the only plausible Objection against the *Bills* of the *old* Tenour, That such *ill·Effects* did attend their *irregular Emissions:* However, as this might be easily prevented, so it ought industriously to be avoided for the future. For the most essential Qualification of Money, in order to make it a just Measure of the Value of all Things bought and sold, is, That *its own Value be fixed;* I mean, that *its Quantity* always bear a due *Proportion* to the *Demand* for it, or that its Quantity and Demand increase and decrease together, and continue fixed to each other: The undeniable Evidence of which would be, its keeping or being kept as near as possible to an assign'd Rate of *Interest*, (for as *Lands* and *Houses* change their Value by any Change in their *yearly* Produce, or *Rent*, so *Money* can no otherwise be said to change it's Value, than by a Change in its Interest) so that when *Goods* rise or fall in the *Market*, the *Change* must be in the *Goods*, and not in or by Means of the *Money:* Which is often the Case in *Silver* and *Gold*, which cannot be fixed, but lose their Value in a more certain (tho' slower progressive) Manner, than Goods in general do.

5. The *Intricacy* of the *Scheme* may be the Means of introducing many *bad Practices* in the Province. The *Bills* are to promise *Silver* at 6 s. 8 d. *per Oz.* when the Province is hardly in a Condition to pay its just *Debts* at Home and Abroad at the Rate of Silver 27 s *per Oz;* are to be paid off at *Five* and *Ten* Years, *without Interest;* to pass *One* for

Three Bills of the *old* Tenour, which are themselves of an *uncertain* or at best a disputable Value; to be *equal* to Bills of the *new* Tenour already extant, payable in *Silver* at 6 s 8 d. *per Oz* in *Five* Years; and above all, equal to *Silver* at 20 s. *per Oz*. at their Emission, *i. e.* 6 s 8 d. of them being to pass for 20 s. is to be received in lieu of an *Ounce* of *Silver*. This strange Perplexity, it 's to be fear'd, among other Things will give great Opportunity for *Stock Jobbing* and *Usury*.

Indeed it is not *impossible* for common Consent to agree in paying and receiving in the propos'd Method, *i. e.* for People to take and give a present *Ounce of Silver* for a *Bill* promising only an Ounce at Five and Ten Years, with no Interest, and the like: But do we find it so in private Trade, or did ever any Community of People act after [22] that Manner? Indeed we had something like it in the Case of the *Merchants Notes*, which tho' promising Silver at their first Emission only at 27 s. 1 d. *per Oz*. yet were received upon the same footing as Bills of the *old* Tenour, which might then purchase Silver at about 22 s. *per Oz*. But this continued only a very short Time, and the Wisdom of the Province has since in a great Measure atoned for that amazing Error, by keeping them up, after they were above *Par*, till a *Premium* was given, tho' they received them when under *Par* without a Discount, both being founded in the same Reason, *viz.* the Promise of the Notes.

Besides the other Things mentioned, the Proportion between *Silver* and *Gold* is not equal; for the Rule in the *Mother Country* (and *Europe* in general) ought to be ours, *i. e.* the Pound *Troy* of *Silver* is made into 62 s. Sterling, and the Pound *Troy* of *Gold* into 44 and a Half *Guineas*, which at 21 s. *per Guinea* is 46 l. 14 s. 6 d. So that where

Silver is put at 6 s. 8 d. *Gold* should be at 5 l. o s. 6 d. *per Oz.* In this Case, he that *pays* in *Gold* to the Trustees, *loses* 2 and an Half *per Cent.* and he that *receives* common Silver from the Trustees, has 2 and an Half *per Cent* less Value than if he received Gold: besides the fineness of Coins is no where mentioned, which might make Difficulties, as the Alloys of Coins are very various.

In fine, *Trade* is the only Means of intorducing *Silver* and *Gold*, the general Treasure of the World.

Trade depends upon *Money*, not only as the Measure of *Value*, but the Instrument or Tool of *Commerce* (a *Sine qua non*) without which it can't be carried on to the general Advantage of the landed as well as trading Party, any more than an Artificer can work to good effect without convenient Tools.

Money is a *Commodity*, and ought proportionably at least to other Countries with whom we trade, and as the Instrument of Commerce, to be the *cheapest* of all Commodities, *i. e.* be let at a *low Interest*: For sometimes the *dearer* the *Produce* or *Manufacture* of a Country be, the *better* (provided their Trade will bear it) as it promotes the general Intercourse of Trade between the landed Man and the Artificer. But without a Sufficiency [**23**] of *Money*, of Consequence *Trade* must in Time dwindle away, and the general Produce of our Lands, as *Cattle* and *Grain*, fall to a very small Matter in this Province, and consequently the Purchase-Value of them; *trading Towns* be depopulated; and above all, *Buildings* for the accommodation of Trade, fall from a good and growing Value, to little or nothing; which will probably be the End of a *Monopoly* of Money, and so the *Crafty* at last catch'd in their own Snare.

The great *Loss* this Province has already sustained by the prodigious *Scarcity* of Money, besides the *Advantages* some of our industrious *Neighbours* have gained over us in a few Years, owing in a great Measure to their emitting *Bills* of Credit, ought to rouse us before it be too late.

For Instance, the Colony of *Rhode-Island* used to take off a very considerable Quantity of *Goods* from us yearly, upon which *we* had the Advantages of *Carriage*, the Merchant's and often the Wholesale-Man's *Profits*, and not only a *Return* partly in Silver, Gold, and other Commodities fit for a *direct* Payment to the *Mother-Country*; but also in some well-known Articles, capable of some additional *Improvements*, and of Use in paying the Mother-Country in a more *remote* Way, and the *Carriage* in our own Vessels: Whereas *now* the Scale is turned, and *they* are not only well nigh able to supply *themselves* with *European* Goods, but of selling a considerable Quantity of some Sorts to *us;* and instead of sending us some Articles *unimproved*, to send them *fully improved*, and to supply some *distant* Places, where we used to supply, and the *Carriage* too in their own Vessels: And they'l find their Account in it, if they should *go on* to emit a sufficient Quantity of *Bills*, at *low Interest*, upon the same capital Stock, and of the same Tenour, but of a much *shorter Period* (in order to have them under Command, to call in and put out, as Occasion should require) the *Length* of which was the only just *Objection* we could have against their *last* Emission, not from any immediate Damage we or others could receive by that single Emission, but from the ill Effects which the further *Continuance* of that Practice might possible in future Times and larger Emissions have produced, which (as was observed) may be easily remedied, and so the Cause of Ob-[**24**]jection cease. That single Advantage of *Money* at a *low Interest* might produce Wonders, not only as to the Improvement of their *own* natural Advantages, but of their *Neighbours* also; and in Time a *Ballance of Debt* might commence against us with relation to *them*, worse than that with the *Mother-Country*: For, after the Payments of Produce and Treasure, our *Lands* might fall into *their* Hands, in proportion to and to make up the Ballance of Debt. And as it is most certain, that those *Colonies*, that have a general Ballance in their Favour, will have the *best Money*, so none more likely to get it into such good Circumstances, than *that* Colony; and having Money enough of their own, none more likely to have it in their Power (as it will be their Interest) to shut out all other Bills from passing amongst them.

I might now, for the further illustrating and confirming all I have said, proceed to a more plain and strict Inquiry into the Qualifications and Operations of *Money*; and show how the *Bills* of the *old* Tenour might be qualified for the true Ends and Uses thereof; and that *private* Notes of the same Nature (having the common Consent of the trading Party in the Province) might be circulated in Trade, and by a due Regulation be of the same or greater Benefit to the Province, towards the general Improvement of our natural Advantages, the regulating of our Trade, and reducing the Price of Silver.

I might also offer some further Thoughts on the Subject of improving and regulating our *Trade*; without which we must be of small Importance, either considered as Part of the trading World, or as a *British* Colony; for the *Mother-Country* chiefly considers us in the View of an advantageous

Trade with them, and aims at the proper Means for that End: But as all Men are liable to Mistakes, it is likely that the Interest of *Great-Britain* with Regard to us, is not always well understood, and I am humbly of Opinion that nothing can have a greater Tendency to hurt our *Trade* (whether with the World in general, or the Mother-Country in particular) than our present *Scarcity* of *Money*. But having already exceeded the Bounds of a Letter, I must for the present defer those Inquiries.

[25] I think I have said enough to show the dangerous Tendency of the Bills proposed, and doubt not but that upon a close Consideration of the Reasons offered against them, you, and every Friend to the publick Interest, will be far from encouraging the Scheme. These are my present Sentiments, until I have further Light: And if I have committed any Mistake, in Point of Fact or Argument, I submit to your candid Censure; who am with much Esteem,

SIR,

Yours, &c.

I B

ERRATA.

Page 1. Line 9 from Bot. read *fully to*. P. 3. l. 17. r. *or though*. P. 4. l. 19. r. *to which*. P. 18. l. 8. r. *one of our*.

NOTE TO "SOME OBSERVATIONS ON THE SCHEME PROJECTED FOR EMITTING £60,000 IN BILLS OF A NEW TENOUR," ETC.

We have already had two reprints of pamphlets which were called out by the desire of the authors to furnish relief to the province from the impending trouble which would inevitably result from the withdrawal from circulation of the greater part of the bills upon which the people depended for a medium of trade.   The first of these, the "Letter to a member of the honourable house of representatives," etc., which I attribute to the pen of Governor Hutchinson, was a clear statement of the case of the hard-money man.   For the first time in this discussion, a man of affairs, familiar with the laws of trade presented his views in a dispassionate manner and without personalities. The "Proposal to supply the trade," etc., is also free from scurrility and the author is entitled to credit for the submission of a scheme which in his opinion would furnish relief to the province.   If this pamphlet is inferior to the other in its treatment of the laws of business, it is at least to be commended for its freedom from personalities.   "Some observations on the scheme for £60,000 in bills of a new tenour" is also to be approved for the scientific — perhaps quasi scientific would be better — method of its arguments.   It is true, that the calculations of the benefits or losses to undertakers, borrowers, possessors and the province, were based upon certain arbitrary assumptions which might not prove acceptable to the reader, but whether acceptable or not they were susceptible of criticism and correction at the hands of those who should reject them.   Dr. Douglass said of them: "I shall forbear any *idle Criticism* upon his Calculations, Figures, and *technical* commercial Words, as being out of the Question.   Here I cannot but observe, that in all his spacious Calculation, he is obliged to make Use of Silver, at a certain Value, and receivable at certain Periods, as a *Basis*; neglecting his darling Paper Currency's Uncertainties, as not qualified for a proper Foundation."   Such moderate disapproval on the part of Douglass indicates that he was not prepared to analyze the calculations.

The discussion in "Some Observations," etc., of what constitutes a true measure of values, the analysis of the proposed scheme for notes of a new tenor, and the general review of the relations of the province with Europe, are full of propositions which would be rejected by the economist to-day and consequently are in many places exceedingly difficult to understand. Some of the arguments of the author are ingenious and even if they are not convincing they represent the speculations of an earnest student of the subject who is hopelessly befogged by the perplexities which surround him.

The scheme which is discussed by the author was one of those projected by the hard-money men about this time with a view to securing if possible a return to specie payments. An account of these efforts is to be found in the paper read before the Massachusetts Historical Society in February, 1899, entitled "A search for a pamphlet by Governor Hutchinson."

This pamphlet is the forerunner of a series consisting of "Observations," an "Essay," an "Inquiry," and a "Discourse," all fortified with Postscripts and all bristling with controversy, which were put forth by the author of this pamphlet in advocacy of a paper currency, and by Dr. Douglass the pronounced supporter of hard-money. Out of this discussion has come renown for Dr. Douglass, but the name of Hugh Vance, whom we are able to identify as the author of this pamphlet, is without distinction and has never been associated in any conspicuous manner with the pamphlets which he contributed to this discussion. The circumstances connected with the discovery that he was the author of this particular pamphlet are set forth in the note to "An Inquiry into the nature and uses of money." "Some Observations," was advertised as "Just Published" in the New England Weekly Journal of March 7, 1738.

The copy was obtained from a pamphlet in my own possession, the leaves of which measure 7¾ by 4⅞ inches. The photograph of the title-page was procured through the courtesy of the Massachusetts Historical Society. Other copies of the pamphlet can be found in the American Antiquarian Society, the Boston Athenæum, the Boston Public Library, the Harvard College Library, the John Carter Brown Library, the Library of Congress, and the New York Public Library.

It ought perhaps to be noted that Sabin attributes this pamphlet to Dr. Douglass and it will be found entered in his list under Douglass, the name of the reputed author. This has led others into the same error, since Sabin was accepted by them as reliable authority.[1]

[1] Palgrave's Dictionary of Political Economy; Economic Studies, American Economic Association, Vol. II, No. 5, p. 289.

An ESSAY,

Concerning Silver and Paper

CURRENCIES,

More especially with Regard to the

British Colonies

NEW-ENGLAND.

BOSTON: Printed and Sold by S. Kneeland and
T. Green, at their Shop over against the Prison.

[handwritten:] A Pamphlet relating to the Affairs of New England

to Dr. Douglass and it will be found entered in his list under Doug-lass, the name of the reputed author.   This has led others into the same error, since Sabin was accepted by them as reliable authority.[1]

[1] Palgrave's Dictionary of Political Economy; Economic Studies, American Economic Association, Vol. II, No. 5, p. 289.

An ESSAY,

Concerning Silver and Paper

CURRENCIES,

More especially with regard to the

British Colonies in

NEW-ENGLAND.

BOSTON: Printed and Sold by S. KNEELAND and
T. GREEN in Queen-Street over against the Prison.

An ESSAY,

Concerning Silver and Paper

CURRENCIES,

More efpecially with Regard to the

Britifh Colonies in

NEW-ENGLAND.

BOSTON: Printed and Sold by S. Kneeland and T. Green, in Queen-ftreet over againft the Prifon.

An Essay, concerning Silver and Paper Currency.

APER Currency at a great Discount has prevailed for several Years in many of our *Colonies*, and by Advocates for it both in Conversation and Print, deluding the People with false Appearances and Representations; it is likely to continue and multiply amongst us to greater Disadvantages than ever: As appears by the late large labouring Emission of 90,000 *l.* in *Maryland*, the enacted but not as yet current Emission of 48,300 *l.* in *New York*, the printed Projection for 180,000 *l.* in *this Province*, and by the Apprehensions we are under of a further *Rhode Island* Emission.

In Affairs of this Nature, a true historical Account of Facts and their Consequences, is called *political Experience;* and as Things are more naturally understood by their Eff cts, than by their Principles: I shall endeavour, by relating bare historical Facts, concerning *Currencies*, with some short Remarks upon the same; to set our *Plantation Paper Currencies*, more especially with **Regard** to this Province, in a true Light.

Silver be ng a staple Merchandize all over the World, as well as an adequate Pledge, did naturally, and by the Consent of all trading Nations, become the *universal Currency* or Medium, by which Goods are bartered and Contracts m de: Therefore *Silver* (ascertained in Weight [2] and Fineness) *Coin* ought to be the only legal Tender in the Trade of all Countries. The Varieties of computative or *nummary Denominations* of different Countries, are no Hindrance; they are reconciled or adjusted by, what is called, the *Par of Exchange*.

Par of Exchange, is the intrinsick Value (in Weight and Fineness) of the *Silver Coin* or Denominations of one Country, reduced to the like Value of Denominations of another Country. Sir *Isaac Newton's* Table of the Assays, Weights, and sterling Values of foreign Coins, published by Dr. *Arbuthnot*, A 1727, is a proper Standard. From this no Country swerves, excepting by a small Variation, called, the *Difference of Exchange*.

Difference of Exchange, is a small *Premium* allowed for the Trouble and Risque of having Silver (that universal Staple and Medium of Trade) remitted to answer the *Ballance of Trade;* according as the Imports and Exports of Countries in other Goods, do exceed one the other. The printed *Prices current* of several trading Towns, from Time to Time informs us of this.

Originally the *nummary Denomination of Silver*, seems to have been the same as its Weight or *ponderal Denomination* It would have been happy and *facile* for the World, if it had so continued; but from the *corrupt civil Administrations* (not from the Ballance of Trade) from Time to Time, in all Countries, the Value of the Nummary from that of the

ponderal Denomination has been altered, *to Defraud Creditors*, and especially to cheat the Creditors of the publick.

In *England* for many Ages before the 14th *Century*, the
nummary Pound was the same with the Pound weight of
Silver (this was in a proper Sense the *natural Pound*) that
is a computative *Pound* Sterling was 12 *Oz* of Silver, a
Mark, or 13 *s.* 4 *d.* was 8 *Oz* of Silver. *Iniquitous Administrations* since the Beginning of the 14*th* Century, have
from Time to Time, reduced the nummary Denominations
to a less Value than its Weight, and cheated Creditors of
some Part of their just Dues and Demands : For the Space
of about 250 Years the Weight of Silver in the several
nummary Denominations, has at Times, been lessened (that
is the nummary Denominations depreciated) excepting in
the Minority of *Henry* VI. when the *Denomination call'd
a Shilling* rose from 142 *Gr.* to 176 *Gr.* of fine Silver; but
during the Confusions occasioned by the hot Disputes,
between the Families of *York* [3] and *Lancaster*, it fell again
to 142 *Gr.;* so it continued until the arbitrary Reign of
Henry VIII, it fell more and more, and *A* 1546 it was only
40 *Gr.*; *A* 1551 by the bad Administration of the *Duke of
Somerset* Lord Protector in the Minority of *Edward* VI. it
was reduced to 20 *Gr.* but immediately after the *Duke of
Somerset's* being beheaded, it rose to 88 *Gr.* and remained so,
until *A.* 1601 it suffered a small Reduction to 86 *Gr.* where
it continues to this Day. Thus *our present nummary
Pound* contains only about 4 *Oz. of Silver*, that is only one
Third of what it originally contained.

In all other Nations the like has been done in bad Administrations. The *Dutch Pond Ulams* (6 Guilders) which
originally contained 12 *Oz Silver*, at present is 2 *Oz Silver*.

The *French Livre* originally was a Pound or 12 *Oz. Silver*, at present it is reduced to 4 *Penny weight of Silver.*

These almost incredible Depravations of the several *nummary Denominations*, had not the least Relation to the *Ballance of Trade*, and the most considerable of them happened in Times prior to their several Nations being much concerned in Trade; excepting, what happened in *France* in the End of *Lewis* XIV. and Beginning of *Lewis* XV. Reigns; *Silver from a Mark or* 8 *Oz at* 27 Livres *was at length* A. 1719 *imposed upon the People at* 120 *Livres*: The Iniquity of the Administration, not the Ballance of Trade was the Cause. Trade has quite a different Operation, and in Fact ever since Trade became extensive in *England*, that is, in the last 180 Years, the nummary Denominations have lost only 2 in 88 *Gr.* The Credit of *Merchants* in the commercial World· is become more sacred, than the Probity of *Ministers* in the civil Administration, and is a Check upon them Ever since the *French* began to have Commerce truly at Heart, which at present they seem to have as much, if not more, than their Neighbours; that is, ever since the Beginning of *Cardinal Fleuri's* Administration, there has been no Alteration in their Coin and Denominations.

In *Europe* all Nations have had the Ballance of Trade sometimes in their Favour, sometimes against them; and each of them more or less at different Times; foreign Wars, civil Wars, Loss of Trade, Increase in Trade; without altering the Value of their *nummary Denominations* in Respect of standard Silver.

[4] In all the *American Colonies* at their first Settling and from some Years thereafter, their *Currency* was the

same, with that of their Mother-Country: But by the *Iniquity* of some Administrations, all of them have *cheated* their Creditors at Home, in lessening the Value of their *nummary Denominations*: Thus the *Dutch Colonies* have cheated 20 *per Cent* a *Holland Guilder* passes with them for 24 *Stivers*: The *French Settlements*, have defrauded their Principles at Home 50 *per Cent*.

In the *British Plantations* originally an *English Crown* was 5 *s.* Denomination; in Process of Time, they remitted to their Creditors at Home a *Piece of Eight*, which is only 4 *s.* 4 *d.* Sterling, at the Rate of 5 *s.*; some Time after that in most of our Colonies this *Piece of Eight* was paid away to their Creditors at 6 *s.* and would have gone further, by *Persons in Debt* getting into the Administration or Power of defrauding their Creditors; if the Merchants at Home had not procured an Act of Parliament called the *Plantation Act*, whereby a *Piece of Eight* in all our Colonies was fixed at 6 *s.* for 6 *s.* 10 *d., per Oz. Silver*: In these Colonies, who upon this Act passed their Silver by Weight only as Currency (*Barbados, Bermudas*, &c.) it continues so to this Day, being 33 *per Cent. Exchange*: But in some of the Colonies (*Leeward West India Islands, New-York, New-England*) not using Weight, they continue to carry on the Cheat by passing a light clipt Piece of Eight for 6 *s.* which is about 8 *s. per Oz Silver;* there being no Bounds to their Clipping, they were obliged to come into the Use of Weights, but continued the Ounce of Silver at 8 *s.* Denomination, is 50 *per Cent. Exchange.* In many of our Colonies they have gone greater Lengths, and by Floods of *provincial Paper Credit* or Money, they have made vile Work of it; *so that Exchange with Sterling is at present in* Jersies *and* Pensilvania 60 *or* 70 per Cent. *Advance*; Maryland 100 *per Cent.*; *the* New England *Colonies and* Nova Scotia 400 *per Cent*; South-Carolina, 700 *per Cent; and* North Carolina *still worse.* (*Virginia* have gone astray the least, being at present only 25 *per Cent.* worse than Sterling) thus that salutary *Proclamation Act* was frustrated: seeing the late Instruction relating to this Affair, to his Governours is not regarded, *we could not complain if the British Parliament should take Cognizance of the same.* This leads me to the Article of Paper Currency.

[5] Because in common Equity, nothing ought to be a *Tender in Trade* in any particular Country, but what is a general Tender all over the commercial World, (Transfers in the *Bank of Amsterdam* are an Exception, because of their universal commercial Credit, and their being better than common Currency) the Wisdom of the *British* Legislature, have not thought it convenient to make our Paper Effects; that is *Bank, East India and South-Sea Transfers; Bank Notes, East India and South-Sea Company Bonds*, a legal Tender: Notwithstanding of their being better than Silver, being at any Time reducable to Silver; so that they, are as *Cash bearing Interest* (Bank Notes excepted) which Silver Cash does not: Hence it is that in Exchange for (Silver) Currency they bear a *Premium.*

I shall, here give some *Instances of the bad Effects of Paper Currency made a legal Tender.* The Arbitrary Government of *France*, after much Damage done to the Subjects in depreciating their nummary Denominations by *recoinages*; did *A.* 1719, to compleat their Misery, embrace Mr. *Law's* Project of a *Paper Currency*; Silver was banished by severe Penalties, Paper was made the only legal

Tender. The Operation was; the Nation reduced to the utmost Confusion, Mr. *Law* and his Abettor Mr. *D'Argenson* were disgraced; Silver again introduced as a Currency, and the only legal Tender.

Baron *Gortz* about 20 Years ago, had reduced *Sweden* to extreme Misery, by imposing *Government Notes* instead of Specie. Upon the King of *Sweden's* Death, the *Baron* suffered capital Punishment, this being one of the principal Crimes alledged against him. The Paper Currency was called in; the Silver and Copper Currency was restored, upon the same footing as before Charles XII. Accession.

We have a very good Instance in one of our own *Colonies*. *Barbados A.* 1702 emitted 16,000 *l. Bills* of Credit on *Funds*, to be brought in again by a *Tax of 3 s. 9 d. on Negroes:* At first they passed at a Discount, but no more being then emitted, and the Time of the coming in being at Hand, they rose again to near Par. Encouraged by this, they made a large Emission of 80,000 *l. Bills* on *Land security* at 4 *per Cent.* payable after 5 Years: These Bills immediately fell to 40 *per Cent.* below Silver; but by an Order from Home they were all called in soon, and their Currency became Silver Value as before. *Ballance of Trade* had not the least Concern here.

[6] *A Paper Credit* well founded and under good Regulations, and not larger than what the Silver Specie Currency will bear; has been found to be a very good Expedient in Business, and it leaves the *Silver Species* at more Liberty to be used as Merchandize, and for petty Occasions. In *Holland* all large Transactions are in *Bank Transfers of Amsterdam*, their Credit being better than that of the Government, and their Bank Money 3 a 5 *per Cent.* better than

the common Currency. The Use and Credit of the *Bank Notes in England* we all know, their Fund being a valuable Depositum, a Call upon Occasion on the Proprietors, and about *Ten Millions* Sterling in the Government's Hands; yet their Notes are no legal Tender. *If Paper Credit exceeds a certain Proportion of the concomitant Silver Currency, its Effects are bad, and ruinous;* by its precarious Loss of Value. The *Bank of Venice* was originally two Millions of *Ducats* given in, and Bills to a limited Sum given out, upon the Security of the same: This Scheme was so good that their Bank Money became 28 *per Cent.* better than common Currency: from this good Success the Government allowed them to issue out more Bills, only to the Value of 300,000 *Ducats;* this small Addition brought down their Bills to 20 *per Cent.* Advance. *N. B.* By continued Additions they might have brought them down to Par, and from thence to Discount, even so low as 400 *per Cent,* as is our Case at present.

Our Province Bills from the various Operations of frequent large Emissions, distant Periods, and Periods postpon'd; are become 400 per *Cent. worse than sterling, and above* 200 per Cent. *worse than themselves* 25 *Years ago.*

All well regulated Corporations are restricted, to issue Bills or Notes not exceeding a certain Value: Thus it is with *English Bank Notes, East-India and South-Sea Companies Bonds;* lest by too large Emissions, they might depreciate their Notes and Bonds, to the Damage of the Society itself, and Creditors. The *King* by an Instruction to his *Governour* of this Province, limits us to 30,000 *l. per Ann.* (to be understood Proclamation Money or its Value) for extraordinary Charges of Government.

The principal Design of a Currency or *Medium* of Trade,

is to avoid the Inconveniencies of *Barter*: Paper Currency
in large Quantities does not answer this End; because of its
Fluctuation, or rather progressive less Value; which obliges
the Merchant at length to return to *Bar*-[7]*ter* again, as being safe and better. In *South-Carolina*, the Quantity of
Paper Currency has so depreciated itself, that all considerable Contracts, are made, not in Province Bills, but in their
Produce *Rice*. In *North Carolina* their Produce, they call
Specie, is 50 to 100 *per Cent.* better than their Paper Currency.

Silver is a staple Merchandize, an adequate Pledge, and
an universal commercial *Medium*. Our *Province Bills* have
no intrinsick Value, and as a Depositum, are no better than
waste Paper; they are no exportable Merchandize, and receivable no where but in *New-England*, being only an ill
contrived provincial or *municipal Medium*. Barter is Merchandize (not so staple, and more bulky and perishing than
Silver) exportable, and upon that Account preferable to
Province Bills as a *Medium*.

In *Virginia, Tobacco* is their *Medium*, and answers better
than Paper, because it is an exportable staple Merchandize.
Let us suppose, that at any Time it should become (as are
our Bills) not exportable, and that Laws should be made
there from Time to Time, for planting of greater Quantities,
to increase their Medium; it would become in Course such
a *Drug*, that more and more of it would be given, for a certain Quantity of Silver or any other Goods, and at length be
of no Value; but if their Government being sensible of their
Error, should forbid planting above such a Quantity, their
Medium would become good as before.

As to the Quantity of Paper Currency which the Silver
Currency will bear, without depreciating its Denominations;

it is only to be learnt by Experience. In *New England* we found that *A.* 1713 there were 194,000 *l.* in Province Bills at *Par* with Silver at 8 *s. per Oz.* When we began to exceed that Sum, our Paper began to loose of its Value: Here we ought to have stopt and kept within that Sum in our future Emissions. *New York* never exceed 40,000 *l.* in Province Bills (at present only about 37,000 *l.*) and so kept up their Value at 8 *s. per Oz. Silver.*

The larger the Paper Currency of any Country, *the more it labours*, and is circulated to the greater Disadvantage. The greatest Quantity of *Exchequer Bills in England* (never were made a legal Tender but in Taxes) at one Time extant was *A.* 1716, being a4,596,184 l. Debt, much of it contracted in the bad Administrations of the latter End of Queen *Ann's* Reign; Notwithstanding of their [8] being above one Fourth of the Nation's Currency, their being receivable in *Taxes* and all Treasury Affairs, and bearing Interest 3 *per Cent. per Annum;* they began to depreciate, and the Government was obliged to allow the *Bank* an Annuity to cancel *Two Millions* Sterling Value of them, and 3 *per Cent. Premium* to circulate, and specify the Remainder while above One Million, and afterwards only 1 *per Cent. Premium. Anno* 1702 there were extant *Two Millions Sterling Value in Exchequer Notes*, the Government allows the Bank 3 *per Cent.* to circulate them while above One Million, and 1 *per Cent.* when not exceeding One Million. Since that Time, if *Exchequer Notes* are at any Time used towards defraying the Charges of the Government, they are honestly paid off next Sessions of *Parliament.* The last Emission of *Exchequer Notes* was *A.* 1730, being 510,000 *l.* towards the Charges of that Year, and were paid off *A.* 1731, the Year following.

If *Paper Credit upon future Taxes or upon Loan,* would answer as a *Medium*; how is it that the Governments in *Europe,* find it so intricate an Affair to raise Money for publick Charges in Time of War, or other extraordinary Occasions? When attempted by arbitrary Governments, they always tend to the Ruin of the Subject: The State Bills of *France* in King *Lewis* XIV. last War, were sold at 50 or 60 *per Cent. Discount.* Baron *Gorz's* State Bills in *Sweden* were Part of the Crimes for which he suffered Death.

Upon any extraordinary Emergency or Charge incur'd by the Government (we were by the King's Instruction allowed to emit, not exceeding 30,000 *l. Proclamation Value per Ann.*) it may be proper to satisfie it, by publick Bills of Credit, to be received again next Year in *Taxes.* This is only good Oeconomy, to lay Part of the extraordinary Charge of a preceeding Year, upon the Taxes of the Year following; they will be as good as Silver Cash, or better, if the Circulation is encouraged by a 5 *per Cent. Premium* or advance Allowance in the Treasury. By this good Management of cancelling the Bills in a Year or two, we kept up their Credit till *A.* 1713.

To emit large Sums of Paper Money, upon Funds of *Taxes* payable after many Years; or upon *Loans* not to be paid in until after 10, 20, or 45 Years, as are the last Payments in *Maryland,* is leaving a heavy Debt of [9] Funds and Loans, contracted by our own Extravagancies and perverse Humours; as a Burden, to be discharged by the succeeding Generation. As it is a natural Instinct in Animals to provide for Posterity, it must be deem'd very *unnatural and wicked* in us, instead of doing so, to contribute to their future Misery.

So much Paper as is current in a Province, *so much really is that Province in Debt;* for the *Funds* Part, the Publick is in Debt; for the *Loans* Part, private Persons are in Debt: It is a Contradiction to assert that a Country may *grow rich by* (Paper Money) *running in Debt?* As neither Publick nor Private are now ashamed to continue in Debt, we may say of those Paper-Money Countries, with Regard to their Mother-Country; what is commonly said, and is in Fact true of many of our Shopkeepers with Regard to the Merchants; if they would be rich they must run boldly in Debt, and not be asham'd of being dunn'd.

If a private Man's Notes or Bonds are negotiated at a Discount, he is deem'd a *Bankrupt* capable of paying only —————— in the Pound. So it may be said of our Colonies, with Paper Currencies at a great Discount; and the Discount encreasing daily, they are in a State of *lawless Bankrupcy.*

Private Credit or Notes on a good solid Foundation, are *better than publick Bills;* the former cannot, *impune*, break their *Faith;* they are under Coercion: The publick is the Dernier resort and in bad Administrations frequently break their *publick Faith.* Hence, the Credit of a well regulated Commerce or Corporation, is better than that of the civil Administration; *the Bank Money of* Venice *is* 20 *per Cent. of* Hamburg 12 *per Cent. of* Holland 5 *per Cent. better than common* Currency.

This private commercial Credit in all polite Nations, is so sacred at present, that the *civil Government stand corrected by it.* The Generality of the *united Provinces* did *A.* 1693 coin alloy'd Pieces called *quaad Schellings* at 6 *Stivers,* being near 10 *per Cent.* above their intrinsick Value. The

Bank retain'd their Integrity, and it again rose to 13 or 15 *per Cent.* this obliged the Government to reduce these *Schellings* to 5 and an Half *Stivers* their intrinsick Value, and have continued so ever since, and the Agio of the Bank fell to 3 or 5 *per Cent.* as formerly. *A* 1720, *France* being in the most dismal Confusion, by their Paper Currency, their Court was obliged to apply [10] to the Merchants and Bankers for their Advice, concerning a Method to be used to find out the natural Proportion between publick Bills and Silver Species, and to *limit their Paper Effects* to a certain Sum.

A plain Illustration, that Private is better than publick Credit, we have amongst ourselves. Our *Merchant's Notes*, so called, being well founded, were 11 and an Half *per Cent.* in *Decemb* 1737, will be 18 *per Cent.* in *Decem.* 1738, 12 and an Half *per Cent.* (3 7ths of them then paid off) in *Decemb.* 1739, 19 and an Half *per Cent.* in *Decem.* 1740, 26 and an Half *per Cent.* in *Decemb.* 1741, and 34 *per Cent.* in *Decemb.* 1742, better than the present Value of our Province Bills at 27 *per Cent.*; because they are continually growing better, until they come to their fixed Value, at which they are to be paid off.

The Scheme for emitting of 60,000 *l. Bills of the new Tenour*, equal to 180,000 *l.* of the common *New England* Bills, by Undertakers or Subscribers, probably will drop, and therefore requires no Disquisition: Only we may observe 1*st.* The Emission is too large, and the Periods too distant. 2*dly.* The Subscribers or Circulators require a good *Premium;* because if let go, at the Rate of 27 *s. per Oz. silver*, the present Value of our Currency, and it is paid in again 1 10th yearly, at 20 *s. per Oz.* Value, allowing for their Profits by Interest; *every* 1000 l. *new Tenour, that is*

3000 *l. common Currency will loose* 262 *l.* 10 *s.*: If Silver rise higher, as it naturally does upon all large Paper Emissions, the Loss will be proportionably greater, after the Rate of 150 *l. for every Shilling advance upon the Ounce of Silver.* 3*dly*. If the *Assembly* our Legislature, being under no Coercion as private Banks are, should *postpone* the Periods of paying the Possessor; the Value of these Bills will further depreciate very much. 4*thly*. The grand Deformity of the Scheme is; that this Money shall *answer all Specialties*, past, present, and to come: The like was never imposed (seeing it is ordered to be printed, it may with Freedom be canvassed) upon the Subject, by the most arbitrary and iniquitous Governments in the World; particularly it is equivalent to a *Bill of Attainder*, against every one of the Committee or Subscribers of the *Merchant's Notes.*

The *Uncertainty and Confusion of Paper Currency* in our several *Colonies*, and in the same Colony at different Times; might be illustrated by the History of the various Paper Currencies of our Colonies; but to avoid Prolixity, we [11] shall only observe; That *Massachusetts Bay* in *New England* led the Way, by an Act of *Assembly* in *Decemb.* 1690, emitting a small Sum in *Province Bills* or Debentures, to satisfy some extraordinary Charges incurr'd by the expensive and fruitless Expedition to *Canada* that Year; afterwards more were issued towards the Charges of the succeeding Years: But were no legal Tender, only receivable for Taxes, and cancelled after a Year or two: Thus they kept up their Credit, and were *at Par* with Silver until *A.* 1713: From that Time, by Funds and Loans in large Sums they lost their Credit, and are at present 27 *s. the Ounce of Silver.*

Barbados followed our Example *A.* 1702, and by a large

Emission upon Loan they run into Confusion; but by an Order from *England* they were cancelled, and the Island came immediately to rights again. *South Carolina* upon their Expedition against St. *Augustine, A.* 1702, began to issue Paper Money; by their subsequent large Emissions on Funds and Loans, and by their vile Breach of publick Faith in Postponings, have arrived to 42 *s.* 6 *d. per Oz. Connecticut* in *New-England,* their first Emission was *A.* 1709. *Rhode-Island* in *New-England,* came into it *A.* 1710, as did *New-Hampshire* in *New-England,* about the same Time; they are all over *New-England* 27 *s. per Oz.* Silver. *New-York's* first Emission was *A.* 1734, as their present Currency does not exceed 37,000 *l,* Silver with them is only 8 *s.* or 8 *s.* 6 *d. per Oz. Jersey's* Bills are at the same Price. *Pensylvania* begun *A* 1723, but do not exceed 69,000 *l.* and are at 8 *s.* 6 *d.* to 9 *s. per Oz* of Silver. *Maryland's* first Emission *A* 1754, was of 90,000 *l.* at long Periods, and are at 10 *s.* to 11 *s. per Oz* of Silver.

A Glut of this Provincial confused Paper Currency, by frequent and large Emissions, did naturally make it a *Drug,* and cheaper than Silver the general Standard of Merchandize: So that the *Merchant* was obliged to advance upon his Goods, bought for Silver, & sold for this Paper; and in Consequence the Consumer of them, obliged to raise the Price of *his Labour and Country Produe,* paid in Paper.

When *Paper Money* is in a continued Course of *depreciating,* all Debts and other *Contracts* are paid in a less Value than they are contracted for; which is an unjust but natural Operation of this false *Medium*; the generous foreign Adventurer or *Merchant,* and consequently Trade in its genuine Sense, is hurt; the Gainers are the *Shop-*[12]*keepers* and

Merchant Hucksters, who have a long Credit from their Merchant, and abuse this Credit.

Large Emissions of Paper Currency, have *encouraged the unwary Merchant* at Home to send large Quantities of Goods, supposing our Money to be good: And therefore has a natural Tendency to make the Ballance of Trade against us, by increasing our Imports.

A large Emission of publick *Paper Credit on Loan*, to be paid at a distant Period or long Credit; gives the desperate and unthinking Borrowers or Subscribers, an Opportunity of *ruining themselves*, by taking up this Money and spending it extravagantly: *Industry and Frugality* (the only Means of becoming rich) are turned aside: In Place of being industrious, our young Men called Gentlemen, follow no other business but *Drinking and Gaming;* many in Quality of Shop-keepers become *Drones;* Tradesmen of all Occupations in *Boston, loiter* away much of their Time; the Husbandmen in the Country spend many idle Days in their little *Rum Taverns.* Frugality is superseeded by Prodigality and Extravagance, as is too aparent in our fine Houses and Furniture, Chaises and other Equipages, Velvets and Scarlets, rich Silks and Laces, &c. The Parliament of *Bretagne* in *France*, in their Remonstrance to the Court of *France, A.* 1719, say, 'That many of their Families are 'ruined by Paper Money, it gives an unbounded Loose to 'Excess in Apparel and other Extravagancies.' This is the natural Consequence of large Quantities of Paper Credit in all Countries.

These *Extravagancies* the Consequencies of our Paper Currency, hurt us as to the *Ballance of Trade* in both Respects: They encourage a Consumption of foreign Com-

modities, that is, they increase our *Imports*; instead of
employing our Paper Credit to produce Exports, and to set
up *Manufactures* and other Improvements; it is expended
in fine Houses, Equipages, and Apparel, or to pay Debts
contracted by a long Credit: The Hands employ'd in fitting
out these Extravagancies, would have been more profitably
employ'd, about Things for *Exports*, or in manufacturing
such Things, as would have lessened our *Imports*.

This leads us, to an *Argument* much used by some, in
Favour of Paper Credit. *viz. The fine Figure Boston now
makes*, in Houses, Equipages, &c. is owing to it. This is
Truth, but not to be boasted of, no Man is the richer [13]
for these Extravagancies, he thereby starves his Trade, and
disappoints his Merchants and other Creditors: We are not
to judge by Appearances only; *Boston* never was more ex-
travagant and gay than at present, but never were more in
Debt, never more incapable and backward in paying Debts.
From the repeated large Emissions of Paper Credit, the
Value of our *nummary Denominations* did continually become less, and the Merchants at Home were from Time to
Time paid a less Value than they contracted for; thus, for a
Debt contracted 25 Years ago, he now receives only 7 *s. in
the Pound*, that is the Debtor (defrauds) retains 13 *s.* in the
Pound of the Merchant's Money, and with this he builds
fine Houses, makes Purchases &c.: Let us not boast of
these Things, lest it may be said of our Posterity, and of
those who are to enjoy them: *Happy is the Child whose
Father goes to the Devil.*

Seeing then a Creditor paid in these *depreciating Denominations*, does not receive the Value he contracted for; is it
possible that any Man (if in his right Senses) of a monied

Estate, that is, in Cash, or out upon Bond or any other kind
of Debt, can desire such a Moth of a Currency. Every Act
for Emissions of large Sums of Paper Credit, unless upon a
solid Fund, or to be cancelled in a Year or two by Taxes;
may properly be called *An Act for the Relief of insolvent
Debtors;* or rather, An Act to encourage and enable Debtors
to defraud their Creditors, by compounding at —— *Shillings*
in the Pound, and every Creditor looses thereby a certain
Portion of his Estate. This is one of the most pernicious
Operations of this Paper Credit, *viz.* That all who have the
Art and Assurance of running in Debt, and postponing
Payments from Time to Time, are in a certain Way of getting an Estate; to the Damage, or Ruin of their Creditors
and Benefactors.

In all Countries where there have been several sorts of
Currencies at a Time; *the basest only remains for common
Currency:* In *Holland, quaad Schellings* are now their common Currency. In our *Leeward-Islands* are two Currencies,
viz. Silver and Gold, upon unequal footing; Silver being
upon the best footing is shipt off, Gold remains; and in
changing of Gold for Silver, there is an Advance upon the
Silver. Where there have been good and bad Currencies in
the same Place; all the good, if Merchandize, is *shipt off,* as
is Silver and Gold; if not [14] Merchandize, but upon a fixed
Foundation as to Value and Period of Specification or Payment, they are *hoarded up,* because daily growing better as
these Periods approach; as is the Case of our *Merchant's
Notes.*

We have no Reason to fear *Want of a Medium,* if the
Grievance of publick Paper Credit were gradually removed.
Trade will find its own *natural proper Medium,* viz. *Silver*

and Gold: They are imported here from Time to Time; when we have no other Cash; Cash is a *Merchant's Tool* or Instrument of Trade, by which he carries on his Trade and Business; and therefore will require no Laws, to hinder its Exportation.

Our Government of *Massachusetts-Bay* in *New England*, from the Inconveniencies, in their own Experience, and from the notorious bad Consequences of the like Practices in other Colonies; are now beginning to reform this Error of a *vague Paper Currency*, by reducing it to a certain *Silver Standard* and Fund. Upon this Occasion I beg Leave to observe; that in our Bills of the *new Tenour*, if *Gold* had been put at 5 *l.* (instead of 4 *l.* 18 *s.*) *per Oz.* it would have been nearer at Par with Silver at 6 *s.* 8 *d. per Oz.*; and the Gold Penny-weight, being thus at 5 *s*, would have been without a Fraction, as is the Silver Penny-weight at 4 *d.* The *Leeward Islands* and *New-York*, have erred on the other Side, *viz.* Silver at 8 *s. per Oz.*, and a Pistole at 28 *s.*

Some harsh sounding Words, are not designed as a *Reflection* upon this Country in general (the Country is not without its Merit, and their People in their natural *Genius* do excel) the Errors of all Countries in bad Administrations, are to be imputed, to the *Iniquity* of Administration, but not to the People in general.

There has lately appeared here in print a small Piece (*Some Observations*, &c.) in Favour of a Paper Currency: But unluckily for the Author and his Cause, most of his Arguments, when cleared of unnatural Incumbrances, recoil upon himself, and they point out the many Inconveniencies which attend a large publick Paper Credit. As it seems designed for the Vulgar great and small; notwithstanding, what I have already related, is a full Answer to the whole; I must by a closer Application, retort his Arguments. I shall forbear any *idle Criticism* upon his Calculations, Figures, and *technical* commercial Words, as being out of the Question. Here I cannot but [15] observe, that in all his spacious Calculations, he is obliged to make Use of Silver at a certain Value, and receivable at certain Periods, as a *Basis*; neglecting his darling Paper Currencies Uncertainties, as not qualified for a proper Foundation.

He introduces these Words, *Ballance of Trade*, upon all Occasions, with no true Meaning and Application.

Ballance of Trade is Cash (Silver and Gold) imported to, or exported from a Country, according as the general Exports or Imports of Merchandize exceed one the other. The Silver and Gold which we send to *England*, are no Part of the Ballance of Trade against us, being truly, as Merchandize only. *England* sometimes exports *Two Millions* Sterling Value of Silver and Gold per *Ann.* to *Holland*, *East-Indies*, &c. by Way of Merchandize; the Ballance of Trade continuing in Favour of *England* notwithstanding. *Ballance of Trade* is also against a Country, not only when they export their Medium, but also when the Country runs in Debt, by expending in fine Houses, Apparel, *&c.* that which ought to have purchased Exports; this is our present Case.

The whole of his Book may be summ'd up in this Sentence, *The sinking Value of our Bills is from and in Proportion to the Ballance of Trade being against us.* Is it possible that a Country should continue to trade, or be capable of trading, when by the *Ballance of Trade* being against them, should meerly upon that Account in 25 Years Time, loose two Thirds of their Substance, as our Bills have lost above two Thirds of their Value. In any Country if the *Ballance of Trade*, is very much against them for a Series of Years; their Merchants naturally become Bankrupts, to the Damage of their foreign Creditors; the Country looses its Credit, and is no more a Place of Trade. *Paper Money cannot satisfy a Ballance of Trade*, it is not exportable or to be negotiated abroad.

If we find that in all our Colonies where is no Paper Credit, that, the Value of their *nummary Denominations*, continues the same; and in all Colonies where Paper Currencies has prevailed, their Denominations have depreciated; Hand in Hand with their repeated Paper Emissions, ought we to have Recourse to any other Conceit (as Ballance of Trade) for its Cause, but only to the Operation of these Bills, would he not be reckoned *a wrong Head*, who should asign any other *Regulator* of [16] the *Tides* but the *Moon*, seeing at all Times and every where they vary *pari passu*, *Barbados* has had its Visicitudes of good and bad Crops; their Planters sometimes rich, sometimes much in Debt: But having no Paper Credit, their nummary Denominations are constantly of the same Value. *Pensylvania* (I mean the three upper Counties) has ever been in a progressive growing Condition: Their nummary Denominations continue of the same fixed (*Proclamation* 6 *s*. 10 *d*. half-penny *per Oz*.) Value; until their Emissions and Re-emissions of Paper Money *A*. 1723, 1724, 1726, and 1729, raised Silver to 9 *s*. *per Oz*., tho' at present their whole Paper Currency does not exceed 69,000 *l*. *Maryland* the last of our Colonies, that has fallen into this Expedient of Debtors cheating their Creditors (a Debt of 100 Weight of *Tobacco*, 10 *s*. Denomination before, is now paid by 10 *s*. Denomination of this Paper, which purchases only, and consequently is worth no more that 50 Weight of *Tobacco*) *A.* 1734 they emitted 90 000 *l.* on a Silver, or *Proclamation* Bottom; but the Emission being too large, and the Payments to the Possessors at too distant Periods (15, 30, *and* 45 *Years*) not being receivable in the Proprietors Quit-Rents, nor in Taxes, and being made a legal Tender; *Exchange* rose directly from 33 to 100 *per Cent.* Where the natural Causes of this Rise are so plain, is it reasonable to introduce some *chimærical* invisible Ballance of Trade, opperating so suddenly and so violently, while their Trade (Imports and Exports) in Appearance is still the same. In *New-England*, by unlucky incident, *in the Fall* A 1733 *Massachusetts Bay* emitted 70,000 *l. Rhode-Island* 104 000 *l*, *Connecticut* 50,000 *l.*: The Operation of these Emissions was exactly the same; *Exchange* rose from 275 to 440 *per Cent.* Imports exceeding the Exports in Trade, is therefore not the true adequate Cause of the *Minoration* of the Value of our *nummary Denominations.* In *South-Carolina* where the Paper Credit is the lowest, 42 *s.* 6 *d. per Oz.* Silver; their *Rice* and *Deer-Skins* or Exports are of much greater Value than their Imports, being now fully stockt with *Negroes.*

He says, *That Province Bills ought to be emitted from Time to Time, and postponed; until the Quantity exceeds the Demand.* This is impracticable in the Nature of the Currency: By Experience we find, that the more Emissions from Time to Time, the Value of these Bills is the less, and consequently the greater Quantity of them is re-[17]quired (that is the Demand is the greater) to carry on the same Business. *A.* 1713, when our Bills began to depreciate, there was current in all *New England* 194,000 *l.* in publick Bills of Bredit, at 8 *s. per Oz.* (the Value at that Time) is

485,000 *Ounces* Silver Value, besides a considerable concomitant Silver Currency: Our Paper Currency at present
(Merchant's Notes not included) is about 580,000 *l.* (triple
the former) at 27 *s. per Oz.* Silver Value, is only 429,629 *Oz.*
without any concomitant Silver Currency; so that our real
Medium of Trade or Currency is considerably less at present,
than it was *A.* 1713; notwithstanding the emitted large
Sums, of this imaginary fallacious nominal Currency. This
is the certain and constant Operation of a publick Paper
Currency in large Quantities, over all our Colonies; that is,
when it exceeds a certain Proportion; the more that is emitted the more it depreciates, and by continued multiplied
Emissions, at length, *Province Bills may become in Value
equal to Waste Paper.*

He says, A 20 *s. Bill is the natural Pound of New-
England.* This ought to be understood no otherways, than
as a *Banter* upon our publick Bills, because they are continually fluctuating; and may be compared to the Inscription,
semper eadem upon a Vane in *Camb dige,* in the Time of the
Administration latter End of Queen *Ann's* Reign. Or in
a more familiar Comparison, of the Loads of Hay brought
to *Boston,* which originally were design'd and understood to
be 20 *Hund. Wt.* or a Tun, at present if a Country Man's
Load is reduced to a Standard Weight, and found to be
only 12 *Hund. Wt.;* would it satisfy the Buyer of this Load
or Tun of Hay, the Country Man's saying, it is all right, this
is my natural Tun or Load: This is what our Author in
another Place says, that every Man may have his own natural
Pound: Which cannot possibly be, until Society is dissolved.

' *Silver falling in infinitum, and Bills growing better in
infinitum* ' This is a *Delirium,* without any Connection or

Meaning; as are sundry other Passages in tha Book, which I do not understand, and therefore cannot presume to explain.

' *The Ballance of Debt against us, will fall our Bills ad infinitum* '. I suppose he means not below the Value of Waste Paper. Where is then the Value of these Bills? Is it not a *Burlesque* upon us, to call a 20 *Shilling Bill* not fix'd, but left free to its Course in the Market, and [18] at length become equal to Nothing; *New England's natural Pound Value?* Are those natural Pounds in any Country, which in the Space of 25 Years have fluctuated or rather sunk from 50 *per Cent* Exchange to 400 *per Cent.,* and may still sink *in infinitum?*

What he calls *Buying with our Silver at a Market Price;* is, in a mercantile Phrase, discounting our Bills at a Market Price, with Silver, which is the fixed universal commercial *Medium;* thus he endeavours to perswade us, that our Bills are of a fixed Value, and that Silver fluctuates; after this same Manner, as if aboard of a coasting Vessel under Sail or fluctuating, he should endeavour to perswade Passengers, that the *Ship* stands still, and the Land fluctuates or alters: He might perhaps from Appearances perswade one who had not the right Use of his Reason. To say this Bill shall be in Value equal to Money without fixing any standard Value, is only saying, *Valeat quantum valera potest. Qui vult decipi, decipiatur.*

Of the same Nature is his Assertion, That *when Goods, rise or fall in our Market, the Change must be in our Goods, but not in Paper Credit.* Whereas in Fact Goods and Produce in this Place, *communibus annis,* have nearly retain'd the same Price (or rather of late are cheaper) for many

Years, with Regard to Silver the universal commercial Medium: That is, the same Quantity of Silver will buy the same Quantity of Cloth, Woollens, and Linnens of any particular Sort, and build the same Tunnage of Vessels (when Silver was at 8 *s. per Oz.* Ships from 200 to 300 Tun to the Builder, cost about 4 *l. per Tun*, and 10 *s.* for Extras as was the Custom at that Time; at present 15 *l. per Tun*, Extras included.) *Labour* is rather cheaper, a Ship-Carpenter when Silver was 8 *s.*, had 5 *s.* a Day, or 5 8ths of an *Oz*; at present has only 12 *s.* a Day, which is not Half an *Oz.* at 27 *s. per Oz*

The Author is a Stranger to the Affairs of *Exchange-Alley* in *London*. He compares the continued great Falls of our Province Bills from 50 to 400 *per Cent.* (I suppose he means the *Bubles A* 1720) to the Changes in the *Stocks* negotiated there, which is only a small Fluctuation, proceeding not from Ballance of Trade, or Variations in nummary Denominations, or Addition of more Stock on the same Fund; but from some *Stock jobbing* little Arts or Tricks He is not acquainted with the Nature of *East-India Bonds:* He says they are not fit for a Market, be-[19]cause they promise Money only at a distant Time, and a supposed Interest of 6 *per Cent.* Whereas the Possessor or *Bond-Holder* may demand at Pleasure (or be allowed in any of their Sales as ready Money) but the *East-India Company* cannot oblige the Bond-Holder to quit (have it discharged) his Bond, but at half Years Notice. Hence it is, that they bear an Interest lower than the common Interest (3 or 3 and an Half *per Cent.*) and sell for a *Premium*; because they are as Cash bearing Interest, which Silver Cash does not.

'*Paper Money not being emitted in Quantities, is the Rea-*

son why the natural Interest amongst us rises.' This unnatural *Medium* in Quantities, has a quite different Operation; from that of the natural *Medium* Silver in Plenty, which effectually lowers the Interest of Money. The Quantity of Paper Credit sinks the Value of the Principal, and the Lender to save himself, is obliged to lay the growing Loss of the Principal, upon the Interest. *Rhode-Island* who have much exceeded us in their Emissions, have for some Time rose their Rate of Interest to 10 or 12 *per Cent.* and give this very Reason for so doing.

'*No Man can say, but that his Money will now bring him in, as much Interest as ever.'* The Matter of Fact is, 100 *l.* in Province Bills 25 Years ago, brought in 15 *Oz.* of Silver *per Ann.;* the same 1000 *l,* at present does not bring in 5 *Oz,* is 5 equal to 15, or 1 to 3.

His *tacit Consent of the Multitude to the Schemes of Paper Money;* is a weak Argument in its Favour. I remember some Years ago, when we had got into the Humour of *Lotteries*: Notwithstanding the Discount upon the benefit Tickets for Charges, and other great Frauds (*v. g.* in one of the First of these *Lotteries,* a House was set at 1600 *l.,* the Proprietors of this benefit Ticket, after this House had been upon Sale many Months, could get no more than 100 *l.* for it, which is a Discount of 37 *per Cent.*) yet without Imputation of *Knavery* on the one Side, or *Folly* on the other; People did continue in subsequent *Lotteries* to sink their Substance, and would have continued longer in the same Manner; if the Wisdom of our *Legislature* had not put a Stop to it.

He alledges that *long Credit (our great Grievance) is from the Scarcity of Paper Money.* No. It is from too great Imports, encouraged by large Emissions. The Merchant or Factor cannot dispose of so much, at a reasonable ready-money Price, and therefore, that their Goods may [20] not lay long upon Hand, are obliged to give a long Credit.

I cannot avoid, by way of Digression, to make some Remarks on *long Credit.* It makes the Unthinking buy profusely. Whereas ready Money, or a short Credit, would not allow a Man to buy and spend more, than his present Earning could afford, consequently he would live frugally, and keep clear of Debt: Foreign Commodities would not be imported in such Quantities, because they could not be consumed faster than our Earnings (our Returns) would admit of; and would answer the Intention of *sumptuary Laws,* which our stated Dependance on a trading Mother Country cannot allow of. Ready Money or a short Credit, makes a quick Circulation; the quicker the Circulation, the less Quantity of a Currency or *Medium* is required to carry on any Trade and Business. This would be an effectual Method, and equivalent to enlarging our Currency.

He alledges also, that *Shop Notes (another great Grievance) were introduced from the Scarcity of Paper Currency.* This is ill judged. Because the *Merchant* to procure a greater Advantage upon his Goods, than if sold for Cash; contracted with the *Shop-keeper*, to take it out in his Way by *Tradesmen's Notes*: The Shop-keeper by imposing upon the Tradesmen and Labourers, Possessors of these Notes, found their Profit in it; this made the Shop keepers chuse to buy, to be drawn out in Notes. The factor also found his Advantage in it, by dazling his Employer with a large Account of Sales, & by encreasing his Commissions. This is become an *Iniquity* as it were by compact.

He encourages the *Rhode Islanders* to more Emissions of Bills, '*And they will find their Account in it, if they go on to emit a sufficient Quantity of Bills.*' He advises this Province to follow their Example, *in emitting a great Quantity before it be too late.* He does not consider that if this Province were to emit a Quantity of Bills in proportion to what ·*Rhode-Island* have emitted, (*Massachusets Bay* Colony being to that of *Rhode Island* nearly as 6 is to 1) they would be so depreciated by their Quantity, as not to answer the End of a Currency, and oblige us to a *Truck Trade;* as in *North Carolina*, where their Truck call'd Specie, passes at a great Advance above their Province Bills; and in *South Carolina*, by reason of their large Emissions, all considerable Contracts are made [21] in their Produce Rice, not in Bills. A Man of a landed Estate perswaded some Merchants his Neighbours and and Friends to accept his Notes for Goods and other Necessaries payable after 10 or 20 Years, and to circulate them all that Time without any *Premium*: And this Man a trading with these Goods to his own private Profit. It is scarce credible that there could be such *Infatuation* on the one Side, and such *bare fac'd Imposition* on the Other. This is the very Case between this Province and *Rhode-Island*. It is in vain to think, that we may follow their Example; it is impracticable so to multiply Bills to our Advantage, unless we could perswade (it is *Folly* to imagine it) all our Continent Plantations, to circulate them; *Rhode-Island* bears no greater a Proportion to this Province, than this Province does to all our other Colonies upon this Continent.

He is an inexorable Enemy to Silver, for the following Reasons, as he says.

Silver has been and may be greatly depreciated by the Excess of its Quantity. Silver is of so universal Demand all over the World; that the continued Additions to it is like throwing of Water into the Ocean, making no sensible Alteration: But a continued Emission of any peculiar provincial Paper Money, above a certain Sum, is like continued Pourings of Liquor into a Cask, which is soon full, runs over, and the Additions are lost. In Fact, the computative or *nummary Denominations*, instead of containing more Silver, as it might be imagined from its Excess, do contain considerably less, *v. g.* in *England* instead of 12 *Oz to a Pound Sterling*, as it was when Silver was scarce, it is at present only 4 *Oz* when Silver abounds: But, as we have already proved, this proceeds from none of the Qualities of Silver; it is meerly from the *Iniquity* of civil Administrations. The Silver Mines of *Potsio* are said to have been first discovered *A.* 1545, the nummary Denominations, as to Quantity of Silver, varied much before that Time, and since *Anno* 1552 (prior to this our Import of Silver was inconsiderable) in *England* they have altered or varied only Two, in Eighty Eight.

Bills are a Commodity, not as a Pledge given but as Value paid, and therefore preferable to Silver. Is it not more natural to say, Silver is as a certain Value paid, as a Pledge, and as Returns or Merchandize; therefore it is preferable to publick Bills, which are only as a precarious Va-[22]lue paid, but no Pledge, and no Returns or Merchandize.

Bills are less bulky and more handy than Silver. Is a Shop-keeper's (whose Notes are already at a great Discount) promisary Note of Hand, better than a Bag of Silver.

Notes on a fixed real Fund, are worse than Notes that have no such Fund; because the former cannot grow better beyond that fixed Standard : But the others being bad, may grow better *in infinitum.* This is ludicrous. I can answer only by a like Story : A certain *Quack* in the Cure of a sick Person, being told that by his Management, the Patient did grow worse and worse: So much the better, answered the Quack, because when Things are come to the worst, then they will mend. The Truth of the Case is, the first can be no worse, than the just Discount for the Distance of the Time of Payment; but the Others may grow worse and worse, *in infinitum.*

If we make Bills promising Silver or any Thing of a certain Value, it will occasion their being hoarded up. It will be so, where there are also current Bills, promising a precarious or no Value; because such will be hoarded up by no Body, but be gladly parted with, even at a Discount, until we discount near the whole, that is until they are of no further Currency or Value: Accordingly in this Province, we are now arrived to a *Discount of more than two Thirds* of what these Bills were first emitted for. That a Bill without Limitation of Value or Period, and continually growing worse, should be preferable to a Bill with the Advantage of Period, and Value certain, and yearly meliorating, as are Bills on a fixed Silver Bottom; is a *strange Paradox.* Some keep up the *Massachusets* Bills and pass away the *Rhode-Island* Bills; are the *Rhode Island* Bills therefore better than the *Massachusetts?* Amongst our present publick Bills, what are tore and defac'd, or suspected, are passed away first; are they therefore a better Currency, than a good fair Bill?

There ought to be no Silver Fund for Bills, because it will rise the Price of Silver, to make good this Fund. That is, all our Banks in *Europe* are ill founded, both Publick and Private; because they are all upon a Silver Bottom.

To pay Contracts according to a fixed Weight of Silver; would have an unavoidable Tendency to raise the Price of it. It does not happen so in *Europe*, where Silver is their only legal Tender. In *New England*, paying of Contracts in Province Bills, does not rise the Price of them.

[23] *Our Bills are better than Silver, because they are by our Acts of Assembly a Tender, and consequently must pass: Silver passes only by Consent, which may be withdrawn.* That is, a forced provincial Tender, passable no where else, is better than a natural, universal and legal (*Proclamation Act*) Tender, from which no trading Consent ever was or will be withdrawn: And 27 *s.* in Bills the present Value of One *Ounce* of Silver, is better than 27 *s.* which was the Value of Three *Ounces and an Half* of Silver Twenty Five Years ago; or in plain Words, One is more than Three.

The following Clauses in his Book I cannot understand, *viz. Province Bills may be fixed to an assigned Interest, and so be made a just Measure or Standard of the Value of all Things bought or sold, which Silver cannot be. — When Silver falls the Government may stop it at any fixed Rate, and make that the Silver Pound or legal tender. Why not also when Silver rises if it were practicable. — Lowering the Price of Silver in* England, *where the nummary Denomination continues of the same Weight in our Coin,* it is a Contradiction in itself. — *By Means of a Paper Currency, to introduce Silver to pass current.*

He concludes thus. That he might now shew, how the Bills of the old Tenour, might be qualified, for the true

Ends and Uses thereof; and the like of private Notes of the same Nature, but having exceeded the Bounds of a Letter, he must forbear. *Cui bono* is the whole, since he concludes without entring upon the main and only Affair?

Most *political* Affairs have some Resemblance, to natural *oscillatory* Motions, when got to their Extent on the one Side; they must return gradually and in the same Path to the other Side. Large Emissions of a bad Currency, long Credit, Insensibility of Discredit, Idleness, Extravigance, and Intemprance, have carried us to the Extent of bad Circumstances: We must return by [23] gradually cancelling our bad Medium, by shortning our Credit, by being more upon the Punctos of Honour and Honesty, by being more industrious, by being more Frugal, and by abandoning the plentiful Use of *Rum*, that execrable Bane of all our Plantations, and perniciously recommended by some of our Practitioners in *Physick*, as more wholesome than Wine.

FINIS.

ERRATA.

Page 4' Line 20. for *for*, read *or*.   p. 11. l. 25. for 1734 r.
1714.   do. l. 31. f. 1754. r. 1734.   do. l. 38. f. *Produe* r.
Produce.   p. 19. l. 25. f. 1000 r. 100.   do. l. 35. f. 100 *l.*
r. 1000 *l.* p. 20. l. 12. f. *stated* r. *State of*.   p. 21. l. 35. f.
Potsio, r. *Potosi*.

NOTE - TO "AN ESSAY CONCERNING SILVER AND PAPER CURRENCIES," ETC.

This "Essay," although anonymously published, is known to have been written by Dr. William Douglass, of whom the statement was made in the note to "Some Observations," etc., that he was the only participant in the contemporary discussion about the currency who has gained renown by his publications.

Douglass was a Scotchman by birth, a physician by profession, and apparently was fond of dabbling in mathematics and economics. He published an almanac, a number of pamphlets in connection with medicine, others in relation to the currency question, and a history of the North American colonies under the title of "A Summary political and historical of the first planting, progressive improvements, and present state of the British settlements in North America." The contents of this work disclose familiarity with contemporary knowledge of physics, and there is evidence of extensive botanical investigation.[1]

His style of writing was peculiarly abrupt, and in polemical discussions he was always aggressive and intemperate. This occasionally led him into difficulty, the most conspicuous instance of which was a libel suit brought against him by Admiral Sir Charles Knowles, for language used in the "Summary," in an account of a riot in

---

[1] Summary, etc., Vol. I, pp. 35, 51, 122, 123, 124, 125, 126, 127, 128, 129, 131, 148. See also note to page 21, Vol. II, where he says he collected eleven hundred indigenous plants for an herbarium.

Boston in 1747 caused by the impressment of a large number of sailors by the admiral.[1] He was discursive and did not hesitate to abandon temporarily his narrative for what he was wont to term a digression. Even in so short a pamphlet as this "Essay," he says on page 20, "I cannot avoid, by way of Digression to make some Remarks on *long Credit.*" In his "Summary" he had opportunity for indulgence in this whim with the result that we have in the first volume alone, "a digression on Whaling" (pp. 56–61), "*A digression. A short history of the* South-Sea *company* affairs" (pp. 74–87), "*A digression concerning sugar,*" (pp. 115–118), "*A digression concerning the* religions *of ancient nations,*" (pp. 162–167), "*A digression concerning the settling of the colonies in general; with an Utopian amusement, or loose proposals, towards regulating the British colonies in the north Continent of America,*" (pp. 233–262), "*A digression concerning the magnetic needle, commonly called the mariner's compass,*" (pp. 262–272), "*A digression giving some further accounts of the late endeavours towards a north-west passage to* China," (pp. 283–286), "*A digression concerning fisheries*" (pp. 294–304), "*A digression concerning some late British Expeditions against* Canada" (pp. 309–316).

It will be seen that these so-called digressions were all of them related, and most of them closely related, to the subject concerning which Douglass was writing. They were rather disproportionate amplifications than digressions, and were not nearly so perplexing to the student who may have been led to consult his "Summary" as his habit of tucking in voluminous notes, concerning topics in which he was interested, in the most unexpected places in the narrative. The currency question, for instance, is treated in the text, and contact with this subject necessarily occurs at two or three points. The annotations at these points are voluminous, but it is evident that while the work was going through the press, allusions in the text to the subject suggested other annotations, and these are to be found scattered in a random way through the pages of the work.

[1] See Douglass's apologetic explanation in the preface to Vol. I. The affair is referred to in the note, pp. 252–255. See also Publications, Colonial Society of Massachusetts, Vol. III, p. 215 *et seq.*

Douglass was a learned man, as the pages of the "Summary" demonstrate, but he was a hasty and careless writer, impatient of delay and indifferent to details so long as his main allegations were correct. An illustration of this occurs in the first volume of the "Summary," where on page 527 he gives a table of the outstanding currency, Christmas, 1748. The information furnished in this table as to the several emissions is probably correct, but the net result of the amount of outstanding currency did not agree with the official figures. Knowing that the table as it stood was in any event approximately correct, he inserted a note, "Here is some small error," and let the volume go to press in that shape.[1]

It is not surprising that certain of our authorities on such subjects, under circumstances like these, should have rejected Douglass's work as untrustworthy. Palfrey terms him "a master of ribaldry," "a conceited censor," "a snarling physician," and "a contemporary Scottish grumbler." Eliot, in his Biographical Dictionary, defines the "Summary" as "a collection of things which came into his head, whether they related to his family, his private squabbles, or the affairs of the publick." Palfrey was impressed by Douglass's intemperate language and infirm temper; Eliot by the digressions, and it may be safely said that historians, accepting these opinions, have been slow in recognizing the real value of Douglass's work. Appletons' Cyclopædia sums up the case of the "Summary," by saying that it is inaccurate and records the author's grievances as well as public affairs. It remained for the economists to elevate him in the repute of the world to the position to which he was entitled. This was done through the numerous reprints of a pamphlet entitled "A Discourse concerning the currencies of the British plantations in America," etc., which was originally published in Boston in 1740, and which is largely based upon the material used in "An Essay concerning silver and paper currencies," etc. The "Essay" is seldom mentioned, but had the "Discourse" not

---

[1] The table itself in the volume before me is full of typographical errors. It may be assumed that Douglass's comment that there was an error in it referred to his own manuscript table.

been published it is probable that Douglas would ultimately have reaped the reward of recognition through its pages.

We occasionally receive a hint in these pamphlets of the daily life and the manners and customs of the colonists. On page 12 of the " Essay," there is a slap at " our young Men called Gentlemen " who " follow no other business but *Drinking and Gaming*," which is followed by references to the " Prodigality and Extravagance " of Boston people. " *Boston*," he says on page 13, " never was more extravagant and gay than at present, but never were more in Debt, never more incapable and backward in paying Debts."

It may be permissible to call attention to Douglass's opinion as to the availability of a paper currency as a medium of trade in the colonies. On page 6 he says: " *A Paper Credit* well founded and under good Regulations, and not larger than what the Silver Specie Currency will bear; has been found to be a very good Expedient in Businefs, and it leaves the *Silver Species* at more Liberty to be used as Merchandize, and for petty Occasions." What the amount was which might safely have been maintained in New England he discloses on page 7: " As to the Quantity of Paper Currency which the Silver Currency will bear, without depreciating its Denominations; it is only to be learnt by Experience. In *New England* we found that *A* 1713 there were 194000 *l.* in Province Bills at *Par* with Silver at 8 *s. per Oz.* When we began to exceed that Sum our Paper began to loose of its Value; Here we ought to have stopt and kept within that Sum in our future Emissions."

The exact date of the publication of the " Essay " is indicated in the advertisements in the New England Weekly Journal of April 4, and April 11, 1738:

IN a few Days will be Published, An Essay concerning Silver and Paper Currencies, more especially with Regard to the British Colonies in *New England.* And will be Sold by *Kneeland* and *Green* in Queenstreet.

THIS DAY is PUBLISHED, An Essay concerning Silver and Paper Currencies, more especially with Regard to the British Colonies in *New England.* To be Sold by *Kneeland* and *Green* in Queenstreet.

The copy of the text was obtained from " An Essay," etc., in my own possession. The leaves measure 7¾ by 4⅞ inches. The facsimile of the title-page was procured through the courtesy of the Massachusetts Historical Society. Other copies of the pamphlet can be found in the American Antiquarian Society, the Boston Athenæum, the Boston Public Library, the Library of Congress, and the New York Public Library.

A
SCHEME
FOR A
Paper Currency.

 EADING in News-Papers, the laſt ſitting of the Honourable Aſſembly of this Province, of a Petition ſign'd by a great Number of the Freeholders of this Town, was preſented to the Court, for Relief under their preſent difficult and diſtreſſing Circumſtances, for want of a ſufficient Medium; whereby the Trade and Buſineſs of the Town is very much decayed, Law-Suits increaſed, and Caſh to purchaſe the Neceſſaries of Life hard to be attained, even by many of good Eſtates among them. It muſt plainly appear, to a Mathematical Demonſtration, that nothing can help or relieve this Town out of its preſent great Diſtreſſes and bad Circumſtances, but Frugality and Induſtry, and purſuing juſt and reaſonable meaſures. For any reaſonable Man living to think that the Printing a few Sheets of Paper, without the leaſt Shadow of Foundation, and calling it Money, will relieve them, they are vaſtly miſtaken, it will only lead them into a vaſt Labyrinth of Evils.

The following Scheme will appear to a full Demonſtration what vaſt Service it will be to this Town.

It muſt be allowed that a Number can perform more than a few, which is juſt and reaſonable: For the Gentlemen in *England*, *Holland* and other Parts of the Trading World, form themſelves into SOCIETIES and COMPANIES for the carry-

The copy of the text was obtained from " An Essay," etc., in my own possession. The leaves measure 7¾ by 4⅞ inches. The facsimile of the title-page was procured through the courtesy of the Massachusetts Historical Society. Other copies of the pamphlet can be found in the American Antiquarian Society, the Boston Athenæum, the Boston Public Library, the Library of Congress, and the New York Public Library.

A
SCHEME
FOR A
Paper Currency.

 EADING in News-Papers, the laſt ſitting of the Honourable Aſſembly of this Province, of a Petition ſign'd by a great Number of the Freeholders of this Town, was preſented to the Court, for Relief under their preſent difficult and diſtreſſing Circumſtances, for want of a ſufficient Medium; whereby the Trade and Buſineſs of the Town is very much decayed, Law-Suits increaſed, and Caſh to purchaſe the Neceſſaries of Life hard to be attained, even by many of good Eſtates among them. It muſt plainly appear, to a Mathematical Demonſtration, that nothing can help or relieve this Town out of its preſent great Difficulties and bad Circumſtances, but Frugality and Induſtry, and purſuing juſt and reaſonable Schemes For any reaſonable Man living to think that the Printing a few Rheams of Paper, without the leaſt Shadow of Foundation, and calling it Money, will relieve them, they are vaſtly miſtaken, it will only lead them into a vaſt Labyrinth of Evils.

THE following Scheme will appear to a full Demonſtration what vaſt Service it will be to this Town.

IT muſt be allowed that a Number can perform more than a few, which is juſt and reaſonable: For the Gentlemen in *England, Holland* and other Parts of the Trading World, form themſelves into SOCIETIES and COMPANIES for the carry-

S

Pa

A

SCHEME

FOR A

Paper Currency.

 EADING in [   ] News-Papers, the last sitting of the Honourable Assembly of this Province, of a Petition sign'd by a great Number of the Freeholders of this Town, was presented to the Court, for Relief under their present difficult and distressing Circumstances, for want of a sufficient Medium; whereby the Trade and Business of the Town is very much

decayed, Law-Suits increased, and Cash to purchase the Necessaries of Life hard to be attained, even by many of good Estates among them. It must plainly appear, to a Mathematical Demonstration, that nothing can help or relieve this Town out of its present great Difficulties and bad Circumstances, but Frugality and Industry, and pursuing just and reasonable Schemes. For any reasonable Man living to think that the Printing of a few Rheams of Paper, without the least Shadow of Foundation, and calling it Money, will relieve them, they are vastly mistaken, it will only lead them into a vast Labyrinth of Evils.

THE following Scheme will appear to a full Demonstration what vast Service it will be to this Town.

IT must be allowed that a Number can perform more than a few, which is just and reasonable: For the Gentlemen in *England, Holland* and other Parts of the Trading World, form themselves into SOCIETIES and COMPANIES for the carrying on *vast* Designs in Trade and Commerce. The *Dutch* are the only People [2] who have got Money by their first Scheme: Their Maxims are thus, when they have a Mind to bring any Manufactury into their Country, they always procure the best Workmen from that Country where that Manufactury is carried on to the utmost Perfection. Having procured Workmen, they perform to those Men their Engagements and Contracts to the least Tittle: And those Workmen finding themselves justly dealt withal, they directly bring that Manufactury to as great Perfection as it is carried on in the Country they came from. And thus from these wise Maxims, which the *Dutch* have followed, they have brought them to that glorious Figure which they now make in the World.

NOW to my Scheme. There is the compleatest Place for
for the Erecting and Building Twenty Mills on of any Place
I ever saw in my Life; it is from the Warehouse of JOB
LEWIS, Esq; near the Fortification, across to his Warehouse on *Dorchester* Point. I suppose, was it possible, that
such a Place could be procured as near *Amsterdam* as this
is to *Boston*, the *Dutch* would give *One hundred Thousand
Pounds* Sterling for such a convenient Place.

Our *Mother* Country will be much pleas'd with this
Scheme, because not one Mill will interfere with any of the
Manufactures in *Great Britain*. I shall explain the great
Benefit and Advantage of sundry of these Mills; which by
the Parity of Reason will explain the rest. It's plain to a
Demonstration, that those Corn Mills which are erected on
the Mill Pond, will in a few Years be of no Service. The
Reason is, Because the Pond fills so fast with Filth, that
there will not be sufficient Water to carry on the said Mills.
And such a fine, beautiful Tract of Land will be more fit to
build Streets of Houses on; and ten Times the Improve-
ment than they are at present employ'd in. And these Corn
Mills, (to be built on the aforementioned Place) may be
built to the same advantage as [ ] in *England*. The Corn
Mills have been vastly improved in *England* with [ ]
Twenty Years. And these Mills being built to the same
Perfection they are now built in *England*, they will grind
more Flour by six lb. Weight out of a Bushel of Wheat, and
make better Flour, than any Mill now built in *America*.
(For all the Mills now built in *America*, are built in the old
Form.) So that the Merchants of *Boston* may purchase
Wheat from the Wheat Countries, and supply the *West-
Indies* Cheaper than either *New-York* or *Philadelphia*.

For the Truth of these Facts I appeal to the Millers and Bakers of *Boston*. A Number of Saw-Mills for the Ship Builders and Joiners, they will be able to demonstrate. Leather Mills, the Gentlemen Leather-Sellers will be able to inform. Linseed Oil Mills, the Consumers of Oil will be able to inform. There being vast Quantities of Iron Bog Ore at the Eastward, Mills to run into Piggs for *Great-Britain*. Bark Mills for grinding Tanners Bark, both for home Consumption and *Ireland*, several Gentlemen will be able to inform. A Number of Logwood Mills, a Number of Merchants will be able to inform: And so by a Parity of Reason all the rest of the Mills are explained. The Place lies entirely on Water Carriage, and has a constant Supply of Water all the Summer, which is the only Time to perform Business. It has already been justly Surveyed, and a Plan taken. And was a Number of Gentlemen to be incorporated by the General Assembly, they might bring this Scheme to Perfection immediately, to the vast Service of this Town and Province in general. I can with Modesty say, this is the best Scheme that ever was on the [3] Tapis since the Colony has been settled. It is not like the Uncertainty of Mine Adventurers, but as soon as these Mills are built they will produce a certain Profit, as sure as the Sun that moves. The Corn Mills at *Bow* near *London*, with twelve Pair of Stones, are let at *Nine hundred Pounds* Sterling a Year, and I will Mathematically prove, that twelve Pair of Stones built on the abovementioned Place will produce as much Profit as the Mills at *Bow*. And such a fine Scituation for Mills cannot be better in any Place in the World. There is now an absolute Necessity for coming into a just Scheme in order to have Money pass for a

Supply of our common Necessities, till such time as by our Frugality and Dent of Industry we bring Silver and Gold to pass as a proper Medium; which was the real Design of his Majesty's Royal Instruction not to make any more Paper Bills, which is absolutely a common Cheat, let them be made in any Form or Shape whatever, without a solid Foundation to support their Value. Was a Number of Gentlemen to be incorporated, and the whole Body liable to be sued as one Man, their Notes of Hand would pass better than any Money to be made by the Province, because the Profits arising by the Mills would be a solid Foundation. I shall only mention one Company in *London*, that is the *New-River* Company, which pays them Twenty *per Cent.* Interest; then, would not the Notes of such a Company pass equal with Bank Notes, or Gold or Silver. I will Mathematically demonstrate to any Man living, that these Mills will produce Twenty *per Cent.* then consequently their Notes must pass equal to Silver and Gold. All Mechanicks are now brought to be proved by mathematical Demonstrations, so that it is impossible to err in building these Mills, for it may be computed to a single Farthing what each Mill will cost. And these Mills being built according to the Mathematicks, then it may be easily demonstrated what each Mill will produce yearly, so that the Company may proceed like wise Master-Builders. And when the above Mills are brought to Perfection, a vast Number of great Schemes may be laid before the Company, which they will naturally come into: For we have a common Proverb, *Mathematical Demonstrations can no Man gainsay.* And it would certainly be for the Interest of *New-England* not to make one Paper Bill more: The Reason is, The Notes of Hand made by the Company will

answer the Ends and Purposes of purchasing all the Necessaries of Life; and these Notes not being made a Tender in
Law, it would absolutely oblige the Merchants to bring Gold
and Silver to answer all Specialties, or else it would be impossible for them to carry on Trade and Merchandize.   For
so long as the Assembly continues to make Paper Bills the
whole Publick will depend on them.   Each Gentleman will
flatter himself he shall be able to procure as many Bills as
will answer all his Designs.   But any Man that knows the
just State of the Province must allow that according to its
present Scituation it requires a Million ready Specie to
carry on the Trade of the Province: It is therefore a meer
Jest to make a few Paper Bills, thinking that will answer
the End, it will only embarrass and entirely Ruin hundreds
of Families, and bring on Law-Suits almost numberless.   It
must be allow'd that a Merchant managed his Affairs with
Prudence and Caution, when he has brought his Trading to
such a Point that his Profits may be large, and his Loss not
considerable.   But should a Man of Traffick put *Twenty
thousand Pounds* on board a leaky Vessel, and send it to the
Spanish West-Indies, through as many Dangers as there are
Shelves in the Sea, or Points in the Compass, with the [4]
bare Hopes of gaining *Six Pence*, would not all Mankind
post up such a Merchant for a mad Man: I leave the Application.

THIS Body Politick may be justly compared to a Mer-
chant beginning the World with *One hundred Thousand
Pounds*, and directly advanceth to a Trade that requires *One
Million* ready Specie.   Notwithstanding the Merchant has
an exceeding good Character in all Parts of the trading
World, and his Credit supported a vast many Years with a

fair Shew, yet in the End it will be the intire Ruin, not only of himself, but of vast Numbers of other Men. The Reason is, It is plain that for want of a sufficient Sum to carry on his Trade, he is often obliged to part with his Goods for less than Prime Cost, besides making use of Userers and griping Extortioners, which will always Prey on him like so many Vultures or Horseleach's: And the poor honest Gentleman, so far from growing Rich for the Reward of his great Pains and Industry, not only sinks his own private Patrimony of *One hundred thousand Pounds*, but a great many Hundreds besides. His Character is entirely ruin'd in all Parts of the Trading World, and his End may be in Ruin and Want. And his Substance, with other honest Gentlemen's, who consign'd to him, got into the Hands of base unworthy Knaves, who have watched all Opportunities to take Advantage of the poor Gentleman's Necessity.

His Excellency *JONATHAN BELCHER*, Esq; our Governor, hath twice recommended to the General Assembly the employing a Number of Men to take an exact Survey of this Province, and the Extent of its Bounds. For this Province is hardly known by our Mother Country. And I can with humble Modesty observe, that the State of this Province was never yet fairly stated.

Our Mother Country never was so full of Men and Money since the glorious House of Hanover came to reign over us. And was a just Plan to be taken of this Province, and laid before the Nobility, Gentry and substantial Farmers in *England*, the young Branches will bring their Fortunes into *New-England* and purchase Lands. For it may be Mathematically demonstrated, for a Gentleman to bring to *New-England Five thousand Pounds* Sterling and lay it out in

Lands, it would in twenty Years time be worth *Thirty thou-sand Pounds* Sterling, if they are improved after the same Manner they are in *England.* For the Lands there are prodigiously improved within these Twenty Years past: For a vast Quantity of Land was then Let for *Eighteen Pence per* Acre, which are now Let for *Twenty Shillings per* Acre. And I will demonstrate to any Man living, that the Lands in *New-England* are as good as they are in *Old.*

As I am obliged to go to *England* with all my Law Suits, for want of a Court of Equity in this Country: And being forc'd to stay some Time there before I can bring my Affairs to a final Issue, I will imploy my Time to lay down before our Nobility, Gentry and Farmers THE GLORIOUS STATE OF THIS PROVINCE, and what noble Improvements they may make for their young Branches. Their Fortunes at home make but an indifferent Figure there, but if laid out in *New-England* will with industrious Improvement produce as noble Estates as the Originals they sprang from. And it is not [5] in the least to be doubted but his Royal Majesty and Parliament will encourage such a noble Undertaking, so much for the Good of OUR MOTHER COUNTRY in Trade and Commerce.

OUR young Nobility, Gentry and Farmers coming now to *New-England,* is not like the Gentlemens first Settling this howling Wilderness, at vast Expence, and the almost insupportable Difficulties. But those worthy good Gentle-men have fairly paved the Way. That as soon as our Gentry shall arrive at *Boston,* they will find no difference, either in Provision or polite Conversation, (without the least Disparagement to any Part of *Great-Britain*) for their Money may be improved Fifty *per Cent.* more than they can be in *Great-Britain*, if it is improved either in Lands or Manufactures. And I suppose further, Was not the Gentlemen of this Province to come into my Scheme of the Mills, I will lay all my Schemes mathematically before several of our Companies in *London*, and they will as certainly come into the said Scheme, as sure as the Sun that moves. For they are all so full of Money, that shew them mathematical Demonstrations, and they will venture their Substance to the Ends of the Earth; so I can with humble Modesty say, provided Almighty GOD spare my Life to bring my Projections to Perfection, to the infinite Advantage of our Mother Country, and to the great Benefit of *New-England*. For I may justly observe, this most noble Province of the *Massachusetts-Bay* is superior to any Province in his Majesty's Dominions in *America*, both for Health and to be improved. And I further observe, these young Branches of our Nobility, Gentry and substantial Farmers, bringing large Substance, would be able to procure all Sorts of Naval Stores for *Great-Britain*, and entirely prevent the *Baltick* Trade. And there is no Merchant but what knows that immense Trade, so much taken Care of by the *Northern* Princes, particularly the Czar of *Muscovy*, after he came home from his Travels, (having taken a Tour thro' *France, England* and *Holland*) observing what mighty Riches they acquired by Trade and Merchandize, and forming a just Idea of these Countries, that they could raise but small Quantities of Naval Stores; and having large Dominions, he immediately gave Orders to all his Subjects to raise prodigious Quantities of Naval Stores, and he being an absolute Prince it was immediately comply'd with: Which was the first Scheme he laid to bring forward those mighty

Schemes which he afterwards compleated. And all Mankind are Witnesses, from those just Schemes formed by him, to what a mighty Figure they make, and at present appear in the World. The Empire of *Muscovy* is in no ways to be compared with his Majesty's Dominions in *America*. And was his Majesty's Colonies to be justly improved by proper Encouragements from our Mother Country, it would make our King one of the greatest Monarchs on Earth. For it must be Men of large Fortunes to proceed on that Scheme of procuring Naval Stores, and not Beggars. For it is plain that the People at the *Eastward* can but just support Nature, by cutting Timber and Cord Wood, so it's plain to a Demonstration what Quantities of Naval Stores we may expect from those People.

FROM the whole, I most humbly conceive it would be the great Interest of this most noble Province, for the Great and General Court to pass an Act to encourage [6] our young Nobility, Gentry and Farmers to come and settle amongst us, setting forth the Goodness of the Land, and the vast Improvements they may make of their Money, and to grant them what Lands they want to improve. Suppose but one single Hundred of our young Nobility and Gentry was to come with *Five thousand Pounds* Sterling in each Gentleman's Pocket, the Moment they arrive in *Boston*, the whole Land will be worth double the Value by their coming; this can be mathematically demonstrated: But I don't doubt but Thousands of our worthy honest Gentlemen's Sons will come and settle to the utmost Bounds of this most noble Province: And then if a French War happen, King GEORGE and *Canada* forever; then his glorious Majesty King GEORGE will have a compleat Empire.

And I verily think that the Opinion of the ingenious Dr. *Mather* will certainly come to pass: For the Doctor in his Letter to one *Anthony William Boheme*, late Chaplain to his Royal Highness GEORGE when Prince of *Denmark*: The Contents of which Letter was this, That Dr. *Mather* had remitted so much Money by Bills of Exchange (collected from private Gentlemen in *New-England*) for the Propagation of the *GOSPEL* in *Mallabar East Indies*: The Money was to be sent to Professus *Frankus* at *Hall* in *Saxony*. After Dr. *Mather* had given a beautiful Description of Church Affairs, he concludes his Letter with political Affairs; and gives a fine Account of this Part of the World; and heartily lamenting the Misfortune of the *Canda* Expedition; (but wholly lays the Blame on the *Old-England* Men) for he declares, That no Men on the Earth could proceed with more Courage and Resolution than the *New-England* Men: But the Dr. concludes with this noble Saying, That I really and verily think, that in less than fifty Years, the glorious House of HANOVER will be Emperors of all *America*, and then it will be the greatest Empire in the whole World. Now to any thinking Man, the Doctor's Thoughts will certainly come to pass: For we see what a glorious Settlement is carrying on at *Georgia*, and how the English Nation are spirited to support that Province. And it is not in the least to be doubted but by proper Application to his Royal Majesty and Parliament, they would come into any Measures to make the Frontiers of this Province a strong Barrier against *Canada*; and then if the *French* and *Spaniards* dare to go to War with *Great-Britain*, so certain we shall take *Canada* and the *Spanish West-Indies*, which will put a final End to all the Villanies committed on us by the *Spaniards*, and there is no true *Englishmen* but hopes and wishes to see that Day.

The worthy ingenious Capt. *Plaisted* informed me he had received a Letter from Mr. *Silas Hooper*, Merchant in *London*, dated *October* 8. 1738. wherein he informs him, That the *Pot-Ash* remitted from *New-England* to him, was allowed to be as good as that Pot-Ash which comes from *Russia*. It appeared by our Book of Entries, there was upwards of Two Thousand Tuns imported from the Northern Kingdoms in one Year: And Pot-Ash being worth *Thirty Pounds* per Ton, (the said 200 Tons at 30 *l.* per Ton, amounts to *Sixty Thousand Pounds*) And as the Pot-Ash pays to his Majesty *Six Pounds* per Ton Duty; I do not doubt in the least for the Encouragement of this Manufactury in these Parts, by properly applying to [7] the Parliament for the Drawback to be taken off, it would be done, and a Royal Bounty granted: And the Gentlemen of this Province coming to a just Way of thinking, they might flow in Riches as they please. And these Gentlemen or Society that are concerned in the aforementioned Mills, might directly bring this Scheme of the Pot-Ash to Perfection; and what glorious Farms would be produced from this Scheme of Pot-Ash?

I had almost forgot to mention one more great Benefit to this great Town of *Boston* in the building these Mills, which all Mankind must allow to be just; that is thus, Suppose it should happen a War, by having such a fine Communication with the Castle, we might soon supply that Fortress with Ten Thousand brave Fellows that would face any Enemy on the whole Earth. And by this Scheme the great Town of *Boston* may be made impregnable. We may see to what a glorious Spirit the English Nation are arrived to, in improving every Thing that's possible to be done for the Good of the Publick; witness the advancing 700,000 *l.* towards building a Bridge from *Westminster* across to *Lambeth*; and there is no Gentlemen, that are thinking Men, but knows the Profits arising by Tole of the said Bridge will not bring in more than Two per Cent Interest; but they all know it's for the Good of their Country, therefore they see it necessary it should be done notwithstanding the Insufficiency of the Premium for such a vast Undertaking. Therefore as the aforementioned Mills can be mathematically proved, to produce Twenty per Cent. it will be look'd upon in England, if it is not done, that the Gentlemen of this Country do not consult their own Interest and the general Good the whole Country will reap therefrom. And for any Person or Persons to send Home any dismal Complaint of the State of the Province, it will be look'd upon as only noisy Faction and Clamour.

I have been always surprized to think what vast Improvements have been performed by the Gentlemen of this Province in one Century. But now, provided our young Nobility, Gentry and Farmers come over, with their Pockets full of Money, what vast Improvements may be expected in the next Century.

I don't in the least doubt but these fifteen Colonies will arrive to as great a Pitch of Glory as those fifteen Provinces of *China.* And as Sir WILLIAM TEMPLE observeth, it must be allowed to be the greatest, richest and most populous Kingdom now known in the World; and will be found perhaps to owe its Riches, Force, Civility and Felicity to the admirable Constitution of its Government, more than any other. The Empire consists of fifteen several Kingdoms, which are govern'd by Vice-Roys, who yet live in Greatness, Splendor and Riches, equal to great and sovereign Kings. In the whole Kingdom there are 145 Capital Cities, of mighty Extent and magnificent Buildings; and 1321 lesser Cities, but all walled round; the Number of Villages is infinite: And no Country in the whole World is so full of Inhabitants, nor so improved by Agriculture and Manufacturies, by infinite Growth of numerous Commodies, by Canals of incredible Length, Conjunction of Rivers, by Convenience of Ways for the Transportation of all Sorts of Goods from one Province to another; so as no Country has so great a Trade.

THERE is a vulgar Error, to the vast Damage [8] of this Province, that the *New-England* Oak is far inferiour to the Oak in *Old England*; and the Error has so long prevailed that it's now really allowed by all Sorts of People to be Fact: And the only Reason I find to Support this Opinion is, that the Ships built in *New-England* will not last so long as those built in *Old*: I grant what they say. Those Ships that have been hitherto built, are not so good as those built in *England*. The Reason is plain to a Demonstration why they are not so good, The People that procure the Timber cut it down in Season and out of Season, for they are obliged to eat it as fast as they cut it. The Ship Builders are poor, and the Merchants will always keep them so, according to the present Scheme they act by; so that it cannot be expected, from the solid Reason of things, these People can build with regular season'd Stuff I can with Modesty say, I understand the just and true Nature and Goodness of Oak, as well as any Man living. And I am fully determined to prove, before the Commissioners of his Majesty's Royal Navy, that there is as good Oak in *America* as any in *Old England.* And that it would save his Majesty some *hundred thousand Pounds* Sterling, by building Fourth, Fifth, and Sixth Rate Men of War in *New-England.* I am certain of destroying this vulgar Error concerning the Oak, and with as much Pleasure as *Daniel* destroyed *Bell* and the *Dragon.* For the English Nation are arrived to a fine Method in polite Reason and Thinking. For in the present Age, no Man that has or really pretends to have the least Shadow or Foundation of common Reason, will by any Means be Hoodwink'd, but shew him mathematical Demonstration and he will come into your Scheme directly, so that any Man that Grounds his Hypothesis on solid Truth will certainly gain his Scheme.

I humbly make bold to make use of an Observation of a worthy, learned Gentleman, who is look'd upon by all Men in the Province to be a Gentleman of solid Knowledge and Learning, he lately wrote an Essay concerning Silver and Paper Currencies; and it is allowed to be compleatly done: He observeth thus on a private Bank. Private Credit, or Notes on a good solid Foundation, are better than publick Bills; the former cannot impune or break their Faith, (they are a Coerusion) the Publick is the Dernier Resort, and in bad Administrations frequently break their publick Faith. Hence the Credit of a well regulated Commerce or Corporation, is better than that of the Civil Administration. The Bank Money at *Venice* is 20 *per Cent.* better than common Currency. This private commercial Credit in all polite Nations is so sacred at present that the Civil Government stands corrected by it. The Generallity of the

United Provinces did *Anno* 1693, Coin alloy'd Pieces, called *Quaad Sckellings*, at 6 Stivers each, being near 10 *per Cent.* above their intrinsick Value.   The Bank retain'd their Integrity, and it again rose to 13 and 15 *per Cent.* this obliged the Government to reduce these *Sckellings* to 5 and half Stivers, their intrinsick Value, and have continued so ever since.   And the Agio of the Bank fell to 3 or 5 *per Cent.* as formerly.   *Anno* 1720, *France* being in the most dismal Confusion by their Paper Currency, their Court was obliged to apply to the Merchants and Bankers for their Advice, concerning a Method to be used to find out the natural Proportion between publick Bills and Silver Species, and to Limit their proper Effects to a certain Sum; a plain Illustration that private is better than publick Credit.   We have among our selves our Merchants [9] Notes, so called, being well founded, were 11 and half *per Cent.* in *December* 1737; will be 18 *per Cent.* in *December* 1738; 12 and half *per Cent.* 3 7ths of them then paid off, in *December* 1739; 19 and half *per Cent.* in *December* 1740; 26 and half *per Cent.* in *December* 1741; and 34 *per Cent.* in *December* 1742, better than the present Value of our Province Bills at 27 *per Cent.* because they are continually growing better until they come to their fix'd Value, at which they are to be paid off.   Thus it will be with these Notes made by the Company for the Building these Mills.

THE worthy Gentleman very justly observeth further, When Paper Money is in a continued Course of depreciating, all Debts and other Contracts, are paid in less Value than they are contracted for: which is an unjust, but natural Operation of this false Medium.   The generous foreign Adventurer or Merchant, and consequently Trade in its genuine

Sense, is hurt; the Shopkeeper and Merchant Hucksters, who have a long Credit from their Merchants and abuse this Credit Industry and Frugality, the only Means of growing rich, are turned aside; in the Place of being industrious, the young Men, called Gentlemen, follow no other Business but Drinking and Gaming; many in Quality of Shopkeepers become Drones; Tradesmen, of all Occupations in *Boston*, loiter away much of their Time; the Husbandmen, in the Country, spend many idle Days in their little Rum Taverns. Frugality is superceeded by Prodigality and Extravagancy, as is too apparent in fine Houses and Furniture, Chaises and other Equipages, Velvets, Scarlets, rich Silks and Laces. Thus far saith that learned and ingenious Gentleman, the Author of the Silver and Paper Scheme.

FROM the whole of this Scheme I observe, and will make it appear to any Gentleman or Body of Gentlemen, that these Mills aforementioned, will produce *Twenty thousand Pounds* neat Profit each Year. But this Scheme is a small trifling one to what I have by me. And as I have drawn all my Schemes to be proved by the Mathematicks, and all Mankind perfectly knowns that Figures will not lye, if rightly placed. And I don't doubt having the Approbation of all solid, wise judicious and thinking Men in all Nations of the trading World. For there is no Parts on the whole Earth, where Money is to be got and improved, more than what is to be got in his Majesty's Provinces in *America*. I shall endeavour, to the utmost of my Power, to forward the Establishment of a Bank, on such a Footing as to bring the wise Men in all the trading Nations to be concerned in it. And I do not in the least doubt of having his Royal Majesty's Approbation, and that great and dernier Resort, our great and august Parliament of *Great Britain,* which Assembly is now the Glory of the whole Earth.

WE may see what a noble Harmony there is between the Parliament and our most gracious KING, by the bottom Clause of his Majesty's Speech, which he recommends thus,

My Lords and Gentlemen,

I cannot but earnestly recommend it to you, not to suffer any Prejudices or Animosities to have any Share in your Deliberations at this important Conjuncture, which seems in a particular Manner to call upon you to unite in carrying on such Measures as will be most conducive to the true Interest and Advantage of My People.

[10] THE most noble LORDS Answer to his Majesty is full of Duty.

We are deeply sensible how unbecoming and pernicious it would be at any Time, to suffer either Prejudices or Animosities to mix themselves with parliamentary Deliberations: And your MAJESTY'S *gracious Recommendation to us particularly to avoid them at this importunate Conjuncture, cannot fail to awaken in us a more than ordinary Caution on that Head.* Great-Britain *hath but one common Interest consisting in the Security of your* MAJESTY'S *Person and Government, and the Welfare and Happiness of your People. And when your* MAJESTY *is pleased to exhort us to Unanimity it is only calling upon us to unite to our own Preservation. We therefore beseech your* MAJESTY *to accept the strongest and most affectionate Assurances, that we will zealously and cheerfully concur in all such Measures as shall be most condusive to those great and desirable Ends.*

THUS answered our most noble LORDS, which is like

Apples of Gold in Pictures of Silver, and a glorious Pattern for all his Majesty's Subjects.

AND as Sir ROBERT LE ESTRANGE justly observeth, Let Error, Corruption or Iniquity be never so strong, never so popular, let the Ignorance of things necessary to be known be never so dark and palpable, we may yet assure our selves, That however Truth and Justice may suffer a temporary Eclipse, they will yet at the long run as certainly vindicate themselves, and recover their original Glory, as the setting Sun shall rise again.

P. S.   *Cum sit alioqui multo deformius,*
          Amittere quam non assequi Laudem.
              Plin. Ep. Lib. 8.
                  I am,
                      Gentlemen,
                          Your most obedient
                              humble Servant,
          Boston Goal, going onward Two Years
              of my unjust Confinement.
                  April 19, 1739.
                                      Richard Fry.

                          [11]

                  POSTSCRIPT.

SINCE the finishing this Scheme, the worthy and ingenious Capt. CYPRIAN SOUTHACK made me a Present of the *New-England Coasting-Pilot.* And as I am informed, the Motive that induced him to make me this Present, was his hearing that I was drawing the present State of the Province: he was willing to forward such an Undertaking as much as lay in his Power. As it is allowed by all Mankind, that Ingratitude is as bad as the Sin of Witchcraft, therefore I think it my Duty to return Capt. SOUTHACK my most hearty Thanks for the Present of his *New-England Coasting-Pilot*, in this publick Manner. And all the Gentlemen of this most noble Province ought to know what a just Value our late most glorious King WILLIAM shew'd Capt. SOUTHACK, for this his noble Undertaking. The following Order of his Royal Majesty will demonstrate it.

At the Court at *Whitehall* the 26th of *February*, 1694.

PRESENT,

The King's most Excellent Majesty in Council.

WHEREAS Capt. CYPRIAN SOUTHACK, *who has been for several Years employed by the Government of* New-England *at Sea, and has performed divers signal Services in several Expeditions; having this Day had the Honour to Kiss his Majesty's Hand; presented to his Majesty a Draught of* New-England, Newfoundland, Nova-Scotia, *and the River of* Canada, *and the Seas and Territories thereunto adjoining, made by himself in the said several Expeditions: His Majesty taking into his gracious Consideration the said* CYPRIAN SOUTHACK, *and for his further Encouragement, is pleased to Order as is hereby ordered the Sum of* Fifty Pounds, *to be paid to him for the Buying a Gold Chain and Medal, as a Mark of his Majesty's Royal Favour; and that the Right Honourable the Lords Commissioners of the Treasury do give all necessary Directions for the speedy Payment of the said Sum.*

JOHN NICHOLIS.

You plainly see what a just Sense of the Merits of this Gentleman his Royal Majesty conceived. And I must humbly observe to the Gentlemen of this most noble Province, that they could not express their just Value and Esteem for our great Deliverer, our late most august and glorious King WILLIAM, than by erecting to his Memory his Majesty's Statue on Horseback, erected on a Pedestal, and placed before the Town House facing *King Street*: And there is not one Man in the Province, that is a Lover of Liberty and Property, but what will contribute towards such a noble Undertaking. The Gentlemen of *Ireland* have, notwithstanding the famous Monument in the City of *Dublin*, erected soon after, and in Memory of his Majesty's glorious Actions, further to perpetuate the same, erected another of glorious Structure in the great River of *Boyne*, where the chief Scene of their Deliverance was, by the Almighty's assisting his Majesty's Arms, fully compleated. From this glorious Example I hope the Gentlemen of this most noble Province will not be wanting to erect a Trophy of Honour, in Memory of him they have express'd so great a Value for by Words; but as for Words we all know they cost nothing. As for the worthy and ingenious Capt. SOUTHACK, I have not heard that he has received any Gratuity by way of Bounty for his great [12] Labour and Pains in serving this most noble Province. Mankind nothing more imitates almighty God, than by rewarding those that lay out their Powers and Faculties in serving Mankind, This *Coasting Pilot* gives me a just Idea of the Coast of his Majesty's Provinces from *New-York* to the Bay of *Funday*. The very Islands are able to contain Millions of People; which absolutely destroys that vile selfish Principle of some People which say they are not for Strangers coming amongst them, because they shall not have Land enough for their Children; which is really a childish Story.

UPON moderate Computation the Gentlemen Farmers have borrowed on Bond and Mortgages upwards of *Five hundred thousand Pounds;* of which the greatest Part is let at 10 *per Cent.* And according to the present Scituation of Affairs, it is impossible for those Gentlemen to pay off their Securities: So that a Gentleman that has Mortgaged his Form for 500*l.* that is worth 2000, his Farm on Prosecu-. tion is certainly forfeited for want of the 500*l.* And it is impossible it should be otherwise whilst the griping Usurers Monopolizes into their own Coffers, the Bulk of that small Quantity of running Specie that is now Extant amongst us. And as the old saying is, The just Value of any Commodity whatever, is what it will fetch. The only Remedy to avoid this great Evil, is for the Assembly of this Province, as I observed before, to lay just Schemes, to perswade and allure our young Nobility, Gentry and Farmers to come and settle among us; and it's not to be doubted, but these Gentlemen would purchase the Farms of those Gentlemen that have involved themselves, and are now in a State of Bondage; and they may put Money sufficient in their Pockets to proceed on the Settlement of new Farms on the out Lands, with Resolution and Vigour. And in a few Years, by common Industry, they will have as good Farms as they at first parted with, and an entire Freedom from the grand Oppression they then labour'd under. And upon the Arrival of a Number of our young Nobility and Farmers, with a Quantity of Money, it would make it a Year of Jubilee for all those Gentlemen that now labour under the present grand Oppressions. For all Gentlemen well knows what a vast Number of Farms must be put to Sale in few Years; And no Purchasers can appear to buy of these Country People: The Reason is, because they will not have Money to pay for them. And further, I observe to the Gentlemen Shopkeepers not to purchase large Quantities of English Goods, for some time, till the Ballance of Trade is brought to a more fix Standard; for it may be mathematically proved, that as certain as any Man buys large Quantities of Goods, so certain he will be ruined: For as some Gentlemen have lately got Estates by the prodigious Rise of Goods, so certainly some Men will be ruined by their great Fall; which will come to pass, as sure as the Sun that moves.

I must observe, by way of Comfort, to the Gentlemen that labour at present under great Oppressions, that we have a common saying, *A desperate Disease must have a desperate Cure*; but if more pacifick Measures can be found out, it will be vastly more pleasing to this Body Politick. For as Harmony and sincere Love are the just Foundation of all Happiness both in this World and the World to come, and as our General Assembly are the proper Physicians, it is not in the least doubted but they will make a sound Cure of this Body Politick, and lay a solid Foundation of Happiness for the rising Generations. And what more noble and grand than to lay great Designs for future Ages to copy after; which will be lasting Monuments of Praise to our great Assembly.

NOTE TO "A SCHEME FOR A PAPER CURRENCY."

One copy alone is known to have been preserved of "A scheme for a paper currency," and this has found its way into that great collection of Americana at Providence, Rhode Island, the John Carter Brown Library. To the courtesy of that institution we are indebted for our copy of the text and for the facsimile of the first page, which is reproduced in reduced form. The pages of the original measure 12¼ by 7⅞ inches.

A curious interest attaches to this production owing to the fact that it is dated from the Boston gaol, and was sent forth by a prisoner confined there for debt, who was then in the second year of his imprisonment. Richard Fry, the author, signs his name to the publication and gives as the date of its birth April 19, 1739. In May, 1739, on the 28th of the month he published the following advertisement in the Boston Gazette:

THIS is to inform the Publick that there is *now in the Press, and will be laid before the Great and General Court, a Paper Scheme, drawn for the Good and Benefit of every individual Member of the whole Province ; and what will much please his Royal Majesty ; for the Glory of our King is the Happiness of his Subjects* : And every Merchant in Great Britain *that trades to* New-England *will find their Account by it* ; *and there is no Man that has the least Shadow of Foundation of Common Reason, but must allow the said Scheme to be reasonable and just* : *I have laid all my Schemes to be proved by the Mathematicks, and all Mankind well knows, Figures will not lye* ; *and notwithstanding the dismal Idea of the Year* Forty One, *I don't doubt the least seeing of it a Year of* Jubilee, *and in a few Years having the Ballance of Trade in Favour of this Province from all Parts of the Trading World* ; *for it's plain to a Demonstration by the just Schemes of* Peter the Great, *the late Czar of* Muscovy, *in the Run of a few Years, arrived to such a vast Pitch of Glory, whose Empire now makes as grand an Appearance as any Empire on the Earth, which Empire for Improvements, is no ways, to be compared with his Royal Majesty's Dominions in* America.

I humbly beg Leave to subscribe myself,
A true and hearty Lover of New England,
Richard Fry.

Boston Gaol May, 1739.

The published "Scheme" bears date April 19, 1739. According to the advertisement of May 28, the "Scheme" was then in press. These two dates a month and upwards apart show a protracted period of preparation, altogether inconsistent with the amount of press work required for the production. This may perhaps be explained by the situation of the author. He had money enough, even though imprisoned for debt, to pay for advertisements, but very likely he found difficulty in providing for the pamphlet itself in addition. In June, however, the assembly became excited at the currency situation, and were influenced by what Fry terms "the dismal Idea of the Year Forty-one." It was close at hand.

Stimulated by the pressing needs of the province for some addition to the circulating medium, over and above what would be furnished by the bills of public credit which were permitted to be emitted for the current expenses of the government, the maximum amount of which to be kept in circulation after 1741 under the royal instructions was limited to £30,000, the representatives, instead of attacking the question of procuring a supply of silver, thought in June, 1739, only of substituting other bills for the bills of public credit. They declared that bills of credit were the only medium of commerce in the province and voted " that a committee be appointed to receive in the recess of the court any scheme or proposals from any persons whomsoever for the furnishing a further medium of trade, in such way and manner, as that the value may be maintained." [1]

The appeal to " any persons whomsoever" was broad enough to include an imprisoned debtor and in June, 1739, Fry addressed himself to the governor and council. It is probable that he submitted his scheme to the representatives at the same time, but at any rate the evidence that he addressed himself to the governor and council remains on file in the archives.

The following is the language of Fry's proposal: [2]

---

[1] Currency and Banking in Massachusetts Bay, Vol. II, pp. 130–131.

[2] The typography follows the method adopted by the Editor of the fifth reprint of the Club for Colonial Reprints of Providence, Rhode Island.

To His Excellency Jonathan Belcher Esq^RE

Cap^T Generall & Governour in Cheife in and over his majesties Province of the Massachusetts Bay in New England & To the Honourable his Majesties Councill.

Worthy & Honourable Gentlemen

I Have Humbly made bold To Lay before you a small scheme ; and as theire is an absolute nessesity for the Gentlemen of this province to come into a Just Scheme for a paper Currency till such time as by frugallity and Dent of Industry Silver & Gold be brought to Pass Amongst us as A Medium, it's plaine to a Demonstration. If the Gentlemen will unite ; they may Directly Emitt such a sufficient Sum by notes of hand, and upon such a solid footing as to be Equall to Gold or Silver, theire is no Person of this Honourable Board, but knows the dismall State the Seven United provinces were Reduced too, not many Ages since ; butt they all united as one man and pursewed Just & Reasonable Schemes and with Indefaticable Industry, hath brought them to make that Glorious figure they now Appear in the world ; they had all theire Ruff Materialls to produce from Other Countrys for theire Manufactury's, butt it is not so with us, we haveing them all within our Selves ; and If the Gentlemen of this province will proceed with the Same vigour and Resolution as they did may in the Run of A few years Arrive to As Great A Pitch of Glory as the United States of Holland, and I Dont Doubt of seeing the New England Company make as Great a figure as the East India Company in Holland, which Boasts of Haveing Subdued more Leagues of Country then there are Acres of Land in all Holland, of haveing Thirty Thousand Souldiers & A Vast number of Ships in its Service of Employing Commonly one hundred Thousand men.

May it Please your Honours haveing nothing more to add, only wishing that Allmighty God will Inspire you with the Same Noble & Generous Resolution and Courage As Guided the States of the once poor, Low & Distressed States of Holland, butt now the most high and mighty ; which is the Earnest and Hearty Prayer

of your Honours most Humble
and Obedient Servant at Command
Richard Fry

Boston Gaol
June
1739

It is not likely that much attention was paid to the scheme by the assembly, for at that very time Fry was pestering them with petitions

for relief in connection with his law suits, and hearings were from
time to time being held. The name of Fry attached to a communication under these circumstances was not likely to secure for it any
very great consideration.

Setting aside any discussion of the plan to rely upon a great in-
dustrial enterprise for the currency of the province, vaguely set forth
in the scheme, one cannot refrain from recognition of the foresight
of the author in his suggestions as to the future of the old Mill
Pond. "Such a fine, beautiful Tract of Land," he says, "will be
more fit to build Streets of Houses on; and ten Times the Improvement than they are at present employ'd in." He quotes from
Douglass's "Essay on silver and paper currencies," and one statement in Douglass's text requires notice. With suitable explanation
the language employed may in this instance be justified, but at the
hands of others the phrase used has caused the commission of error.
Allusion to it has already been made elsewhere, but the reader may
or may not have made note of it. Douglass is in this instance
speaking of the increase in value of the Merchants' Notes of 1733.
These notes had their value expressed in weights of silver at a fixed
price per ounce, and were payable in instalments, three tenths in
three years, three tenths in six years, and the remaining four tenths
in ten years. In the "Scheme" itself the payment of the instalments was described as follows: "Three Tenth Parts at the End of
the first Three Years, Three Seventh Parts of the Remainder, at the
End of the first Six Years; and the whole of the Residue at the End
of the aforesaid Ten Years." The Weekly Journal of the 17th of
September and the News Letter of the 20th of September, 1733,
both described the notes as "three Tenths at the end of the first
three Years, three Sevenths at the end of the first Six Years, and the
rest at the end of ten Years."[1] The dropping of the words "of
the remainder" from the words describing the time of payment of
the second instalment completely changed the character of the plan.

In the quotation from Douglass which has brought about this
necessity for an explanation, the author says, speaking of the second

---

[1] The Merchants' Notes of 1733, reprinted from the Proceedings of the Massachusetts Historical Society, April, 1903, p. 24.

payment on the Merchants' Notes, "⅜ths of them then paid off," which clearly is wrong if he was speaking of the entire emission. Douglass was writing, however, at a time when the first instalment was past due, and the possible justification of his language would consist in the inference that his allusion was to the amount of the notes then outstanding.   Three tenths having been paid off, three sevenths of the remainder was equal to three tenths of the whole. This absurd fraction, used by Douglass, then recently seen in my examination of the "Scheme," led me, with full knowledge that it had been the downfall of others, to make use of it in my description of the notes given in the Introduction to Fry's "Scheme," printed by the Club for Colonial Reprints,[1] of Providence, Rhode Island, where they are said to have been payable three sevenths in three years, three sevenths in six years, and the balance in ten years. The sevenths should of course be tenths.

Notwithstanding the fact that the fifth reprint of the Club for Colonial Reprints, just above referred to, contains an account of Fry's career in Boston and describes the litigation which was the cause of his confinement in the Boston gaol, it is desirable to say something about him in this note.

Richard Fry was an Englishman, who describes himself in an advertisement as "Stationer, Bookseller, Paper-Maker, and Rag Merchant." Winsor in the Narrative and Critical History of America alludes to him as a printer.[2]   Winsor probably got his information from Thomas, who practically says that all that he knows about the matter is derived from an advertisement in the Weekly Rehearsal in which Fry says "I have Printed the most beautiful Poems of Mr. Stephen Duck."[3]   Fry was obviously a scheming adventurer, who launched plans and suggested enterprises from which he hoped to make himself and others rich.   It is not necessarily to be inferred from his being found in gaol that he was dishonest.   His letters clearly indicate that he believed himself to have been persecuted. It is as paper-maker rather than printer that he figures in the scenes

---

[1] Page xxviii.
[2] Narrative and Critical History of America, Vol. V, p. 137.
[3] History of Printing, Vol. II, pp. 432–433.

of his life which are revealed to us. According to his own statement, he arrived in this country in 1731, and not long after his arrival he published an advertisement containing directions for gathering rags. October 17, 1734, he says in another advertisement, "it is now almost three years since I published an advertisement," etc., thus fixing the date of his first public announcement that he was in the market for paper stock. We know nothing of the advertisement in the fall of 1731, which must have been published very shortly after his arrival in this country, except that it contained directions to the public for gathering rags. This however is of some importance as it indicates in which direction his business thoughts were then turning. What that direction was is also shown by the direct statement made in the advertisement relied upon by Thomas as authority for classing him as a printer, which was inserted in the Weekly Rehearsal [1] published in Boston May 1, 1732, and which reads as follows:

T*HIS is to give Notice, That* Richard Fry, *Stationer, Bookseller, Paper-Maker & Rag Merchant from the City of* London *Keeps at Mr.* Tho. Fleet's, *Printer, at the Heart & Crown in* Cornhill, Boston ; *where the said* Fry *is ready to accommodate all Gentlemen Merchants and Tradesmen with Setts of Accompt Books after the most neatest Manner.* And whereas *it has been the common Method of the most curious Merchants in* Boston, *to procure their Books from* London. *This is to acquaint these Gentlemen,* that *I the said* Fry *will sell all sorts of Accompt Books done after the most acute Manner, for Twenty* per Cent. *cheaper than they can have them from* London. I *return the Publick Thanks for following the Direction of my former Advertisement for gathering Rags, and hope they will still continue the like Method, having received upwards of Seven Thousand Weight already. For the pleasing Entertainment of the Polite part of Mankind, I have Printed the most beautiful Poems of Mr.* Stephen Duck; *the famous* Wiltshire *Poet. It is a full Demonstration to me, that the People of* New-England *have a fine Taste for good Sense and polite Learning, having already Sold* 1200 *of those Poems.*

Rich. Fry.

It will be observed that Fry does not describe himself as a printer in this advertisement. He calls himself, amongst other things, a book-seller, and it was probably as such that he "printed" Stephen

[1] The same advertisement in the New England Weekly Journal, April 24, 1732.

Duck's poems. At any rate the only copy of Duck's poems that Sabin found bears the following imprint: "Boston. Printed and Sold by S. Kneeland and T. Green. 1732." The volume was advertised in the New England Weekly Journal, March 27, 1732, as follows: Stephen Duck's Poems "to be sold by S. Robinson in Marlborough Street over against the South Brick Meeting-House."

This venture in the publishing line on the part of Fry was followed by an attempt at another of a more pretentious character which was to be based upon subscriptions and which was specifically set forth in the New England Weekly Journal of June 5, 1732, in the following language:

This is to Acquaint the Publick, that I have Printed a Specimen of a new Sett of Letters, lately Imported from *London*, on which I propose to print the SPECTATORS by Subscription, at *Three Pounds* the Sett, neatly Bound; and that the Publick may be intirely satisfied, the Subscriptions in *Boston* are to be taken in at the Office of Mr. *Joseph Marion*, Notary Publick, & Deposited in his hands. It will be needless to acquaint the Learned and Polite part, that nothing more demonstrates the fine Genius of a Country, than to have the curious Art of Printing brought to Perfection, wherein the present Age have Opportunity to convey their Ideas in fine Characters to succeeding Ages. The vast Returns the Dutch make only in this Branch of Trade is most prodigious, for they Print for all the Known parts of the World; and it was really the *Grand Oppressions* they suffer'd that gave them that Keen Edge, to such a pitch of Industry, as hath brought them to make that glorious Figure they now make in the World: Therefore the Rod is sometimes very Convenient to reform Commonwealths of those things which would certainly be destructive of their Happiness: and there is no way of bringing any Commonwealth out of any Calamity but Industry, and jointly to promote every Art and Science that has the least view of being useful to the Publick: Therefore I don't doubt but every Gentleman that is a true Lover of his Country will Subscribe. And I justly flatter my self I shall have a Number of Ladies Subscribers, the Authors of these Books having always been justly esteem'd among them.   *Richard Fry*

N. B. Subscriptions will be taken in at *Newport, New-York, Philadelphia, Piscataqua*, and *South-Carolina*, and after Three Hundred Subscriptions, the work to be committed to the Press, and finish'd with all possible Expedition. 20 *s.* to be paid at Subscribing, & 40 *s.* at Delivery.

These two advertisements indicate plainly enough that Fry, finding that the paper-making business was not likely to develop as rapidly as he had hoped, then turned his attention to publishing, in which the minor success achieved with the 24-page edition of Duck's poems led him to embark upon the more ambitious enterprise which has just been set forth. Since there is no known Boston edition of the "Spectator" of that date, we may assume that his scheme failed, but out of this activity came some reward. There are claims set up by Fry in some of his suits that he was induced to come to this country as a paper maker with the promise of employment. His advertisement containing directions concerning the collection of rags, and his announcement that he had already gathered in seven thousand pounds, would indicate a belief on his part that there would be in the near future some place where he could use them. Whether this be so or not, we find him in 1734 treating with two Maine capitalists for the establishment of a paper mill in Maine. Samuel Waldo, one of these capitalists, was the owner of an extensive domain in the district of Maine, having within its limits water power and saw mills. Thomas Westbrook, the other, owned lands on the Stroudwater just west of Falmouth, a place now known by the name of Portland. Negotiations ensued between Waldo and Westbrook on the one part and Fry on the other which resulted in the lease by them of a paper mill on the Stroudwater to Fry, the term of which began, as appears in the papers in the suit against Fry, on October 14, 1734. On the 17th of that month, Fry inserted the following advertisement in the Boston News Letter:

To the Inhabitants of the Great Town of *BOSTON:*

IT is now almost Three Years, since I Published an Advertisement, to shew you the excellent OEconomy of the Dutch, in the Paper Manufactory, in order to induce you to follow so laudable an Example; but I am sorry to say, I have had *but small Effects of as yet: When Gentlemen have been at great Expense to serve the Public, as well as their own private Interest, it is the Duty of every Person, as much as in them lies, to help forward so useful a Manufactory; Therefore I intreat all those that are Lovers of their Country, to be very careful of their Linnen Rags, and send them to* Joseph Stocker *in* Spring-Lane, *Boston, and they shall receive ready Money for the same.*

Richard Fry.

This advertisement was repeated November 8, and actually meant business. Fry was in charge of a paper mill and had use for the rags which he was collecting. Then follows a sequel much of the sort that might have been predicted. He made some paper ; got behind on his rent; was sued; judgment was rendered against him in the lower court; he appealed; lost his appeal, and, August 9, 1738, execution was issued against him. If the suit was commenced with arrest, he was then a prisoner in Boston gaol. During his imprisonment his restless spirit kept courts, assemblies, the gaol itself, and all places where his influence could reach, in lively commotion.

One gleam of light was shed upon his life while in confinement. He won a suit, and at once hastened to announce the fact to the Boston world through the medium of the newspapers. The New England Weekly Journal of August 22, 1738, contains the following :

THIS is to Acquaint the Great Town of *Boston* and all those that are Lovers of Justice, and Haters of Cruelty and Oppression that the Case between Mr. *Joseph Plaisted* High Sheriff for the County of *York* Plantiff, and *Richard Fry* late of *Falmouth* Defendant ; after a Tryal of twelve Hours, the Jury brought in their Verdict for the Defendant Eight Hundred Pounds Damages and Costs of Court. It was on a Review.

I can with Pleasure acquaint the Publick, that my Scheme for Erecting sixteen sundry Sorts of Mills, from Mr *Job Lewis's* Wharfe- near the Fortification, to his Warehouse on *Dorchester* Neck, the Plan hath been laid before a Number of Gentlemen of solid Judgment and judicious Understanding, and they all allowed the Scheme appeared to a full mathematical Demonstration and the only Means to help this now distressed Country out of a Number of its many Difficulties. Next Thursday Evening at 5 o'Clock, a Number of Gentlemen are to meet at the Green Dragon near the Mill Bridge, any Gentleman that hath the least Objection against this Projection, may come and be heard. I beg leave to subscribe my self a true Lover of Liberty and Property.

Richard Fry

From his cell in the gaol Fry summons the citizens of Boston to meet and discuss his plans for settling the currency question. His advertisement does not show this fact, but, when he addresses his proposals to the governor and council, he dates them at the Boston gaol. Such was the man and such were the principal incidents which connect him with the subject under discussion. Many details concerning his law suits and prison life which cannot be reproduced here are to be found in the fifth publication of the Club for Colonial Reprints of Providence, Rhode Island. The advertisements of June 5, 1732, October 17, 1734, and August 22, 1738, have been unearthed since that publication appeared.

THE

NUMB. 663.

New-England *Weekly* JOURNAL.

Containing the moſt Remarkable Occurrences Foreign & Domeſtick.

TUESDAY January 1. 1740.

To the Publisher of the WEEKLY JOURNAL.

Boston, Dec. 28. 1739.

S I R,

Several Gentlemen being disposed to come into the following Scheme, it is published that such Others as shall think it will be for the common Interest, may know and [   ] *in it.*

Yours, *&c.*

*W*HEREAS *the Silver and Gold, which formerly were our Medium of Exchange have been exported to our Mother Country, in Payment for the Manufactures we have received from thence; and for many Years our Affairs and Business have been transacted with Bills of Credit in Lieu thereof. And for as much as the Bills of Credit emitted by the Province of the* Massachusetts-Bay, *are grown scarce by their Return into the Public Treasury, according to the Periods that have already arrived, and in a short Time the Remainder is by Law required to be bro't in and consumed to Ashes; and whereas it seems very difficult, if not impracticable, so suddenly to procure Silver and Gold sufficient for the Management of our Trade and Commerce,*

THEREFORE, for Remedy in this Case, We the Subscribers have agreed on the following Articles, *viz.*

THAT as soon as conveniently may be, there be
emitted *Three Hundred Thousand Pounds* in
Bills or Notes of Hand of the following Denominations *viz Two Hundred Thousand Pounds*
in *Ten, Seven, Five* and *Three Pound* Bills, *Eighty Thousand Pounds* more in *Forty, Thirty, Twenty,* and *Ten Shilling* Bills ; the remaining *Twenty Thousand Pounds* in
*Eight Shilling and Six penny, Six Shilling and Six penny,
Three Shilling and Six-penny,* and *One Shilling and Six-
penny* Bills, all to be redeemed and paid with coined Silver
of Sterling Alloy, at *Twenty Shillings* per Ounce, or coined
Standard Gold at *Fourteen Pounds fifteen Shillings* per
Ounce both Troy Weight by the last Day of *April,* Anno
Domini, One Thousand seven Hundred and fifty five.

II. Fifteen Gentlemen shall be chosen by the Subscribers, to be a Committee or Directors in this Affair, who
shall sign the Bills or Notes, and become obliged to the
Possessors or Proprietors of them, not less than Eight of
which Directors shall sign each Bill of the largest Plate, not
less than Six those of the middle Plate, nor less than Four
those of the smallest Plate, the Tenour of which Bill shall
be as follows, *viz*

20 S.   20 S.

*We jointly and severally promise, for our selves our Heirs,
Executors, and Administrators, to pay
or Order in* Boston, *one Ounce of coined Silver Sterling
Alloy, or thirty two Grains and an Half coined standard*

Gold, both Troy weight by the 30*th of* April, *Anno Domini,* 1755 *Value received.* Boston, New England, March 31 1740.

20 S.   20 S.

III. To enable the Directors or Signers of the Bills to redeem or pay them as before, and defrey the incident Charges, every Subscriber or Undertaker for *One Thousand Pounds*, shall Annually during the space of Fifteen Years from April 30*th* 1740, Pay to the said Directors, Eighty eight Ounces and an half of Silver, or six Ounces of Gold, both of the quality respectively, and weight as aforesaid; and shall execute fifteen Bonds accordingly, and every Undertaker for a less or greater Sum, shall be obliged to pay in proportion, the Bonds to be made payable in each Year by the 30th day of *April*; nevertheless it is understood and agreed, that the said Directors may Covenant with, and shall accordingly execute Instruments to the Undertakers, That in as much as the said Directors will have great occasion for Silver or Gold one Month sooner annually, than the Undertakers are obliged by the aforesaid Bonds to pay them) They the said Directors will accept of Sixty seven Ounces & an half of Silver, or Four Ounces eleven penny weight and thirteen grains of Gold both of the respective quality and weight aforesaid, from the Undertaker of *One Thousand Pounds*, if he shall pay them annually by the thirty first of *March*; and the Directors may agree with the Subscriber or Undertaker for a less or greater Sum to pay in the same proportion.

IV, The Security to be given by the Undertakers or Subscribers and Borrowers shall be made to all the aforesaid

Directors or Signers of the Bills or Notes, except what is given by any of the Directors, which shall be made to the Remainder of the Directors. The Security both from Undertakers and Borrowers to be either Real or Personal to the acceptance of the Directors: if it be Personal, there shall be two sufficient sureties with the Undertaker or Borrower, all bound jointly & severally, if the security be Real, it shall be Land worth double the Sum it is mortgaged for, exclusive of all Buildings, and other things being and growing upon it, and the Mortgager, if an Undertaker, shall give fifteen Bonds for the payment of the several annual Sums as aforesaid, and his Mortgage as a colateral security for the payment and discharge of those fifteen Bonds; if the Mortgager be a Borrower of Silver or Gold herein after mentioned to be let out, he shall give his Personal Bond for the same, and the Mortgage as a colateral security for the Bonds discharge.

V. Every Subscriber or Undertaker shall be come obliged to the aforesaid Directors to indemnify and save them harmless, as to any damage they may sustain in redeeming or paying the said Notes or Bills to be Emitted, or in letting out the Silver or Gold as herein after directed, or by any deficiency or other neglect of the Company or either of them, the said Damages or Deficiencies to be paid or made up in proportion to each ones Subscription.

VI. Whereas at and after the Expiration of the first of the aforementioned fifteen Years, there will be considerable Sums of Silver or Gold in the hands of the Directors, it is agreed and Covenanted, that the said Directors may let or hire out the said Silver or Gold to such Inhabitants of this Province as shall desire the same for the space of thirteen

Calendar Months and no longer at one time, the Borrower giving full and undoubted Security for the Payment of it within that Term, with Interest at the Rate of six per Cent. per Annum: Nevertheless it is agreed and concluded that if the said Directors shall judge that they shall have Occasion for said Money sooner than the said Bond specifies, they may agree to give any proper Instrument to the Borrower to secure & assure him, that upon paying the Sum borrowed with Interest at the Rate of four per Cent. per Annum, so much sooner than by Bond he is obliged, as the Directors Occasions require, and the Instrument they give the Borrower specifies, his Bond shall be delivered up to be cancelled.

VII. The Directors shall keep fair Accompts of their Doings in the Service of the Company, and the Company shall meet annually on the first Monday in *May* at some suitable Place in the Town of *Boston*, of which they shall have convenient Warning from the Directors if in *Boston*, or within four Miles, when and where they shall lay before the Company the State of the Company's Affairs from Year to Year, and at the Expiration of the aforesaid Term of fifteen Years, shall deliver and pay to each Subscriber or Undertaker his Executors or Administrators his proportionable Part of all the Net Profits of the aforesaid Emission of Notes, and of their letting or hiring out the Silver or Gold aforesaid, or any other way arising from the Company's Interest as aforesaid.

VIII. No person shall be chosen a Director unless he subscribes or undertakes at least for *One Thousand Pounds*, and whosoever is chosen shall before he enter on the Service covenant and agree that in Case of his Death or that an other is chosen in his Stead, he the said Director his Heirs, Executors or Administrators will resign to the Company or their Order every Thing in his Hands belonging to the Company as soon as may be, not exceeding one Month after his Death or Removal: And it is hereby agreed and to be understood that the Company may at any annual Meeting in *May*, during the first fourteen Years of the Term of fifteen Years aforesaid, if they shall find it needful chuse one or more new Directors in the room or stead of one or more who were Directors before; the Company giving sufficient Security to indemnify the deceased or removed Director or Directors his or their Heirs, Executors and Administrators from all Damages which may arise from what he or they may have done in the Service or at the Desire of the Company.

IX. No person shall subscribe or undertake for less than *five Hundred Pounds* nor more than *ten thousand Pounds*, and every Subscriber for *five hundred Pounds* shall have one Vote, and all the other Subscribers shall vote in proportion; but it is to be understood that no Person who by Purchase Inheritance or otherwise may be Owner of more than *ten thousand Pounds* shall have more than twenty Votes how great soever his Interest may be.

X. Whereas, we are very apprehensive, that the receiving and passing the Bills of the Neighbouring Governments, which have not any good Foundation to secure their Value, promiscuously & indifferently with these, will greatly prejudice this Province, and very much tend to depreciate these Bills, tho' on the most sure Bottom; and whereas the Law of this Province prohibits the receiving and passing any Bills emitted by the Neighbouring Governments in the

Year 1738, or that shall hereafter be emitted not founded on, or redeemable by Silver or Gold; and whereas the Government of *Rhode-Island* have emitted a large Quantity of such prohibited Bills, dated 1738, and if these should pass currently, may go on to emit more of such ill founded Bills; wherefore we the Subscribers agree & promise, that we will neither directly nor indirectly by our Selves or any for us, receive any Bills dated 1738, emitted by *Rhode-Island*, nor any Bills that shall be emitted hereafter by the Neighbouring Governments unless redeemable by Silver or Gold, and that we will carefully and diligently inform of and prosecute all Persons whomsoever, that shall receive or pass any such prohibited Bills; and as to Bills emitted before the Year 1738, by the Neighbouring Governments, we agree and promise that we will either totally refuse such Bills for Debts due and in Trade, or otherwise receive and pass such sorts of them and with such Allowance or Discount as this Company shall agree upon by major Vote from Time to Time, at two Meetings yearly, one in the Month of *May*, and the other in the Month of *November*, and will do every other thing as much as in us lies to make this Emission a common currency, and prevent these Bills being hoarded up or depreciated.

XI. Every Subscriber or Undertaker shall be obliged at the Desire or Demand of the Company or Directors to give such further and better Security as they shall judge needful.

XII. The Directors may call a Meeting of the Company at any Time when they shall judge it needful, giving due Notice thereof, and shall be obliged to call a Meeting at any other Time when the Undertakers of one Quarter Part of the Sum emitted by the Company shall desire it by writ-

ing under their Hands signifying the Occasion of their
Desire : and it is agreed and understood that in every
Meeting of the Company before they shall be capable of
acting there shall be present either in Person or by Proxy
in Writing under the Hands of the Undertakers so many as
shall make one Third Part of the original Subscription.

XIII. The Directors shall be allowed and paid
per Annum, for their Service besides their Allowance for
signing the Bills, and shall be allowed a Clerk or Clerks,
and other Officers as shall be judged needful, who shall be
paid by the Company.

XIV. The Directors shall from Time to Time take Care
that every Undertaker Subscriber and Borrower fully comply with his Obligation, and on Failure shall forthwith put
his Bond or other Obligation in Suit.

XV. The Company may at their annual Meeting in *May*
make such By Orders and Rules as they shall judge for the
Benefit of the Company and at any other Meeting, provided
Notice be given of the Rule or Order desired in the Warn-
ing for the Meeting, always provided that no such Rules or
Orders shall be any Way inconsistent with any Article or
Articles in this Scheme, which are hereby declared to be
fundamental and unalterable.

XVI. The Directors shall let to Hire no Silver or Gold
belonging to the Company at any Time in the two last
Years of the aforesaid Term of fifteen Years, and shall at
the Expiration of the fifteenth Years of said Term, pay to
every Possessor or Proprietor of a *Twenty Shilling Bill* or
Note of the aforesaid Emission, one Ounce of coined Silver
of Streling Alloy or thirty two Grains and an half of coined
standard Gold, and to every other Possessor or Proprietor

of a less or greater Sum in the same Specie and Proportion at their delivering the said Bills or Notes to them the Directors, upon which they shall be consumed to Ashes in the Presence of said Directors and a Committee for that Purpose specially appointed by the Company.

XVII. Every Subscriber or Undertaker shall have Liberty for the first thirteen Years of the aforesaid Term of fifteen Years in Lieu of Silver or Gold, to pay, in Flax, Hemp, Iron, Copper, Tanned Leather, or Sail Duck, which Commodities shall be disposed of by the Directors for Silver or Gold Coin as aforesaid, the Directors taking two and half per Cent. for their Trouble, and upon the Expiration of the annual Term of Payment taking Bond of such Subscribers for the Sums due in the same Manner as of other Borrowers, and as soon as the Commodities are converted into Silver or Gold, indorsing the Sums they fetch, on the Bonds they have given as Borrowers.

XVIII. The Company may at any annual Meeting in *May* release a Subscriber or Undertaker, his Executors or Administrators at his or their Desire, on his or their bringing a Person to their Acceptance to stand in his or their stead, and perform his or their Obligations.

To the Publisher of the WEEKLY JOURNAL.

SIR,

THE distressed State of the Province and this Town in particular for want of a proper and sufficient Medium of Exchange has of late been the common Subject of Conversation, and has also stirred up several Gentlemen of a

Schematizing Genius, to exercise their Skill in finding out some happy Expedient to redress our growing Difficulties.

No less than 6 or 7 *Schemes*, I think, have been exhibited in publick Print, wherein the Authors, however different in their Sentiments, have, I doubt not, sincerely endeavoured to promote our common Welfare. —— I shall by no Means presume to make any Observations or Remarks on the Performances of Gentlemen, in Understanding so much superior to my self; but in order to introduce my Design, I shall make one Observation, wherein I am sure of the Concurrence of every reasonable Man; *namely*, That no Scheme whatsoever, or howsoever wisely calculated, can *alone* bring us out of our present Embarrasments, but that together with the best projected Schemes we must join both *Industry* and *Frugality*, as Means absolutely necessary in order to obtain the desired Relief: For by *Frugality*, we shall gradually lessen our Consumption of the Growth of other Countries; and by *Industry* we shall proportionably increase the valuable Produce of our own. However, it is I think, acknowledged by all, That *some* Medium of Trade is absolutely necessary; in as much as tho' it be not altogether impracticable to carry on an extensive Commerce in a Way of Truck or Barter, yet we know that such a Method of Trade will be forever attended with great Unrighteousness and Oppression, it being in the Power of every Man in his Turn, [ ] over reach and oppress his Neighbor[] That we think *some* Medium to be necessary, is evident from our greedily takin[ ] such great Numbers of the *Rhode-Isla*[ ] Bills, which derive their Value chiefly not wholly from the Currency we ha[ ] been pleased (or rather necessitated) to gi[ ] them. And as a proper Medium is t[ ] only one we can expect in our present C[ ]cumstances, so it is doubt-less our Wisdo[ ] to furnish ourselves with one that is agre[ ]able to the best Schemes we can projec[ ]

In erecting a Bank of private Cred[ ] (and we have no Prospect of Relief a[ ] other Way) the following Points are to [ ] carefully regarded. First, that the Bills o[ ] Notes be of some real and substantial V[ ]lue; I mean that they promise somethin[ ] certain on which the Possessors may depend, tho' at a distant Period; this I think is necessary to their obtaining a genera[ ] Currency. In the next Place, that they be well guarded against the *voracious Grip* of the *Hoarders*, lest they take the same Turn as the Merchants Notes, which in Fact never were a Medium of Trade, (I had almost said, never design'd to be) but have eventually prov'd such a Snare to so many Persons, and perhaps will yet be *Bitterness in the latter End* —— And lastly, that there be proper Encouragement for the Undertakers to carry on so good a Work; for we cannot reasonably expect that Gentlemen of large Substance will encumber their Estates without a Prospect of considerable Advantage to themselves.

Agreeable to these important Hints, the following Scheme is offered to Consideration.

First, It is propos'd, That 100,000 *l.* in Bills or Notes be struck off, of the following Denominations, and no other [ ] vi[ ] 5 *l* 3 *l.* 40 *s.* and 20 *s.*

That every Subscriber first pay in 1 per Cent. in the present passing Bills to defray the Charge of carrying on the Work.

That the Subscribers take out in Notes but two Thirds of the Value of their Lands (exclusive of Houses) which they shall Mortgage to the Managers or Directors (call them which you please) for the Use of the Society.

That no Person take out more than 3000 *l.* nor less than 200 *l.*

That the Subscribers pay to the Treasurer annually for every 100 *l.* 4 Ounces of Silver or Gold in proportion.

That the Managers and Officers be as few as may be to prevent Charges.

That Meetings and Votes be regulated by the Society.

By this Scheme it appears, that at the Expiration of twenty Years, there will be 80000 Ounces of Silver, or Gold equivalent in the Treasurer's Hands, equal to 120000 *l.* of our present Bills to pay out to those who shall then be possess'd of these Notes. This will be a charming Bait indeed to allure the *Hoarders!* And therefore our next Care must be if possible to prevent them.

In order to which as it is apparent that these Notes will annually rise in Value, so the Subscribers must strictly bind themselves to take them at higher Rates as the Grand Period draws on. Therefore it is propos'd, that the Tenor of these Notes or Bills shall be as followeth; *viz.*

No. ———   V *l.*

We the Subscribers, in behalf of ourselves and the rest of the Society do promise, That we will receive this Bill of Credit in all our Trade and Commerce, at the several Times and Rates herein expressed; namely, *From the tenth of* April 1740, *to the tenth of* April 1745, *for* five Pounds five Shillings, *Province Bills; from thence to the tenth of* April 1750 *for* five Pounds ten Shillings; *from thence to the tenth of* April 1755, *for* five Pounds fifteen Shillings; *and from thence to the tenth of* April 1760, *for* six Pounds *of the Bills aforesaid. At which Time the Possessor hereof shall receive of the Treasurer 4 Ounces of Silver or Gold proportionable.*

The Bills of the lesser Denominations, must be of the same Tenor, according to their respective Value.

It remains now in the last Place, that we enqaire into the *Profits* that will result to the Undertakers, according to this Scheme. And here it is propos'd, that the Silver or Gold which is annually paid in, may again be let out to Interest; but then, the utmost Care must be taken, that it be on Security as cannot possibly fail. This second Interest, from the End of the second Year, to the End of the eighteenth, will amount to 32480 Ounces of Silver, or 48720 *l.* in Province Bills; as the Curious may inform themselves, by making a Computation. And when the eighteenth Year is compleated, it is propos'd, that the whole Silver or Gold be secured in the Society's Treasury, ready to be paid out to the Possessors of the Bills, at the Expiration of the grand Period, which will be *then* near approaching — This 48720 *l.* will be intirely for Undertakers, and enable them to sustain some Loss (if any should arise) from unforeseen Fluctuations that may possibly happen; tho' it is to be hop'd Silver will never exceed 30 *s.* per. Ounce.

Thus, I have offer'd some Tho'ts (rude and undigested as they are) on a Subject which, I confess, **is** somewhat forreign to the common Course of my Studies and Business in the World. —— If my Sentiments are disapprov'd, and my Scheme has the Misfortune to be *damn'd*, I hope I shall patiently share the Fate of better Men. — And I am sure, no Man will envy me the Happiness of these Reflections, —— That, had I any Interest in the World, it should fall a willing Sacrifice *to serve the Publick*: —— That what I have here offer'd, *was honestly design'd*, without the least Prospect of personal Advantage or Applause.

Yours &c.

Boston, Dec. 27. 1739.

NOTE TO TWO COMMUNICATIONS IN THE NEW ENGLAND WEEKLY JOURNAL OF JANUARY 1, 1740.

On the 18th of March, 1739–40, a committee of the general court was appointed "to investigate the several projections for emitting notes." The scheme contained in the first of the foregoing communications published in the New England Weekly Journal, January 1, 1740, was one of the projections which caused the appointment of this committee. The paper-money advocates had been aroused by the comprehensive nature of a resolution passed by the house of representatives June 28, 1739, in which provision was made for the appointment of a committee "to receive in the recess of the court any scheme or proposals from any persons whomsoever for the furnishing a further medium of trade, in such a way and manner, as that the value thereof may be maintained." This awakening was shown by the presentation to the general court at a session begun December 5, 1739, of a petition for a Land Bank, which was headed by John Colman, with whose name we are already familiar as an advocate of a paper-money currency, and which was signed by nearly four hundred other persons. The petitioners desired incorporation. A broadside was issued by the managers of the enterprise dated March 10, 1739–40, in which the details of their proposed Land Bank were set forth, and on July 30th the company organized by electing officers, there being at that time upon their subscription lists the names of more than eight hundred subscribers. Ultimately the number reached upwards of a thousand. It being evident that it was impossible for the Land Bank to secure a charter from the government, the company proceeded in August to emit bills and to transact business as a mere partnership. On the eighth day of September, 1740, the directors of the company executed an instrument in which the meaning and intention of their scheme were set forth in twenty-three articles.

The form of the bill proposed to be emitted was not set forth in this document. Specimens of the bills which have been preserved show that they were in the nature of promises on the part of the subscribers to the scheme to receive each bill for its denominational value " at six shillings and eight pence an ounce " and to pay the same at that estimate to Mr. Joseph Marion, or order, at any time after twenty years from the date, September 9, 1740, in the produce or manufactures enumerated in the scheme. The bills were all endorsed in blank by Joseph Marion, and the list of articles in which they were ultimately to be paid was to be found in the third article of the scheme and was repeated in the first subdivision of the second section of the sixth article of the same.[1] The organization was to be composed exclusively of borrowers and the interest of the separate individuals of which it was to be formed was measured by the amount of their borrowing. The price of silver on the market was then between twenty-eight and twenty-nine shillings an ounce in old tenor. The circulation of the bills was probably effected on this basis, although this discount was hardly an offset for the postponement for twenty years of a payment, which could then be made in produce.

The hard-money men of the province, in their several movements to secure a return to specie payments, or to check the upward flight of the price of silver, had not been aggressive. Their several plans had been suggested as defensive operations to protect the community from the hazards of existing evils. For that reason it is fair to assume that the preliminary movement towards the organization of what was known as the Silver Bank was not for the purpose of securing profit through the circulation of the notes, but with the intention of supplanting the emissions of the Land Bank with something on a better foundation. A contemporaneous writer, speaking of the Silver Bank, says: " This Scheme appears to have taken its Rise from the *Land Bank* Scheme, and indeed to have been formed

---

[1] Currency and Banking in Massachusetts Bay, Vol. II, pp. 268, 270. A form for a bill was suggested in the preliminary broadside issued by the company March 10, 1739–40, *Ibid.* p. 133.

upon near the same Plan. . . ."[1]   It will be seen from the dates heretofore given that the preliminary announcement of the scheme for a Land Bank was made public March 10, 1739–40, while the matured scheme published by the directors was dated September 8 of the same year.   If we turn to the reprint of the first communication in the Weekly Journal[2] of January 1, 1740, we find that the date of the preliminary proposition of the Silver Bank was December 28, 1739, while the matured scheme, if we accept the date given on the face of the bills as the probable date of that instrument, was executed August 1, 1740.[3]   It thus appears that both in preliminary organization and in perfected scheme the Silver men anticipated the Land Bank men.   This seems to militate against the suggestion of the priority of the Land Bank scheme and apparently makes the attitude of the Silver men aggressive and not merely defensive. The more prompt action of the advocates of the Silver Bank, when once aroused, was, however, to be explained by the fact that they were smaller in numbers, were nearly all Boston men, were more homogeneous, and, as a body of men, were more intelligent. Seeing that their adversaries had gone so far that they must go farther, they took the field and anticipated them in the completion of their work.   The scheme of the Silver Bank as finally adopted closely resembled the preliminary proposition given above.   Changes of phraseology, changes of dates, and changes of amounts were made in different articles.   The amount of bills to be emitted was cut down from £300,000 to £120,000 and the tenth article was very decidedly mollified in tone.   The nineteenth and twentieth articles were added, the former being an attempt to provide for the currency of the bills at the constantly changing values caused by the changes in the silver rate which would necessarily take place during the term of the bills in consequence of their phraseology.   The

---

[1] An Account of the Rise, Progress and Consequences of the two late Schemes, etc., 1744, p. 7.

[2] The Scheme was also published in the Gazette of the 7th of January.

[3] A copy of the Scheme taken from the General Magazine and Historical Chronicle for January, 1741, is given in Currency and Banking in Massachusetts Bay, Vol. II, pp. 277, 286.

twentieth article was merely an agreement of the subscribers to sustain the bills according to the terms of their issue.

The price of silver when the bills were issued was 28 *s.* 4 *d.* an ounce. This measure of value is in "old tenor," in which bills all values were then stated. The bills of the Silver Bank were emitted on this valuation of silver. They ran for fifteen years and were then payable in silver at the rate of 20 *s.* an ounce. That is to say, if a person had in his possession August 1, 1740, 28 *s.* 4 *d.* of these bills, the equivalent of an ounce of silver, and if he retained the bills until the 31st of December, 1755, when they were redeemable, he could get his ounce of silver with 20 *s.* of the bills and would have 8 *s.* 4 *d.* left over, which was convertible into silver on the same terms. All of the bills were drawn payable December 31, 1755, and all were payable to the order of Isaac Winslow and were endorsed in blank by him.

We are able to find traces of the progress of the organization during its earlier stages·in the newspapers of the day. Advertisements showing that twice each week agents would be in attendance at certain hours at the Orange Tree in Boston to receive subscriptions were inserted in the New England Weekly Journal, January 15, 22, 29 and February 5, 1740.

There was no special provision in the preliminary proposition, published in the Weekly Journal of January 1, 1740, for a recognition by the company of the constantly appreciating value of the bills while in circulation, due to the fact that they were emitted at one specie value and were to be redeemed at another. The nineteenth article in the scheme was framed to cover this point. A schedule of appreciation from year to year, covering the duration of the bills, was constructed, and by the terms of the nineteenth article the subscribers to the scheme agreed to receive the bills according to the terms of that schedule. It was thought that this agreement between the subscribers was not adequate to protect possessors of the bills not subscribers, and under the influence and persuasion of Governor Belcher an additional instrument was executed by the directors of the Silver Bank November 5, 1740,[1] in

[1] Currency and Banking in Massachusetts Bay, Vol. II, p. 287.

which the directors asserted that they would at all times comply with the terms of the nineteenth article and would on demand exchange and give in bills of common currency to any and all possessors of their bills according to that article.

The second communication in the Weekly Journal of January 1, 1740, which is reprinted above, is from a person who admits that six or seven schemes for the relief of the currency situation have already been promulgated by "Gentlemen of a *Schematizing Genius.*" Nevertheless, he has another proposition to offer even though the subject " is somewhat foreign to the common Course of my Studies and Business in the World." His project is like all those of which we have had cognizance in connection with the proposals for relief at this time, an organization to be composed exclusively of borrowers. They were to emit bills running from £5 to 20 s. in denominational value, payable twenty years after date in silver at the rate of 30 s. an ounce. The bills were in the form of an agreement between the subscribers to the scheme, to receive their own bills in trade on a sliding scale of appreciation, expressed in the case of the five pound bill as follows: during the first five years from the date of the bill, it would be received in lieu of five pounds and five shillings in province bills; during the second five years for five pounds and ten shillings of the same bills; during the third five years for five pounds fifteen shillings. The bill contained a promise that at the end of the twentieth year the possessor should receive for the bill, which would then be worth six pounds in province bills according to the scheme, four ounces of silver.

To meet the expenses of organization subscribers were to be assessed one per cent of their borrowings, and they were to pay for their borrowings four ounces of silver per annum for each hundred pounds borrowed. The writer furnishes calculations to show that the scheme, in his opinion, would be feasible and profitable.

The copy of these two communications was obtained at the Boston Public Library, the original being damaged in places indicated by square brackets.

DISCOURSE

Concerning the Currencies

OF THE

British Plantations

IN

A

which the directors asserted that they would at all times comply
with the terms of the nineteenth article and would on demand
exchange and give in bills of common currency to any and all
possessors of their bills according to that article.

The second communication in the Weekly Journal of January 1,
1740, which is reprinted above, is from a person who admits that
six or seven schemes for the relief of the currency situation have already been promulgated by "Gentlemen of a *Schematizing Genius.*"
Nevertheless, he has another proposition to offer even though the
subject is somewhat foreign to the common Course of my Studies
and Business in the World." His project is like all those of which
we have had cognizance in connection with the proposals for relief at
this time, an organization to be composed exclusively of borrowers.
They were to emit bills running from £5 to 20 s. in denominational
value, payable twenty years after date in silver at the rate of 30 s. an
ounce. The bills were in the form of an agreement between the
subscribers to the scheme, to receive their own bills in trade on a
sliding scale of appreciation, expressed in the case of the five
pound bill as follows: during the first five years from the date of
the bill it would be received in lieu of five pounds and five shillings
on present bills. During the second five years for five pounds and
ten shillings of the same bills; during the third five years for five
pounds fifteen shillings. The bill contained a promise that at the
end of the twentieth year the possessor should receive for the bill,
which would then be worth six pounds in province bills according
to the scheme, four ounces of silver.

To meet the expenses of organization subscribers were to be
assessed one per cent of their borrowings, and they were to pay for
their borrowings four ounces of silver per annum for each hundred
pounds borrowed. The writer furnishes calculations to show that
the scheme, in his opinion, would be feasible and profitable.

The copy of these two communications was obtained at the
Boston Public Library, the original being damaged in places
indicated by square brackets.

A

DISCOURSE

Concerning the Currencies

OF THE

Britiſh Plantations

IN

America.

Eſpecially with Regard to their PAPER MONEY*:*

More Particularly,

In Relation to the Province of the

Maſſachuſetts-Bay,

IN

NEW ENGLAND.

By Douglaſs

BOSTON: Printed and Sold by S KNEELAND & T. GREEN, over againſt the Priſon in Queenſtreet. 1740.

A

DISCOURSE

Concerning the Currencies

OF THE

Britiſh Plantations

IN

America.

Eſpecially with Regard to their PAPER MONEY:

More Particularly,

In Relation to the Province of the

𝕸𝖆𝖘𝖘𝖆𝖈𝖍𝖚𝖘𝖊𝖙𝖙𝖘-𝕭𝖆𝖞,

IN

NEW ENGLAND.

BOSTON: Printed and Sold by S KNEELAND & T. GREEN, over againſt the Priſon in Queenſtreet. 1740.

A Diſcourſe concerning the Currencies of the British Plantations in *America* &c.

THE many *Schemes at present upon the Anvil in* Boston, *for emitting enormous Quantities of Paper Currencies; are the Occasion of this Discourse. The Writer does not vainly pretend to dictate to Government, or prescribe to Trade; but with a sincere Regard to the publick Good, has taken some Pains, to collect, digest, and set in a proper Light, several Facts and Political Experiences especially relating to Paper Currencies; which tho' plain in themselves, are not obvious to every Body. If any Expressions should sound harsh, they are not to be understood as a Reflection upon this Province in general: It was always my Opinion, That the Province of the* Massachusetts-Bay, *is by far the most vigorous and promising Plant (with proper Cultivation) of all the British Plantations; in the best of Countries at Times, bad Administrations, and private evil Men of Influence have prevailed. The Author is not a transient Person, who from Humour or Caprice, or other Views may expose the Province; but is by Inclination induced, and by Interest obliged to study the Good of the Country.*

[4] All Commerce naturally is a *Truck Trade*, exchanging Commodities which we can spare (or their Value) for Goods we are in want of. *Silver it self is a Merchandize*, and being the least variable of all others, is by general Consent made the *Medium of Trade*. If a Country can be supposed to have no Dealings but within it self; the Legislature or tacit Consent of the People, may appoint or receive any Currency at Pleasure: But a trading Country must have regard to the universal commercial Medium, which is Silver; or cheat, and trade to a Disadvantage: It is true, that in some Countries of Europe *Billon* (a base mixture of Metals) is used for small Change, but not as a Medium of Trade.

Every Country or Society have their own peculiar Regulations, which may be called their *Municipal*, or By-Laws in Trade: but the universal trading Part of the World, as one tacit Confederacy have fallen into some *general Rules*, which by Custom of Merchants are become as Fundamental: One of these is a *Silver Medium of Trade*, that all Contracts (Specialties excepted) are understood to be payable in this Medium, being always of the same fixed Value, or easily adjusted by the *Par*, and accidental small Differences of Exchange from one Country to another.

There can therefore be no other proper *Medium* of Trade, but Silver, or Bills of Exchange and Notes of Hand payable in Silver at certain *U'sos* or Periods, which by a currant Discount are reducible to Silver ready Money, at any Time. The Debitor Party (I am ashamed to mention it) being the prevailing Party in all our Depreciating-Paper-Money Colonies, do wickedly endeavour to delude the unthinking Multitude, by perswading them, that all Endeavours of the Governour, or Proposals and Schemes of private Societies, to introduce a Silver Medium, or a Credit upon a Silver Bottom, to pre-[5]vent the honest and industrious Creditor from being defrauded; are Impositions upon the Liberty and Property of the People.

Depreciating of the Value of *nummary Denominations*, to defraud the Creditors of the Publick and of private Persons; by Proclamations of Sovereigns, by Recoinages, and by a late Contrivance of a depreciating Paper-Credit-Currency; were never practised but in notoriously bad Administrations.

All over *Europe* for many Ages preceeding the 14th Century, the *nummary Pound*, and the *Ponderal* or Pound Weight of Silver were the same: but in some following Ages in bad Administrations the Values of nummary Denominations were gradually reduced; as in *England* to 4 oz. Silver value (upon all Occasions I use the nearest round Numbers) one third of its original Value; in *Holland* the Pound *Ulams* (6 Guilders) to 2 oz. Silver being only one sixth of its original Valuc. A general Stop has been put to those notorious publick Frauds ever since Trade began to flourish; the civil Governments becoming more polite, found it their Interest in Affairs of a *Medium* of Trade, to be advised by the more knowing and experienced Traders: Thus, since the Reign of *Edward* VI. *in England*, the Shilling Denomination hath lost only 2 gr. Silver. We have two or three Instances of late in *Europe*, that have deviated from that *Maxim* of a fixed Value of Silver in Trade; these were in arbitrary Governments, under most arbitrary Administrations. 1. *France by Recoinages* from A. 1689, to the wise Administration of *Cardinal Fluery*, was obliged to defraud the Subject, to maintain unjust Wars and Rapines upon its Neighbours, and lessen'd the Value of nummary Denominations from a *Mark* of Silver at 27 *Livres* to 80 *Livres*. 2. *The King of Spain* A 1688 lowered his Denominations 25 *per Cent.* a heavy Piece of *Eight* formerly 8 *Ryals* Plate, passed for 10 *Ryals* [6] currant. 3. *Sweden* under the Administration of Baron *Gortz*.

In all Sovereignties in *Europe* where *Paper-Money* was introduced, great Inconveniencies happened; upon cancelling this Paper Medium all those Inconveniencies did vanish. 1. In *Sweden, Baron Gortz*, by imposing *Government Notes* (and *Munt tokyns*) reduced the People to extreme Misery (this was one of the principal Crimes alledged against him when he suffered capital Punishment) but these being called in, and the *Coin* settled upon the same Foundation as it was before *Charles* XIIth Accession, *Sweden* flourished as formerly. 2. The late *Regent of France*, by the Advice of Mr. *Law*, did form a Project *A.* 1720, and by his arbitrary Power, endeavoured to put it on Execution; to defraud State Creditors and others, by banishing of Silver Currency, and by substituting a *Paper Credit*: the Effect was, the greatest Confusion, and almost utter Subversion of their Trade and Business: The *Remedy* was (Mr. *Law* having sneak'd off, became a *Profugus*, and at last died obscurely) after a few Months the Court of *France* were obliged to ordain, that there should be no other legal Tender but Silver-Coin; and Commerce has flourished in *France* more than ever. At present, under the wise Administration of Cardinal *Fleury* (who allows of no Paper Currencies, nor Re-coinages, which had the same Effect in depreciating nummary Denominations in *France*, that frequent and large Emissions of Paper-Money have in our Colonies) their

Trade bids fair to outdo the Maritime Powers (as *Great Britain* and *Holland* are called) and has a much better Effect in advancing the Wealth and Glory of *France*, than the *Romantick* butcherly Schemes of Conquest over their Neighbours, under the Administrations of *Richelieu, Mazarine* and others, in the Reigns of *Lewis* XIII and XIV.

3. In *Great Britain* A. 1716, were current [7] four and a half Millions of Pounds Sterling in *Exchequer Notes*, being the largest Quantity current at one Time: although they bore about half of legal Interest, and not equal to one third of the concomitant national Silver Currency; they laboured much in Circulation, and the Government to prevent their being depreciated, was obliged to give considerable *Premiums* to the *Bank* for cancelling some of them, and circulating the remainder.

It is not easily to be accounted for, how *England, France* and *Holland*, have tacitly allowed their several *American Colonies*; by *Laws* of their several Provinces, by *Chancerings* in their Courts of Judicature, and by *Custom*; to depreciate from Time to Time, the Value of their original Denominations, to defraud their Principals and Creditors in *Europe*. The *British Plantations* have not only varied from Sterling, but have also very much varied from one another; to the great Confusion of Business, and Damage of the Merchant. This will appear plain by inserting at one View the State of the Currencies in the several British Plantations; whereof some are per *Exchange*, some in *Spanish Silver* Coin, and some in *Paper Money* called Colony or Province Bills of publick Credit.

Originally and for some Years following in all the *English American Colonies*, 5 *s.* Denomination was equal to an English Crown Sterl. after some Time *Pieces of Eight*, being the general Currency of all foreign American Colonies, became also their Currency; and they remitted or gave Credit to the Merchants at Home (by Home is meant *Great Britain*) a Piece of Eight (value 4 s. 6 d. Sterl.) for a Crown or 5 s. Sterl. *this was a Fraud of* 11 *per Cent.* In sundry of our Colonies were enacted Laws against passing of light Pieces of Eight; these Laws not being put in Execution, *heavy and light Pieces of Eight passed promiscuously;* and as it always happens, [**8**] a bad Currency drove away the good Currency; heavy Pieces of Eight were ship'd off. This current Money growing daily lighter, a Difference was made between heavy Money which became Merchandize, and light Money in which they paid their Debts gradually from 10, 15, 20, to 25 per Cent. as at present in *Jamaica: this was another and continued Course of cheating their Creditors and Employers at Home.* From a Complaint of Merchants and others dealing to the Plantations; Q. *Anne* by Proclamation, and the Parliament of Great Britain afterwards by the *Proclamation Act*, ordered, that after *A.* 1709, *A heavy Piece of Eight and other Pieces in Proportion to their Weight, in all our Colonies should pass not exceeding* 6 s. *Denomination.* This Act continues to be observed in none of our Colonies, excepting in *Barbadoes*, and *Bermudas. Virginia* Currency was formerly, and continues still better than what the Act directs.

In *NEWFOUNDLAND*, all large Sums are transacted in *Sterling Bills of Exchange*; small Dealings are in *English Coin* Sterling Value, and in *Pieces of Eight* at 4 s. 6 d. being the Sterling Value.

In *NOVA SCOTIA :* The *Sterling Bills of Exchange* on the pay of the Troops, Garrison, and Train, Supply there with what they may have occasion for from *New England :* Small Dealings are in *New England publick Bills, and in French Coin* from Cape *Breton ;* one *Livre* equal to 4 s. New England Currency: at *Canso* Fish and Oil are purchased by *Bills of Exchange New England* Money upon *Boston.*

In the four Colonies of *New England,* viz. *New Hampshire, Massachusetts Bay, Rhode Island* and *Connecticut,* their Currency being Paper, is promiscuously the same.

[9] *NEW HAMPSHIRE* (too diminutive for a separate Province, of small Trade and Credit) their *Publick Bills are so much counterfeited* they scarce obtain a Currency; hence it is (the Governour's Instruction is also a Bar) that at present, their outstanding Bills of publick Credit, some on Funds of Taxes, some on Loan, do not exceed *l.* 12;000, gradually to be cancelled by *December* 1742. Their ordinary Charge of Government is about *l.*1500 *New England* Currency per Annum.

MASSACHUSETTS-BAY: This being more especially the scene of our Discourse, we shall be more particular. At the first settling of the *New England* Colonies; their Medium was Sterling Coin at Sterling Value, and Barter; some Part of their Taxes was paid in Provisions and other Produce, called *Stock in the Treasury.* When they got into Trade a heavy Piece of Eight passed at 5 *s.* A. 1652, *They proceeded to coin Silver Shillings, six Pences, and three Pences, at the Rate of 6 s. to a heavy Piece of Eight;* Silver continued current at this Rate by sundry subsequent Acts of Assembly till *A.* 1705, by a Resolve of the General Court Silver was to pass at 7 s. *per Oz.* *A.* 1706 the Courts of Judicature chancered Silver to 8 s. *per Oz.* in satisfying of Debts, being nearly after the Rate of 6 s. a light Piece of Eight as then current. At this Rate Silver and Province Bills continued upon *Par* until *A.* 1714, the Assembly or Legislature fell into the Error of making from Time to Time large superfluous Sums of *Paper Money upon Loans*, and the Emissions for Charges of Government not cancellable for many Years, so that these *Publick Bills have been continually depreciating for these last 26 Years, and are now arrived to* 29 s. *per Oz. Silver.*

Massachusetts-Bay was the Leader of Paper Currencies in our Colonies. Their first Emission was of 40,000 *l.* *A.* 1690 & 1691, to pay off the publick [**10**] Debts incurr'd by that expensive, tho' unsuccessful, Expedition against *Canada*; of this Sum 10,000 *l.* was cancelled and burnt in *October A.* 1691: In the following Years no more new Emissions, but some Re-emissions of the remainder, and that only for the necessary Charges of Government, called in by Rates or Taxes within the Year; the last Remission of these Bills was *A.* 1701, of 9,000 *l.* Bills all this Period continued at the Rate of 6 s. a heavy Piece of Eight, and were called *Old Charter Bills.* *A.* 1702 began new Emissions of Province Bills; but, as it ought to be in all wise Administrations, cancelled by Taxes of the same and next following Year, until *A.* 1704, the Rates for calling them in, were in Part postponed two Years; they began *A.* 1707 to postpone them in Part for three Years; *A.* 1709 for 4 Years; *A.* 1710 for 5 Years; *A.* 1711 for

6 Years; *A.* 1715 for 7 Years; *A.* 1721 for 12 Years; *A.* 1722 for 13 Years : *Thus unnaturally instead of providing for Posterity, they proceeded to involve them in Debt.* This long publick Credit and the enormous publick Loans, have depreciated our Province Bills to the small Value they bear at present; the Issues and Cancellings of their Bills being for a long Series of Years too tedious to be particularly and minutely inserted.

The Province of the *Massachusetts-Bay* besides the Emission & Re-emissions of the 40,000 *l.* old Charter Bills, have since *A.* 1702 emitted and re-emitted Bills of publick Credit, 1,132,500 *l.* upon Funds of *Taxes,* and 310,000 *l.* upon *Loans,* being in all near one and a half Million; whereof about 230,000 *l.* still outstanding, and if publick Faith be better kept will be gradually cancelled by *A.* 1742. The ordinary Charges of Government may be about 40,000 *l.* *New England* Currency per Ann. *Exchange with Great Britain* 4.50 *per Cent. Advance,* or five and an half *New England* for one Sterl.

[11] *RHODE-ISLAND,* their first Emissions were *A.* 1710, towards paying more readily their Quota of Charges on the Expedition against *Port Royal* (now *Annapolis Royal*) in *Nova Scotia,* and have emitted from Time to Time, in all 399,300 *l.* whereof only 19,300 *l.* upon Funds of *Taxes* for Government Charges, and 360,000 *l.* upon *Loans,* whereof there is at present outstanding (all upon Loans) 330,000 *l.* circiter; which, if their publick Faith should chance to be kept in Time coming, will not be finished cancelling until *A.* 1759. The Interest of those publick Loans defreys the Charges of Government, and of their Towns.

I shall embrace this Opportunity of exemplifying the Iniquity of Colony publick Bills of Credit by the Instance of Rhode-Island, a small Colony containing about 18,000 Souls, under an old Charter very lax and general; they admit of no Instructions from the *King*, Council, or Board of Trade and Plantations; the *King* having no Representative or *Commissioned Governour* in their Legislature. This handful of People have lately made a *very profitable Branch of Trade and Commerce by negociating their own Paper Money in various Shapes:* their Money being Loans of Paper Credit called Bills, from their Government to private Persons upon Lands Security; to be repaid not in the same real Value, but in the same depreciating fallacious Denominations.

1. Their first Loan was *A.* 1715 for 10 Years, but have by subsequent Acts postponed and prolonged the Payments, so that the last Payment was *A.* 1738, Thus *A.* 1715 Exchange was at 65 *per Cent.* with *England, A.* 1738 Exchange was at 400 *per Cent.* Advance; that is for 100 *l.* Sterl. Value received, they pay only after the Rate of 33 *l.* Sterl. Suppose further, that the same Person upon the same Land Security, borrows again of the new Emission *A.* 1738, this 33 *l.* Sterl. value; and, as formerly by repeated large Emissions, Exchange becomes as at present in [12] *North-Carolina* 10 for 1 Sterl. by *A.* 1758 the Period of this Loan, *the original* 100 *l. Sterl. Value will be redeemed with* 16 *l. Sterl. Value.* And if this Paper Money Loan Trade, could be supposed to continue, the Land Security would gradually vanish, *the Land redeem'd and the Debt paid with nothing.*

2. They who take up this Loan Money are called *Shar-*

ers; and for the first ten Years pay into the Treasury 5 *per Cent.* per Annum Interest; and for the other ten Years pay 10 *per Cent.* per Annum of the Principal, without Interest. The *Sharers* let out this Money, in their own & neighbour. ing Colonies at 10 *per Cent.* for the said twenty Years (some let it at a higher- Interest) is at the Expiration of the twenty Years 300 *l.* for every 100 *l.* Loan, Principal and simple Interest; for which only 150 *l.* is paid into the Colony Treas- ury, & 150 *l.* is clear Gain: *So that in this Shape for every* 100,000 *l. Emission, their People in the space of twenty Years, have after the Rate of* 150,000 *l. clear Profits.*

3. In another Shape; upon a new Emission, Interest is made with the *Managers*, to obtain Shares in the Loan: the Sharers immediately sell (or may sell) their *Privilege*, as it is called, for *ready Money Præmium;* at the Emission *A.* 1738 the Præmium was 35 *per Cent:* that is, *the Emission of* 100,000 *l. does immediately produce after the Rate of* 35,000 *l. ready Money profit.*

4. *Rhode-Island* purchases from their neighbouring large Province of the *Massachusetts-Bay*, all Sorts of British and Foreign Goods with this Paper Manufacture which costs nothing, which enables them to rival us in Trade, partic- ularly in that valuable Branch of it to the West India Islands, and to which by some unaccountable Infatuation we give a Currency; while at the same Time our Mer- chants cannot make Returns by any Colony Paper Money, for these Goods; it is true, sometimes they bring us Molasses from the Sugar Islands. We have a late [13] good Law against the Currency of such Bills, but not being put in Execution, is of no Effect. *The only Reason that can be assigned for giving the Rhode-Island Bills a Currency,* is,

that they are received in all Payments by Consent: The same Reason may hold good for passing of any Bills, even the 500,000 *l.* lately proposed without Fund or Period; and of counterfeit Bills, as in Fact some Bills of *Connecticut* of small Denominations, tho' known to be Counterfeit, have a currency.

CONNECTICUTT, a Charter Colony of industrious Husbandmen, having, with much Prudence emitted only small Quantities of Bills; Silver would have continued with them at 8 s. per Oz. as it did in *New York* their neighbouring Government westward, if their People had not given a Currency to the publick Bills of their Brethren, in the neighbouring Colonies of *New England. Connecticut* emitted Bills only for the present necessary Charges of Government upon Funds of *Taxes*, until *A.* 1733, having granted a *Charter* for Trade and Commerce to a Society in *New-London*, this Society manufactured some Bills of their own, but their Currency being soon at a Stand; the Government were obliged in Justice to the Possessors, to emit 50,000 *l.* upon *Loan* to enable those concerned in the Society to pay off their Society Bills in Colony Bills; their Charter was vacated, and a wholsome Law enacted, *That for any single Person, or Society of Persons to emit and pass Bills for Commerce or in imitation of Colony Bills, Penalty should be as in Case of Forgery, or of counterfeiting Colony Bills.* Their first Emission of Colony Bills was in *A.* 1709, and may have emitted in all 155,000 *l.* whereof only the above 50,000 *l.* upon Loan. There are at present outstanding about 60,000 *l.* which will be gradually cancelled by *A.* 1742, if the present good Assistants (Council) continue to be annually elected. They have at

Times been [**14**] guilty of emitting small Sums for the present Supply of Government (by oversight and not with any sinister Design) without annexing a Fund or Period; but have soon after been cancelled by Taxes. Their ordinary Charge of Government does not exceed 3,000 *l. New England* Currency per Annum.

N. B. This promiscuous Currency in the four Governments of *New England,* that is, one Colony giving a Currency to the enormous Paper Credit Emissions of one of the other Colonies, has the same Effect as if that Colony did emit Bills of its own: thus *the King's Instructions to the commissioned Governments are evaded,* by the popular Charter Governments, rendring them of no Effect, having as it were no Dependance on the Crown. *A Parliamentary Regulation is the only adequate Remedy.*

NEW-YORK chancered Proclamation Money to 8 s. per Oz. of Silver, at the same Time and for the same Reasons, as has been said of *Massachusetts-Bay Government: A.* 1709 towards the Charge of an intended Expedition against *Canada* (upon this same Occasion, began the first Paper Money Emissions of *New Jerseys & Connecticut*) they issued 13,000 *l.* publick Bills of Credit bearing Interest: *A.* 1710 the Interest was taken off upon pretence, that it occasion'd them to be hoarded up as Bonds, and did frustrate their Currency; and 10,000 *l.* more Bills without Interest were issued. All these Bills being small Sums and faithfully paid off & sunk in Taxes, *did not affect Exchange with England.*

A. 1714. By *collusion* of the Governour, Council and Representatives, a large Sum of 27,680 *l.* in Bills, was issued, to pay off Government Debts, whereoff some Part consisted of *their own ill founded Claims*; gradually to be cancelled by *Excise* on Liquors to *A.* 1734: these were issued with the *Royal* Assent.——*A.* 1717 for paying of Government Charges & Debts were issued 16,607 *l.* without waiting for the *Royal* [15] Approbation, gradually to be cancelled by a *Duty* upon Wines and Rum for 17 Years and *Excise* continued from *A* 1734 to *A.* 1739: this Emission was connived at by the *Boards* of Council, Trade and Plantations at Home; lest many Persons who had *bona fide* received them for valuable Considerations, might suffer by their being suppressed. Which Indulgence this Government have abused, by never waiting for the Royal Assent in their future Emissions.

In the intermediate Years were some small Emissions for Charges of Government, and regularly cancelled. — *A.* 1734 issued 12,000 *l.* in Bills for *Fortifications* to be gradually sunk before *A.* 1746 by *Imposts* — *A.* 1738 issued 48,300 *l* Bills, whereof 40,000 *l.* upon Loan; all to be sunk and paid in by *A.* 1750: this rais'd Exchange to 70 *per Cent.* and Silver to 9 s. 3 d. per Oz. *The Lieut. Governour to obtain of the People a Governour's Allowance consented to humour them in this Emission,*

A. 1739, the Funds being otherways applied, it was found that *contrary to publick Faith*, 15,000 *l.* of the Emissions *A.* 1714 & 1717 were still current, and fifteen Years more upon *Excise* were enacted to cancel them. So that now there is about 70,000 *l.* in Bills of *New-York* current.

NEW JERSIES, A. 1709, issued 3,000 *l.* publick Bills of Credit upon the intended Expedition against *Canada;* and *A.* 1711 upon another intended *Canada* Expedition 5,000 *l.* more Bills were emitted, to be cancelled gradually

before *A.* 1713; but were by Acts of Assembly *postponed*,
& many Bills of both Emissions were currant *A.* 1723.

A. 1724 emitted 40,000 *l.* in Bills whereof some small
Part was to cancel the old outstanding Bills, and the rest
upon Loan, to be paid in gradually in twelve Years. This
being *too large an Emission* for a small Colony, their Bills
became of less Value than those of *New-York*; but being
yearly *in good* [16] *Faith*, sunk, they became equal, and after
some Years 2 s. in the Pound better than *New-York* Bills.
This is a Demonstration, that the Quantity of Paper Money
increasing or faithfully decreasing, sinks or raises the Value
of it.—*A.* 1733, was issued 20,000 *l.* more upon Loan to
be gradually paid in sixteen Years: this Emission *fell* their
Bills to near Par with *New-York.*—*A.* 1734, the first Loan
of *A.* 1724, being near sunk, the Assembly enacted a 40,000 *l.*
Loan, but was not issued till *A.* 1736, having then obtain'd
the *Royal* Approbation, and *passed scarce at Par with New-
York;* but upon the *New-York* Emission of 48,300 *l. A.*
1738, the *Jersey* Bills are 6 d. in the Pound better than
New-York Bills, and 1 s. in the Pound better than those of
Pensylvania.

The *Jersey* Bills keep their Credit better than those of
Pensylvania and New-York for these two Reasons, 1. *New-
York* Bills not being current in *Pensylvania*, and *Pensylvania* Bills not current in *New-York;* but *Jersey* Bills
current in both, all Payments between *New-York* and *Pensylvania* are made in *Jersey* Bills.   2. In the *Jerseys* failure
of the Loan Payments, at the Days appointed; is equivalent
to Judgment, and thereafter only 30 Days Redemption of
Mortgages is allowed.

The 5 *per Cent.* Interest of publick Loans defrays all

Charges of Government. In the *Jerseys* at present about 60,000 *l.* in publick Bills current all upon Loan.

In the two Governments of *PENSYLVANIA* their Currency continued Silver Proclamation Value, until *A.* 1723: The three Upper Counties (strictly called *Pensylvania*) emitted upon Loan 15,000 *l.* in Bills, and *A.* 1724 emitted 30,000 *l.* more; but A. 1726 finding that in strictness of the two preceeding Acts 6100 *l.* part of the Capital of 45,000 *l.* was sunk, the Encouragers of Paper Money procured an Act for re-emitting what should be an-[17]nually paid in of the remainder by the Borrowers; and *A.* 1729 emitted 30,000 *l.* which have generally been continued out by *re-emitting Acts* from Time to Time. *A.* 1739 they made an Addition of about 11,100 *l.* upon Loan on the same Terms: so that at present they have 80,000 *l.* all upon Loan. Exchange with *London 75 per Cent.* before Emissions of Paper Money it was only 33 *per Cent.*

The three Lower Counties have also Paper Currency in small Quantities, and upon the same footing.

In MARYLAND Silver continued at Proclamation Value until *A.* 1734, with a considerable Concomitant *Truck Trade* as a *Medium*, viz. *Tobacco*; they then emitted 90,000 *l.* in Bills, which tho' payable to the Possessors in Sterling well secured, the Sum being too large, and the Periods too long, viz. three partial Payments of 15 Years Periods each; *Exchange immediately rose from 33 to 100 per Cent.*

VIRGINIA has the same considerable *Truck Trade Medium*, viz. *Tobacco*; and with regard to Silver Currency have kept their Integrity better than the other Colonies. It is true, *Lord Culpeper* their Governour, about *A.* 1680, by an arbitrary Proceeding in the Quality of the King's Representative, did, by virtue of his own Proclamation, alter the Value of their Silver Coin for his own Profit, to defraud an English Regiment then paid off and disbanded, (this Regiment was sent from *England* to quell an Insurrection or Mutiny in *Virginia* under *Bacon*) but soon finding, that it occasioned much Confusion in Business, and did particularly affect his own Perquisites; he reduced it again to the former Standard.   Silver a few Years ago was 6 s. a Crown British, or 6 s. 3 d. per Oz. Silver, at present it is 6 s. 8 d. per Oz. of Silver, and 5 *l.* per Oz. Gold; *is 25 per Cent. worse than Sterling.*

[18] *NORTH CAROLINA*, an inconsiderable Colony scarce capable of any Fund for Paper Emissions; have notwithstanding 40,000 *l.* upon *Loan*, and 12,500 *l.* upon Funds of *Taxes*.   At present Exchange is settled by their Legislature at 10 *North Carolina for* 1 *Sterling.*

In SOUTH CAROLINA their first Emission of publick Paper Credit was *A.* 1702, towards the Charges of an Expedition against *St. Augustine.*   Their Legislature have been most *notoriously guilty of breach of publick Faith* in not cancelling their Bills.   Besides the Emissions for ordinary Charges of Government, and their Expeditions against the *North Carolina Indians A.* 1711, and against the *Southern Indians A.* 1715, they have large Sums upon *Loans.* They may have at present outstanding about 250,000 *l.* in Province Bills (whereof above 100,000 *l.* without Fund or Period) besides private Notes of substantial Merchants negociated, payable upon Demand in Province Bills; they have also a valuable *Truck*, viz. *Rice.*   Their present Exchange with *London* as settled by their Legislature to ascertain the Value of Debts contracted, is 8 *South Carolina for* 1 *Sterling*.

In the new Colony of *GEORGIA*, their Currency are the Trustees *sola Bills Sterling*: the Funds are the Allowances by Parliament, and private Subscriptions to carry on the Settlement.

PROVIDENCE including the rest of the *Bahama* Islands is scarce reckoned a Colony.

In *BERMUDAS* a Colony of Sea Carriers; their *Currency continues Proclamation Value.*

BARBADOES: Their Currency is Proclamation Value, by weight 6 s. 10 d *farthing* per Oz. Silver. By the Advice of Mr. *W.* from *New England*, they [**19**] made the Experiment of a Paper Currency, and emitted 16,000 *l.* upon the Negroe *Tax* Fund, and soon after 80,000 *l.* more upon *Loan;* these Bills immediately fell 40 *per Cent.* below Silver, and upon Complaint were directly suppressed by an Order from *England*; *and some of the Possessors who gave them a Currency* have Quantities of them to show as a Monument of this Folly, and of Paper Money becoming waste Paper.

Here as in all our Sugar Islands, *Sugar* according to its Quality at the Market Price, serves as a *Truck Medium* to pay Debts. *The Par of Exchange is* 33 *per Cent.* but generally lower and in favour of *Barbadoes*.

The *CARRIBEE LEEWARD ISLANDS* of *Antegoe, Newis, St. Christophers, Montserrat, & the Virgins*, have depreciated from Silver Proclamation Value to 8 *s.* per Oz. in the same Manner as has been said of *Massachusetts-Bay;* but never proceeded to that Fraud, Paper Money: light Pieces of Eight are current by Tale. *Exchange* 50 *per Cent Advance.*

In *JAMAICA* formerly a heavy Piece of Eight current at 5 s. but light Money taking Place as a Currency; the heavy Money was ship'd off in course of Time at 10, 15, 20, & 25 *per Cent.* as at present, Difference. At this Time a light Piece of Eight passes at 5 s. a heavy Piece of Eight at 6 s. 3 d. and Silver at 7 s. 2 d. per Oz. *The Par of Exchange with London is about* 36 *per Cent. difference,* but generally higher and in favour of *London.*

Thus we see, that particularly in our Paper Money Colonies, the Currencies have incredibly depreciated from Sterling, and from one another. Exchange with Great Britain *being at this Time* (Febr. 1739) *in New England* 450 *per Cent. in New-York, Jerseys, & Pensylvania* 70 *to* [20] 75 *per Cent. in* Maryland 100 *per Cent. in North Carolina* 900 *per Cent. in South Carolina* 700 *per Cent. worse than Sterling.*

To make a Bill or Note bearing no Interest, and not payable till after a dozen or score of Years, a legal Tender (under the highest Penalties as in *New-York* and *Jerseys*) in Payment of Debts, is the highest of *despotick* and arbitrary Government: *France* never made their State Bills a common Tender. Our Paper Money Colonies have carried the Iniquity still further; the Popular or *Democratick* Part of the Constitution are generally in Debt, and by their too great Weight or Influence in Elections, have made a depreciating Currency, a Tender for Contracts done many Years before; that is, *they impose upon the Creditor side in private Contracts,* which the most despotick Powers never assumed.

An Instance of a still further arbitrary Proceeding in relation to Paper Money was an Act of Assembly in *New Jerseys A.* 1723, whereby *Executions for Debt were stayed until Paper Money should be issued.*

The Mystery of the infatuation of our Colonies running Headlong into a depreciating Paper Currency may be this: In many of our Plantations of late Years, by bad Management and Extravagancies, the Majority of the People are become *Debtors*, hence their Elected Representation in the Legislature have a great Chance to be generally of the Debtors Side: or in other Words, the *Representatives* being generally Freeholders, and many of them *much in Debt*; by large Emissions their Lands rise in Denomination Value while their Debts become really less, and the Creditor is defrauded in Part of his Debt. Thus our Colonies have defrauded more in a few Years than bad Administrations in *Europe* have formerly done in some Centuries. The great Damage done to the generous Merchants at Home, and to the [21] industrious fair Dealers amongst our selves; call aloud, for some speedy and effectual Relief from the supreme Legislature the *Parliament of Great Britain.*

There is an Argument, which tho' not much attended to here, may be of some Weight at Home, viz. *That the Government at Home ought to connive at Paper Money in the Colonies*, because by indulging them in this Error, all the Silver which they acquire from Time to Time is sent to *Great Britain*; and by the *chimæra* of a fallacious Cash, Extravagancies are encouraged in favour of a great Consumption of British Goods: *This ought to be an Argument with us against that Paper Currency*, which tends to turn the Ballance of Trade so much against us. It is true, That *Great Britain* naturally ought to reap some Profit by its Plantation Improvements: but a good Farmer improves his Lands not by working them out of Heart (as the Term is) but by manuring them, that they may yield the better Crops: besides, what the British Merchants lose in their Returns by the Colony Bills depreciating, and by the Bankruptcy of their Factors and Dealers here; is much more then what *Great Britain* gets, on the abovesaid Accounts.

In the Sequel of this Discourse, I shall 1, Enumerate the Inconveniencies and bad Effects of our large Emissions of Paper Money.   2. Endeavour to remove the Prejudices which some designing Men have infused into the Minds of the Populace in favour of Bills of Credit.   3. Consider several Projections or Schemes to rectify our Currency and present Circumstances, or to prevent their growing worse.

The Mischiefs arising from a large Paper Currency are, 1. With regard to *the particular and immediate Sufferers thereby.*

[22] 1. *The Labourers and Trades-men,* who in all Countries, are the Heads which feed the Belly of the Common Wealth, and therefore *deserve our chief Regard.* How much they have suffered and continue to suffer is obvious: For Instance, a Carpenter when Silver was at 8 s. per Oz. his Wages were 5 s. a Day all Cash. The Town House *A.* 1712 was built at this Rate; whereas at present *A.* 1739. from the bad Influence of Paper Money Silver being 29 s. per Oz. he has only 12 s. a Day, equal only to 3 s. 4 d. of former Times; and even this is further reduced, by obliging him to take one half in Shop Goods at 25 per Cent. or more Advance above the Money Price: this Iniquity still grows,

by reducing the Goods Part to the least vendable; the Shopkeeper refusing to let them have Provisions, West India Goods, or Goods of *Great Britain* that are in Demand.

To make the Case more familiar, Suppose a Tradesman laying in his Winter Store, when Wages were at 5 s. with one Day's Labour he purchases 15 Pound of Butter being 4d per Pound (I use Butter because it rises the most uniformly of all Provisions) at present his 12 s a Day purchases only 7 Pound of Butter at 20 d a Pound. *The Clergy* or settled Preachers to Congregations in *Boston*, no Offence in classing them with Labourers, when Silver was at 5 s. had 3 *l.* per Week, at present Silver at 29 s. per Oz. they have only 6 *l.* to 8 *l.* equal to 40 s. of former Times.

The *Shopkeepers* are become as it were Bankers between the Merchants and Tradesmen, and do impose upon both egregiously. Shop Notes that great and insufferable Grievance of Tradesmen, were not in Use until much Paper Money took Place: this Pay in Goods which gnerally are of no necessary Use (Provisions and West India Goods at this Time are removed from that Denomination) encourage Extravagance in Apparel and Furniture much above our Condition.

[23] 2. *The Merchants of Great Britain Adventurers to New England, because of their largest Dealings have suffered most.* Their Goods are here generally sold at a long Credit, while the Denominations of the Money in which they are to be paid, continues depreciating; so that they are paid in a less Value than was contracted for: thus our Bills have successively depreciated from 8 s. per Oz. Silver *A.* 1713,

to 29 s. in this Year 1739; that is, if we could suppose the same Person to have constantly followed this Trade (without extraordinary Hits) for that space of Time, *he must have reduced his Estate after the rate of 8 s. only for 29 s.* For every Shilling in the Pound that Silver rises in Price, or, which is the same, for every Shilling in the Pound that the Denomination of our Paper Money depreciates, the Creditor actually looses 5 per Cent. of his Debt.

There have been from Time to Time *seeking Factors,* who to procure Business from Home, have entred into Engagements which could not possibly be complied with: these having little or nothing of their own to loose, soon make desperate Work of it; become Bankrupts, and from a general insensibility of discredit, do notwithstanding keep their Countenance as before.

Many *Factors* to dazle their Employers for a Time, and in the mean while to procure more Consignments; send Home a high Account of Sales, by the Shopkeers giving a great Advance in Consideration of a very long Credit, and to be drawn out in Shop Notes. This Practice has so much prevailed, that it is now become a fixed tho' pernicious and ruinous Custom.

As Paper Money pays no Debts abroad, the Factor is obliged to give an extra Quantity of it, to purchase Silver, and other Returns; which can be exported, to satisfy Debts; in this Shape also the Merchant becomes a Sufferer.

[24] 3. *Widows, Orphans, Funds for Charity* at Interest, and all other Creditors; by Bonds, Notes & Book Debts, acquired by Industry, good Management, and Frugality; are great Sufferers from Time to Time: For Instance, from Autumn *A.* 1733 to Autumn *A.* 1734 Silver rose from 22 s. to

27 s. per Oz. this was a Loss of 23 per Cent. of the Principal.

II. *The repeated large Emissions of Paper Money are the Cause of the frequent rise of the Price of Silver and Exchange ;* that is, of the publick Bills of Currency depreciating in all the Paper Money Colonies; which do as regularly follow the same, as the Tides do the *Phases* or course of the Moon. When no larger Sums are emitted for some Time, than what are cancelled of former Emissions; Silver and Exchange are at a Stand; when less is emitted than cancelled (which seldom happens) Silver and Exchange do fall. This is plain to a kind of Demonstration, from the Instance in the History of our Paper Money Emissions in *New England.*

After Silver had rose *A.* 1706 to 8 s. per Oz. by light Pieces of Eight superseding the heavy Pieces ; it continued at that rate, while Paper Emissions did not exceed a due Proportion to the current Silver. *A.* 1714 we emitted 50,000 *l.* upon Loan, and *A.* 1715 in *Rhode Island* 40,000 *l.* besides Emissions on distant Funds for Charges of Government; in the Autumn *A.* 1715 Silver became 15 per Cent. Advance above 8 s. that is about 9 s. 2 d. per Oz. *Massachusetts-Bay A.* 1717 emitted 100,000 *l.* upon Loan and a very long Period; Silver rose to 12 s. per Oz *A.* 1721 *Massachusetts-Bay* emitted 50,000 *l.* and *Rhode-Island* 40,000 *l.* upon Loan, Silver *A.* 1722 became 14 s. per Oz. From that Time a chargeable Indian War, required large Emissions, and Silver rose to 16 s. per Oz it continued at this Rate till *A.* 1728, Emissions not being larger than Cancellings. *A.* 1727 *Massachusetts-Bay* emitted 60,000 *l.* and

A. 1728 *Rhode-*[25] *Island* emitted 40,000 *l.* upon Loans; Silver became 18 s. per Oz. *A.* 1731 *Rhode-Island* emitted 60,000 *l.* upon Loan. (*N. B.* Besides the several Loans in the course of this History, all the Charges of the four Governments, were defrayed by Paper Emissions) and Silver became *A.* 1732, 21 s. per Oz. *A.* 1733 *Massachusetts-Bay* emitted 76,000 *l.* upon Funds of Taxes, *Rhode-Island* 104,000 *l.* upon Loan and Taxes, *Connecticut* 50,000 *l.* upon Loan, and *A.* 1734 Silver became 27 s. per Ounce. From *A.* 1734 to *A.* 1738 more Bills were cancelled than emitted, Exchange fell from 440 to 400 per Cent. Advance. *A.* 1738 *Rhode-Island* emitted 100,000 *l.* upon Loan, Silver rose from 27 s. to 29 s. per Oz.

In *New England,* as in all other trading Countries, from some particular Accident and Circumstances, there happened at Times, some small fluctuations in Exchange, without any Regard to Emissions of Paper Money. At all Times, when Returns in Ship Building, Whale Oil and Fins, Naval Stores &c. turn out well at Home; Silver and Exchange here suffer a small fall: at other Times when these prove bad Returns, Silver and Exchange rise a small Matter; the most noted Instance was *A.* 1729, when the usual Returns to *Great Britain* turned to bad Account; the Merchants from Home, directed their Factors here, to make Remittances in Silver or Exchange only, and at any Rate; together with an Agency from this Province and that of *Connecticut,* fitted out with a Silver Supply; Silver rose very considerably, but after a few Months fell again to the former Price.

The Instance of *Barbadoes* must put this Assertion beyond all Dispute with sober thinking honest Men. *A.* 1702 by the Perswasion of Mr. *W.* from New England, *Barbadoes* emitted 16,000 *l.* Bills of publick Credit on a Fund of 3 s. 9 d. Negroe Tax; at first they passed at a Discount, but no more being emitted, and the Period of cancelling being short, [**26**] they rose again to near *Par:* this encouraged them to make an enormous Emission of 80,000 *l.* Bills on Land Security at 4 per Cent. Principal payable after 5 Years: These Bills immediately fell 40 per Cent. below Silver: by an Order from Home, they were soon suppressed, and their Currency became Silver Value as before. That Province has ever since kept their Currency up to Proclamation Value, Ballance of Trade in their Favour, Exchange to *Great Britain* being generally under 33 per Cent. the Par.

III. *Large repeated Emissions of publick Bills of Credit, called Paper Money, is no addition to the Medium of Trade.* No Country can have an indefinite or unlimitted Credit; the further a Country endeavours to stretch its Credit beyond a certain Pitch, the more it depreciates. The Credit of a Country may be compared to that of a private Trader; if his Credit is equal to 100,000 *l.* Sterl. his Notes of Hand for 100,000 *l.* will be as good as Silver; if it be known that he passes Notes of Hand for 200,000 *l.* Sterl. their full Credit will be suspected and eventually be worth no more than his real Credit 100,000 *l.* Sterl: if he can be supposed to utter 500,000 *l.* Bills or Notes, his 5 *l.* Note will be worth only 20 s. Sterl.

In *New England A.* 1713 there were about *two thirds* Bills to *one third* Silver current, equally to 8 s. per Oz Silver Value; there being an Allowance of 5 per Cent.

in all publick Payments in favour of Bills only, gave them a Credit beyond their natural Stretch. At that Time the publick Bills of the four Provinces were about 175,000 *l.* at 8 s. per Oz. Silver Value (we use always the nearest round Numbers) is 438,000 Oz. Value, with 219,000 Oz of Silver Currency is 657,000 Oz. Silver Value. *A.* 1718 the publick Bills of *New England* were 300,000 *l.* (Silver all drove away by the worse Currency of Bills) at 12 s. per Oz. Silver; is 500,000 Oz. Value in Silver. *A.* 1731 [**27**] *New England* publick Bills were 470,000 *l.* at 20 s. per Silver, is 470,000 Oz. Silver Value. *A.* 1739 the current Paper Money of *New England* was 630,000 *l.* at 29 s. per Oz. Silver is in Value 434,000 Oz. Silver. Here it is plain that the more Paper Money we emit our real Value of Currency or *Medium* becomes less, and *what we emit beyond the trading Credit of the Country does not add to the real Medium, but rather diminishes from it, by creating an Opinion against us, of bad Oeconomy and sinking Credit.*

A Country may exceed in any Commodity or *Medium*, excepting in that universally Staple Commodity and Medium Silver; and a smaller Quantity of any other Commodity or Medium will turn to the same or better Account than a larger. In *Holland* upon a too large Importation of Spices, they destroy some Part, to keep up the Value of Spices. Not long since in *Virginia*, finding that Tobacco (their Currency as well as Export) by its too large Cultivation began to depreciate; by Act of Assembly they restricted it to 1000 *l.* wt. per Annum per Tythable. In *Maryland A.* 1734 & *A.* 1735 for the same Reason they burnt 150 *l.* wt. per Rateable. If our House of Representatives allow our Paper Money to be cancelled in Course, and be sparing in the Manufacture of more; the Value of the remainder, would be equal to the Value of the whole now current, or proposed to be added to the Currency.

It is therefore vain and inconsistent to make *Provincial* or Municipal Bills of Credit, for a Medium of general Trade: Merchants know how to find their own Tools or *Medium* of Trade, better than any Civil Administration can prescribe: in Fact, they who call out loudest for this Paper *Medium*, are not our large Traders; but such as would take up Money at any bad lay, *viz.* the Idle, those in desperate Circumstances, and the Extravagant; who never can have any other Claim to Money but by [28] Fraud; we must except some who tho' naturally honest are misguided. Publick Bills of Credit in a proper Sense are only to defray the incident Charges of Government which may accrue, before the proper Ways and Means of Taxes can take Place; but so soon as can be, to be cancelled by those Taxes. We know of no Country in *Europe*, where Exchequer Notes, State Bills, or other Bills of publick Credit, have been issued by the Government for a *Medium* of Trade.

IV. *This infatuation in favour of Paper Money has had a mutinous bad Effect upon the Civil Government, in several of our Colonies.* The Representatives of the People, have frequently refused to provide for the necessary Charges of Government, and other wholesome Laws; because the Governours & Councils, would not (in breach of their Instructions from the Crown) concur in emitting large Sums of Paper Money to defraud the industrious Creditor and fair Dealer. I shall mention only a few Instances. In *S. Carolina A.* 1719, the People deposed the Proprietors Governour

on this Account: it is true, the *King* did not much resent
this Mutiny; perhaps, that the Proprietors might be weary
of their Property and Government; and accordingly seven
of the eight Proprietors, for a small Consideration, did *A.*
1729 resign and sell to the Crown: Upon Governour *John-
son's* arrival in *S. Carolina A.* 1731, there had been no
Supply granted in the four preceeding Years. The Government of the *Massachusetts-Bay*, has from Time to Time
been distressed, by our Representatives refusing Supplies
for the necessary Charges of Government, and other publick
Affairs neglected on this Account: *Our present Governour's
Fortitude and steady Adherence to the King's Instructions,
& his having shortned the long Periods of Emissions for
Charges of Government (I am under no Obligation to flatter) are highly laudable.* New Hampshire Representatives
for [29] five Years preceeding *A.* 1736 granted no Supply.
As the French humour of building Forts, to protect their
Settlements against an Enemy; and as the Spanish humour
of Devotion, in building Churches and Convents, is perverted, by their becoming Nurseries of Idleness and other
Vices; so the *English Liberty and Property of the Subject*, in
many of our Plantations are somewhat abused, to levelling
and licentiousness; it is true, all Men are naturally equal,
but Society requires subordination.

V. *Long Credit, is not one of the least of the bad Effects
of Paper Money.* People run in Debt, endeavour after a
long Credit, and refuse paying their Debts when due; because while Bills are continually depreciating, the longer
the Debt is outstanding, they pay their Creditors with a less
and less Value, than was contracted for. Sir *Alexander
Cumings* in his Defence wrote *A.* 1729, says, that in his

Time in *South Carolina*, pay, after twelve Months, was reckoned as ready Money. Long Credit thus obtained, does in its turn, forward a bad Currency, they go Hand in Hand. A Creditor after being long out of his Money, chuses rather to take the bad Currency and run the Risque of passing it off again (as was the Case of the *Rhode-Island* Emissions *A.* 1733 & 1738) than of losing his Debt, if another Creditor should take it, and the Debtor afterwards become Insolvent.

With ready Money or short Credit, Business goes on brisk and easy. *Long Credit* occasions the unthinking of all Conditions and Occupations, to involve themselves. A Merchant over-trades himself, a Shopkeeper buys more Goods, and at a greater Advance than he can afterwards comply with; the Countryman buys and Mortgages Lands, to his final Ruin.

[30] VI. *Insensibility of Discredit, does naturally follow long Credit:* All Shame and Modesty is banished even in the Creditor; who, tho' formerly a modest forbearing Man, is now obliged to Dun incessantly or lose his Debt. Ready Money and short Credit, give a quick Circulation; the quicker the Circulation, the less Quantity of *Medium* is required to carry on the same Trade and Business; long Credit, and insensibility of Discredit, have the contrary Effect. There are at present extant of *New England* publick Bills of Credit about 630,000 *l.* a much larger Sum than ever was extant at any other Time; yet Money was never so scarce and Debts worse paid: *People chuse rather to hoard it up*, and wait for better Times, than put it out and not be able to recover it again, but after an unreasonable Length of Time and much Trouble; Money hoarded up,

is the same as if not in being, as to Currency.   If a Shop-
keeper does not clear with his Merchant, till after two or
three Years due; he is notwithstanding esteem'd as honest
as his Neighbour: Our Courts are full of plain Bonds, and
Notes of Hand; Appeals on them are allowed, Executions
delay'd &c.   This insensibility of Discredit, breaks all Friendship; it makes a Man cautious of lending his Money to his
best Friend, and nearest Relation.

A general Clamour for a depreciating Paper Currency, is
a certain Sign of the Country being generally in bad Circumstances, that is, *in Debt;* because all Creditors who by
their Industry and Frugality have acquired Rents, Bonds,
Notes and Book Debts, loose by its depreciating; and the
Debtors (the Idle and Extravagant Part of the People)
come off easy by the Creditors loss.   Seeing they who are
desperately in Debt, and want to pay a smaller Value than
contracted for, or *they who have nothing to loose, are generally
of the Party for Paper Money;* this ought to be a strong Prejudice against it, with sober thinking Men.

[31] We have *some prevailing Customs and some Laws in
force,* which seem to encourage this *insensibility of Discredit*
in Debtors; 1. *A Maxim amongst Shopkeepers;* That the
most ready Way to grow rich, without any Expence of Industry; is, to run boldly in Debt, procure a long Credit, after
Time of Payment is elapsed to bear Dunning with a good
Face, and finally to let the Debt take its full Course in the
Law, which further requires twelve Months or more, at a small
Cost: Notwithstanding this Chain of Iniquity, the Debtor
keeps his Countenance, and many Factors continue to trust
him with their Employers Goods as formerly.   2. *Estates too
easily allowed to be represented as Insolvent;* whereby Credi-

tors are defrauded of some Part of their Due. 3. *Appeals upon plain Bonds, Notes of Hand, and Defaults,* to the great Relief of the fraudulent Debtor, and Damage of the honest Creditor. 4. *Sheriffs* impune *delay of Executions,* while the Creditor is allowed neither Interest nor Damage upon the Debt. 5 *The too general Laws for the relief of insolvent Debtors,* whereby the Fraudulent, the Idle, and the Extravagant, when sent to Goal; are too soon, and at too easy a Rate turned loose to follow the same Courses. What I have here said, *cannot be understood in contempt of our Legislative Authority;* because of that valuable Privilege belonging to our Constitution, viz. of repealing, amending, or explaining what Laws from Experience may be found to require the same.

The Arguments current amongst the Populace in favour of Paper Money are,

I. In most of the Paper Money Colonies one of the principal Reasons alledged for their first Emissions; was, *to prevent Usurers imposing high Interest upon Borrowers, from the scarcity of Silver Money.* It is true, that in all Countries the increased Quantity of Silver, falls the Interest or Use of Money; [32] but large Emissions of Paper Money does naturally rise the Interest to make good the sinking Principal: for Instance, in the Autumn *A.* 1727 Silver was at 26 s. to 27 s. per Oz. but by a large *Rhode Island* Emission, it became in Autumn 1739, 29 s. per Oz. this is 7 per Cent. loss of Principal, therefore the Lender to save his Principal from sinking requires 13 per Cent. natural Interest (our legal Interest being 6 per Cent.) for that Year. In Autumn *A.* 1733 Silver was 22 s. per Oz. by large Emissions it became 27 s. in the Autumn *A.* 1734; is 22 per

Cent. loss of Principal, and the Lender to save his Principal requires 28 per Cent. *natural Interest* for that Year. Thus *the larger the Emissions, natural Interest becomes the higher;* therefore the Advocates for Paper Money (who are generally indigent Men, and Borrowers) ought not to complain, when they hire Money at a dear nominal Rate.

If Bills were to depreciate after a certain Rate, Justice might be done to both contracting Parties, by imposing the loss, which the Principal may sustain in any certain space of Time (the Period of Payment) upon the Interest of a Bond or Price of Goods: but as depreciations are uncertain, great Confusions in Dealings happen.

II. *That the Merchants arbitrary Rise upon the Price of Goods, does from Time to Time depreciate the Denominations of our Paper Money*, is imposed upon the unthinking Part the People, as a certain Truth, by designing Men. It is certain, that in all Countries of *Europe*, where by Recoinages or Proclamations, the current Specie has been debased; the nominal Price of Goods did naturally rise in Proportion: is it not more natural to say, that formerly in *France* their re-coinings or lessening the Value of their Denominations, did rise the Price of Goods; than to say that the Rise of the Price of Goods, was the Cause of their Recoinages. A con-[33]tinued Rise on Goods in general is from a depreciating *Medium*; but fluctuations in particular Goods, are from the Quantities and Demand; thus *A*. 1739 Provisions the most Staple of all Commodities have been cheap, *viz.* Wheat at 10 s. per Bushel, Silver being 29 s. per Ounce, whereas *A*. 1738 Wheat was at 18 s. per Bushel, when Silver was only 27 s. per Oz.

When a large Emission can be foreseen the Price of

Goods rises; because being sold upon long Credit, the effects of the Emission will take Place before the Time of Payment: hence it is that *generally the Price of Goods Advances, before Exchange and Silver do rise;* Exchange and Silver being bought with ready Money, cannot take Place until the Addition is made to the Currency by this new Emission, and then only gradually as the Merchant receives his Pay; thus the large Emissions of *A.* 1733 did not bring Silver to its heighth, 27 s· per Oz. until Autumn, *A.* 1734: Hence proceeds that inculcated Fallacy of the Advance on Goods rising the Price of Silver and Exchange. The same Reason for Lenders of Money, imposing a high Interest, holds in the Rise of the Price of Goods: Custom has given a long Credit, Insensibility of Discredit makes it still longer, and before the Merchant is paid, the Currency is become much depreciated.

III. *The Sticklers for Paper-Credit requiring long Periods, as well as large Emissions is a most unnatural Desire.* Some of the *Massachusetts-Bay* Loan, of *A.* 1717 is still outstanding *A.* 1739: The several *Rhode-Island* Loans do not terminate in less than 20 Years: By this unnatural Contrivance they oblige Posterity to supply the Extravagancies of their Parents and Ancestors, instead of the common and natural Instinct of Parents providing for their Children.

[34] IV. *It is not repeated large Emissions of a base Paper-Currency, but our Imports exceeding our Exports, that occasions Silver to be ship'd off in Ballance; therefore we are not to expect a Silver-Currency supposing all Bills cancelled.* Before Paper-Money took Place in *New·England,* Silver abounded in Currency as much and perhaps more, than in

many of our Colonies: Our Exports are always in Demand, viz. Ship-building, all Branches of Fishery, Naval-Stores to *Great Britain*, Logwood from the Bay of *Honduras*, Lumber, Stock, and other Provisions to the other Colonies; and (*Bermudians* excepted) our Navigation is the cheapest of all Carriers. Silver began to be generally ship'd off as Paper became the Currency; which gave the Merchant the Liberty of shipping off his Silver as Merchandise, which otherways he must have kept as Cash, seeing no Business can be carried on to Advantage without Cash. In all Countries if a bad *Medium* is introduced, People take care to secure the better *Mediums* and they are no more current.

The Fallacy of Quantities of Paper-Money, has increased our superfluous Imports, much beyond what was in former Times. The *seeking Factors* upon a large Emission, advise the Merchant in *Great Britain*, that Money being now very Plenty, a large Quantity of Goods will sell: Accordingly a Glut of Goods is sent to *New England*, more than can be sold for ready Money and short Credit; the Consequence is, a long Credit, with its consequential Multitude of Evils; that is Returns or Exports in full, are never, or not, till after a long Time, ship'd off.

Our Paper-Money being only passable amongst our selves, is the Reason, why, *they who deal only in buying and selling a Shore, get the most Money;* all their Profits are upon our selves, and run no Risque of Precarious Returns; while the generous Merchant looses upon his Exports to a foreign Market. This is a ruinous Case.

[35] *As Paper-Money grows scarce, Imports will be less, and be sold cheaper;* no Country can want a true real Medium of Trade, while their Exports exceed their Im-

ports: Let us then lessen our Imports by our Frugality, and add to our Exports by our Industry; and we shall have no occasion for this *chimerical ill founded Medium, Paper Money.*

V. *The goodly Appearance, which* Boston *and the Country in general at present, make in fine Houses, Equipage, and Dress, is owing to Paper Money.* All our Plantations from some Infatuation, are inclinable to run into Prodigality, Profuseness, and Show: these Paper Loans (from publick or private Schemes) upon long Periods, give the unthinking and unwary, Opportunities of involving themselves, by thus sinking what they have borrowed; by repeated Emissions, they have Opportunities of paying a former Debt, by running further in Debt, till at length they become Insolvents. People do not consider, that all Emissions upon Funds of Taxes or upon Loans, is running the Country more and more in Debt, and will in Course fall heavy upon every Individual. Never were greater Complaints of want of Money, while at the same Time, never more extravagance in Equipages and Dress. *Boston, like a Private Man of small Fortune, does not become richer but poorer, by a rich goodly Appearance.*

What Part of these Emissions have we laid out in Improvements of Produce, or Manufacture? Not any. It is true, it gave some Men Opportunities of building Vessels and running into Trade; but their Education and Experience not laying that Way, and having no other Bottom of their own, they soon became *broken Merchants.*

Expending in fine Houses & Apparel what ought to have purchased Exports, is one of the Reasons, why Ballance of Trade is against us.

[36] *There is another Fund for all this finery,* and of which we ought not to boast, but be ashamed. By the Means of a depreciating Currency the Merchant at Home, has been paid in less Value, than was contracted for; his Loss was our Gain. Several Factors from Time to Time, have by Artifice, & Assurance, procured large Commissions from Home, and with Effrontery and Insensibility of Discredit, have become Bankrupts: Thus the Produce of these Effects remained here, and makes good in some Sense, that Position of Dr. *Mandevilles*; Private Vices are publick Benefits.

VI. *This Country formerly had but a small Trade, now our Trade being much enlarged, we require a large Medium.* This like all the Arguments commonly used to pervert the People, is very unnatural: because the more a Country grows in good Trade, the more true *Medium* of Trade it acquires, and would have no Occasion, to have recourse to a fallacious *Succedanium* or Shift. Notwithstanding the vast Floods of Paper Money lately emitted, and our Trade also more general; we find that in former Times, the People were more willing and able to pay high Rates, than at present. The first Assembly upon the new Charter, did in *June A.* 1692, lay a Tax of 30,000 *l.* (equal to upwards of 120,000 *l.* present Currency) payable within the Year, *viz.* one half before 25th of *December A.* 1692, and the other half before 1st of *May* 1693; towards paying off Charges formerly incurred by the *Canada* Expedition and Charges of that Year. *A.* 1694 the Tax was 17,589 *l.* (equal to upwards of 70,000 *l.* present Currency) towards paying off the Government Charges of that and the preeceding Year. Whereas, we who reckon our selves so much increased in Trade at present *A.* 1739 refuse a small Rate of about only 50,000 *l.* towards paying Government Charges incurred *A.* 1728, *A.* 1733, and *A.* 1737.

[**37**] VII. *How can we pay our Taxes and Debts, if the Government do not make large Emissions of Paper Money?* In all Countries excepting in Paper Money Colonies, the People support the Government: it is absurd to imagine that a Government finds Money for its People, it is the People who by their Trade and Industry, provide not only for their own Subsistence, but also for the Support of Government, and to find their own *Tools* or *Medium* of Trade. It is true, the Government, that is, the Stewards of the Publick, may by the Consent of their Principals, the collective Body of the People; raise Money upon the Credit of the Real and Personal Estates of the People: but this in Propriety of Speech, is not making (or acquiring) of Money as we term it, but the reverse: A Prodigal who involves his Estate to raise ready Money, is it not ridiculous to say he has made so much Money; whereas in effect he has spent so much Money by sinking some Part of his Estate. The unthinking Part of our People do not consider, that *every Emission of Paper Credit called Money, is laying a heavy Tax upon us,* which in Time will contribute to our Misery: and is really analogous to the Negroes in *Guinea,* who sell their Progeny into Slavery, for the sake of raising some ready Pence.

Our present Rates, are only a calling in Bills formerly Emitted, and therefore are supposed in being, and do not require a new Emission. This Cry is the same, as if a private Person borrows of another 100 *l.* payable after some Time, and in the mean while by profuseness and bad Oecon-

omy, becomes incapable of satisfying the Debt when the
Term of Payment is come: but says to the Lender, you use
me very ill, if you do not lend me 200 *l.* to enable me to pay
the first 100 *l.* and for other Occasions: If the Lender proceeds thus to indulge the Borrower, this bad Husband must
at length be reduced to a State of Bankruptcy: *Province
Bills are as much a* [**38**] *Debt upon the collective Body of the
People; as a private Man's Bonds and Notes of Hand, are a
Debt upon himself.*

VIII. *The Emission of* 35,000 *l.* to 40,000 *per Ann. for
the ordinary Charges of Government, is a small insignificant
addition to our Currency; publick Loans have been found in-
convenient; let us then emit large Sums in Province Bills
(the Charge of making Bills is a Trifle) towards publick Edi-
fices, Fortifications, Guarda Costas, Bridges, Castles in the
Air, or any Thing, tho' of no Use or Consequence: they will
draw out larger Sums, and considerably increase our Currency.* They do not consider, that this contracting a large
unnecessary Debt, to be redeemed after some Years, by heavy
Rates and Taxes, will occasion a Clamour, perhaps a Mutiny,
worse than the present groundless Complaints of Oppression.
Such unnecessary Impositions are frequently Grounds of
Complaint in the People against some Governours; but
that the People should thus impose upon themselves, is one
of the unnatural Effects of Paper Money.

IX. *Seeing, there is like to be no Stop to our Infatuation
in receiving the depreciating Bills of* Rhode-Island; *why
should they reap all the Profit in our Ruin: why should not
some of our merciful Selves* (as the Authors of the 500,000 *l.*
Scheme call themselves) partake with them in the Plunder,

by taking the Advantage of our present Indispositions & Weakness, Carry the Imposition further than that of *Rhode-Island*; even beyond what could have entred into the Heart of Man, at any other Time or Place, to conceive: I mean the emitting of 500,000 *l.* in Notes without Fund or Period; a Project, to outdo the *Rhode-Islanders* in Fraud, & to make these Bills more current, because worse than those of *Rhode-Island*: it is almost incredible to what a Pitch of Iniquity some People are arrived, even prophanely to lard their Proposals with Scripture Phrases, *to impose upon the Vulgar waste Paper, instead of a valuable Medium.*

[39] *The several Projections or Schemes which occur at present, towards rectifying our Currency, or at least to prevent its growing worse, are*

I. Of a publick Nature.

1. *Is palliative, to prevent its growing worse, by bringing it to a Standard.* By Act of Assembly let *the Governour and Council be impowred, with the Advice of Merchants, to settle once or twice a Year the Price of Exchange to London, or of Silver, in Province Bills*; all Bonds, Notes, and Book Debts when paid, shall be received in Province Bills equal in Value to the Exchange or Price of Silver, as it was thus settled at the Time of contracting: For Instance, if I contract for 500 *l. New England* Bills of Credit when Exchange is settled at 5 *New England* for 1 Sterling, and when the Contract is to be satisfied, Exchange is settled at 6 for 1; I must pay the true or Sterling Value, which is 600 *l. New England* Bills: this is strict Equity and natural Justice, it will effectually obviate the fraudulent Practices of those who are constantly clamouring for more Province Bills, and prevent the neighbouring Colonies from imposing their depre-

ciating Bills upon us. Both *Carolina's* have given us a successful Precedent.

2. As private Credit, being under Coercion, is better than publick Faith, which being above the Law, is lawless. *Let the Legislature give a Sanction to some Society, of good substantial Men, who may be willing to emit Bills upon a good Silver Bottom*, continually meliorating at a small Rate, *v. g.* 3 per Cent. per Ann. to prevent their being hoarded up; and receivable in Taxes and all publick Payments: Such Bills will soon bring a Discount upon all other Bills. We have at this Time (*Christmas A* 1739.) a remarkable Instance of private Credit being good, and publick Faith of no Account: *Merchants Notes* (a private Emission some Years ago upon a Silver Bottom) are sold at 33 per Cent. Advance, their true Value above common Currency; at the same [40] Time, *our Province Bills of the new Tenor*, which in *good Faith* are 25 *per Cent.* better than the other Currencies, pass promiscuously with the bad Currencies at *Par.*

3. Let *Massachusetts-Bay Bills* only, be receivable by the Treasurer of the Province, Counties, & Towns; all Bills of the old Tenor when brought into their Treasury, to issue no more: *that all publick Bills hereafter to be emitted, be of the Nature of our late Bills of a new Tenor*, with this additional Clause, "And after the last of *December A.*---- the Treasurer is hereby directed, without further Advice or Order, to pay to the Bearer ---- Silver or ----- Gold upon Sight": The Fund for bringing in this Silver and Gold from abroad, to be Impost upon Goods, Tonnage, and Light-House Money, payable in Silver or Gold only. At the several Emissions, let there be an equal Sum taxed on subsequent Years within the Period; and these Taxes at

the same Time assessed on the several Towns, ordering the Province Treasurer at the stated Times to issue out his Warrants accordingly without further Order; to prevent breach of Faith in future Assemblies, refusing to assess the Taxes of the Year, which is the same as postponing. Thus all these Bills will have the *Credit of a Silver Bottom*, tho' in their Nature they will be cancelled in Course by Taxes, before the Period of redeeming them by *Silver* arrive; that is, *there will be none left to make a Demand upon the Treasury:* the Silver lodged, will, after the Period, be ready for any Exigency of Government. In Fact, if breach of publick Faith do not intervene; *the present Bills of the new Tenor will, by the end of* December *A.* 1742 *bring Silver to* 20 s. *per Oz.* — Let all new Emissions be in *Bills of a second new Tenor*, two for three of the first new Tenor, payable in Silver or Gold after the last of *December A* ----- if not paid in by Taxes as above. Thus *Silver will be brought to* 13 s. 4 d. *per Oz.* ----- Finally, after some Years let [**41**] all future Emissions be in *Bills of a third new Tenor* 1 for 2 of the second Tenor, payable in Silver or Gold after the last of *December A.* ---- with the forementioned Circumstances; *Silver will then be* 6 s. 8 d. *per Oz.* It is plain, that 100,000 *l.* of this last Money, will be a larger *Medium* of Trade, than 400,000 *l.* of the present Currency. *This promises best, and would be a gradual, gentle, and easy Method of making our Currency as valuable as that of Virginia*, which is the most valuable of all our Colony Currencies.

4. *The Parliament of Great Britain* are at this Time, perhaps, taking some more *summary Method* of setling our *Plantation Currencies* towards redressing the injured Merchants at Home, and the fair Dealers in the Colonies; they

made some Steps towards it last Sessions of Parliament. It is probable they may abridge the Plantations of this Privilege which they have assumed, of making their *publick Bills of Credit, a Tender* at any Rate they please to impose, which is *equal to the King's Prerogative in Coins.* And to prevent private Societies, from *bubbling* the People; perhaps, they may extend, the Act 6th *Annæ*, to the Plantations, viz. *That no Partnership exceeding Six shall act as Bankers.*

II. *Private Schemes.* It happens unluckily for our Paper Money Advocates, that, at this Time when the Parliament are about redressing these Grievances, they should *madly* advance many more Schemes (some fraudulent, some foolish, and some good, but impracticable) than ever before for multiplying of Paper Money; this makes good the old Saying, *Quem Deus vult perdere, prius dementat.*

All *Private Banks* for large Sums upon Subscription, have the same bad Consequence which attends publick Loans, viz. *a Snare to the People,* by giving the unwary, and the Prodigal, Opportunities of borrowing, that is, of involving & ruining themselves. [42] Our *Legislature* from Experience, are become sensible of this Error, and for many Years have issued no publick Loans.

i. *Land Banks.* The famous Mr. *Law,* noted for his Knowledge in the Chances of the Games called Hazard, and for these Fallacies called Sharping: in favour of a Land Bank, being preferable to Silver, says, That *Land Mortgaged serves for Money, and Culture,* or Produce at the same Time; whereas Silver cannot serve for Money, and Plate at the same Time. As he did not understand Trade, he did not consider that *Silver serves for Money and Merchandize* at the same Time, and that Trade is more profitable than

Agriculture. A Land Credit or Bank may do in a Country of no Trade: but it is ridiculous to imagine that it can serve as a *Medium* for foreign Commerce: it cannot be shipt off as Merchandize or Returns, as is the Case of Silver; it cannot be transferred by Bills of Exchange; for so many Ounces of Silver received in *Boston*, I can draw upon my Correspondent for so many Ounces of Silver payable in *London*, but for so many Acres of Land made over to me in *New England*, I cannot draw upon *England* for any Number of Acres, quantity and quality adjusted.

In a Country where the Denominations of their Currency depreciates, Land being fixed in itself, rises in Denomination Value, whilst what is owing upon the Land becomes so much less as the Denominations do depreciate: Hence it is, that a Land Bank is so much desired, by those who are in Debt or Mortgage, or who desire to run in Debt by Mortgaging their Lands.

2 *A Credit or Bank of Produce*, and Manufacture, will never answer in a Country where Idleness and Indolence prevails; a late large *Bounty upon Hemp* did not encourage the raising of any considerable Quantity thereof: it would prove a most perplexed labouring Affair, *viz.* inspecting the Quality, set-[43]tling from Time to Time the Market Price, Deficiencies in Case of bad Crops, and other Misfortunes: Notes payable at these *unweildy Stores*, would be of the same Nature, and attended with the same Inconveniencies, as the so much deservedly exclaimed against Shop Notes. In the Infancy of Countries, particularly of this *Province*, some Part of the Taxes were paid in Produce, called *Stock in the Treasury;* but as our foreign Trade did grow, it was found most convenient to discontinue it.

I shall exmplify our present Projections of Banks upon Land, Produce, or Manufacture; by only one Instance. *The Bubble of* 450,000 *l. upon Land and Produce*, which fills by Subscriptions a great Pace; the Subscribers by their Articles, give their *Twelve Directors a Negative in the whole Management*; a Power never before heard of in any Society of Bankers or joint Stocks; it is true, they deserve it; because, by the Face of their Bills, the Directors or *Signers promise to circulate the whole* 450,000 *l.* But is it possible, that any Man who gives himself the Trouble of thinking seriously, can imagine, that 12 Men of small Fortunes (who perhaps do not trade for 30,000 *l.* per Ann.) should in their Trade, immediately circulate 450,000 *L.?* Can it be supposed possible to *negotiate Notes of so great a Sum, upon so small a Bottom?* In short, this Scheme is so full of Inconsistencies, that it seems to *exceed any of the Bubbles* (which were upwards of 100 in Number) projected in *London*, in that Year of Bubbles *A.* 1720.

3. *A Credit upon a Silver Fund* well regulated as to Periods and Discounts, would answer, if there were no concomitant bad Currency: but as a bad Currency already prevails, and will in all probability increase; by two Years Charges of this Government to be emitted at once; by a 100,000 *l. Rhode-Island* Emission, which they may throw in upon us at Pleasure; and by a new Emission of 100,000 *l.* [44] from *Connecticut*, which they have been endeavouring from Time to Time, by trying to drop a majority of the present *Assistants* or Council; Silver will then rise in Price, and these Notes on a Silver Bottom becoming more valuable, will be hoarded up, lie dormant, and *answer no Design of a Currency:* It is true, *they will secure to the Possessor,*

his Principal with a growing Interest; but as to Currency they are worse than common Bills, which being daily let upon Bond to circulate and promote Business, tho' at the same Time the Owner or Creditor sinks part of his Principal, by its depreciating; and his Interest is ill paid from a general insensibility of Discredit. *Such Bills will never obtain a Currency, until they force a Discount upon the bad Currency.*

An Experiment of this Kind, has already been made by the *Merchants Notes* so called, without any good Effect: they never became a Currency; they prov'd a Snare to many of the Subscribers and Borrowers; Silver did rise in Price as much and perhaps more, than if they had never been emitted. Any Scheme of this Nature if upon a longer Period, will on that Account, be the more defective.

If the Scheme for emitting Company Notes or *Bills, to be paid after* 15 *Years, with Silver at* 20 *s. per Oz.* can be so contrived, as to bring a growing Discount upon the bad Currency; it will be of the greatest Service to this Province. It seems to bid fair for it (I am no Undertaker nor Promoter thereof, and therefore may be deemed *impartial*) the Undertakers are Men of known Probity, of the best Estates and of the largest Trade in this Place: by their Articles they oblige themselves under high pecuniary Penalties, to circulate these Bills at a certain annually growing Value, until they arrive at 20 s. per Oz. and, in conformity to a late Law of this Province, to refuse all future Emissions of the neighbouring Governments, unless founded upon a Silver Bottom.

[45] *It may perhaps be advisable to suspend the Execution of any Paper Money Schemes, as the Affair of Colony Paper Credit, is this present Sessions, under the immediate Consid-*

eration of the Parliament of Great Britain, our supreme and absolute Lawgiver: lest the Subscribers (Undertakers) or Possessors of these Bills and Notes should suffer some considerable Damage, by their peremptory Suppression.

The Projectors of the many various private Banks for Currency, seem to presume too much upon the Indulgence or *Connivance of our Legislature:* Some audaciously question their Power to prevent the People from *bubbling* one another, (being as they call it) an *Act of Liberty and Property to pass and receive Notes of Hand;* others impudently impeach the Integrity of the Majority of the Legislature, as being in a private Capacity Promoters and Encouragers of these *Bubbles.* Doubtless our Legislature, as the *natural Guardians* of the People, will compassionately prevent their ruining themselves; by proper Laws, such as those in *Great Britain* 6*th Annæ* against Bankers, and sundry Acts against Bubbles; or to go no further for a Precedent, that of our neighbouring Colony *Connecticut, A.* 1733, against private Society or Bank Bills. There seems, at least for the present, an absolute Necessity to suppress those which will unavoidably have a riotous Consequence; I mean the passing upon the unwary, for a valuable Consideration, *Bills without any true Fund or Bottom:* Such Bills soon stop in Currency, and the poor innocent Possessors, the Tradesmen and Artificers, who for special Reasons (as they express it) are made their *Dupes,* will be provoked to use the Persons and Effects of the Projectors and Signers of those Bills in a *riotous* Manner. Our Assembly did formerly effectually suppress the pernicious Bubbles of private *Lotteries.* Our Law enacted in *January, A.* 1738, may be extended, so as to comprehend [46] private Societies amongst our selves. *This Act forbids* *passing or receiving Bills to be issued by the neighbouring Governments, unless redeemable by lawful Money,* (Silver Proclamation Value) *upon good Security,* (*to appear upon the Face of the Bill*) *within ten Years after their first Emission.*

While this Affair of *Colony Paper Money* is under Consideration of Parliament for Redress; it will appear as a *daring Presumption*, to proceed to large Emissions, especially in those Colonies who have *valuable Charters* to lose. I mention this with a particular regard to *Connecticut*, who have hitherto behaved well; but at present their Eastern Borders being tainted by a bad (I had almost said *abandoned*) Neighbourhood, the Colony in general ought to be upon their Guard.

In redressing this Error, in which many of our Plantations have obstinately persisted for many Years: it is to be hoped the *Parliament of Great Britain*, will not use any rigorous sudden Methods; but give us Time gently & gradually to extricate our Selves; That we may be allowed upon any sudden extraordinary publick Exigences to emit *Government Notes* to be a Tender only in publick Taxes, and to be called in as soon as may be by subsequent Taxes: that publick Bills may never be a Tender in Trade and Business. As to the calling in of publick Bills already extant; in those Governments where the Periods are short (*in New-Hampshire, Massachusetts-Bay, and Connecticut*, they do not extend beyond *A.* 1742) they may be allowed to run their Course: Where the Periods are long; if upon *Taxes*, as the Governments have the Privilege of Taxing at any Time, they may be required to assess the same at any Time sooner; if upon *Loan* the Borrowers may be obliged to pay in yearly for a few Years a certain Part of the Debt, but if they insist upon the original long Period, let the [47] Governments give Premium's upon all such Bills, as they are brought in; thus few or none of these Bills will be left with the Borrowers, and at the Expiration of the Periods of the Loans, they must pay in lawful Money Proclamation Value; which they will by all Means endeavour to avoid, by paying as is directed.

FINIS.

NOTE TO "A DISCOURSE CONCERNING THE CURRENCIES,"
ETC.

On the 18th of March, 1740, the following advertisement appeared in the New England Weekly Journal:

Just Published and, Sold by Kneeland *and* Green, *over and against the Prison.*

A Discourse concerning the Currencies of the British Plantations in America: Especially, with Regard to their PAPER MONEY. More particularly in Relation to the Provinces of the *Massachusetts Bay* in *New England.*

This was, without much doubt, an announcement of the first appearance of Douglass's "Discourse," etc., a pamphlet which earned fame for its writer, and concerning the date of the first appearance of which bibliographers have had doubts.

According to Sabin the "Discourse" was originally printed in

London in 1739.[1]   The date of this London edition, which was fifty-
four pages in length, was purely conjectural, there being no date given
on the title-page, and the assignment to 1739 was unquestionably erroneous.   This assignment was probably due to repeated statements
made in the pamphlet itself that it was being written during the year
1739.   A closer analysis of these statements would have shown that
its publication in London in 1739 was impossible.   It may be inferred
from the contents of the pamphlet that its composition was begun
early in the year 1739 and finished in the first part of 1740.   The
references by page which I shall now give are made to the Boston
edition which came out, as appears from the above advertisement,
March 18th, 1740, and which was forty-seven pages in length.

On page 19 Douglass says, "Exchange with Great Britain being
at this time (Febr. 1739); " on pages 23, 33, and 36 he mentions
the year 1739 as being the year in which he was writing; on page
32 he gives the price of silver "in Autumn 1739; " on page 39 he
says, "We have at this time (Christmas *A*. 1739)," etc.   In other
words, in February, 1739, he was at work on the nineteenth page.
He had certainly reached the thirty-second page in the autumn of
the year, and by Christmas he had reached the thirty-ninth page.
Then followed the interval required for the remaining eight pages,
and for the type setting and press work on the pamphlet in preparation for its being placed before the public on the eighteenth of
March, 1740.

The assignment by Sabin of priority to the London edition
relegated the Boston edition to the subordinate position of a reprint, and inasmuch as it came out early in the year almost necessitated the use of the date 1739 for the London edition to make this
possible.   Mr. Wilberforce Eames is authority for the statement that
this undated London edition has been variously put in different
catalogues under the years 1739, 1740, and 1741.[2]   If we should
adopt the natural order of issue and assign priority to the Boston
edition, the London edition would then become the reprint and
might easily have been published in 1740.

[1] Dictionary of books relating to America, under " Douglass."
[2] Currency and Banking in Massachusetts Bay, Vol. II, p. 178.

Sabin in describing the different editions of the " Discourse " says that one of them was printed in Boston in 1740, with a postscript. This is true, and yet it is not strictly true. It does not tell the whole story. The " Discourse " was originally printed in Boston without any postscript, a feature that made it almost unique among the controversial pamphlets of the day, but a postscript with continuous pagination, separately published and separately advertised, was put on the market three months after the appearance of the pamphlet.

The " Discourse " was reprinted in London in 1751, with the postscript, which fact was stated on the title-page. The Boston pamphlet, originally 47 pages in length, was swelled to 62 pages with the added postscript. The London edition of 1751 preserved this number of pages.

In 1857, J. R. M'Culloch edited a collection of tracts which was published by Lord Overstone.[1] He reprinted the " Discourse " and thus refers to previous editions on his title-page: " Boston, printed MDCCXL, and London; Reprinted MDCCLI."

In 1897, the American Economic Association reprinted the " Discourse " in Number 5 of the second volume of Economic Studies. The value of this edition was greatly augmented by the admirable annotations of Professor Charles J. Bullock, the editor, and was enriched by a carefully prepared sketch by Mr. Bullock of Douglass's life [2] in which the writer did full justice to Douglass's learning and capacity. Professor Bullock very naturally accepts the date assigned by the bibliographers, 1739,[3] for the appearance of the first London edition, and also includes " Some Observations on the Scheme for emitting 60.000 l.," etc., among Douglass's writ-

---

[1] A select collection of scarce and valuable tracts and other publications on paper currency and banking, etc., London, 1857.

[2] Douglass in the first paragraph of the " Discourse " says, " *The Author is not a transient Person.*" To this statement the following written annotation is appended in the margin of my copy of the Discourse: *Dr. Douglass transibat ab Edenburgia in Scotia ad Jamaicam, & inde inter Insulas Caribbeanas — deinde p Provincias anglo-marinas — domum Bostoniâ Demoratus est.*

[3] I myself have never before ventured to dispute this assertion. The language used in the Introduction, Vol. I of this series, p. 85, will show, however, that I had some doubts.

ings, for which he refers to Sabin as authority. On page 284 Professor Bullock says, "Although the Discourse Concerning the Currencies of the British Plantations was published anonymously in London, Douglass's name appeared in the Boston edition, in 1740," and follows this up by putting the name on the title-page of the "Discourse." The Boston edition does not contain any avowal that Douglass is the author, but most of the copies that I have seen have the fact endorsed on the title-page in writing. This error is probably chargeable to a copyist.

In the "Essay," etc., Douglass undertook to reply to the arguments set forth in "Some Obversations," etc. It would seem as if he considered while writing the "Discourse" that the author of "Some Observations," etc., was finally disposed of. He nowhere alludes to that pamphlet and nowhere indicates that it is entitled to further consideration. His analysis of the arguments of the paper money men is general in its character and he rehearses the various familiar propositions put forth in support of Land Banks by the projectors of Blackwell's Bank, by the supporters of the project of 1714, by Colman in his "Schæme" in "The distressed state of the town of Boston once more considered," and still more recently by the proponent of the plan for a Land Bank contained in "A proposal to supply the Trade," etc., without however specifying in any way the particular writer whom he was at the time criticising.

In his discussion of the private schemes for supplying a currency to the province, he refers to Land Banks in general, and to the various attempts which had been made in the past or were then being advocated before the public. He divides his subject so as to treat of Land Banks in general, of the Connecticut Land Bank of 1732, of the Merchants' Notes of 1733, of the Land Bank and Manufactory Scheme, and of the Silver Bank. The only scheme of this nature of any historical importance which had been up to that date actually inaugurated in New England during this period and which had proceeded to emit notes for currency, that does not find mention was the project of the Portsmouth merchants in 1734, which was actually put in operation and emitted notes sometimes called the New Hampshire Notes, and this enterprise never amounted to much.

The reference by Douglass (p. 38) to a scheme for the emission of £500,000, "without fund or period," for the purpose of heading off the Rhode Island Notes cannot be satisfactorily identified with any project that I have seen. That which comes nearest to the demands of Douglass's paragraph is the plan for a bank of £500,000 in "A proposal to supply the trade," etc. His classification of the scheme, and the language that he uses in speaking of it, would indicate that he was dealing with some proposed government emission. Except for this his description tallies well with the scheme of the pamphlet mentioned above.

The Connecticut company referred to by Douglass was entitled "The New London Society United for Trade and Commerce in Connecticut in New England." In 1729 a petition was made to the Connecticut assembly for a charter for a company of somewhat similar name which should permit the emission of bills of credit for currency. The petition was not then granted, but in 1732 a second petition, which did not ask for the privilege of emitting bills, but purported to seek for the organization of a company for trade and commerce, was more favorably received and the charter was granted. The company organized and soon disclosed the fact that the special trade and commerce that it desired to foster was in the nature of circulating the bills of credit of the company.

Governor Talcott, as soon as he heard what was going on, summoned a special session of the Connecticut assembly and secured the passage of an act dissolving the charter of the company and providing for winding up its affairs. In the course of the discussion in the assembly some very interesting law questions were propounded. One of them was "Whether it was within the authority of the government of Connecticut to make a company or society of merchants?" In other words, could a mercantile company like Connecticut create a corporation?

In addition to the proceedings through which the "New London Society," etc., was closed up, the Connecticut assembly in 1733 passed an act prohibiting any persons or societies from striking or emitting bills of credit of the tenor of the bills of public credit. This act was printed in the Weekly Rehearsal of November 19, 1733, in connection with an opinion of Attorney-General Northey as to the legality of such emissions.

After reciting the act in full the article in the Rehearsal concludes as follows:

> Quaere, *Whether any Number of Persons by Way of Partnership can Emit Bills on Land Security, not having the Sanction of the Government?*
> I am of Opinion small Numbers as Goldsmiths in Trade may Keep Cash, and give out Cash Notes, but a great Number cannot unite together and have Directors or Managers, and act as a Bank, without a Royal Charter, or Act of Assembly.
>
> *Edward Northey.*

The prompt action of Governor Talcott in securing the suppression of the New London Company, and the prohibition in Connecticut of any and all companies whose purpose was to emit currency, relieved that colony from participation in the struggles that shook Massachusetts to the centre a few years later. The story of the New London Company has been told in full elsewhere.[1]

The Merchants' Notes of 1733 have been so frequently mentioned in this volume that no special description of them is required. They produced one effect, however, which is worthy of notice. They stimulated the people of Portsmouth, New Hampshire, to form, in 1734, a similar organization and to emit notes for circulation as currency. These notes bore interest at one per cent per annum and were payable in 1746 in silver and gold, at the then current price or in passable bills of credit on the provinces of New Hampshire and Massachusetts and the colonies of Rhode Island and Connecticut. Legislation was effected in Massachusetts prohibiting the circulation of these notes, but the province act was disallowed by the Lords of Trade on the ground that the notes were emitted " by a set of private men, who according to our information are of the best estates and rank in New Hampshire " and who had entered " into the Association for issuing Promissory Notes or Bills

---

[1] Currency and Banking in Massachusetts Bay, Vol. II, p. 102 *et seq.*; A Connecticut Land Bank of the Eighteenth Century, Quarterly Journal of Economics, Vol. XIII, October, 1898.

bearing an interest of one p^r cent p^r annum, which notes no man is obliged to accept in payment, having in themselves no currency in law, but are left to stand or fall according to the credit of the signers, and may be taken or refused at pleasure."[1] This support of the Board of Trade did not prove to be of much service to these notes.

After dealing generally with Land Banks, Douglass, in his "Discourse," devotes an article to what he terms "*A Credit or Bank of Produce, and Manufacture.*" He says in this article, "I shall exemplify our present Projections of Banks upon Land, Produce, or Manufacture; by only one Instance. *The Bubble* of 450.000 *l. upon Land and Produce*, which fills by Subscriptions a great Pace . . ." In this he can only refer to what is generally spoken of as the Land Bank of 1740, which, in its original broadside appealing to the public, stated that it was "proposed to set up a Bank on Land Security;" which in the articles of association finally adopted was denominated in the heading "The Manufactory Scheme," and in the text of the articles "The Manufactory Company;" the stock of the bills to be emitted by which in both broadside and articles was limited to £150,000; and which in consequence of this joint character was not infrequently called "The Land Bank and Manufactory Scheme." Douglass was in the habit of stating his values in "old tenor." The "first new tenor" notes were then in circulation and were receivable by the government on the basis of three of the old tenor bills for one of the new. The new tenor bills and the Land Bank bills were stated to be worth in denominational value the equivalent of silver at six shillings and eight pence an ounce. Douglass probably converted the nominal valuation of the bills to be emitted into old tenor by multiplying by three, thus giving them a value to which they were not entitled.[2]

[1] Acts and Resolves, Province of Massachusetts Bay, Vol. II, pp. 746, 747. See also Currency and Banking in Massachusetts Bay, Vol. II, pp. 126–129.

[2] In a similar way a writer in 1744 says: "the Sum in Notes of Hand proposed to be emitted by the Land Bank Company, being *l.* 150,000 to pass as lawful Money (that is) equal to *l.* 600.000 in Bills of Credit of the old Tenor . . ." At the time this was written the new tenor bills of later issue than the first were receivable by the government on the basis of four old tenor for one of the new.

It is not possible within the compass of this note to give any idea of the remarkable story of the Land Bank of 1740. A suggestion has already been made in the note to the communication to the Weekly Journal of January 1, 1740, as to what the project was. The social and political contest precipitated by its appearance upon the scene was practically the history of the province for the next few years. We shall deal with other pamphlets in which the events that justify this assertion will be discussed, and through their pages the reader will be able to learn facts which will enable him to comprehend what that contest amounted to.

The Mr. W. who persuaded the government of Barbados to emit notes, and who is alluded to by Douglass on pages 18 and 25 of the "Discourse," was the Reverend John Woodbridge. For further details concerning him see Volume I of this series, pp. 118, 119.

The first London edition of the "Discourse" is very rare. There is a copy in the John Carter Brown Library. The Boston 1740 edition can be found in the following libraries: American Antiquarian Society, Boston Athenæum, Boston Public Library, Harvard College Library, John Carter Brown Library, Library of Congress, Library of Massachusetts Historical Society, and New York Public Library. The copy of the text from which this reprint was made was taken from a volume of my own. The photograph of the title-page was procured at the Boston Public Library. The leaves measure 7⅞ by 5¼ inches.

An Inquiry

INTO THE

Nature and Uses of Money

More especially of the *Bills of Publick*
Credit, Old *Tenor.*

A PROPOSAL ... ief in the
preface Explained.

To which is added,
A Reply to the *Essay on Silver and Paper*
Currencies.

B O S T O N: Printed and Sold ... over against the ...

An Inquiry

INTO THE

Nature and Uses of Money

More especially of the *Bills* of Publick
Credit, *Old Tenor*.

Together with
A PROPOSAL, of some proper Relief in the
present Exigence.

To which is added,
A Reply to the *Essay on Silver and Paper
Currences*.

BOSTON: Printed and Sold by S. KNEELAND & T. GREEN,
over against the Prison, in Queenstreet. 1740.

An Inquiry

INTO THE

Nature and Uſes of *Money*;

More eſpecially of the *Bills* of Publick
Credit, *Old Tenor*.

Together with
A PROPOSAL of ſome proper Relief in the
preſent Exigence.

To which is added,
A Reply to the *Eſſay on Silver and Paper
Currences*.

B O S T O N: Printed and Sold by S. KNEELAND & T. GREEN,
over againſt the Priſon in Queenſtreet. 1 7 4 0.

[ ]

An Inquiry into the Nature and Uses of *Money*, &c.

 HE Title-Page sufficiently shews the Reader the Design I have in Hand. To pursue it in the clearest Method, I propose

First, to treat of the *Value* or *Estimation* of Things.

Secondly, of the *Changes* in the comparative Value, or Price of Things in the Market.

Thirdly, of *Money*.

Fourthly, of *Banks*, with a PROPOSAL.

Finally, I shall make some Observations on a Piece, intitled, *An Essay on Silver and Paper Currences.*

Of these in their Order: And

I. Of the *Value* or *Estimation* of Things.

All Things that are in Use in the World, have their Value or Estimation from two different Causes, *viz* either

1st from the craving *Necessity*, or 2dly from the voluntary *Choice* of Mankind.

Those of the *first* Sort have a *real* and *intrinsick* Value or Estimation, which is unchangeable and cannot be withdrawn: but those of the *second* Sort have only an *accidental* or *circumstantial* Value or Estimation, which is changeable, and not only may be, but often is withdrawn.

Of the first sort of Things the most remarkable Articles are Air, Water, necessary Provisions &c. which as they are absolutely necessary to our being and well-being, we must value or esteem them highly, and [2] readily part with all other Things in our Possession (which have only their accidental Value) for a present Supply of any of them, when it happens to be in the Power and Pleasure of others to with-hold them from us; or in other Words, we find by Experience that there is a certain Virtue in the Things themselves, which we cannot but value or esteem: And this I take to be the true meaning of *intrinsick* Value, tho' in common Speech it is often otherwise applied; as we say, that one Piece of *Silver* has more intrinsick Value than another Piece; by which we mean no more than that one Piece *weighs* more than another, when they are both of the same *fineness*; or that one Piece has more *fine* Silver in it than another, when they are both of the same *weight*. We say also that *South Sea Stock* rose above its intrinsic Worth, meaning no more than that it rose higher than its *Dividend* was worth.

We must add one Instance more, which particularly relates to our present Case, *viz.* in *New England* we commonly say, that *Silver* has an *intrinsick* Value, and *Bills* of publick Credit have not: and why? because Silver will pass generally throughout the trading World, and Bills of Credit only in *New England*. But that is wrong, for the universal Currency of Silver (strictly speaking) gives it no intrinsick Value, and the Value of each is only accidental, as we shall shew anon.

Of the *second* Sort of Things, *viz*. Those that have only an *accidental* Value or Estimation, there are innumerable Articles, as Diamonds and other curious Stones, Jewels of all Sorts, Silver and Gold, also every Degree of Finery, in the several Species of Manufactures, beyond what is absolutely necessary; and in short, every Article of Provision, Cloathing, or Lodging, upon which there is more Cost bestowed than is needful. These have their Value or Estimation from the *voluntary Choice* of Mankind, guided either by Reason, or meer Humour & Fancy, in choosing one Thing and neglecting or refusing another at one Time, and again choosing what they before neglected or refused.

Some of these Articles have obtained a very *general* Value in the World, as Silver and Gold, Time immemorial; others have had it only in *particular* Places in a more changeable Manner; and a third Sort change with the Fashion for the Year or a particular Season, and either go into disuse, or at least are greatly reduced in their Price [3] till the Return of the Fashion brings them in use again. Thus we may probably suppose, *Silver* was first brought into use as a *Metal*, and in Time it was used as *Money*, passing by Weight (either in unequal *Pieces*, or else in Coins, where the Weight and Fineness of each Piece is ascertained) till it obtained the common Consent of the trading World; and so long as that continues, it will have an accidental Value; but when

·it is withdrawn (if ever) Silver must go into disuse, and be of no Value.

Under this Head of the second Sort of Commodities, are our *Bills* of publick Credit, of the old Tenor, to be ranked: They have not an intrinsick Value, as *Air* and *Water*; but an accidental Value, as *Silver* & *Gold*, founded partly upon the Promise of this Government, but principally on the common Consent of this and the other Colonies that are pleased to receive them. They are not *universal* Commodities, as Silver, Iron, &c but *local*, or confined to these Provinces which : however makes no material Difference in the present Case, as we shall show in the Sequel.

I am perswaded, that in order to form a right Judgment of the Cause of the present Difficulties in the Trade of this Province, and find out a proper Remedy, nothing can give greater Light, than the right Understanding of this Point; and therefore shall further pursue the Argument, and endeavour to make it plain and obvious to the Understanding of every Body.

And here,

1st. That the Bills are a *Commodity*, will appear by *comparing* their Promise with the Promise of any other Commodity. For Example, the implicit Promise of an Ounce of *Silver* is, that it will be received universally in exchange for Wheat or any other Commodity at the Market-Price, so long as common Consent shall continue to value Silver; but the *Bills* have a twofold Promise, *viz* An *explicit* Promise on the Face of them, and in the Acts by which they were emitted, *That the Government will receive them in all publick Payments, or for any Stock* (as Wheat, &c.) *at any Time in the Treasury,* meaning to be disposed of at the Market-

Price; and the Bills can never go into disuse, because there is a Demand for every Shilling of them, founded in the Acts of Government, and they must for ever be a lawful Tender for publick Taxes, so long as any of them are extant. And besides this explicit, the Bills have also an *implicit* Promise foun-[4]ded in the *common Consent* of the Colonies where they pass.

But great Stress is laid upon that Part of the Promise, *shall be in Value equal to Money*; — that is (say some) shall be made good to the Possessor at the Rate of Silver-Money at *eight Shillings* per *Ounce*, which I reckon might in the Year 1702 be near the Rate Silver passed at in the Market; and so they would put the Bills on the Foot of the common *promissory Notes* in Trade.

But that they are not common promissory Notes, is plain; for these must express the Thing promised, as so many Ounces of Silver, Pounds of Iron, of a certain Fineness &c. besides the Time when, and the Place where they are to be paid off: neither of which are to be found in the Bills, nor in the Acts of Government; all which will appear upon Examination. For in the Year 1702, the Government first began to emit the Bills, now called old Tenor, and the general Reasons assigned in the Act then, and in the subsequent Acts for and relating to the Emissions, were *the extreme Scarcity of* (Silver) *Money, and the Want of other Media of Commerce*: And in 1704 they say, *and the Impossibility that the Money, Plate and Bullion within this Province, can support the Charge of the War*: And in 1716 they say, *All the Silver-Money which formerly made Payments in Trade easy, being now sent into* Great Britain, *to make Return for Part of what is owing there; by Means of all which the Trade of the Province is greatly obstructed, and the Payment of the publick Debts and Taxes retarded, and in a great Measure rendered impracticable* &c. Thus far for the Design of the Government; and next for the Tenor of the Bills themselves, *viz —This indented Bill of Twenty Shillings, due from the Province of the Massachusetts-Bay in New England, to the Possessor thereof shall be in Value equal to Money. and shall be accordingly accepted by the Treasurer, and Receivers subordinate to him in all publick Payments, and for any Stock at any Time in the Treasury* Boston, *November 21st,* 1702. *By Order of the Great and General Court or Assembly.* I R. E. H. N E *Committee* — Now from the foregoing Quotations it is very plain, that the Government intend no more than this, *viz* That inasmuch as there was not Silver-Money sufficient to carry on the Affairs of the Province, they proj cted those Bills, and promised to give them the same Credit as they did Silver-Money, i. e. where they owed *twenty Shillings* in Silver they paid it by one of their [5] *twenty Shilling* Bills, and where any Person owed them *twenty Shillings* for Taxes, or had bought any Commodity of them to that Value, they received the same *twenty Shilling* Bill back again in Payment. And indeed to have emitted special promissory Notes, as Affairs were thus circumstanced, would have intirely defeated the chief Design of the Government, *viz.* That their Bills should be negotiated without Discount, and serve as well for the Trade, as publick Taxes; and the Consequences of such Bills would have been to introduce *Stock jobbing* and *usurious* Practices, to the Damage both of the political and trading Interests of the Province.

Indeed there is no mention made of their being received
as a *Commodity*, but only as Money; however, that is sufficiently imply'd: for the more general Definition of Money is
briefly this, *viz* Any one Commodity (or a Number of
Commodities) chosen out of all others, and received either by
the trading World in general, or any Community of People
in particular, more readily than all other Commodities passing in Trade, and that for which Contracts or Agreements
are usually made.   The Notion of a Commodity is insep-
arable from that of Money; they differ only in Degree,
being of the same Kind.   All Moneys are Commodities:
but all Commodities are not Moneys; because the latter by
common Consent will be more readily received than the
former.   Thus as the ingenious Mr. *Lock* well observes,
" Amongst all other Commodities passing in " Trade, Money
is truly one ".   For Example, Silver, Iron, and Lead,
are all Commodities generally in Use, but Silver is used
as the Money, or the most general Commodity in the
trading World; and here in *New-England* having no
Silver, nor other fit Commodity for Money, our Bills
of Credit are received as the most general Commodity,
or Money.

2dly. As *other* Commodities are *distinguished* by their
Weight, Fineness, Measure &c. and have a greater or less
Value in Proportion thereto (i. e. two Ounces of Silver will
purchase double the assigned Quantity of other things in
the Market, that one Ounce of the same Fineness will do,
and so on)   In like Manner our *Bills* are distinguished by
their *Quantity* or Number, as *twenty* and *forty Shillings*
&c. (the last will purchase twice as much as the first) and
by their *Impression, Subscriptions*, and other Marks of

Distinction; by all which they are as well secured, if not better than any other Commodity, from Counterfeits.

[6] I must here observe by the Way, that they are not such a Commodity as hath its Value only from the *Usefulness* of its *Matter* (which indeed is most agreeable to the vulgar Notion of a Commodity) as *Iron*, which is made into a vast Variety of useful Manufactures: But we have already shown, that it is in the Power, and the usual Practice of Mankind, by common Consent to give an *accidental Value* to Things for different Reasons, as to *Diamonds*, and other curious Stones, for the Sake of their Colour; to *Silver* chiefly as qualify'd for Money; and to set these Things at a vast Degree of Value beyond *Iron*, tho' the most useful of any Thing that comes under the Head of accidental Value.

3dly. They are a Commodity *the best qualified for the true Ends and Uses of Money*, of any other Commodity whatever. But the Proof of this I must defer till I come to the Head of Money.

And finally, Without labouring the Point in Hand, the Fact is *self-evident*, and must appear so to every one in Trade. For supposing any Man in this Province possessed of any Quantity of *Wheat, Silver, Iron*, or any other Commodities, and *Bills* of Credit, he cannot be insensible that although the first three Articles are in general Demand, yet the *Bills* are by far the most useful, will be vastly more readily received, and may be negotiated to much better Advantage, than those or any other Commodities whatever in Trade.

I shall only add here, the Bills were in the Year 1702 *received* by the common Consent of the Province, as a *Commodity*, passing among others in the Market, or as *Money*, the most general Commodity in Use among us. At their first Emission *eight Shillings* in *Bills* were made equivalent (suppose) to one Ounce of *Silver*, thirty two Pound of *Iron*, and seven Pecks of *Wheat;* or in Words more adapted to our common Way of Speaking, equivalent to *Silver* at *eight Shillings* per Ounce, *Iron* at *three Pence* per Pound, and *Wheat* at *four Shillings and seven Pence* per Bushel, and to other Things at the then current Market Price. And having been thus established in Credit, and continued so ever since, they never could change their Value, but by the *same Means* that all other Commodities always have, and still continue to do; which brings me to consider the *second* Thing proposed, namely, [7]

The CHANGES *in the comparative Value of Price of Things in the Market.*

HAVING finished the Distinction of *real* and *accidental* Value, I have now to do with the *comparative* Value, or (as it is commonly called) the Price of Things in the Market; this being the common Notion of Value, and understood by every Body, I shall proceed to the Matter in Hand.

All Things in Use in the World, whether they have a real or accidental Value, *change* their comparative Value or Price in the Market, from the *same Causes, viz.* either from the *Plenty* or *Scarcity* of the Commodity to be sold, or from the greater or smaller Number of *Buyers*; but more fully and clearly expressed thus, by Means of any Change in the *Proportion* between the *Quantity* to be *sold*, and the *Demand* for that Quantity.

By the *Quantity to be sold*, we must understand the present Quantity of Goods that the *Sellers* are inclined or forced to part with; and by the *Demand*, the present Quantity of Goods, which the *Buyers* are under Obligations at the same time to purchase. For the deferring the Sale or Purchase of Things till tomorrow, or the next Month, or Year, has no Effect upon the present Market.

The true Proportion between Quantity and Demand, as to any Commodity, is rarely known; because no Man can tell what Obligation or Disposition other People may have to sell or buy. We can only form a general Judgment of the Circumstance of the Market; but may be fully satisfied that a Change in the Price can proceed from no other Cause, but a Change in the Proportion of the Quantity and Demand: For Example, Suppose a Man went to Market yesterday and bought Wheat at *ten Shillings*, and to day was obliged to give *eleven Shillings*, he might easily discover that there was less Wheat, or more Buyers, at Market to day than yesterday. The exact Change in the Proportion, between yesterday and to day, none can tell; but every one must necessarily conclude, that the Change in the Price was the Effect of the Change in the Proportion of the Quantity and Demand. Many Incidents may contribute to raise or lessen the Demand for a Commodity, besides its own natural and common Circumstances. For Instance, the short Crop of *Indian* Corn and Rye may [8] be supplied by good Crops of *Wheat*, and consequently the Demand for *Wheat* increased thereby: As on the other hand, a Plenty of fresh *Fish* or wild *Pigeons* will have a Tendency to lessen the Demand for *Beef*, and consequently affect the Price of it: But these and all other the like Circumstances are included in the Notion of Quantity and Demand.

All *exportable* Commodities, common to the World in general, change their Value by Means of any Change in the Proportion between the Quantity and Demand in the whole trading World; but such as are *not* exportable, change their Value from the same Cause, within any particular Country.

Of the *first* Sort are Wheat and other Grain, salted Provisions, as Beef, Pork, Butter, and Fish, Metals of all Sorts, and innumerable other Articles. The Price of these, when taken for a Number of Years, is comparatively the same in all Places where there is Freedom of Trade; as having only this Difference, that those Countries that have the Commodities *imported* to them, must pay all Charges, besides a reasonable Profit to the Importer; at least the Merchant always adventures upon that Supposition. And thus the Price of a Quintal of Cod-Fish in this Province is governed by the Proportion of the whole Quantity carried every where, to the whole Demand every where within the Compass of the Fish-Trade. As we are *Exporters*, we save the Charge of Transportation, as to what is consumed among us; which we should pay, were it imported to us from other Countries. And the Merchant must make a Judgment from his former Experience, and the best present Advices he can obtain.

Of the *second* Sort of Things, *viz* Those that have only a special or local Value, the most remarkable Articles are Houses and other Buildings, Lands under most Circumstances, Mutton, Fowl wild and tame, fresh Fish, Roots, Herbage, Fruits &c. these being either not exported at all, or but rarely, change their Value in every Country, as the Quantity is greater or less within themselves in Proportion to the Demand, & many Times with as little Regard to the Prices of the same Kind of Things in other Countries, as if they were unknown to all the rest of the World. The most remarkable Instance in this Part of the World is our *wild Pigeons*, which are sold at one T me for *five Shillings* per Dozen, and in two or three Weeks, or perhaps Days, fall down to *five Pence*, [9] and so by Degrees return to *five Shillings* again; and yet there is no Article in Trade but under the same Circumstances would undergo the same Changes.

There may be some Exceptions to the foregoing general Rules, and particularly in this Province, *viz.* Our Beef, Pork, Butter, and many other Articles, which are usually exported, have their Value from the Quantity and Demand within this Province, because we have not yet a Surplusage of them to send abroad to foreign Markets; our own Demand being equal to the Quantity: and sometimes we are obliged to import Butter in particular from *Ireland.* Whereas if we depended on a foreign Market for the Sale of a Surplusage of Beef, the Price of *fresh* Beef in this Province would be govern'd by the Price of *salt* Beef in the Markets to which we exported it; which is the present Case of our Cod-Fish. And here I cannot but make a short Remark, of what vast Importance our *trading* Interest is to our landed Interest, and how solicitous our Country-Gentlemen ought to be to support it; for if they depended chiefly upon foreign Markets for the Sale of their Produce, the Prices thereof must fall at least to half, if not a third of the present Money, (*viz.* Silver at *twenty-nine Shillings* per Ounce) and their inexportable Articles to a very trifle (compared with the Prices in the Mother-Country, and other trading Countrys) and the Purchase Value of their *Lands* fall in Proportion to the Fall of their *Produce.*

The Rents of *Houses* and *Lands* are governed by the Proportion of Quantity and Demand, and the Purchase-Value is governed by the Rent: For Example, if a House bring in *one hundred Pounds* a Year neat Rent (supposing the common Rate of Houses twenty Years Purchase) it may sell for *two thousand Pounds;* but if by a Change in the Quantity, or Demand, it bring in *two hundred Pounds* a Year, it will then sell for *two thousand Pounds* &c.

The same may be said of *Money.* There is one Way of Judging of the Change of its Value, by *comparing* it with other Things in the *Market;* and another Way of Judging of it, by the Change of its yearly *Increase* or *Interest*: For agreable to Mr. *Lock, Money* is fitly compared to *Land;* Mankind by common Agreement or publick Authority having added a Faculty to it (which naturally it has not) of increasing yearly so much per *Cent*: In the Land it is called Rent, in the Money Use or Interest.

[10] Of these in their Order.

1st. As to the Change in the Value of *Money,* when *compared* with *Goods* in the *Market.* Mr. *Lock* observes, "That the *natural Value* of Money in *exchanging* for any one *Commodity*, is the *Quantity* of the trading Money of the Kingdom, *designed* for that Commodity, in *Proportion* to that single *Commodity* and its *Vent*". This is certainly true: and therefore it is exceeding difficult to judge when the Change is in the *Money,* and not in the *Commodity* for which it is given.

It is equally difficult to judge of the *general* Change of Money in the Market of the trading World: For, tho' it be certain that many Things have *risen* in Value, in some Proportion to the Increase of *Silver* (the common Money) in

Europe, yet it is equally certain that many Things have *fallen* in Value, more especially of later Years, notwithstanding the yearly Increase of Silver. For *Money* has this extraordinary Faculty, that altho' it be the Cause of a *greater Demand* for many Things, yet (as it circulates vastly quicker than any other Commodity) it gives a Spring and Encouragement to the *Invention* and *Industry* of Mankind, and so becomes also the Means of *increasing* the *Quantity* of many Things, equal to, and often vastly exceeding, the most extravagant Demand.

A further Reason for the Difficulty of Judging in this Case, take from Mr. *Lock*: "For Money (meaning Silver Money) being look'd upon as the *standing Measure* of other Commodities, Men consider and speak of it *still* as if it were a standing Measure, tho' when it has *alter'd its Quantity* (meaning in Proportion to Demand) it's plain it is *not*."

But the best and clearest Notion, that we can have of the Change of the Value of *Silver Money*, is by the *Influence* it has on the *Mode of Living* in all Countries where it is in Use: For upon a new Accession of Money, People require not only a greater Number of Articles, but a greater Degree of Finery in the same Sorts; so that the yearly *Expence* is considerably *increased*, even tho' some Articles should continue at the *same*, or even *fall* in their *Price*. Thus in *England*, and more particularly in *London*, the Difference in the Mode of Living, since the opening of the Spanish Mines in *America*, to this Day, may probably be as *one* is to *thirty*, if not more, for Men of the same Rank and Employment: And yet many Articles, more especially those that are raised in the *American* [11] Plantations, are sold for a trifle of *Silver* now, to what they were then sold for.

2dly. As to the Change in the Value of Money with Regard to its *natural Interest,* or *yearly Increase.*

By *natural* Interest I mean the *Market-Rate* of Interest, which subsists in all Countries, and is sometimes *above,* and sometimes *under* the Rate of Interest assigned by *Law.* The Law nevertheless may be founded on Justice and Equity, and a necessary Rule where Bonds and Specialties, upon which Interest becomes due, are sued for in the Law : But tho' that forbids a Transgression of the Rule by *Excess,* when it is in the Power of the *Lenders* to have more (as in this Province) it nevertheless establishes Contracts for *less* than the Rule, where the Parties have agreed it should be so: The Reason of this is because Money is an absolutely necessary Instrument for carrying on Trade; and the lower the Rate of Interest, the better the Instrument. Therefore all Countries strenuously endeavour to have it as low or lower than any of their Neighbours, because of the superior Advantages it gives them in Trade.

The Change of the natural Rate of *Interest,* is an undeniable Evidence of the Change in the *Proportion* of the Quantity & Demand of Money, and therefore of the Change in the Value of Money from time to time. For if a House changes its Purchase-Value from a Change in its yearly Rent, undoubtedly Money must be allowed to have a Change in its Value upon any Change in its natural Interest: And therefore if (agreeable to Mr. *Lock*) in the Year 1691 the natural Interest of Silver Money in *England* was eight to ten per *Cent* (say nine at a Medium) and now as I am informed but about three per *Cent* (the Government have it so, and the Stocks in general produce thereabouts, in proportion to the Purchase-Money given for them) then upon this Supposition we may truly say that an *Ounce* of *Silver* of the same Fineness now as it was in 1691, is worth but one *third* of an *Ounce* at that Time, when compared with the great Capital Stock, *viz* the Lands and other real Estate of *England*; besides what other Changes it may have undergone for the worse, by Means of the Change in the Mode of Living, uncertain, yet doubtless very considerable.

But to proceed,

I have but one Change more to speak to, and that is not a Change in the natural Proportion of Things, but a [**12**] *forced* Way of *Rating* Things under some Circumstances in Trade, and that chiefly with Regard to a State of private or publick *Bankruptcy*.

For Instance, The Standard for Silver Money in *Great Britain* is *five Shillings and two Pence* per *Ounce*, or three Ounces, seventeen Penniweight, ten Grains assigned to the Money *Pound*: But supposing Silver there (to avoid a Fraction) at *five Shillings* per *Ounce*, or four *Ounces* to the Money Pound, and that *N* owes *one hundred Pounds* Sterling, or four hundred Ounces of *Silver*, but it happens that he has but two hundred *Ounces* of Silver, and can pay no more but half his Debt, by Composition. Now there are two Ways of expressing the Case of *N*, *viz*. one Way by keeping to the Standard of *Great Britain, five Shillings* per *Ounce*, and saying that *N* pays *ten Shillings* in or for the *Pound*, or that he pays half a Pound instead of a whole one. But there is also another Way of expressing *N's* Case, commonly in Use in this Province, when we talk of Money, *viz*. that *N's* Silver is *raised* to *ten Shillings* per *Ounce*, (instead of *five Shillings*) and therefore *his* Money Pound (agreeable to his Circumstances) is only equal to Silver at *ten Shillings* per *Ounce*, and so his two hundred *Ounces* of Silver at the Rate of *ten Shillings* per *Ounce*, is just equal to one hundred of his Composition *Pounds.*

Again, suppose *N* owes one hundred Yards of *Cloth*, (the Standard Measure being thirty-six Inches to the Yard) and has but fifty Yards to pay his Debt: In this Case also *N* pays half his Debt according to the Standard Measure; or in other Words he pays by a Yard (agreeable to his Circumstances) of but eighteen Inches: for fifty Yards of thirty-six Inches are just equal to one hundred of *N's* Yards of but eighteen Inches.

Thus we see that *N's* Circumstances put a new Rate upon his Money, the Measure of the Value of Things; and upon his Yard, a Measure of the Quantity of Things: and every Thing he has, must be rated according to the Quantity he is able to pay in Proportion to the Demand. And this, as has been observed, makes no Alteration in the natural Worth of his *Silver* and *Cloth* in the Market, but they continue as they were.

This brings me to the chief Thing to be considered under this general Head *viz.* our B I L L s of publick Credit, of the *old Tenor.* I shall therefore, agreeable to the foregoing Method with Regard to Silver Money, consider them in two different Respects.

[13] 1st. As to the Change of their Value with Regard to the *Purchase of other Goods in the Market.* And in this Regard I shall endeavour to prove that they have not undergone any other Change, than that which is common to all other Commodities. For let it be observed,

In 1720 *eight Shillings* in *Bills* was equal to *eight Shillings* in *Silver*, in *Iron*, in *Wheat*, and all other Commodities : And now in 1739, *eight Shillings* in Bills is still equal to *eight Shillings* in these and all other Commodities.

Eight Shillings in *Silver* has now but eight twent-nine Parts of the *Quantity* of Silver it had in it in 1702. *Eight Shillings* in *Iron* has likewise about the same eight twenty-nine Parts, and *eight Shillings* in *Bills* but eight twenty-nine Parts, of the Value they had, when compared with these and other Commodities.

By the Year 1715 Silver at sundry Times by the Scarcity of it in Proportion to Demand, and by no other Means, rose from *eight Shillings* to *nine Shillings* per *Ounce*, and so the Silver Money Pound was reduced from two *Ounces* and half, call it fifty Penniweight, to forty four Penniweight and seventeen Grains. By the Year 1728 it rose to *twenty Shillings* per *Ounce*, and the Money Pound was reduced to twenty Penniweight. By this current Year 1739, it has risen to *twenty-nine Shillings* per *Ounce*, or the Money Pound reduced to thirteen Penniweight and nineteen Grains. And this is truly our *natural Silver-Money-Pound*; such a one as our trading Circumstances, or our Market affords ; and which must for ever be govern'd by the Market. While that affords a *Quantity equal to Demand*, it will then be *fixed* in its Quantity, but upon any Variation will contain more or less Silver in Proportion *ad Infinitum ;* only with this Reserve, when the Quantity *exceeds* the Demand, it will then be in the Power of the Government and People (and no doubt all would be willing) to agree upon a certain assigned Quantity of Silver that it has fallen to, for the Pound ; but otherwise it is impossible for them to fix it.

Or if we take any other Articles of our Exports, shall we not find the same Changes ? As supposing (what is absolutely necessary in all Cases of this Kind) that *Tarr* had all along kept the same Proportion to its Demand in the trading World, must it not nevertheless have risen *here* in Proportion to the general *Deficiency* in our Returns and kept pace with *Silver*, gradually rising from [14] *eight Shillings* to *nine Shillings*, *twenty Shillings*, and *twenty nine Shillings* per Barrel?

Or, on the other hand, Can it be imagined that *Britons* who buy and sell with a Regard to the Rate of *Silver* in all Places, should not be allowed to raise the Rates of their *Goods* by common Consent, in *Proportion* to the Changes in the Rates of Silver? And accordingly when Silver was *eight Shillings* per *Ounce*, to sell at about one hundred per *Cent* advance (above the Par of *Great Britain, five Shillings and two Pence* per Ounce) and Silver *nine Shillings* per *Ounce*, Goods at one hundred and twenty-five per *Cent*; and so on to this present Year, Silver at *twenty-nine Shillings*, Goods at six hundred per *Cent*, or *seven hundred Pounds* of our Standard for *one hundred Pounds* Sterling-Standard, in the Sale of Goods?

Or finally, Could it possibly otherwise have happened but that the *Bills*, which are a Commodity passing among other Commodities in the Market, should keep pace with all other Commodities, whether common or special? most certainly it could not be otherwise.

But it will be *objected*, that in 1702, *eight Shillings* in *Bills* were equal to an *Ounce* of *Silver*, but now *eight Shillings* in *Bills* are only equal to five Penniweight twelve Grains and half, of Silver; therefore the Change must be in the *Bills* and not in the *Ounce* of *Silver*.

I answer, This is all true: But it has *no Relation* at all

to the present *Case*; because an *Ounce* of Silver is a *fixed* Measure, but all *our* Measures are *changed*, as in the Case of *N*. For Instance, the old Measure for *eight Shillings* was an *Ounce* of Silver, but the new or forced Measure is but five Penniweight twelve Grains and half of Silver: And this is as truly the common Measure of *eight Shillings*, as if the Government had enacted it, and common Consent concurred in it. So that whether we say, we pay *five Shillings and six Pence half Penny* in the Pound, when we compare the new Measure with the old, or say that we now pay by a new Measure of five Penniweight twelve Grains and half for *eight Shillings* (that is thirteen Penniweight nineteen Grains to the Pound) it amounts to the same Thing; and the Change is alike in every Thing in Use among us, as well as in the Bills.

This Province has not been obliged to pay *more* to the Mother Country, than its just Debt, but rather *less*, by Means of those *Changes;* for if we *formerly* gave *Great Britain one hundred* per *Cent* Advance for Goods, and [15] paid them in *Silver* at *eight Shillings* per *Ounce*, and other Things in Proportion; and *now* give them *six hundred* per *Cent.* Advance, and pay them in Silver at *twenty-nine Shillings* per *Ounce*, it amounts to near the same Thing. And as the Trade of this Province has first caused the Change, and the Mother-Country has follow'd the Course of Trade, so the former has had much the Advantage of the latter in that Regard

The *greatest Loss* has been to those who *agreed* for *Bills* of Credit, or for Money *indefinitely*, without Regard to the *Rate* of Silver or any other Commodity: For, as we have already shown, *our Measures* are all virtually *changed.* And in this Respect those that have *Salaries*, and *Fees* of Office appointed by the Government, have been great Sufferers, and (where they have not already) ought to be relieved in such a Way as to Equity (all Circumstances considered) appertains: For which I do by no Means think the Change in the Rate of Silver is the best Rule; but rather the different Circumstances of an Office on one Hand, and the Change in the Mode of Living on the other.

But for *all other* Persons, who have been left to their *Liberty*, to make Contracts for a certain Rate of Silver, or other Things, either where Moneys were lent, or Goods were sold, they have an Exception or Reserve made in the *Acts*, for Bills being a lawful Tender, purposely for them (viz. *Specialties and express Contracts in Writing always excepted*) and the Law has ever supported them in such Agreements. Therefore they must blame themselves; and not the Government, who have not yet succeeded in any Methods to stop the Changes in the Rates of Things. *Orphans* must blame their Guardians; *Widows* their Advisers; and *money'd* Men themselves; for they might always have let their Money at a certain fixed Rate, if they had not (its to be feared) been too covetous in expecting, besides 6 per *Cent* (or more) Interest, a further Advantage of the Borrower in the Fall of the Rate of Silver. Upon this Score the *Clergy* have in many Regards been *less free* than other People, and ought to be honourably supported by their Hearers *under all the Changes* of Things.

This Province (simply considered) has so far been a great Loser in Trade, as that all our *Treasure* (Silver and Gold) which is the chief Encouragement and Reward for Industry in all Countries, has been constantly carried off [16] (and often all too little) for the Payment of our Debts, due to the Mother-Country. But yet (excepting that Case) at the same Time our *capital Stock* has prodigiously *increased in Value*, since the Emissions of Bills, chiefly by their Means, and next to impossible it should have been brought about without them : And we may reasonably suppose, that we are now capable of exporting three times more Produce in Quantity, and the general Estate of the Province is three times more valuable (when compared with Silver) now than in the Year 1702.

On the other Hand, not only the Mother-Country, but the Province has greatly suffered ; the most laborious and industrious among us, Widows and Orphans consider'd as such, and in general every Body, save the Shopkeepers and a very few money'd Men, have been greatly *distressed* by Means of the *Want* of a Sufficiency of *Bills* : by having their Debts postponed ; by being obliged to take Goods (and in a much greater Degree of Quantity and Fineness than their Inclinations or Circumstances required) in lieu of Bills ; by being obliged to purchase Goods or borrow Money at a much higher Rate than in other Countries, where they have a Competency of Money ; and in fine, by being put under a Necessity of pursuing a despicable Trucking (and naturally a cheating) Trade.

There is another *Objection* very commonly brought against the Bills, *viz.* That on sundry *large Emissions* Silver and other Returns have *risen* in a very extraordinary Manner, which would *not* have happened *without* those Emissions.

To this I answer, That (agreeable to my own Argument) the *sudden* & *large* Emissions, as in the Loan-Money, might have a *proportionable* Influence on the Prices of Returns to the Mother-Country, and ought for ever to be industriously *avoided* in the Regulation of Bills.   However, still I am of Opinion that the Market-Rate of Things would have *risen* to the *same* Height by *slower*, yet equally *certain* Degrees, *without* the Help of such Irregular *Emissions*, and by the mere *Operation* of our *Trade*.

For consider,

1. *Every trading Country must at all times have a Sufficiency of Silver to answer all Demands*, whether they be great or small, more sudden or more gradual; else upon *Failure* thereof, *their Rates* of Silver must undoubtedly be *raised.*   Now if this Province had been in *such* Circumstances, let the *Emissions* have been never so large and [17] sudden, *they* would not have affected the Price of *Silver*, the Quantity thereof being still equal to the Demand: But as they have generally been otherwise, we might expect sudden and great Changes at times.

2. Another Reason, to the same Effect, may be this, that *the general Quantity of Bills*, current at any Time in the Province, has been vastly *less than the Demand* (as we shall show anon) so that often *between* the several Emissions a great *Scarcity* has happen'd : And as they were the *chief Money* for which *Contracts* were made, it was impossible but that many *Debts*, due to the *Mother-Country* must have been *postponed;* so that upon a *new* Emission, obtained with great Difficulty, after long Sollicitations, perhaps *L.* 100000 was immediately applied to the Purchase of *Silver* and *other Returns;* and the Quantity being *unequal* to such Demands, the Prices *rose*.   Whereas, if there had been a moderate Quantity of *Bills always extant*, the *Demand* would have kept a more *regular* Pace with the *Quantity*.

3. The *Instances* hinted at in the Objection, are vastly *too few* to make a settled *Rule*. For *Changes* in the Price of *Silver* have been *daily*; it has not one Day been *fixed* to an absolutely certain Rate, as in the Mother-Country; since the Year 1702 (and many Years before any Emissions of Bills of any Sort) no *two* Men hardly selling at the *same* Price for *one* Day. And this was not only obvious to every one all along, but will still admit of Demonstration every Day: that is, we shall find the Sellers and Buyers acting in the same Manner with Regard to the Sale or Purchase of *Silver*, as they do with Regard to *all other* Commodities, and the Proportion of Quantity and Demand every Day operating on the Price of Silver in the same Manner, as on every other Commodity; and consequently more or less *Bills*, *Iron* &c. given for the same assigned Quantity of Silver on one Day than another, without the least Regard to the Quantity of Bills extant.

But supposing that the irregular Emissions *had* produced these bad Effects, *this does not at all destroy the Scheme of Bills*. There is nothing in the Operation but what is common to all Moneys : for there is not one new *Ounce* of *Silver* added to the old Stock in the trading World, but what has a *natural* Tendency to *increase* the *Demand* for many Things; as, on the other Hand, the same Tendency to increase the *Quantity* of many Things. The same [18] Tendency must also be allowed to our *Bills*, and indeed in a lower Degree to *all* Commodities whatever. For there is not a single *Cow* or *Horse* added to the Capital Stock of this Province, but what has the same Tendency. As contrariwise, the *Reduction* of Silver-Money in the trading World would have a natural Tendency to *lessen* both the Demand and Quantity .

of many Things; but still *worse*, when the Quantity of Money is so reduced, that it is utterly insufficient for the Instrument of *Trade* (as in this Province) to make Money become the Instrument of the greatest *Oppression*, and to force People upon Contrivances to supply that Defect by other Commodities, or to run into a general Barter in Trade equally pernicious, and which must end in a general Ruin. For, what Mr. *Lock* says of Silver, that it is the Measure of the Quantity or the Extent of Trade in the World, the same may be truly said of *Bills* in this Province.

Some will *object*, that according to the general Observation of judicious Men, many People upon the *first Emission of Bills* ran into an *extravagant Use of English Sh p-Goods*, more than the *Exports* of the Province were sufficient to pay for, and consequently *Returns rose*, and plainly by *their Means*. I answer, I have already assigned two different Effects to Money, *viz.* both the Rise and Fall of Things: Which of these two were most prevalent, is difficult to tell; but we are sure, that the Silver from 1702 to 1715 rose but from about 8 to 9 *s.* which is no great Matter, considering the Benefit the Province might otherwise have by the *Bills*, more especially in increasing the Quantity of Returns But by the best Information I can have from Men of Credit then living, the Fact is truly this, *viz.* about the Year 1700, *Silver-Money* became exceeding *scarce*, and the Trade so embarassed, that we begun to go into the Use of *Shop-Goods*, as the Money. The *Shopkeepers* told the Tradesmen, who had Draughts upon them from the Merchants for all Money, that they could not pay all in Money (and very truly) and so by Degrees brought the Tradesmen into the Use of taking Part in Shop-Goods; and likewise the *Mer-*

chants, who must always follow the natural Course of Trade, were forced into the Way of agreeing with Tradesmen, Fishermen, and others; and also with the Shopkeepers, to draw Bills for *Part* and sometimes for *all* Shop-Goods: And the Continuance of this pernicious Practice (the unavoidable Consequence of the Want of a Sufficiency of Silver-[19] Money, or Bills of Credit) has always been, is now in a surprizing Manner, and for ever will be the Bane, and in the End the Ruin of this unhappy Province, by forcing us into a vile Trucking-Trade, or to trading without any other Measure, than such a one as every Man is either willing, or thinks himself obliged by Way of general Reprizal, to try to impose upon his Neighbour, and operates in many Respects as if we had no Laws for the Measures of Justice, no Yards nor Bushels for Measures of Quantity, but every Man left free to do what seemed right in his own Eyes.

The greatest Quantity of Bills extant at one Time was in 1721, and probably fell considerably short of 90 *thousand Pounds* Sterling; and yet at that Time the general Run of Ship building, the greatest Article of our Returns, was for half Money, half Goods, or more. The Merchant indeed at that Time might have possibly had ready Money for his Goods, and paid the Tradesmen in the same; but every Body knows that even then (and now much more) no Man could live by the Trade, because of the great Abatements in Proportion to the Prices for Money upon them, or for those Notes. And now the Sum of Bills extant may be about *l.* 250000, and equal but to *l.* 45000 Sterling; and no Ways proportionable to the Demand.

Finally, With Regard to the common Observation of Men in Trade touching the Changes of Commodities in the Market, I may appeal to the Experience of every Body, whether the *Bills* have not always been the *scarcest* Commodity whatever; whether a Man that wanted ready Money, has not generally been put to great Difficulty, and obliged to sell at a very low Rate; or when he wanted to buy any Thing upon Credit, for want of ready Money, whether he has not been obliged to purchase his Credit very dear, and at a Rate vastly exceeding the Usage in other Countrys, where they have a Competency of Money.

2 I am to consider the Bills with Regard to the Change of their *yearly Interest*, or *Increase.*

The *lawful* Interest in this Province is 6 per *Cent.* No Man since the first Emission had occasion to let his Money *under:* He might always have *that* (which by the Way is comparatively exceeding *high*) with very good Security, none better in the World, than in this growing Province; and his Bills fixed, as in *Europe*, to an assigned [20] Rate of *Silver:* But how much *more* than 6 per *Cent*, the Borrowers and Lenders can best inform us; it is so well known that I need say nothing more upon it. But that the Bills have never exceeded in *Quantity*, even on the greatest Emissions, is evident; for if they had, their *Interest* must undoubtedly have *fallen*; because the *natural* Interest follows the *Proportion* of the *Quantity* and *Demand*, as the Shadow does the Body. They have a mutual Dependance, naturally lead to, and illustrate each other.

Besides the foregoing, we might offer another Argument, indeed not so certain, but abundantly sufficient to prove the Point in Hand, and that is from a Comparison of the supposed *Numbers* of People, yearly *Expence*, and Quantity of *Money* in *Great Britain*, with those of *this Province.*

Suppose in *Great Britain* 9 Million of Souls, the yearly Expence from the highest to the lowest *l.* 8 by the Head, and the current Money (which is so variously reported, that I am at a Loss what to say; having found it computed from 30 Million and upwards down to 18 Million) say at a Medium, 24 Millions Sterling, or *l.* 2. 13 *s.* 4 *d.* by the Head; besides immense Sums in Bills and Notes passing in Trade, equal to and on some Accounts better than Money; that, while they have but a general, tho' small Ballance of Trade, and a wise and faithful Administration, might be extended to any Length, even beyond what the Kingdom might at any Time have Occasion for. Besides they have an old Country abounding in all Sorts of Cultivation and Manufacture, in many Respects beyond the Vent of their Trade. Now, on the other Hand, suppose we have in *this Province* 125 thousand Souls; the yearly expence *l.* 40 per Head; and the Money *l.* 250000. In that Case *they* have a Sum of Money equal to one third of their yearly Expence, and *we* only a Sum equal to one twentieth Part of *ours*; or nearly, but one seventh Part, in Proportion to what they have. The Quantity of our Bills cannot be *enlarged*, as their Silver-Money virtually is, by the Help of *Banks*, they being already a compleat Instrument of Trade, And we labour under many other Disadvantages from the yet comparatively Infant-State of the Province; together with the Irregularities in emitting and calling in the Bills, which makes them liable to many and great Stagnations *&c.*

[21] By this Instance it appears, or even taking the whole *New England* Colonies complexly, and more critically comparing their Circumstances with those of the Mother-Country, I doubt not but it might be made appear, that

we have not one tenth Part of Money in Proportion to them.

Before I leave this Head, it will be needful further to explain what I mean by comparing the trading Condition of the Province to a State of *Bankruptcy;* which I was forced to do out of mere Necessity : For I know of no other Comparison, that would have clearly illustrated the Subject And I would not be understood to mean a *total* Bankruptcy, as in the Case of a private Man when all his Estate real and personal is not equal to the Demands his Creditors may have upon him : For the real and personal Estate (or Capital Stock) of the Province is vastly more valuable than all the Demands upon it in the present Case.   Therefore,

By a State of *partial* Bankruptcy, or Bankruptcy in in our *Trade*, I mean only, that at certain Times the whole exportable Produce, the whole Silver and Gold to be purchased in the Market, or all exportable Things whatever put together, are *less* in *Quantity* than the *Demand* for them, and of Necessity the Prices of them must rise in the Market in Proportion to their Scarcity. For Example, Suppose that last *February* the Rate of *Silver* in the Market was 27 *s.* per *Ounce*, and *Tarr* 27 *s.* per Barrel, and all other Returns in Proportion : And that *N*. had sold *l* 100 worth of *British* Goods to *P*. at an Advance agreeable to the then Rate of Silver, to be paid this *February*; which accordingly is done by *P*. and *N*. goes to Market in order to purchase Silver, but there he finds that by the Scarcity of it in Proportion to Demand it has risen from 27 to 29 *s.* per Ounce, and Tarr and all other Returns in Proportion; and that he can no otherwise make Returns than by purchasing Things at the Market-Price. Now in this Case *N sold* by a Measure of 27 *s.* per Ounce, and *receives* only by a Measure of 29 *s.* per Ounce: Or in other Words, receives only *l* 93 for 100, or a Composition of about 18 *s.* 9 *d.* in the Pound.

This unhappy and dishonourable State may be called by another Name, *viz* A *Ballance of Composition;* or to give it the softest Name, a *Ballance* (not of Trade, but) *of Debt,* as I formerly called it upon another Occasion; by which I mean, a certain Part of our provincial Debt, [**22**] due to the Mother-Country, virtually remitted or forgiven us at Times: As in a most remarkable Manner in the Year 1734 when Silver rose from 22 *s* 6 *d.* to 27 *s.* and all that had Debts out when the Change happened, were obliged to take their Composition in Proportion thereto.

The Ballance of *Trade* is only the *Difference* between the Value of the *Produce* and *Manufacture* traded for between two Countrys, which is paid or received in *Silver* or *Gold* the general Treasure of the World: For Example, if *Great Britain* exports in one Year to *Spain l.* 100000 in Produce and Manufacture, and takes back in Return but *l* 90000 worth of the Produce & Manufacture of *Spain*, she must then receive *l.* 10000 in Silver or Gold, to ballance that Years Account of Trade; and nothing is forgiven *Spain*: But it has happened some Years in the like Case that *we* have had *l.* 10000 forgiven this Province, in the Manner above; which for the Future I shall call by the Name of a Ballance of *Debt*: which is the one and only Cause of the Changes in the computative Value or Rate of Things in our Market, and while continued must still have the same Effect, and that whether we have Bills of Credit extant or not. But it's time to proceed to the next Thing proposed, *viz.* to treat

Of MONEY.

THE *Definitions* of Money are very various. I shall collect a few of them, from Mr. *Chambers*, and others.

Money is any Matter, whether Metal, Wood, Leather, Glass, Horn, Paper, Fruits, Shells, Kernels &c *which hath Course as a Medium of Commerce.*

Most of the Ancients are frequent and express in their Mention of *Leather*-Moneys, *Paper*-Moneys, *Wooden*-Moneys *&c.*

This is a good general Definition of Money; & agreable not only to the Usage of ancient Times, but even of the present. Look into our *British* Plantations, and you'll see such Money still in Use. As, *Tobacco* in *Virginia*, *Rice* in *South Carolina*, and *Sugars* in the *Islands;* they are the chief Commodities, used as the general Money, Contracts are made for them, Salaries and Fees of Office paid in them, and sometimes they are made a lawful Tender at a yearly assigned Rate by publick Authority, even when [23] Silver was promised. And the same may be said of *Shop-Goods* in this Province, in several Respects sufficiently known among us.

Paulus the Lawyer defines Money, *a Thing stamped with a publick Coin, and deriving it's Use and Value from it's Impression, rather than it's Substance.*

This Definition must be confined to the Construction, which the *Law* puts upon Money: that is, whatever assigned *Quantity* of Silver, Gold, Copper *&c.* the publick Authority of any Country have given to the *Pound, Livre,* or *Guilder,* and whatever Changes they shall think fit to make as to *Matter, Weight,* and *Fineness* at any Time; yet the Piece of Matter having the publick Stamp for a *Pound*, shall be a *lawful Tender* for so much. In this Definition he seems to countenance the Custom of reducing the Weight or Fineness of Coins, by Recoinages, which (when made to take in past Contracts) is a publick Fraud.

Or if we take him in a general Sense, he is notoriously wrong: For Money derives both its Use and Value from the *common Consent* of Mankind Neither Silver, Copper, nor Iron have any other Value than what common Consent gives them: nor will they ever give the same Value to *one* Ounce of Metal, which they do to *two* Ounces, or receive one Ounce of *baser* Metal equal to an Ounce of *finer*.

Indeed if a Method could be found to fix an Impression upon any Metal, easily to be distinguished from all other Impressions, next to an Impossibility of counterfeiting, then an assigned Quantity of that Metal might be raised to any Value, and the common Consent of the People (if they stood in good Terms with their Government) might be obtained to such a national or provincial Scheme; and the Money continue for ever to pass, with as little Variation as all other Commodities have. But this is next to impossible to be done upon Metals: So that an Ounce of Silver or other Metal can never pass for more in Coin, than in Bullion. And therefore those Princes, who have attempted to introduce Copper-Species at a great Disproportion, have been forced to use the most violent Means; as in the well known Case of the late King of *Sweden*, when a *Farthing's* worth of Copper was ordered to pass for 32 *Pence* of their Money, upon Pain of Death.

Mons. *Boizard* defines Money, *a Piece of Matter to which publick Authority has affixed a certain Value and Weight, to serve as a Medium of Commerce.*

[**24**] By *certain Value*, I suppose, he means a certain *Dé-nomination*, as Pound, Shilling *&c.* and also an *assigned Weight.* For the Value of Coins in the Market is equally uncertain with other Things. This is also an Assertion of the Right of publick Authority to make and alter their Coins or Money.

Mr. *Lock* says, *Silver is the Instrument and Measure of Commerce*, in all the civilized and trading Parts of the World. It is the *Instrument* of Commerce by its *intrinsick Value.* The *intrinsick Value* of Silver, considered as *Money*, is that *Estimate* which *common Consent* has placed on it; whereby it is made *equivalent* to all other Things, and consequently is the *universal Barter*, or Exchange, which Men give or receive for other Things, that they would purchase or part with for a valuable Consideration: And thus (as the wise Man tells us) *Money answers all Things.* Silver is the *Measure* of Commerce by its *Quantity*; which is the *Measure* also of its *intrinsick Value*: If one Grain of Silver has an intrinsick Value, two Grains have double that intrinsick Value *&c.*

The Meaning of all this (I humbly conceive) is, that as *Silver* by common Consent is made a *universal Commodity*, so People measure the *Value* of every Thing *by* it, and usually say that Things are dear or cheap in Proportion to the greater or smaller Quantity of Silver they cost in the Market, and for the same Reason they choose Silver, rather than any other Matter, as the *Instrument* for carrying on their Commerce.

The ingenious Author does not by this mean, that *Silver* is either a *fixed Measure* or Standard of the *Value* of all Things bought or sold, as a *Yard* and a *Bushel* are fixed

Measures of *Quantity;* nor that it is the *best Instrument* for expediting Commerce: For as to the *first* he is frequent and express in it, that Silver changes its own Value in a Course of Years, more than almost any other Commodity; and every one knows that *Bank-Bills* and *Transfers* are a much better *Instrument* of Commerce. Therefore he only means that Silver is the *received* Measure or Instrument of Commerce. And we must all allow it is one of the best universal Commodities, the general Treasure of the World, the Measure of the Quantity of Trade carried on in the c m-mercial World (as our Author elsewhere observes) and indeed in a great Degree the Measure of the Power and Influence of every Country in the political World.

[25] Mr. *Law* defines *Silver the Measure by which Goods are valued, the Value by which Goods are exchanged, and in which Contracts are made payable.* By which he Means neither *a fixed Measure* of Value, nor the *best Instrument* of Commerce; but that Silver is the *received Measure* by which Goods are valued, and the *agreed Value* or universal Commodity (by common Consent) for which Goods are exchanged, and in which Contracts are made payable. For he not only reckons that it *falls* in *Value*, but that it is in danger of *losing* its *Use* as Money, and of being reduced to a mere Commodity; and that it is *far* from being the *best Instrument* of Commerce. But to proceed,

Money is a Measure of the Value of all Things bought and sold and *a necessary Instrument for facilitating Commerce.*

It is a Measure of the *Value* of Things, in some sort as a Yard or a Bushel are Measures of the *Quantities* of Things.

It is an *Instrument* of Commerce; an Expedient, without which Trade can never be carried on to good Purpose.

In these different Regards Money must be subjected to Rules, as all other Measures are.

The *Qualifications* of Money may be reduced to the four following ones; *viz.*

1. That its own *Value* be *stable*

2. That it be made of *convenient Matter.*

3. That it be received by *common Consent* within the Community for which it is intended.

4. That it have the Sanction of *publick Authority.*

Of these in their Order.

1. *Money must have a stable Value.* Now in Order to have any Commodity a of stable Value in the Market, it must have its own *Quantity* as near as possible always equal to the *Demand* for it; because otherwise it cannot be the *Measure of the Value* of other Things: No more than a *Yard* or a *Bushel*, that by Means of some Imperfection should at Times grow longer or shorter, bigger or less, would be just Measures of *Quantity.*

There's no Commodity, left free to its Course in the Market, but what must for ever be liable to change its Value: And no assigned Quantity of any one Thing will long continue just equal to an assigned Quantity of another Thing Even *Silver* and *Gold* are naturally as far from holding an exact Proportion to one another, as any other Commodities: But in asmuch as the *European* Nations have thought fit to receive Gold in Payments in a [26] certain Proportion to Silver (the Standard) every Kingdom is obliged to be very vigilant in observing the Proportion that is fixed by the Maritime Nations, or the Majority, to keep to that, and change as they do; else they run a Risque of having the less valuable Species imported to them, and the more valuable carried off to their Loss. As for Silver, how can it ever be made a stable Measure of Value? Since it is introduced without any Regard to the Proportion there ought always to be kept up between the Quantity and Demand, and loses its Value every Year by the Influence it has on the Mode of Living, and on the Rate of Interest.

Mr. *Lock* reckons that *Silver* is reduced to one tenth Part of the Value it had in the Reign of *Henry* VII (about the Time of opening the *Spanish* Mines in *America*) when compared with *Wheat*, which he reckons a Commodity the least liable to change, when taken for a Number of Years. And Mr. *Law* reckons that *Silver-Money* is worth but one twentieth Part of the *Goods*, & one fifty-seventh Part of the *Land*, it was worth about 200 Years ago. But in Mr. *Law's* Calculations, Allowance must be made for the lessening the Quantity of Silver in the Coins from time to time. There are many strange Instances to this Purpose, so well known, that I need not mention any more.

Some think that the Rate of *Labour* is a Standard-Measure of the Value of Things: But I am of a different Opinion. For we find that even this undergoes as many and as great Changes as other Things do, and from the common Causes, *viz.* the Changes in the Proportion of the Number of Labourers to the Demand for them, in the different Imployments of Life: And it may be said to differ in *Great Britain* from a *Groat* to a *Guinea* a Day. Indeed in the first Contrivance of Things, the Labour to be bestowed on them, must always be considered as one, and often the chief Article of the Cost of them: Yet notwithstanding, when the Husbandman has produced his, Wheat, and the Clothier has perfected his Piece of Cloth, and both are carried to the

Market, they must be sold there according to the Proportion of Quantity and Demand.

A Commodity, that is to be made the Measure of the Value of other Things, must besides its natural Qualifications, have a considerable deal of Art and Pains added to them. And I know of no one Thing in Being, that [**27**] can be so well managed for that End, as our BILLS of publick Credit, put under proper Regulation: They may be made almost a perfect Measure of Value, by being fixed to an assigned Rate of Interest (say 3 to 6 per Cent) and may be emitted or called in always in Proportion to the Demand every Day at the assigned Rate; and whilst they were so managed, they could not be said to *change* their *own* Value, nor to be the *Cause* of the Change in the Value of *other* Things, whether directly or consequentially. Nor on the other Hand, could they *fix* the Rate of any Commodity: For this can only be done by the common Consent of a Community, or by special Agreement among private Men. But in one Word, they would be the *Measure* of the Changes in every other Thing, as being fixed themselves.

However strange this Doctrine may seem to those, who have either wilfully or ignorantly tantalized this unhappy Province by calling in Question, whether the *Bills* may be said to have *any* Value at all, contrary to the daily Evidence of their own Senses; branding them as *Waste-Paper*,-- *Pen, Ink & Paper*, and the like childish Stuff: And however plain we have proved the contrary, yet I shall not desire them to rely on those Evidences, but will call in the Judgment of the great Mr. *Lock*, who perhaps was the first, at least in *England*, that ever wrote judiciously. on the Subject of Money, which has all along been kept as a great *Mys-*

tery, as he somewhere observes, and (as we have already hinted) supposed to be just what an iniquitous Ministry and a crafty Mint would have it to be, for their own Advantage.

The Author speaking of a Standard-Measure of Value, says, that *Wheat* in *Europe* (& that Grain which is the general Food of any Country) is the *fittest* Measure to judge of the *alter'd* Value of Things in any long Tract of Time; then shews what would be such a Measure in an *Island* unknown to the rest of the World; and proceeds to observe. That if in any Country they use for Money any lasting *Material*, whereof there is not any more to be got, and it cannot be increased; or being of no other Use, the rest of the World does not value it, and so it is not like to be diminished; *this* also would be the steady standing *Measure* of the *Value* of all *other* Commodities. — Which is a Case full in Point. *Such a Material* I propose (that need neither be increased nor diminished, will not be exported, and sufficiently lasting, or when [28] damaged by any Accident capable, of being easily renew'd) for an Instrument of Commerce. But the ingenious Author presently stops his Prosecution of this Point, and gives the Reason, Because *Silver* and *Gold* have already *obtained* in *England*, and the trading World, and he is not for *altering* (nor should I neither if we were on the same Footing, because of the great Difficulty of such a Transition in most Countries) but adds, Though it be certain that that Part of the World, which *bred most* of our Gold and Silver, *used least* of it in Exchange (meaning for other Goods) and used it not for *Money* at all.

Take also the Judgment of Mr. *Law*, who wrote admirably well upon Money in the Year 1705, about 14 Years after

Mr. *Lock*, and as many before the fatal *Missisippi*-Scheme; father'd upon him, but more likely to be the Device of the then Regent of *France*, I mean the iniqu tous Part of it. He says, If a Money be established, that has no intrinsick Value, and its extrinsick Value such as that it will not be exported, nor will not be less than the Demand for it within the Country, Wealth and Power will be attained; and 'twill be less precarious Money, not being liable to be lessened directly nor consequentially; and Trade not liable to decay consequentially; so the Power and Wealth of that Country will only be precarious from what may be directly hurtful to Money. Again, That a Nation having established such Money, having also the other Qualities necessary in Money, they ought to have no Regard what Value it will have in other Countrys; on the contrary, as every Country endeavours by Law to preserve their Money, if that People can contrive a Money that will not be valued abroad, they will do what other Countries by Laws (meaning with Regard to their Silver Money) have endeavoured in vain.

This is also full to the Purpose: And though we must not dream of Wealth and Power in this Province, yet I am satisfied that a sufficient Quantity of *Bill-Money* for the Improvement of the great natural Advantages of the Province, a moderate Ballance of Trade with all the World in our Favours, a Competency of Silver and Gold for common Safety, would all have a direct Tendency to promote the Interest of the Mother-Country, as well as our own; that the Want of either of them would be vastly prejudicial; but that the Want of a Sufficiency of Money would be the absolute Ruin of our Trade. We may also learn from this and other Passages of Mr. *Law*, [29] that it is better to have

Silver in any Country passing on the Foot of a *Commodity*, than as *Money*. Which brings me to the second Qualification of Money;

2. *That it be made of convenient Matter.*

As Money is the Instrument or Tool of Commerce, convenient Matter is absolutely necessary. It must be of little Bulk and Weight, both for the Convenience of Carriage and Keeping: Durable or not liable to waste or perish: Capable of being divided, without Loss, for small Change: Capable of taking a plain lasting and not easily counterfeited Impression, that the Receiver may be sa isfied that the Measure offered him is according to the Standard.

In most of these Regards, *Bills* have much the Advantage of *Silver*. For the Imperfection of Silver is the true Cause of the Introduction of *Banks*; which have been of great Service to Trade, by avoiding the Expence & Risque of Carriage, the Charge of Cashiers, and the Danger of bad Money, which are considerable Articles; and therefore in all great Places of Trade, the Merchants would rather pay the Bankers for keeping their Money, than be without them.

In this Province we have not one Article of Produce, Manufacture, or imported Commodity, to serve as a fit Instrument of Commerce. Our *Silver* is all carried off, and some particular Years we may want above 50000 Oz. to pay our full and just Debt. If we had *Iron, Copper*, or *Lead*, they might be put into Magazines, and Notes taken out promising them at a certain Rate and Fineness, and they would change their Value as Silver and all other general Commodities do *Wheat* or *Hemp* might be negotiated something after the same Manner; but they are more liable to perish: Nor have we a Surplusage of these,

or any other Things for the Purpose, but either export or
consume all of them. Our *Lands*, and other real Estate,
cannot be exported, and will not commonly be taken for the
Payment of a foreign Debt; tho' they may so far as relates
to Money, be of Service: Of which more hereafter.

For want of Silver, or Bills of Credit, as an Instrument
of Commerce, People have in a Manner been forced into a
much greater Consumption of *Shop Goods*, both as to the
Kinds and Degrees of Fineness, than they would have
chosen; which has introduced all Sorts of Prodigality
among us, one Step therein naturally leading to another.

[30] Trading People in general, are obliged to pursue this
Method, as they cannot make, but must follow the natural
Course of Trade. But the *Shopkeepers* have reaped by far
the greatest Advantages by it, as being virtually possessed
of the current Money of the Province, and in that Regard
may fitly be compared to the *Bankers* in *Europe ;* only that
they have greater Advantages than them, by having Goods
put into their Shops upon Credit, and without Interest, and
virtually the same taken back again in Payments, that is,
Shop-Goods, or the Produce of them in Provisions, Tradesmen's Work, and the like, with very little Money, and a
considerable Profit allowed them. And in this Regard they
ought not to be blamed, since they act agreable to the Plan
of our Trade: For as all People that are concerned in Trade,
will unavoidably lay hold of any bad Matter, and use it as
Money, when they have no better to use, so most certainly
upon the Want of Silver or Bills, even in any Degree of
Proportion to the Demands of Trade, Shop-Goods will be
negotiated as Money; tho' in the Main the Hurt and Ruin
of all our Trade.

Some few People have traded chiefly for Money; others for a greater or lesser Part in Money, and the Remainder in Goods: But in the End the chief of the Labour of the Province has been paid for in *Shop-Goods*, and the Labourers have been the greatest Sufferers, by spending a great Part of their Time in attending the Shops, giving great Discounts for Money in lieu of Goods, and permitting many hurtful Conversions of Money into Goods, which has introduc'd great Extravagance and Idleness, to say no worse.

In some particular Places the *Name* of Money has been kept, but a quite *different* Thing intended: For Instance, *Shop-Notes* that have specified half Money, half Goods, have been by iniquitous Custom construed to signify half English Goods, half Provisions. I have heard of almost incredible Discounts allowed by the poor Tradesmen for ready Money in lieu of such Notes.

Another great Inconvenience consequent to the Want of Money is a *Trucking*-Trade, which brings with it insurmountable Difficulty. For as a great Number of People depend upon Money to go to Market for their daily Provisions, & other necessaries, and as that Defect can by no other Means whatever be remedied than by proper Money, so it will be a Miracle if our Trade do not sink under [31] the Burden, to the vast Damage of the landed Interest of this Province, and proportionably also of the Trade of the Mother-Country.

In fine, The Want of an adequate Instrument of Commerce has been the first and great Cause of all our Extravagance, the Rise of Silver, and a shameful Ballance of Debt; besides many base Practices, bitterly aggravated by our Enemies, and sufficiently complained of by our Friends.

3. *Money must be received by common Consent, within the Community for which it is intended.*

That Money should have the common Consent of the People, where it is to pass, is very obvious to every one; and why I restrain it to a particular Community, as a Kingdom, Province, &c. will appear from the following Considerations.

It is necessary in the trading World, that there should be one or more Commodities of universal ready Acceptance, in which the different trading Countries might pay or receive their respective Ballances of Trade with each other: For it is impossible that any two Countries can exchange yearly just an equal Value in Produce and Manufactures; and in this Regard Silver and Gold have the natural Advantages of all other Commodities. They are also of great Advantage, as being the Commodities, which all Nations have agreed upon to be used in the Course of Exchange; the Weight and Fineness of the Coins of one Country adjusted to those of another, being the Basis or Par of Exchange; and the Variation from the exact Standard, called the Rise or Fall in the Course of Exchange; and finally, they are the best Commodities to be transmitted from one Country to another, whose Trade or Policy requires they should.

Again, It would be of considerable Advantage to Trade, if all the *European* Kingdoms at least could agree in a fixed Proportion of Alloy to their Silver and Gold, and upon a certain Weight to their Coins; as supposing the highest of Silver to be exactly an Ounce, Troy-Weight, and subdivisions by tenth Parts as low as they conveniently could; and that all their Measures of Quantity were also fixed to one Standard.

Such a general Regulation might possibly be brought about: But a Regulation of Money as a just Measure and fit Instrument of Commerce, never could be accomplished. No universal Commodities, as *Silver*, *Gold*, &c. can [**32**] be so managed. Every Country must choose a special or local one, and in this Regard *Bills* of Credit have the Preference of all others.

4 The last Qualification of Money is the *Sanction of Publick Authority*.

It is the undoubted Prerogative of the civil Magistrate, to appoint all the common Measures of Quantity and Value, and to change them as just Occasions require, and more especially to order what shall be adjudged Money in the *Law*. But then it is not the Act of Government, that gives Value to Silver: For that depends wholly upon common Consent, and no one would receive it of the Government, if it had not that Consent.

In like manner, it is not the Act of Government that gives Value to our Bills of Credit in the Market; but the common Consent of the People. For the Government can and do only say, that so far as they pay or receive, the Bills shall be valued, and any one or more Men may emit Bills to the same Import. They have (and it is their undoubted Right) said, that the Bills shall be a *lawful Tender* where Money is promised, but have justly excepted *special Contracts*; for otherwise they would strike at the very Root of Trade. They may order that the Bills and no other Things shall be received in Taxes, and so every one would be obliged to purchase some of them for that End: But the People might notwithstanding refuse them as Money in Trade. I am next to offer my Thoughts

Of BANKS. *With a Proposal.*

FOR some Years past People in general among us have run into the Notion of a *Bank*, and some Attempts have been made: As the Scheme for the *Merchants Notes*, promising *Silver*, at 19 *s.* per *Ounce*, 3 10ths in 3 Years, 3 10ths in 6 Years, and 4 10ths in 10 Years, without Interest: Also a Proposal for *L* 60000 in Notes promising *Silver* at 20*s.* per *Ounce*, half in 5 Years, and half in 10 Years, without Interest; not to mention the Province-Bills of the *new Tenor*. All such Schemes promising *Silver*, at a certain fixed Rate, and distant Time, having a direct Tendency (under our present Circumstances) to to raise the Rate of Silver, and to oppress the Debtor, the Success of them has been answerable. However, I am of Opinion, that a Bank (erected either by one sufficient [33] Man alone, or by a Number of such Men associated together) contrived with a just Regard to our present unhappy Circumstances (for otherwise it would be of hurtful Consequence) might be of great Advantage; is indeed the first and most necessary Step towards our Relief, and would contribute, by the Favour of Providence, to the mutual Benefit of our selves and the Mother-Country. I shall therefore proceed to the Consideration of *Banks*, and examine how far they may be *practicable* and *useful* in *New-England.*

There are *two Sorts* of Banks in common use in the trading World, *viz* those that make *effective* Payments of *Silver* or *Gold* on Demand, and those that make *no* effective Payments, but only a bare *Transfer* of an assigned Sum upon the *Bank-Books*, from one Man's Account to another, as every one has Occasion to pay or receive a Debt.

Of the *first* Sort are the Banks of *England* and *Scotland*, established by Acts of. Parliament; the private Bankers or Goldsmiths *London*, *Dublin*, &c All founded upon the *Estate*, but chiefly the Credit of the respective Bankers.

The general *Plan* of such a Bank is —— to begin with, and always keep in Hand *such a Sum* of Money, as may answer all reasonable *Demands;* to lend Money, and discount Bills and Notes, in the *shortest* and *safest* Way; so that if a Run upon them should happen (either by a Diffidence of their Credit, or the Malice of other Bankers) they may be provided, and have a Supply of Money equal to all Demands.

They emit Notes *promising Money on Demand;* and may be assured, and while their Credit is good, and there is a competent Proportion of Silver in the Country where they live, the trading Party will bring them in *more* Money than they carry out. For the *Trader* is greatly benefited by the Bank: as having all the Bills or Notes, due to him, punctually negotiated by the Bankers without any Charge; ready Money advanced upon them occasionally at a moderate Discount; the Convenience of easier and quicker Payments, by a Draught on the Bank; saving the Expence of Cashiers, Baggs and Carriage; and having his Money more safely lodg'd, in Cases of Fire or Robbery, the best Measures being taken for that End. And besides these Advantages to the private Trader, the *Publick* is also greatly benefited; For by Means of the Bank the *Money* of a Country is virtually much *increased,* [34] *Interest* kept *lower*, the *People* better

imployed, and consequently under a wise publick Administration, Wealth and Power easier attained, establish'd and
promoted.

The Bankers Notes bear *no Interest,* because they pay
upon Sight, without Delay ; and the Advantage of negociating a Sum greater than their Stock, is the just Privilege of a Trade or Business, of all others one of the most
useful.

Mr. *Lock* makes mention of a *private Banker,* that had
circulating at one Time *l.* 1100000 Sterling, in Notes signed
by his *Clerk* : A Sum equal to *six Million* of our Currency,
from which he might draw great Profits (natural Interest
being then from 9 to 10 per Cent.) and no trading Man in
the Kingdom might better deserve them.

It is impossible for *us* to have a Bank of this Sort, under
our present Circumstances : Having no *Silver-Mines,* nor a
general *Ballance* of *Trade,* as the Means of importing and
keeping it in the Country, but some Years a considerable
Ballance of *Debt* against us ; so that no Man can either *purchase* a sufficient Sum as a *Fund* for a Bank, nor can he *keep*
such a Sum in his Hands, if already purchased, without proportionably *increasing* the *Demand* for *Silver.* If all the
Exports of the Province were made by its *Inhabitants* only,
and they all should agree to make *no Returns* but in *Silver,*
yet unless they could prevent the usual *Importations* of
Goods, there would probably be a *Demand* for *all* the *Silver,*
and *more* ; and so the Price rather rise, than fall : But if one
Man, or a Number of Men, should *stop* 10 or 20000 *l.* Sterling, as a *Fund* for a Bank, this would *raise* it to a great Degree, and such a Bank would speedily be exhausted, to the
Loss, rather than Profit of the Bankers.

It is obvious to even the meanest Capacity, that every *new Demand* must have a Tendency to *raise* the Price of *Silver*: And we have frequent Instances of the Fact. To mention but one, I have known at the yearly Payments of *Impost-Money*, which in the whole was but a small Sum, yet consisting of a greater Number of small Payments (from about one Ounce and upwards) Silver rose *pro Tempore*, from 27 *s.* to 31 *s.* per Ounce, the Purchasers being numerous, the Sums generally very small, and the Sellers knowing the Pinch of the Matter right well.

But tho' our *Trade* cannot supply a *Bank*, yet some think that our *Lands* might easily do it. Suppose then a [35] Number of Men should go upon *this Method* (which would be easiest for the Province, and the Bankers) *viz.* to procure a *Credit* from the Bank of *England*, for *l.* 100000 Sterling, at 3 or 4 per Cent interest, upon *Land-Security;* and to draw out the said Sum *occasionally;* the *Interest* to commence from the Payment of their Drafts. When they have so done, then proceed to emit *Bills* for a Currency, promising a certain Sum *payable* in 3 or 6 Months, to the Possessor, in *Sterling-Drafts* (this short Distance of Time, considering our Condition, would bring them under little or no Discount) and let them out upon *Land-Security*, to pay in the *same* Money, and 6 per Cent. Interest.

This would be the *cheapest* and *easiest* Way of *borrowing*, and yet I believe next to *impracticable*. Supposing the Sum could be had at Home, which is very uncertain (for we have found by Experience, that the Mother-Country will sooner make us an *Abatement* in our Payments for Goods, than take *Lands* without it) the Province would be charged with a *new Debt*, for the Interest and Principal, and I doubt neither Undertaker nor Borrower here would find their Account in it.

The *nearest* and *safest* Method for a *Bank* Circulation of Bills promising *Silver* at a certain Rate, may be this that follows.

One or more Men having good Credit with the People, to emit Bills promising *Silver* at a certain Rate (suppose 29 ƨ. per Ounce) or an Equivalent in the same *Bills*, at the End of *one Year*: Then to *call in* all their Bills extant, and make *Allowance* equal to the *Change* in the Rate of *Silver* for the Worse (if any) for that Year; and this, either according to the *different Changes* it may have undergone from *Week* to *Week* throughout the Year, taking the whole Number of Weeks upon an Average-Computation, or else according to the Rate of Silver at the *Time of Payment*, which of the two shall be thought most equitable: And having so done, return to the *Possessor* his *Bills* back again with the *Addition*: And proceed after this Manner from Year to Year. Thus far as to the Possessor.

Again, to emit their Bills wholly upon *Loan*, with indisputable *Security*, at the Rate of 4 per Cent. *Interest*, conditioned to pay *Silver* at 29 *s.* per Ounce, or an *equivalent* at the End of every Year, for the *Difference* of Principal and Interest, on the same Foot that the *Bankers* allow to the *Possessors*.

[36] I put *Interest* at 4 per Cent, partly because it is the undoubted *Benefit* of all Countries to have it as *low* as they can, and partly because the *Borrower* makes the *Rate* of Silver *good*, which may possibly be *costly* to him.

This Scheme, I confess, would be very laborious and chargeable to the *Banker:* And how far it would operate upon the *Price* of Silver, is uncertain; the *Payments* not being *effective* as to Silver at the Year's End, and People being forced to do as they can in some Cases. However I am of Opinion, that such a Scheme as I have hinted at, might be put in Execution. But I proceed,

2. To consider the *other* Sort of *Banks*: And of these the Bank of *Venice* is the oldest, and perhaps the best model'd in the World. A short Account of it will be entertaining to the Inquisitive, and is well worthy of our Attention.

Many Years ago the State or Republick of *Venice*, by a solemn Edict, established a Bank, to consist of two Million of *Ducats*. Those that had a Mind to encourage it, carried in their *Money* to the Bank, and had *Credit* given them for their respective Sums upon the *Bank-Books*: Which *Credit* one might *dispose of* to any other Person, in the Way of *Payment of a Debt*, or by Way of *Sale;* and that by a bare *Transfer* upon the Books from his own Account to the other Person's, without any *effective* Payment of Silver or Gold. So that the *first Capital* has been in continual *Circulation* from one Creditor to another, and remains the same intire Sum of Credit, only belonging to different Persons, to this Day.

They enacted, that all Payments in the *Whole-sale Trade*, and for Bills of *Exchange*, should be made in *Banco*, that is, in these *Transfers*.

Their small or *retail* Payments are in *Silver* and *Gold*, as in other Parts. — He that wants to dispose of his *Credit* on the Bank-Books for *Silver*, must sell it in the *Market* on the best Lay he can; and he that wants to purchase a Credit, must also buy it there as he can.

The *Advantages* of this Bank were so great, that after the first Subscription there arose an *Agio* or *Premium* on Bank-Money, of 28 per Cent: which, doubtless, came on gradually, as of 1-8th, or 1-4th of one per Cent at a Time, occasioned by the great Opinion the People had of the Scheme, but chiefly by the Shortness of the first Subscription, in Proportion to Demands of Trade. This Advance the State did not like; and it's said, endeavoured, [37] to restrain it by *Laws*; but without Effect, till they took in a second Subscription of 300000 *Ducats* more, which reduced it to 20 per Cent, and it has since never exceeded this. But I am of Opinion, that it was *not* the *Effect* of that small Subscription, nor of a Law restraining the Rise of the Agio, that reduced and kept it under, but some *effective Method* to *supply* the Person that wanted a Credit at 20 per Cent, when he could not purchase it so in the *Market*: For otherwise it might have continued rising to this Day.

Mr. *Chambers* says, The State has now five *Million* of the People's Money, and *without Interest;* which is a great publick Advantage, and no Body hurt by it: For every Man may let his *Credit*, as he does his Money, to Interest.

It is generally believed, there is *little* or *no Money* in the Bank-Treasury, but that the Government have long ago disposed of it for publick Uses; and very likely: Yet it does not, nor ought to *lessen* the Credit of the Bank.

Besides the general Calamities that attend all Countries, by which the Creditors of the Bank might suffer in common, I know but *one Case* which might affect the Fall in the *Agio*, or make a Run upon the Bank, and that is a Ballance of *Debt* against the Republick, or the Want of a sufficient Quantity of Silver, and other moveable Effects, to pay their *foreign* Debts, (which is the Case of our Province) but this is next to impossible to happen, while they are a *State*: For as the Evil might easily be foreseen, so it might also be prevented by regulating their Imports and Exports, making sumptuary Laws, borrowing Money of other Countries, and even obliging People to part with their superfluous Finery, by selling it off to other Countries for the publick Good; and upon a sudden Diffidence and Fall of the Bank-*Agio*, they might engage to pay Interest to the Creditor, computing the 100 Ducats at 120, which would probably keep up its Credit, and tax the Subjects for the Payment of the Interest. So that there is not the least Probability of the Fall of their Bank-Money, or that Silver and Gold shall be in equal Value with it.

Of later Years they have erected a *Cash Bank*, for the Advantage of Trade: where the Merchants may keep their running Cash for domestick Occasions, and they or Foreigners may be supplied with such Sums or Species, as [38] they want for Exportation; which has also been found beneficial.

Some have said that they emitted *Bills*: But this is a Fact I must call in Question. However, that makes no essential Difference in the general Plan: Only as it appears to me, the *Transfer* is preferable, and in some Cases it would be necessary to have both Bills and Transfers, as the Creditor pleased.

Now let any Man seriously consider this Scheme of the Bank of *Venice*, and I am persuaded he will find all the *essential* Parts of it in the Scheme of *our Province-Bills* of the *old Tenor*. Thus, for Instance, *Their* Foundation was a Depositum of *Silver* & common Consent: *Ours* only the *common Consent* of the Government and People, which is *tantamount*, as being the Foundation of the Value of Silver, and almost all other Things; and if need were, we could make a greater and better Depositum in *Lands*, equal to double the Value of our Bank-Circulation. Both their *Transfers* and our *Bills* were made a *lawful Tender*. —— Neither *they* nor *we* make *effective* Payments. *Transfers*, if left free to their natural Course in the Market, would be liable to change their Value every Day, as being virtually established upon the Footing of a Commodity; that is, according to their Way of Reckoning, would rise or Fall every Day so much per Cent. In like Manner, *our Bills*, being (unavoidably) left free to their Course in the Market, do change their Value daily. *They* would compute this Change by the Method of so much per *Cent*. And *we* do it by the different Rates of *Silver*, which amounts to the same Thing in different Words. Their *Agio* is now fixed: But our Rate of Silver cannot be so under our present Condition. *Their Scheme*, which was projected when they were in *flourishing* Circumstances, in order to the facilitating and further Improvement of Trade, *succeeded* in producing the designed Effect *Our* Scheme, which was projected when the Government was in very *low* Circumstances, having little or no Silver, and no other fit Matter to serve as Money, for the payment of publick Taxes, the Support of the War, and carrying on Trade, *succeeded* too, and fully answered the Ends proposed by it, especially the last mentioned, by the Improvement of the natural Advantages of the Province to a surprizing Degree. —— Their *Transfers* rose to 28 per Cent, above common Money, till they were effectually restrained: Our *Bills* indeed after some Years sunk in [39] Value, yet not by the Imperfection of our Scheme, but the Ballance of Debt, which it has not been in the Power of our Government (at least no effectual Attempts have hitherto been made) to prevent. Otherwise, had our Trade produced a Ballance in our *Favour*, it would have been next a Miracle, if our *Bill-Money* had not been *better* now than at the first Emission, or (in other Words) if *Silver* had not *fallen*, as the Quantity increased above the Demand. —— Thus, it appears, that the Schemes have virtually both the same Foundation and the same Tendency in their own Nature: Tho' the Success has been very different, owing intirely to the differing *trading* Circumstances of the two Countries, and no other Cause whatever.

The Bank of *Amsterdam* is nearly built upon the same Plan. Common Moneys have been and still are taken in by the Bank at an assigned *Agio*, generally from 3 to 4 per Cent above *Par*: But the Man that wants a Credit may either purchase it at the Bank-Rate, or the Market-Rate, as he can make the best Bargain. They have never made *effective* Payments: But People may lodge particular Species of Money in the Bank, not exceeding six Months, and have the same returned to them again, paying about 15 *d.* upon *l.* 100 Sterling, for keeping. The Magistrates and City are made responsible for the safe Custody of the Moneys deposited, and they are secured from the fraudulent Practices of Under Officers by sufficient Sureties and capital Punishments. The Creditor may have a Bill or Note from the Commissioners, certifying that he stands Creditor so many *Guilders* (in a certain Folio) on the Books, upon which he has his future Payments endorsed; or he may keep a running Account with the Bank. All Bills of Exchange (inland and foreign) are by Law made payable in Bank-Money. The

Charge of this great Bank is chiefly (if not wholly) supported by small contingent Payments, collected agreeable to the Rules: As 20 Guilders for opening every Man's first Account, one Penny for every future Entry, 6 *d.* if the Sum be less than 300 *Guilders* (about *l.* 27 Sterling) and 6 *d.* for Business done out of Office-Hours, Forfeitures where a Man over draws his Ballance *&c.* This is also a Bank of *pure Credit;* founded upon common Consent; *no Silver* taken out, nor will it probably ever be the Interest of any Man to demand it: And for the Substance it is the *same* as the Scheme of *our* Bills of publick Credit. The different [40] Success is owing to no other Cause, but the different trading Circumstances: Which will further appear by the following Considerations.

Supposing there could be found in this Province, of wrought Plate and Bullion, to the Value of *L.* 50000 Sterling, and that every Man should bring in his particular Parcel, and take *Credit* for the same on the Books of a *Bank* erected for that Purpose, at the Rate of 29 *s.* per Ounce for Silver *&c.* and then *dispose* of that Credit, as already mentioned; that would be doing the *same* Thing as they do in *Venice* and *Amsterdam*; this in the best Manner would answer the Ends of Money; and in all Countries where they have a Ballance of Trade in their Favour, this would soon rise above the Rate of common Money, if not restrained. And thus it would certainly be in this Province, if we had the Ballance of Trade in our Favour: But in the contrary Case (as there would be no *effective* Payments) *Silver* might rise to 40 or any other Number of Shillings, in Proportion to the Ballance against us.

Again, Supposing *Lands* were mortgaged for half their

Value in *Silver* at 29 *s.* per *Ounce,* to remain as a perpetual Security to the Creditor of the Bank, and to be negotiated as above; yet neither would that, nor any other Security, how great soever, affect the Price of Silver in the Market.

Now as I think these Consequences cannot be deny'd, so this affords us another strong Argument, that the Cause of the Rise or Fall of *Silver* is not from the *Bills,* but wholly from our *trading Circumstances.* —— Wherefore I shall now proceed to offer a few general Hints for

A SCHEME.

PErhaps the only Plan, that can be contrived agreable to our present Circumstances, and which I am perswaded will have the most direct Tendency to extricate us out of our present Difficulties is this.————

Let a Number of men associate themselves together, and emit Bills of the following Tenor, *viz*

WE the Subscribers, for our selves and Partners, promise to receive this Twenty Shilling Bill of Credit in all Payments for Debts due to us, where Bills of publick Credit of the old Tenor were promised, and in all our future Dealings as Money: Specialties and express Contracts in Writing always excepted.

[41] Possibly that Part of the Bill (*in all Payments for Debts due to us, where Bills of publick Credit of the old Tenor were promised*) may be a Stumbling Block to many among us, who have large Sums due to them upon the Footing of the old Bills, and have hopes that the Government will do something in their Favour on that Head; therefore rather than the Scheme should be clogg'd by that

Clause, it might be left out, and the Bills only made to look forward.

The undertakers to give sufficient Security, that they will always receive the Bills according to their Tenor.

The Undertakers to be bound to the Signers of the Bills, as they are to the Possessor, in such a Manner as may give general Satisfaction.

No Undertaker to take out above 10 *per Cent of the Sum he subscribes; and for that too to give his Bond or Note bearing Interest, on the same Footing as other indifferent Borrowers: For as he is justly intitled to his Share of the Profits, and liable to pay his Share of the Charges and Losses, his Depositum ought for ever to remain intire, as a Security to the Possessor.*

The Company to lend out their Bills on good Security at 6 *per Cent Interest; and to discount private Bills or Notes at the Rate of--per Cent, on Conditions to pay in the same Bills again, or in Silver at the current Market-Rate, when purchased with the said Bills: And the Bank to take no other Bills but their own, or Silver as above.*

That they immediately enter into a constant Course of Business, which is essential to a Bank Their Loans to be regulated by the assigned Rate of Interest

As to *Managers, Clerks, Meetings* &c. there will be little Difficulty: So I shall not detain the Reader on these Heads.

Such a Scheme as this I take to be the most agreable to our present Case. I am firmly in the Belief, that no other general Plan than this, can ever take Effect, so as to answer the Ends of Money; and that sooner or later the Distresses of the Province, and the woful Effects of some other Schemes, much talk'd of, will force us into such a one as the foregoing, when our Affairs are much worse than even now : And further that such a one, if wisely managed, with an honest View to the publick Good, would have the most direct Tendency to promote *Frugality* and *Industry* (without which the best adjusted Schemes will be oflittle Significance) to turn the Scale of [**42**] Trade in our Favour, and make us a happy People : Particularly I look upon it the *only Means* to destroy the most pernicious Practice of *Shop-Notes*, or rather *Shop-Money*.

We have lately had a Variety of Schemes propos'd. The prevailing one at present, promoted by some particular Gentlemen, is that for *l.* 300000. the *Bills to promise to the Possessor Silver at* 20 *s.* (the now current Market-Rate being 29 *s.*) *payable at the End of fifteen Years, without any Interest.*

Now, according to the universal Rule, when *these Bills* are computed by *lawful* (compound) *Interest* of 6 per Cent, (not to mention the *natural* Interest, which is equally the universal Practice) they will then be *only* equal to Silver at 47 *s.* 9 *d* per Ounce on the Day of their first Emission, and would sell for no more in the Mother-Country, if Interest were at that Rate. — The *Effects* of such an ill judged Scheme may be easily foreseen by the Success of some of the like among our selves, and other *British* Plantations : For it is next to impossible that such Bills should *long circulate* as Money, and but that they should be the Means of *raising* the Rate of *Silver*, promoting usurious Practices, and bringing this Province into great Disreputation at Home, as they who trade hither are like to be none of the least Sufferers.

Some among us are for *no* Bills of any Sort, but for leaving the Trade to its own natural Course; as thinking that the Necessity of the Thing will naturally oblige us to alter our present Mode of Living, and keep our Silver among us to serve as Money. But this Supposition is absurd and intirely groundless: For as the next and most handy Way of carrying on our Trade (in the Default of *Silver* or *Bills*) is that of the *Shop-Money*, so of Consequence this must prevail (as it has all along) in Proportion to the Scarcity of others, and by this Means Extravagance Increase, Silver rise, and finally the landed as well as the trading Interest of the Province be hurt to a prodigious Degree.

We have had some Accounts lately of a Design on Foot to petition the *British Parliament*, in order to have the Case of the Plantations, with Respect to their *Bills* of Credit, taken into Consideration: And as the Colonies in general, and this Province in particular, are of great Importance to the Mother-Country, doubtless they will give great Attention to an Affair of that Kind

[**43**] Our common Opinion is, that it would be well, if the Parliament should *proportion the Quantity of Bills to every Colony* (that are in the Use of them) and *fix their Value*.

As to the *first* of these, our common Complaint is, that our neighbouring Colony of *Rhode Island*, tho' of small Extent, and much less Trade than we, yet have made and are still allowed to make Emissions of Bills without Restriction; while we are restrained by his Maj sty's Instructions to his Excellency our Governour, and of Necessity are obliged to take theirs, which greatly promotes their Trade, and equally discourages ours. The first Part of this Complaint I shall now consider, and the latter Part, *viz.* with Regard to our Restraint, will naturally follow in the Sequel.

I much question whether our bringing a Complaint against the *Rhode-Island* Emissions would not have an Air of Envy, and hurt our Cause; and whether they might not easily set aside all our Arguments on that Head, by showing that they have only done what a wise People ought to do, in emitting Bills for the Improvement of their own natural Advantages, and carrying on as great a Part as they can of the Trade of the Plantations, which the Mother-Country has in great Wisdom left equally free to all, whilst all their Neighbours are equally free to their Trade, and at their Liberty to take or refuse their Bills.

There are two *Irregularities* in their Emissions, which yet hitherto have had few or no ill Effects; these may and ought to be remedied for the Future; *viz.* their emitting of *considerable Sums* (as about *l.* 20000 Sterling) at *one Time*, and *immediately dispersing* the Bills; together with their letting out the Bills on *Loan*, conditioned to repay the whole in 20 Years (as I am inform'd) in *certain partial Payments*. For Money ought to be emitted *gradually*, and the general Quantity so managed that it may be call'd in, or let out, as the *Trade* requires.

However, as to the *Quantity* of Bills now extant there, altho' they are vastly more in Proportion than in any other Colony, being I suppose about *l.* 330000: Yet this Sum, only equal to *l* 59000 *Sterling*, may be thought in the Mother-Country but a very *moderate* or *small* one to carry on their enterprizing Trade.

I have spoken with the greater Freedom & in stronger Terms in Relation to *Rhode-Island* Bills, from a firm Persuasion, that all attempts to stop their Currency will [44] be fruitless, except that of having a *Sufficiency of our own*, and that Delays in this Case may be vastly hurtful to us both in our trading and landed Interests.

I am now to consider the *fixing* of the Rate of Silver by *Law*: And this I take to be impossible in our present Case, for we have already a Law of this Province (of old standing) fixing the lawful Tender of Pieces of Eight of 17*dwt.* to 6 *s.* that is nearest 7 *s.* 3 *f.* per Ounce, and much later than that, an Establishment in Queen *Anne*'s Reign, making Pieces of Eight of 17 *dwt.* & half a lawful Tender for 6 *s.* that is 6 *s.* 10 *d.* two sevenths per *Ounce*, commonly called *Proclamation*-Money; which Act or Order came too late: For before the Commencement of it, Silver was got to 8 *s.* per Ounce. Neither of these have been sufficient to regulate the Price of Silver, for the Reasons already given; in Effect, that a *Bankrupt's* Pound or Money must be according to what he is able to pay: and this is common, at least in private Affairs, to all Countries. For Instance, in *Great Britain*, *Silver* being established by Law at 5 *s.* 2 *d.* per Ounce, the Man that pays 10 *s.* in the Pound, his Money is only equal to Silver at 10 *s.* 4 *d.* per Ounce. Or if he pays only 3 *s.* 7 *d* in the Pound, it is but equal (as ours is) to *Silver* at 29 *s.* per Ounce.

The *Remedy* then, that I would humbly propose to be apply'd for, is this, in brief: —

That we might be allowed to emit Bills of Credit, *fixed to assigned an Rate of Interest;* agreeable to the foregoing Plan, or in such Manner as shall be thought most proper.

That all Schemes for Bills promising Silver, at a certain Rate, and distant Time, without Interest, or other than by Law allowed, be discountenanced; & that the Courts of Law be required to regulate their Judgments in Conformity thereto.

That they would be pleased to allow us a certain Sum yearly, to be drawn for in Bills of Exchange, for such a Continuance as shall be thought needful (or until we can reduce Silver to the Proclamation-Standard, and have a sufficient Quantity of it passing in Trade) at an assigned Interest. Or else *that we may be allowed and encouraged to make such* Laws *to regulate our Trade, as may effectually bring the Ballance in our Favour, so far as to answer the aforesaid Ends.*

These are some of the necessary Helps, that I would join in requesting from our indulgent Mother-Country: [45] And the rather because her own Interest is so nearly concerned, and probably would be advanced in the End. But the chief and greatest Favour would be to allow us a sufficient Quantity of *Bills* emitted on a well regulated Plan: Without which all other Expedients might fail of Success.

Thus I have finished what I had principally in View: And think I have sufficiently obviated the common Objections as I went along. However, having promised the Reader a Reply to a late printed Piece, on the same Subject, I must now proceed to

Remarks on the *Essay concerning Silver and Paper Currencies, more especially with Regard to the British Colonies in* New-England.

I Shall not imitate the Author in introducing my Reply with *sarcastical* Reflections on his Performance. Nor do I design any *idle Criticisms* upon it. My Inducement in taking Notice of it is, chiefly because it seems calculated to promote such Measures with Relation to our *Bills*, as in my Opinion will be prejudicial to the publick Interest. Though, I confess, another Motive is, because the Author has pretended his Essay is a full Answer to a small Piece I had publish'd, *viz* OBSERVATIONS *on the Scheme for l.* 60000 *&c.* My principal Aim in which was (as the Occasion led me) honestly to represent the dangerous Tendency of any Scheme for Bills promising *Silver* at a certain Rate and long Period, and to shew that *such* Bills would never answer the Ends of *Money.* In order to this, I was obliged to enter a little into the Consideration of *Money* in general, and of *Bills* in particular.

I shall now as briefly as I well can (having already gone to a Length much exceeding my first Intentions) in a *general* Way point out some material *Differences* between the *Essay* and my *Observations*, and then make other more *particular* Remarks.

I am first to give the Reader a *general* View of the material *Differences* between us. The following Instances may suffice.

I had in my Observations argued and sufficiently shown, that our *Bills* of the old Tenor, were established by Government and common Consent, upon the *same Footing* with all other *Commodities* and *preferable* to all [46] other Commodities being received as the *most general* Commodity or *Money* of the Province — But the *Essayer* takes no Notice of this necessary Distinction and Definition: Only from the Beginning to the End of his Piece he calls them *Paper Currency, Vague, Fluctuating, Imaginary, Fallacious, Nominal; Bills promising a precarious or no Value; a forced provincial Tender; an ill contrived unnatural false Medium, and as a Depositum no better than Waste-Paper; a Moth of a Currency* &c.

In my Observations (p. 6 &c.) I plainly show'd, the

special Cause of the *Rise* of the Rate of Silver and other Things in the Market to be from the Operation of *the Ballance of Debt against us*: And *not* at all from any Operation of the *Bills*, they having *never exceeded* the due Proportion in Quantity — But the *Essayer* on the contrary, imputes the *Rise* of the Market to *a Glut of this provincial confused Paper Currency*, and gives it as his Opinion, *that we ought not to have Recourse to any other Conceit (as Ballance of Trade) for its Cause, but only to the Operation of these Bills.*

My *general Cause* assigned throughout the whole Letter, for the *Changes* of the *Value* of all Things in the *Market*, is the *Change* in the *Proportion* of their *Quantity* to *Demand*. And I shewed that any *Commodity* or *Money* when *fixed* in that Proportion, would be an *unerring Measure* or *Standard*, by which to judge of the Changes of all other Things, not fixed after that Manner.

This only and unerring Rule he seems to be an utter Stranger to, and incessantly talks of the *Excess* of the *Quantity* of Bills in the *N.E.* Colonies, without considering the *Demand* for them, in a most surprizing Manner. For to the meanest Capacity it is evident, by all proper Ways of Judging, that the Quantity at any Time hitherto extant has been but very small in Proportion to Demand.

For *Remedy* of our present Calamity, I proposed to have a *sufficient* Quantity of *Bills*, *regulated* by an assigned Rate of *Interest*, and managed with Prudence, as the *first* and absolutely *necessary* Expedient.

The *Essayer* delivers his Opinion (p. 6, &c.) That a *Paper-Credit well founded and under good Regulation, and not larger than what the Silver Specie Currency will bear,* has been found to be a very good *Expedient in Business*: But that *if it exceeds* this *Proportion, its Effects are bad and ruinous*. And yet by sundry Passages in his Essay he seems to deliver his Opinion intirely *against all* further [47] Emissions of Bills; declares *Barter* it self on some Accounts *preferable to Province Bills as a Medium*; and expressly says, *We have no Reason to fear Want of a Medium, if the Grievance of publick Paper-Credit were gradually removed*: Thus *Trade will find its own natural proper Medium,* viz *Silver and Gold.* Which is in Effect to say, that we shall have no Money at all, but the Province be left to their last Shift, *viz.* Shop Notes, and finally be ruined; for we have not one Ounce of Silver to serve as Money.

In a Word, The favourite Notion of the *Essayer*, which runs through and animates his whole Piece, is, That the *Bills* being *depreciated* in Proportion to and hand in hand with the *multiplied* and *large* Emissions, *this,* and this *only*, is the *true adequate Cause of the Rise of Silver; Ballance of Trade against us* (which I call Ballance of *Debt*) *not at all concerned in it.* Which is the grand general Point in Controversy between us, and is in direct Opposition to the whole Tenor of my Letter. The Force of what he has offered to support his Opinion, I shall have Occasion to consider in the Sequel.

Not to take notice of some *other* material Points in the Controversy, which he has passed over in Silence, the fore-going Hints may suffice for a *general* View. I shall now proceed to make some more *particular* Remarks on his *Essay.*

His first Paragraph, *Paper Currency at a great Discount*

has prevailed in many of our Colonies; and by Advocates for it deluding the People with false Appearances and Representations, likely to continue to greater Disadvantages than ever: As appears by Emissions in Maryland, New-York *and* Rhode-Island.

The Word, *Currency*, is in common Use in the Plantations (tho' perhaps least of all in this Province) and signifies *Silver* passing current either by Weight or Tale. The same Name is also applicable as well to Tobacco in *Virginia*, Sugars in the *West Indies* &c. Every Thing at the *Market-Rate* may be called a *Currency;* more especially that most *general* Commodity, for which *Contracts* are usually made. And according to that Rule, *Paper-Currency* must signify certain Pieces of Paper, passing current in the Market as *Money*. Thus he *tantalizes* the Province under its present unhappy Circumstances, and would insinuate that our Bills, emitted upon the best Plan (for the Substance of it) that the World ever saw, and of the greatest Service to our Well-being, are *no better than* [**48**] *Waste-Paper*, as he elsewhere expresses it. Surely according to this Way of Speaking, he might call Silver common *Earth;* so the best Bond in the Province a *Paper-Bond*, and our provincial Charter a *Parchment Charter*, from the Matter on which they are wrote.

The Want of giving a proper *Name* to our *Bills*, has given the *Essayer* and others a Handle to impose such Names as convéy a very wrong and delusive Idea of them. I shall therefore, by Way of Digression, endeavour to set that Matter in a just Light.   And

First, They are often called *a Medium of Exchange* Now tho' the Word *Medium* may be brought to signify a

Means or *Instrument* of Commerce, yet it does not convey a just Notion of *Money*, as a *Measure of Value*, & much less as a *Commodity* passing in Trade. For the natural and obvious Notion of a *Medium* in Trade, is a *Bill, Bond* &c. given as a Pledge, Security, or legal Evidence of the Thing promised in the Bill or Bond at a distant Time. For Example, If a Man gives an assigned Quantity of *Silver* for an assigned Quantity of *Iron*, he then immediately *exchanges* one Commodity for another: But if he gives Iron for Silver to be delivered at a *distant Time*, and takes a *Note* for the Payment, he then receives only a *Medium* for the present. In like Manner, if a Man exchanges our *Bills* for Iron, I see no *Medium* in the Case; but one Commodity is immediately given for another. Whereas if he sells *Iron* condition'd to pay *Bills* for it at a distant Time, by Book-Debt, Note, &c. he then receives only a *Medium of Exchange* for the present.

Secondly, They are called in the *Acts* for their Emissions, *Bills of publick Credit*: which Name upon their *original* Emission was very proper, in asmuch as they were at first established upon the *Credit* to be given them by the Government for *Taxes* &c. and that only. But when afterwards in the Year 1712 they were with common Consent made a *legal Tender* as *Money*. (special Contracts necessarily excepted) and seeing that, agreable thereto, the Government then and ever since made Emissions with a *Design* to supply the Trade with them as *Money*, I say for those Reasons the naming them Bills of *Credit* seems not so proper now.   Therefore

Thirdly, Their only *true* and *adequate* Name, I reckon, ought to be *Bill-Money;* being certain Instruments in Writing received by common Consent as *Money*, or a *general Commodity* for which *Contracts* are made in this Province. But to return from this Digression.

[49] He says, "*Paper-Currency at a great Discount.*" That our Bills have undergone any *Discount*, is a wrong Supposition. For (first) By *Discount* on a Bill is generally understood an *Allowance* of —— per Cent. made to the *Debtor*, provided he pays the Sum express'd in the Bill *before it is due*. Now as our *Province-Bills* promise no otherwise than as all other Commodities do, and differ as much from a *promissory Note*, as an Ounce of *Silver* or Pound of *Iron* does, so it is equally uncommon, and unintelligible, to say that our Bills have undergone *a great Discount*, as it would be to say, in Case an Ounce of *Silver* purchased a Bushel of *Wheat* yesterday, and will purchase but half a one to day, that therefore *Silver* has had a *Discount* to day of 100 per Cent. Indeed the Bills in *Maryland* have, strictly speaking, had a *Discount* upon them: and very justly: For they promise *Sterling* Money instead of (6s. 8d.) their old Money, yet the Payments are extended, *viz* half to fifteen Years, and half to thirty Years, by Means of which, Exchange has risen from 33 to 150 per Cent. above *Sterling*. But the *Rhode-Island* and *New-York* Bills in this Sense have had no Discount.

But (*secondly*) if by *Discount* he means, that they will not now *purchase* so much *Silver* as formerly, I answer, It is already proved, that the *Change* of the *Rate* of *Silver* has been by Means of the *Ballance of Debt*, or its own Scarcity in Proportion to Demand; that the *Bills* had no Tendency to *raise* it; but otherwise, a direct one to keep it *down*, by Means of their constant Scarcity too: That *their* Rate is changed only in *common* with all other Things; and 20 s. in *them* always have been and still are as good or better than 20 s. in *Silver*, or any other Commodity in the Market.

His next Paragraph, " *In Affairs of this Nature a true historical Account of Facts and their Consequences, is called political Experience* " &c. The Meaning of this is; he first gives a *delusive* Account of the *Bills*, and then proceeds to support it by historical *Facts*, either *foreign* to our Case, without any fair State or Application, and some of them odious in the Comparison, or else proving nothing against us, but rather *for* us (which I shall show in the Sequel) When every Body must know that in a Case of this Kind, the Facts and Experiences to illustrate the Nature and Operation of our Bills must chiefly (if not wholly) be collected within this Province.

[50] Next Paragraph " *Silver being a staple Merchandize all the World over* " &c. That Silver is an *universal Merchandize*, I allow, and therefore that all Countries partaking of the general Trade, must and ought highly to esteem it, as being one of the best Commodities, in which they can receive or pay their respective Ballances of Trade, and carry on foreign extraordinary Affairs: But it by no Means follows, that *Silver and nothing else* (as he affirms) *ought to be the only legal Tender.* For the Reasons assigned by Mr. *Lock* and Mr. *Law*, why the World used *Silver* as *Money*, were its being lighter and cleaner than other Metals, capable of taking a plain and lasting Impression, divisible without Loss &c. And the Example and Success of the Banks of *Venice* and *Amsterdam* sufficiently shew, that it is *better* to have it passing in Trade as a *Commodity*, than as *Money*. And I make no doubt but all the World would gladly re-

duce it at least in a great Degree to a common Commodity, if they could with Convenience introduce such Schemes as the aforesaid *Banks*, or even our *Province-Bills*, in lieu of it. But it is hardly practicable in many Countries. Besides it is plain, that it's neither the best *Measure* nor the best *Instrument* in Commerce. However, a sufficient Quantity of it in this Province, at least to pay our just Debts to the Mother-Country, or use as Money (if it be found needful) is what I do now and always have contended for.

Page 2. "*Formerly in* England *the nummary Pound was the same with the Pound Weight of Silver : This was in a proper Sense the* natural *Pound.*" I presume, by this he intends to obviate my saying, that a 20 s Bill is the *natural* Pound of *New-England*, which he takes Notice of *Page* 17 &c. And so far as relates to the Money in *England*, he is right. But surely he ought to consider, that *our* Case exceedingly *differs* from theirs. We can have no *fixed* Pound under our present Circumstances : And such a *natural Pound*, as I mentioned, *viz.* Such as a private Man under *bad* Circumstances can pay, always has fallen out in *England*, as well as in this Country. For a Man that then paid but one Shilling in the Pound, his natural one was Silver at 33 *s.* 4 d. per Ounce, instead of 1 *s.* 8 d. per Ounce.

Page 2, 3, 4. He introduces his *historical Facts*, and gives a long Detail of sundry *Reductions* of *Silver-Coins*, that is, making them lighter *by Recoinages at the Mint, by iniquitous corrupt civil Administrations, in order to defraud* [51] *Creditors, and more especially to cheat the Creditors of the Publick :* And instances in *England*, *Holland* and *France*, and their respective *Plantations*.

That many Male-Practices of this Kind have been used

in *Europe*, cannot be deny'd nor vindicated. But what Relation has this to the *British* Colonies? For, excepting a Coinage of *Shillings* (3*dwt.*) &c. in this Colony (*Anno* 1652.) I never heard of any *Coinages* or *Recoinages* in the Plantations, or that this or any at all, ever took the *other Way* of cheating Creditors, *viz.* that of *Proclamations*, making the *Pieces of Eight* when passing in Trade at 4 s. 6 d. to become a *lawful Tender*, in publick & private Payments, at the Rate of 5, or 6 *s.* or the like. So that all the Benefit we could have from such *historical Facts* would be, to show the Curious the different Changes in the Rate of Silver in the English Mints, & by taking Mr. *Lowndes*'s Extracts from the Indentures of the Mint, mentioned by Mr. *Lock*, and adding the present Proportion of Alloy, now in Use, it would then have appeared that *Anno* 28. *Edward* I. *Silver* was 20 d. per Ounce, or 285 Grains to the Shilling: *5 Edward* VI. at 22 Shillings per Ounce, or 21 (6--10) Grains to the Shilling: 43 *Eliz.* at 5 *s.* 2 d. per *Ounce* or 93 Grains to the Shilling; and continued so ever since.

Page 4. "That in all the *American* Colonies, at their "first Settling and for some Years thereafter, their *Currency* "was the *same* with their (respective) *Mother-Countries:* But "by the *Iniquity* of some *Administrations* all of them have "*cheated* their *Creditors* at Home; and that in the *British* "Plantations, in Process of Time, *they remitted* to their Cred- "itors at Home a *Piece of Eight*, which is only 4 s. 6 d. Ster- "ling, at the Rate of 5 s. afterwards at 6 *s.* and would have "gone further *by Persons in Debt getting into the Administra-* "*tion or Power of defrauding their Creditors*, if the *Procla-* "*mation-Act* had not been obtained by the Sollicitations

"of the Merchants at Home; and finally, that in many of
"our Colonies they have gone greater Lengths, and *by*
"*Floods* of provincial Paper-Credit or Money they have
"made *vile Work of it,* &c.

These are the general *Plantation historical Facts,* by
which agreable to his *political Experience,* we are to know
how our Silver rose or Bills came to be depreciated, and
which he has constant recourse to upon all Occasions, Now
tho' I might justly object against this [52] Method, and tie
him down (as usual in like Cases) to the Evidences where
the Facts happened; yet for the sake of the Ignorant in
such Affairs, and those that are easily imposed upon by
Appearances that seem to gratify their present Interest, I
shall once for all consider his general Account of the Plantation Moneys and our own in particular.

That our Plantations *begun* with *Sterling Money,* &c.
Silver 5 s. 2 d. per Ounce, I allow: But the *Account* he
gives of the Causes of the Changes, I utterly deny. Let us
consider it distinctly.

First, " *They remitted*" &c By (they) we can understand
none other than *Agents* or *Factors* for the Mother-Country,
making Returns to their *Constituents.* (For all others that
remitted on their *own* Accounts, to pay a Sterling-Debt, are
out of the Question.) Now there are only two Things to
be supposed in the Case: *viz.* Either (1.) That they remitted Silver at the *Market-Rate,* and were obliged to give
5 or 6 s. for a *Piece of Eight,* instead of 4 s. 6 d. If so,
they acted *honestly,* and the *Rise* was owing to some *other*
Cause. Or (2) that they bought at 4 s. 6 d. and *charged*
their *Constituents* 5 or 6 s. —— Which to say of them, is
flatly calling hard Names. And yet all this could have no

Effect upon the *Market*, unless he also prove them *Idiots*, as giving one Man 5 s. for a Piece of Eight, when they might have had as good from another for 4 s, 6 d.

Secondly, "*Persons in Debt getting into the Administration or Power of cheating*" &c. In this he leaves us as much in the Dark, as he did with Regard to Factors. Therefore we must suppose they raised the *computative* Value of their *Coins* by provincial *Acts* (for *Recoinages* they had none) ordering that the *Piece of Eight,* when passing at 4 s 6 d. should be a *legal Tender* at 5 or 6 *s.* or the like. Now in this Case he ought to have cited the particular Acts: And not only so, but likewise proved that they were made to take in all *past* Contracts, as well as future ones. For other wise no Body could be hurt, as being left free to make their Bargains, agreable to the new Regulation of the Rate of Silver, in all future Contracts. But so far as ever I have heard, and according to the present Circumstance of some of our Plantations, there never were any such Acts made.

Thirdly, "*By Floods of provincial Paper Credit many of our Colonies have made vile Work of it.* That there have [53] been *Floods* of Bills emitted in any of the Colonies, he has not proved : And I am of Opinion that in general the Quantity has been too little, tho' the Emissions something irregular. But I have proved that the Quantity extant in the *New-England* Colonies has been but comparatively diminutive, and the Scarcity of Bills the Cause of great Oppression: And in Reality, neither have the *Factors* remitted Silver at a higher Rate than the Market-Price, nor the *Government* from time to time enacted that it should pass at a higher. So that the whole Account he gives of the Plantations seems to be full of Mistakes. And the true State of the Case is as follows.

All our Plantations at their first Settlement did, and many of them do to this Day, labour under great Difficulties by a Scarcity of Money. At first doubtless they received Pieces of Eight at the Rate of 4 s. 6 d. to 8 d. in Proportion to the Rate of them in the Mother-Country, and *Bits* (or Reals of Plate) being 1 8th Part at the Rate of 7 d. But by Means of their Difficulties in Trade, they were soon obliged to take *light* Bits, and *light* half Bits by common Consent. And upon this (as there are in all Places People that know the Difference between light and heavy Money, and how to make Advantage of it) some People *hoarded* up the heavy Pieces, and when the Merchants wanted to purchase Returns, insisted on 1 d. or 2 d. Difference between the light and the heavy Money, which the Merchants found their Interest to give. But in Time their Pieces of Eight (as well as small Money) were *clipt*, and in like Manner the heaviest always kept up and sold with a *Premium*, and People in Trade forced against their Wills to take such Money as passed, and even to make Contracts agreable thereto. And thus by Degrees *Silver* is got from 5 s. 2 d. to 6 s 10 d. 2 f. per Ounce in *Barbados*, to 7 s. 3 d. in *Jamaica*, to about 9 s. in *Antigua*, and neighbouring Islands, without any Emissions of *Bills*, or *iniquitous Administration*: And the same Cause (call it Ballance of *Trade*, or *Debt*, or *both*, at different Times, which you please) will produce the same Effects; & that altho' Money pass by *Weight*, as in *Barbados* (the Want of which, he seems to insinuate, has contributed much to the Rise of Silver.) And it would be next to a Miracle if it should happen otherwise.

As to the *Colonies* that have gone into the Use of *Bills*, it is plain, *that* the *Reason* for their so doing was, either (1.) a common Ballance of *Trade* against them, which [54] unavoidably occasioned a great Scarcity of Money in Proportion to the Demand for the Improvement of their natural Advantages, as in *New York:* Or (2.) an actual Ballance of *Debt* against them, as having comparatively no Silver-Money at all, for the Support of Government and Trade (and even sometimes being obliged to collect their Taxes in *Indian Corn*, and other Produce) as in the *New England* Colonies, and probably *South-Carolina, Pensilvania* &c. And the same still continuing, what should hinder the Rise of Silver? And under these Pressures, what could the Government do by any *Act* for the *fixing* the Rate of Silver (or what could the *Plantation-Act* do, however wisely intended) even tho' the Breach of it had been made *Felony?* Surely our Plantation-Governments could do no otherwise than they have done, as this, and (I believe) most others, *viz.* to oblige every Man that makes a *special Contract* for Silver-Money at a certain Rate, to fulfil it, and where that is wanting to give Judgment for *current Money*, as Bills of Credit, or Silver at the current received Rate in the Market. The Instance he gives of *Maryland*, is an Exception to the general Rule: For their Bills promise Sterling Money, instead of 6 *s.* 8 d, Money, half in 15, and half in 30 Years, and have justly been depreciated by Means of their distant Promise from 33 to 150 per Cent above the *Par* of Sterling.

Page 5. He proceeds to show the *bad Effects* of Paper-Currency being made a *legal Tender*. But if he had considered *his own* Account of the Banks of *Venice* and *Amsterdam*, he would have found no Occasion to apply the following Instances to our Case.

" *Baron* Gortz *about twenty Years ago had reduced* Sweeden *to extream Misery by imposing Government-Notes instead of Specie : For which, among other Crimes, he suffer'd Death.*" This he again puts us in mind of *Page* 8. How he came by this Piece of History, he does not tell us. I was in *Stockholm*, the Capital, in the Year 1718, being the last of *Charles* XII. and never then nor since heard of any *State-Bills* passing about that Time ; the Moneys then current were *Copper Coins*, not so large as an English Farthing, called according to their Mark *Dollars S. M.* (*Silver Mint*) of 32 *Stivers* or Pence (their Money) and sometimes *Mint Tickets* This Fact is universally known. Mons *Devoltiere* says, They were called *Gortz's Gods* by the People ; which is true. And they have been frequently mentioned in Print, more especially in the Affair of [55] *Woods's* Half-Pence in *Ireland*, which were compared to K. *James's* Shillings, and *Gortz's* Copper-Coins. —— They were made a legal *Tender* (I think, only for *future* Contracts) upon Pain of Death ; and a Man at *Gottenberg* (I was informed) suffered capitally for the Breach of the Laws relating thereto : All the Produce and Manufactures of the Kingdom were taxed to a certain Rate by the King's Officers respectively, and the People obliged to take their Pay in this Sort of Money.

Some Time after the first Coinage (for I have seen 4 or 5 Sorts of them, and have some of them now by me) they either were really *counterfeited*, or the Ministry gave out that they were so, by a foreign Country ; upon which they made a *new* Emission, of the same Weight and Fineness, to

pass at the same Rate, and *reduced* the *old* ones from 32 to
.1 Stiver, and upon that Foot I have frequently received
them. And thus they went on through several Coinages:
—— No Man of any Estate in the Kingdom, but detested
such iniquitous Practices; all People that could lay down
their proper Businesses, did it; Strangers forsook their
Ports, until in the aforesaid Year the King granted Passes
(chiefly with a View to supply his own Stores with Provisions) promising to pay the Importers in *Iron* and other
Produce at the King's Tax or Rate, which was strictly performed by his Officers in *Stockholm* and other Ports.

Now to run a Comparison between these *Coins* and our
Bills, would be odious and detestable: They differ as much
as Roguery from Honesty, as Folly from Wisdom, and Dark-
ness from Light.

Again, " *The arbitrary Government of* France (he says)
did Anno 1719 *embrace Mr.* Law's *Project of a Paper-Currency; Silver was banished by severe Penalties, and Paper
made the only Legal Tender. The Operation was, the Nation
reduced to the utmost Confusion, Mr.* Law *disgraced* &c

What the Particulars of Mr. *Law's* Scheme were, he does
not tell us, nor could I ever perfectly learn. But according
to my present Thought, such a Scheme as the Bank of
Venice, &c. could not effectually be put in Practice in
France, where the People have had so much Reason to
be diffident of the publick Faith. I have heard it said,
that Mr. *Law's* Scheme, was in it self *good* and *practicable*,
but *perverted* by the Ministry. Or however that was, I am
positively assured by Gentlemen of Credit then [56] at *Paris*,
and now in *Boston*, that the Bills had not only universal
Consent, but were for some Time *better* than *Silver*, and a

Premium of 5 to 10 per Cent above *Par* given for them. But the Fate of them was this; The *Ministry* having obtained their *Ends*, paid off the national Debts, and drawn in a great deal of Money into the Treasury, *broke up the Scheme*, upon the Appearance of great Numbers of *Counterfeits* in different Places at once, said to have been done by a neigbouring Country, refused them publick Credit, and left the Possessors to a total Loss.

Now to make our Case parallel to theirs, the Government in 1702 should have emitted a profuse Quantity of Bills, made them a legal Tender in all publick and private Payments, and to be received in both with a Premium of 5 per Cent above Silver, paid off the Province-Debts with them, given them out of the Treasury for Silver at *Par*, and lent them upon Loan; and after they had carried their Scheme as far as they could, then upon a sudden Appearance of many Counterfeit-Bills in different Places at once, said to be done by the *Mohawk* Indians, have dissolved the Scheme, refused the Bills publick Credit, and left every Possessor totally to bear his own Loss. — This is another of his *historical Facts*, by which we are to have our Bills, according to *political Experience*, set in a true Light. But to proceed with out Author. —

 " *Barbadoes emitted l. 80000 Bills on Land-Security at 4 per Cent, payable after 5 Years, which immediately fell 40 per Cent. below Silver: But by an Order from Home were all called in* " &c.

These were *promissory Notes*, and quite different from our Bills. The People were wise in taking them only at that Discount: For as lawful Interest was then 10 per Cent, so by allowing Compound-Interest *l* 141 1*s.* of them was then only equal to *l* 100 Current-Money on their first Emission : And their Sentence from Home (which I have from good Hands) being that instead of 5 Years they should be paid off in 18 Months, was truly equitable, and ought to be a Warning Piece to some among us who are always hankering after *such* Bills.

Page 6 "*Our Province-Bills from the various Operations of frequent large Emissions distant Periods, & Periods postpon'd; are become 400 per Cent. worse than Sterling*" &c.

As for *large* and *sudden* Emissions, I declared against them in my *Letter*, as what ought industriously to be [57] avoided; and propos'd their being emitted in a *regular progressive* Way so as not hurt the Trade by a sudden Flood. But for the *general Quantity* of Bills out at any one Time in the 4 *New-England* Colonies, it is far from being large. I could make him almost any Concessions on this Head, and I'll suppose there may be now extant and actually passing (tho' it's self evident that the Bulk of them are kept in a State of Stagnation) in the whole l. 650000; a Sum, when computed at the Rate of Silver 29 s per Ounce, only equal to l. 116000 Sterling; which considering the Numbers of the People, improveable Ad- of these Colonies &c. is by all true Ways of Judging but comparatively a very *small* Sum in Proportion to Demand. Now this being the Case, it must be observed, that commonly before a *new* Emission at any Time, could be obtained, *Trade* (by Means of so great Scarcity) *laboured, Debts* were *postpon'd* &c. and what could be the *Consequence* upon a *sudden* Emission, but that People receiving their *Debts* in a much *greater* Proportion, and purchasing *more Returns*, than usual, the *Silver* and other Returns should remarkably *rise*; which is what the *Essayer* means by our *Province-Bills* becoming *worse?* (Surely this must have been the Event, except we had happened at such Times to have *more Silver* at Market than even the *extraordinary Demand;* then it could not have risen.) And yet (as I have once and again observed) if there had always been a sufficient Quantity of *Bills* extant, and People gone more *uniformly* to Market, *Silver* by Means of the constant *growing* Demand would eventually have risen to the *same* Height, in an equally certain, tho' *slower* Manner. Besides, we have sundry Instances wherein *Silver* has *risen* even when *Bills* as to Quantity have been at their lowest *Ebb.* But the daily Operation of the *Market* puts the Matter beyond Dispute: For there we find Silver every Day changing its Rate, as all other Commodities do, without any Relation to the Quantity of Bills extant. And to what other Cause can any Man rationally impute the *general Change,* but to the Operation of the *Ballance of Debt* against us?

" *Distant Periods, and Periods postpon'd* " — Here and throughout the whole Essay he goes upon the Mistake of comparing the *Bills* to special *promissory Notes;* from which they differ as much as a Commodity in Hand does from a Note promising that same Commodity at a distant Time.

[58] The only Thing to be considered with Regard to the *Periods* of the *Bills,* is, whether at any such Periods the Quantity extant was greater than the Demand. That it never exceeded, but fell vastly short at all Times, is obvious to the Understanding of every one. Therefore the *Postponings* are mere *circumstantial* Facts; and have never operated to lower the Value of the Bills, but otherwise. How strange then is the Complaint in this Case? What

Reason have we for it, more than the *Venetians* have to complain, that *effective* Payments have been postponed for many Centuries, when they can every Day in the Market have the Amount of the original *Depositum* in Silver for their *Transfers*, with 20 per Cent. more than the Sum deposited: Especially since our *Bills* are of the *same* general Nature with their *Transfers*; both equal to Things in the Market at the current Rate; the *Rise* of *theirs*, and the *Fall* of *ours*, with Regard to their first *Par*, being wholly owing to *different* trading Circumstances, and to no other Causes whatever? *Postponings* not in the least concerned here, as to either Case.

Page 9. "*So much Paper as is current in a Province, so much really is that Province in Debt*".——— This is a strange Delusion: In what Sense can a Province be said to run in Debt, by necessary Emissions of Bills? Are they indebted thereby to *other Countries*? Or is their *capital Stock* thereby *diminished*? No certainly, their landed and trading Interests have been thereby greatly increased in Value: So that it would have been *good Husbandry* even if they had *borrowed* upon *Interest* a Supply of Silver, or Bills where they were to be had, equal in Value to their Emissions. The *Funds*-Part are absolutely necessary for the Support of Government, and vastly more convenient for the Payment of Taxes (having no Silver) than *Indian Corn* and other Produce. And for the *Loans*-Part, supposing some People have made a bad Use of their Moneys borrowed, & suffered their mortgaged Lands to go in Payment, is not this common to all other Countries? Bad Husbands will sell or mortgage to their own People, or any other, that will lend them Money: And in such Case it is a publick Advantage, that their Estates should get into better Hands. The *Essayer's* Way of arguing is as odd, as if a Man possessed of 1000 Acres of *waste Lands*, which bring in nothing, should refuse to mortgage 20 of them, by Means of which he might be enabled to carry on the Settlement of the whole to good [59] Purpose; saying, No, let the Lands lie waste; if I borrow Money upon them, I shall but *run in Debt.* ——

To go on.

Page 14 " *We have no Reason to fear Want of a Medium, if the Grievance of publick Paper-Credit were gradually removed: Trade will find its own natural proper Medium,* Silver and Gold " *&c.* —— If our Trade were well regulated, it might in a Course of Years get into prosperous Circumstances, and then it would produce *Silver* to pass as Money. But in order to this, it is indispensably necessary, in the mean time, to have *Bills* (having no other convenient Matter) as the Instrument for carrying on our Commerce, and improving our natural Advantages. And can any Man conceive but that upon the *Want* of Bills we must run into the further Use of *Shop-Notes*, which have an infallible Tendency to increase the Ballance of Debt against us, and to drive away the most valuable Part of the Community, Artificers, Labourers, and even Husbandmen, to other Colonies and Parts, where they have Money of one Sort or other to receive for their Labour? An Attempt of this Kind might in a dozen or a score of Years reduce the Value of the capital Stock of the Province to half its present Worth, when compared with Silver.

Having fully answered the Substance of the *Essay*, I shall now proceed to consider the *Author's* particular Remarks upon my *Observations*.

The first I shall take Notice of, is that Reflection (P. 15) "*He introduces these Words,* Ballance of Trade, *on all Occasions with no true Meaning and Application*". The Ballance of *Trade* is not what I mention'd : *Our* Case being in Fact a Ballance of *Debt,* and largely explained. However, as the *Essayer* seems to mean the *same* Thing by a Ballance of *Trade,* that I do by a Ballance of *Debt,* and as the Force of his Objection turns upon that single Case, I shall give his Remarks on it a full Consideration.

"*Ballance of Trade is Cash* (Silver *and* Gold) *imported to or exported from a Country, according as the general Exports or Imports of Merchandize exceed one another.*" This I allow; and every *Ounce* of Silver imported to or exported from a Country is by *Means* of a Ballance of Trade *for* or *against* them, and this may be taken for a Day, Month or Year &c.

Again, "*The Silver and Gold which we export to* England, *are no Part of the Ballance of Trade against us, being truly as Merchandize only.* England *exports 2 Million* [60] *to* Holland *and* India, *as Merchandize, the Ballance of Trade continuing in Favour of* England *notwithstanding.*" The Meaning of this is, that a Country may have a *particular* Ballance *against* them, with *one* Country and *another,* and yet a *general* one at the same time in *their Favour* with all the World. But this is *not* our Case : We have it *for* us with some Parts of the World; and yet upon the whole we want it in *general,* with *England* &c. *Every Ounce* we export, call it *Merchandize,* or what you please, goes in the Ballance of *Trade;* and what we send Home being all together not sufficient, there still rests a Ballance of *Debt* against us.

· Again, "*Ballance of Trade is also against a Country, not only when they export their Medium, but also when a Country runs in DEBT, by expending in fine Houses, Apparel* &c. *that which ought to have purchased Exports : This is Our present Case.*" Which Observation, if *introduced with any true Meaning and Application*, must signify that *we* run more in *Debt* to *England* than we are able to pay (a Thing allowed by every Body) and is in Effect the same Definition I gave of the *Ballance of Debt* against us; differing only in *Words*. Now, as by this he allows us to be in a State of partial *Bankruptcy*, or the Demand for Returns in the general greater than the Quantity, must not the Rates of Silver and other Things by necessary Consequence be *raised* proportionably thereto, as in the Case of *N.?* Notwithstanding throughout the whole of his Remarks, he cavils at the plain, natural and unavoidable Inferences.

He objects to sundry Observations in my Letter. As, Pag. 15. "*The sinking Value of our Bills is from and in Proportion to the Ballance of Trade* (or Debt) *against us. —* Pag. 17. *A* 20 *s. Bill is the natural Pound of* New-England — Ibid. *Silver falling and rising* ad infinitum. All his Cavils at such Passages evidently and naturally arise from his not understanding his own *Ballance of Trade*, by Means of which *Silver* and *Bills* must for ever change their *Market-Rate*, and 20 s in Bills or Silver be just what the Ballance for or against us makes them.

.Pag 18 He pretends to quote that Passage out of my Letter; *When Goods rise or fall in the Market, the Change must be in the Goods, and not in the Bills.* He refers me to no Page, and I find no such Assertion : But the contrary. *Obs* P. 18 "The Pound-Value (or the Value of 20 *s* : in the

" Market) is changed in all Goods, as well as in [61] the
" Bills: And 20 *s.* in them are as good as 20 s. in any other
" Things.

Pag. 16. *Bills ought to be emitted from time to time, and
postponed till the Quantity exceed the Demand.* — A sufficient
Quantity of Bills, regulated by an assigned Interest, I did
and do contend for. But as to *postponing*, I said in Substance, that in as much as the Government have taken upon
them to supply the Province with Bills, they ought to have
kept always a sufficient Quantity out, upon Funds or Loans,
to answer the Demands of Trade. As the Bills promise no
effective Payments, the *postponing* can no otherwise be hurtful than by an *Excess* of the general Quantity extant (which
never happened) and in that Case, whether they *call in* the
Funds punctually, and at the same time *emit* more, or else
postpone the *Funds* already out, it amounts just to the same
Thing. In this Case the Funds or Loans are only *circumstantial* Things, and the *calling in* (not the postponing) in
my humble Opinion is rather the *publick Fraud* and *iniquitous Administration* he so frequently complains of. And
as the natural *Consequences* of thus *reducing* the current
Money of the Province, without any other good Matter substituted in its Place, must be *long Credit, excessive Usury*
and *Extortion, Idleness,* and *Intemperance*; the Use of *other*
Colony Bills, so as to bring a Ballance of Trade against us,
for which both our *Silver* and *Lands* must go in Payment
to them; the ruinous Practices of *Shop-Notes* and a *Trucking Trade;* I say, as these are the plain and unavoidable
Consequences of a Scarcity of Money, the *reducing* the
Money of the Province may be said to be virtually *establishing those iniquitous Practices by a Law*, much more (I 'm

sure) than the largest *Emission* of Bills hitherto may be said to have been.

Pag. 23. "*The following Clauses* (*and elsewhere many* others) I *cannot understand; as, Bills made a fixed Measure of Value, which Silver cannot be.* Again, *When Silver falls, the Government may fix the Rate of it* — Now is it not plain to the meanest Capacity (and allowed by every Body) that a general *Commodity* or *Money* having its own *Quantity* and *Demand* always kept *equal,* must be a *perfect Measure* of the Value of Things; and likewise that supposing *Silver* to fall to 20 s. per Ounce, and the Government and common Consent agree that an Ounce of Silver shall be the *N E .* nummary (or Money) *Pound,* what in the World (so long as we have no Ballance [**62**] against us) should hinder it to *continue* so for ever, as in *Europe?*

But to take in the Substance of all that he says with Regard to the *Bills* being *depreciated,* I must take Notice of one Passage more, Pag. 15. "*If we find that in all the Colonies where is no Paper-Credit, the Value of their nummary Denominations* [or the Rate of Silver] *continues the same, and where Paper-Currencies have prevailed, their Denominations have depreciated* [or Silver risen] *hand in hand with their repeated Emissions, ought we to have recourse to any other Conceit* (*as Ballance of Trade*) *for the Cause, but only to the Operation of these Bills* "? — The Fact is, he himself owns, as I do, that Silver *rose* in the Plantations even *before* the *Plantation-Act;* we differ only as to the *Cause*: And it is notorious that it has also risen *since* that Act in many of them, and still continues so to do; that is, By Reason of their general *Scarcity* of Money, they are obliged to take *light* Pieces, both Silver & Gold, which is as much *raising* the computative Value of their Coins, as if the Government did it by their Province-Acts. And as to those that are in the Use of *Bills*, we have a fresh Instance to the contrary of what he says, in the last *New-York* Emission of l. 48000 in Bills (Silver about 9 s. per Ounce) which was not only very irregular as to the *Method*, being put in Circulation all-at once, and as to the *Quantity* double the whole Sum they had then extant in Bills, but also by comparing the whole Quantity & Demand in our four Colonies with that of *New-York*, might be thought an excessive large Emission: Yet no remarkable Change followed. I have heard of Silver being sold as high there before that Emission, as since: And Exchange has only risen from 165 to 170 l. the highest (for l. 100 Sterling) after two Years Trial; the Reason, because they had Silver enough to answer all Demands for Returns, and so no Ballance of *Debt* against them: Which makes a vast Difference between *their* Case and *ours*. We are assured of a Balance of *Trade* against us by the Demand we every Day see for Silver in Returns to the Mother-Country: And by the general Deficiency we are equally sure of a Balance of *Debt* against us. To no other Cause can we rationally ascribe the Variation of the Rate of Silver among us, but to the greater or smaller Operation of this Balance of Debt, as the Demand and the Quantity of Silver in the Market bear a Proportion to one another greater or less: From hence we may as certainly conclude that the [63] Balance of *Debt* for or against us will for ever affect the Price of Silver in this Province, as that 3 and 2 make 5.

Page **21**. *He is an inexorable Enemy to Silver, because it has been and may be greatly depreciated by the Excess of its Quantity.* — This is intirely wrong: For *changeable* tho' it be, yet I all along aimed at the proper Means of introducing it, and expresly gave it its due Praise. For Instance, I say (*Obs.* Page 22.) *Trade is the only Means of introducing* Silver *and* Gold, *the general Treasure of the World* &c. — I might on this Occasion fairly retort upon him, and say at least with equal Truth and Reason, *He is an inexorable Enemy to Province-Bills.* — But I forbear. And shall close with this single Remark :

That in many Cases it's very plain he does not understand the *Operation of Quantity and Demand,* and therefore one of the most unfit to write *Essays upon Money.*

POSTSCRIPT

WHILE the foregoing was in the Press, the Publick has been offered *A Discourse concerning the Currencies* &c. I presume by the Author of the *Essay*, and upon the same Plan, but I think with no great Improvements in Point of Reasoning. Now altho' I have in my *Inquiry* fully obviated and answered every Thing of Moment he has advanced in Opposition to our *Bills*; yet it may be needful for the sake of the *Unwary*, and others led by a delusive Prospect of *Gain*, who easily take up with any specious Appearances of arguing from *Fact* and *Experience*, to make some Remarks on this Piece also.

I observe, he still entertains a wrong Notion of the Nature of our *Bills*, and in the whole Tenor of his Discourse puts them upon the Footing of common *promissory Notes*, and even *such* as have no solid *Fund*, payable at distant and uncertain (postpon'd) *Periods*, and also without any Allowance of *Interest* for Forbearance: From which sort of *Notes*, it is self-evident, they *differ* in all these Regards; as having the best Fund, *viz.* common Consent, by which they are made equivalent to all Things at all Times bought and sold in the *New-England* Markets; and thus are virtually paid off every Day; and also may be every Day let at an high Interest, either on Condition to receive Silver at a fixed Rate as in *Europe*, or to receive the same sort of Bills as he lent, which he pleases. — From the same Mistake also our Author calls them, as usual, " *Base Paper-Currency, fallacious Cash, chimerical ill-founded Medium* &c."

He seems also still utterly unacquainted with the Operations of Quantity and Demand; constantly complains of *frequent* and *large Emissions of Bills, enormous publick Loans* &c. and yet allows (Page 26, 27.) that the Value of the whole Bills and Silver Cash extant in the 4 *New-England* Colonies, *A.* 1713, was equal to 657000 Ounces of Silver; *A.* 1718, to but 500000 Ounces; and now *A.* 1739, the Bills extant only equivalent to 434000 Ounces [65] of Silver, or about two thirds of the Value in current Cash at this Day to what there was then. Now as I suppose, every one will allow that we may require at least three times *more* Money in Value to negotiate our Affairs *now*, than at that Time; so according to all rational Ways of judging, we ought *now* to have three times more *Bills* in Value, than we then had: More especially since the *Quantity* did not then *exceed* the *Demand* (but probably was *less*) as may be known by the then Rate of Interest. Not that I propose the above Method as a certain Way of judging in this Case; no, the Rate of *Interest* is the unerring Rule. And if we had a proper *Bank-Circulation*, much less Money would answer the End in that Way, than in any other.

As to the *Ballance of Debt*, the great Matter in Controversy, he introduces it in effect, *Page* 34 (and other Places) by Way of Objection, " It is not repeated large Emissions of a base Paper-Currency, but the Imports exceeding the Exports, that occasions Silver to be ship'd off in Ballance; therefore we are not to expect a Silver-Currency, supposing all Bills cancelled " &c. Under this Head he virtually owns my Ballance of *Debt*, by his Concession, that our Imports *exceed* our Exports, and proposes very justly the proper Remedy (*Page* 35.) *Let us then lessen our Imports by Frugality, and add to our Exports by Industry* &c.——— But at the same time he imputes the *Cause* to the *Bills*, as giving the *Merchant Opportunity to ship off the* Silver, *which Necessity would otherways have obliged him to keep as Cash.*——— A strange Way of arguing! Was it ever known in any Country, where they had only a common Ballance of *Trade* against them, much more where they had an actual Ballance of *Debt* against them, as we have, but that *Silver* was ship'd of in Payments? Does not the Exigence of the Case necessarily and inevitably infer it? And is it not so in many of our Colonies, that have had *no Bills*? What a very trifle of *Silver* and *Gold* (and that exceeding *light* too, or else they would probably have none) have they in Proportion to their *Trade*, which may be negotiated chiefly by their *Produce*, which *ours* cannot? What a hard Case would he reduce the Merchants to! *Necessity* (says he) *would have obliged them*, were there no Bills, *to keep their Silver as Cash*: And yet *Necessity* too obliges them *to ship it off as Merchandize*, to pay their Debts at home. ——— Thus he does but trifle with the Objection, he proposes [66] to answer: and he overlooks the natural obvious Consequence of Imports exceeding Exports, *viz.* the Rise of the Rate of Silver and other Things: A Consequence, that in such a State of Affairs is unavoidable. And therefore how *staple* soever our *exportable Commodities* are in the trading World, whether we have *Bills* extant or not; yet the *same Cause* just mentioned, if continued, will undoubtedly produce the *same Effect, viz.* the Rise of the Rate of Silver *ad infinitum*; as the contrary Cause will the Fall of it: And as we are now circumstanced it is next to impossible, to regulate our Trade, or carry it on to any good Purpose, without a Sufficiency of *Bill-Money*.

The grand Point, which he labours throughout the whole Discourse, is to prove by several *Facts & political Experiences* relating to Paper-Currencies, that (as in *Page* 24.) *the repeated and large Emissions of Paper Money, are the Cause of the frequent Rise of the Price of Silver* and Exchange; further, that the *Emissions* and *Cancellings* of Bills, have governed them both, and raised, lower'd and fixed them, as the Course of the Moon does the Tides, plain to a kind of Demonstration, from the following Instances in *New England.*——*After Silver had rose (A.* 1706) to 8 *s. per Ounce it continued* (till 1714) *at that Rate, while Paper-Emissions did not exceed a due Proportion to the current Silver.*" Here in the same Breath he flatly contradicts his own Assertions: For he allows (*Pag.* 26) that *A.* 1713, the *Bills* extant in all the *N. E.* Colonies were in Value (only to be regarded) equal to 438000 Ounces of *Silver*, which is a trifle more than the Value of those now extant, and never exceeded but *A.* 1718, and that only by 62000 Ounces; and *A.* 1731, by 32000 Ounces of *Silver*: Besides that even in that short Period (from 1706 to 1714) there were not only *large Emissions* of Bills, but (*Page* 10) a Number of *Postponings*, and yet after all *no Change* in the Rate of *Silver*; the Reason he gives, is, because there was *a due Proportion of Concomitant Silver passing with the Bills.* And what else is this, but to acknowledge the *Ballance of Debt* (allowed by all) and in effect to say, that from *A.* 1706 to 1714. we had *Silver*, either as Money or as Merchandize, sufficient to *answer all Demands* for Exportation, and therefore it did *not rise;* but that afterwards becoming *less* than the Demand, it rose proportionably, and continues so doing to this Day; the infallible *Phases* of Emissions &c. not all influenital [67] in the Case!—— Or in more general Terms, that from the first Settlement of *New-England,* by Means of their own *Trade,* and in a good Measure by the Help of *providential Supplies* (in which their Trade was not concerned) as *Silver* and other Effects imported by Means of *Wrecks, Pirates* and *Privateers, Settlers* &c. these Colonies were enabled so far to keep their Credit with the Mother-Country, that the Rate of Silver was only changed from 5 s. 2 d. to 8 s. per Ounce, till the Year 1714. But that after the *War* most of those Supplies *fail'd* and our prodnee by Degrees *fell* exceedingly in the foreign Markets, and finally for Want of a Sufficiency of *Bills* in Proportion to Demand, we were forced into the Use of *Shop-Notes* to serve in lieu of *Cash,* and so into an excessive Importation of *European* Goods, which enhanced the Ballance against us, till *Silver A.* 1739, was raised to 29 s. per *Ounce.*

N. B. As to our Author's Assertion relating to the *concomitant Silver,* viz. 219000 *Ounces, A.* 1713 (mentioned *Page* 26.) I am apt to think it is but ill founded: For the Government in all their *Acts* respecting *Bills,* make high Complaints of the extreme Scarcity of *Silver,* and expressly say (*A* 1712) that *all the Silver,* was ship'd off in Payment of Debts to *Great-Britain,* and that the Trade in general had been carried on from 1705, to that Time by Means of the *Bills*: So that the Quantity then in the Market, could be at most but comparatively small, and used only as Merchandize; not as Cash in Circulation *concomitant* with the Bills.

In the same Paragraph he proceeds to say; " *A.* 1714 *we emitted* &c." Here follow seven Emissions in *Massachusetts*, *Rhode-Island*, and *Connecticut*, according to which the Bills were depreciated (*Pari passu*) till *A.* 1739. One of them one Year, others 3, 4, 5, 6 Years distant from each othtr. At one Period Silver rose 1 s. 2 d per *Ounce*; at others 2, 3 & 6 s. without any Relation to the Quantity of the Emissions, or the Demand for them. Now the *Application* of these Facts, supposing his Account of them to be right, I take to be meer *Delirium*. The *Connecticut* and *Rhode-Island* Emissions were never taken notice of as influential in the Case, till *A.* 1733: The Reasons for doing it then, are well known. Besides in his Account of that Year's Emissions he leaves out one historical Fact, very material, I mean, the *Merchants-Notes*, value above l. 100000, and which may with more Justice be charged [68] with being the whole Cause of the late extraordinary Rise of Silver, than all the other Emissions: For it is a known and remarkable Fact, that *Silver* rose *within about nine Months time*, that Year, from 21 s. 6 d. to 27 s. which was to a very trifle the Value of those Notes, when reduced by nine Months Discount. Not that I would be tho't wholly to exclude the natural Operation of *Trade* out of the Case: But the Observation I have made, may help to supply a Defect in the Author's History and Argument, and ought to have Weight with such as impute the Rise of Silver to the meer Operation of the *Bills.*—— As to the last *Rhode Island* Emission in 1738, Silver did not actually rise till the latter End of May 1739, and the Cause of its rising was evidently the great Number of Payments in *Silver* and *Gold* at the annual Collection of the *Impost*-Money &c.

His Instances in the next Paragraph (*Page* 25) in *New-England* &c. are strong Evidences for what I have alledg'd: For if *Returns in Shipping, Whale-Oyl,* &c. *be large, and bear a good Price abroad,* has not that a direct Tendency to *lower* the Prices of *Silver* &c.? As on the contrary, the Demand for *Silver* to supply *Agencies,* or other political Occasions, has it not the same Tendency to *raise* Silver? The whole of this is in some Degree the natural Operation of the *Balance of Debt.*

He instances in the Case of *Barbados,* to put his Assertion out of Dispute; which I have already consider'd, and in Fact it has no Relation at all to the Case.

The utmost that can be said on this Head, is, that upon some new Emissions in this Province Silver rose in *Boston* a small Matter, and the plain *Cause* (for which I appeal to Men in Trade) was the preceeding great *Scarcity of Bills,* by Means of which *Debts* due here and *Returns* to the Mother-Country were greatly *pospon'd,* so that on the new Emission People were *generally* put in Cash, the *sudden Demand* for Returns *greater* than usual, and the Market *proportionably* affected.

The *unerring Evidence* in the Case, is the *Merchants* and *Goldsmiths* Books, to which I appeal: and doubt not but they will show, that *Silver* has been every Day in a *changeable* State; without Regard to Emissions of Bills.

I might here *recapitulate* something of what I said on this Head in the foregoing Inquiry, *viz.* That the Bills are established upon the Footing of a general Commodity or Money, and cannot be changed any otherways than [69] they are; that there has been no Change in them for the worse by Means of a Change in their natural Proportion to other Things, or the Excess of their Quantity above the Demand; but they have undergone a forced Change, in common with other Things, *viz.* in the Way of rating them. That the Bills are virtually, and may actually be put upon the Foot of the Transfers of *Venice,* and *Amsterdam,* & have operated the same Way; different trading Circumstances alone making the Odds; all which Observations carry Demonstration along with them.

It is well known, that *dealing in Silver has been a Business among us,* and that frequently it has been raised by that Means; also that Silver has risen remarkably in the *Spring* and *Fall,* on Account of the *largest Remittances* being made at those Times.

To conclude this Head, I must observe, that some have said in Conversation that *they could raise Silver* from time to time, if they pleased This is what ought, I know, to be mention'd with Caution, but is a melancholy Truth. Such a Thing, trading Men are appriz'd, might be done, and that whether the Bills be gradually sunk, or there be none extant: I say, *none at all,* because when *Bills* grow a little Scarcer, they will then become a private Property, and *Silver* be sold in the *trucking* Way as other Things are, and he that wanted to *monopolize* it, would have at least a good Chance to sell it for such Commodities as would purchase *Silver* again: And whence comes the unhappy Affair, but from the *Ballance of Debt,* by Means of which our Imports of Silver are small, and the Demand frequently greater in Proportion? And by no Means from the Operation of the Bills. But to proceed —

The long and formidable Account he has given of the *depreciating* of *Bills*, upon *Emissions*, in those other Colonies, that are in the Use of them, as it may possibly have a bad Effect to *biass* some of his Readers, I shall therefore take some Notice of it. But a cursory View will suffice to evidence that nothing remarkable has happen'd as to the *Rise* of *Silver*, excepting in *South-Carolina* and *New-England*: And in this Case, I shall not follow him through his political Remarks on their *Emissions, Postponings, Cancellings* &c. Having already given (as I think) the most conclusive Proofs, that the *general Cause* of the Rise of Silver, was the Operation of the *Ballance of Debt*, in them all; and he having offered little or nothing either to prove that the *Bills* were the Cause of it, or to [70] shew *how* they could *operate* to produce the Effect he imputes to them.

In *New-York, New-Jersies* and the two *Pensilvania* Governments, *Pistoles* (the greatest Article of their current Species) of 4 dwt. 6 gr. pass for about 28 *s.* and in *Antigua, St. Christophers, Montserrat, Nevis* & the *Virgin Islands* (which never had any Bills) *Pistoles* of but 4 dwt. pass too or 28 s. — So that the former, taking all their Species together, I reckon have the Advantage of the latter.

Maryland is intirely out of the Question; their Bills being on the Foot of *promissory Notes;* and the Difference of the Rate of Silver there may justly be called a *Discount* for prompt Payment.

North-Carolina, — As to this Government I agree with our Author, that they have no great Fund (Vent) for *Bills* of Credit, those formerly emitted were disregarded by the People, ill-contrived, and much counterfeited: So that their

Trade has all along been in the Way of *Barter* and their *Imports* and *Exports* raised upon *each other* in *Denomination*, without the Influence of *Bills*; their naval Stores sold on the Footing of their common Trucking-Trade, and their best Exports (as Tallow, Deer-Skins, Wax &c.) bartered on the Footing of *Virginia-Money*, Silver at 6 s. 8 d. per Ounce.

Thus it appears that there are but two remarkable Instances, among all the Colonies that are in the Use of Bills such as ours, viz. *South-Carolina*, and the *New-England* Colonies, whose Bills all pass in common: And it may not be amiss particularly to take some Notice of the Causes of the Rise of Silver in *South-Carolina;* having already said enough upon the Case of *New-England*.

I never could learn that frequent and large Emissions of *Bills* were any Cause of the Rise of Silver in *South-Carolina;* but have often heard, about the Year 1733, that they were so very scarce that no less than 20 per Cent Interest was given for them, and the People in great Distress and Confusion, till in Part relieved by a Set of compassionate publick-spirited Gentlemen, who circulated their own Notes in the Way of a *Bank*, tho' not without great Opposition, and Attempts of divers Kinds to defeat their charitable Intentions. But the Causes generally allowed are these — (1.) Large Importations of *Negroes;* (2) The great *Fall* of the Value of their Produce: Either of which were sufficient to have brought about those bad Effects. And (3.) Considerable *Remittances* Home by [**71**] private Persons, for the Purchase of Estates, and as a Depositum in the Stocks. Lastly, A considerable (both necessary and superfluous) Importation of *Materials, Cloathing* &c. from the Mother-Country; together with chargeable Negotiations, Travels, foreign Education &c. all which belong to their general Account of Trade. And yet under all these Inconveniencies, *South-Carolina* taken in a complex View, has been one of the most flourishing Settlements, their capital Stock increased in Value to a prodigious Degree; and this in a great Measure owing to the Bills of Credit. The same might justly be affirmed of this Province, till such unaccountable Notions, as those of our Author, so detrimental to the Common-Wealth, were received and industriously propagated among us.

There's little else remarkable in his Piece, but what I have already obviated. His supposed *Mischiefs* arising from a large *Paper-Currency*, his *Arguments* (as he says) current among the *Populace*, together with his *Proposals* for rectifying our Currency, his abusive *Reflections* &c. are all but the native Consequence of his bad Politicks, and Ignorance in the Subject he writes upon, sufficiently obvious to any judicious & impartial Reader. — Therefore I shall only take notice of a few Passages, and conclude.

Page 26. "*Large repeated Emissions of Bills are no Addition to the Medium of Trade.*" Here he again contradicts his own Assertion, that in 1713 there was one half more in Value of Money, passing then, than what there is now, and yet we may require three times more in Value now in Proportion to Demand. It is the Quantity of Money in *Value*, not in *Denomination*, that we must regard; and every private Man, as well as every Community of People, requires a certain Proportion (in Value) of Money to carry on their Affairs. Supposing then, that *Great Britain* required 20 Million in Silver at 5 s. 2 d. per Ounce, and

Silver raised from time to time by Recoinag s, Proclamations, or a Ballance of Debt, to 29 s. per Ounce, must they
not in that Case have 112 Million in Silver, new Money, or
the same Sum in Bills of Credit? And would there be in
that Case one superfluous Shilling, whether of Silver or
Bills?

Page 27 "*People who never can have any other Claim
to Money, but by Fraud, the Idle, Extravagant* &c. *call out
loudest for a Paper-Medium*". This is an unjustifiable Reflection: For in Fact, every Body knows, that the *Labourers*
[72] and *Tradesmen*, who (as he well observes) are the
Hands which feed the Belly of the Common-Wealth, have
been oppressed to a crying Degree, for Want of honest and
punctual *Money-Pay*. The industrious *fair Traders* have
suffered greatly, by having their just Debts long postpon'd,
by being forc'd to take Goods at great Disadvantage in lieu
of Money, and often to lose their Debts by Insolvencies:
Widows and *Orphans*, and even the *Clergy* many of them,
have suffered much by the distressing Scarcity of Money:
All these have a good Right to desire a reasonable Currency.
And the *real* Estates in *Boston*, and the Province in general, have of later Years been reduced incredibly in their
Value, by the Operation of the same Cause. As for the
Shopkeepers, they have least Reason to complain, and some
of them fairly own that a Trucking-Trade is best for them.
All Men that have indisputable *Security* to give, are intitled
to Money; and all Countries endeavour they should have it
at as *low* an *Interest* as possible. We are perhaps the only
Country, that ever dreamt of *reforming* their Trade by a
Scarcity of *Money*, when a Sufficiency of it must be ac-
knowledged the best Means of *Industry* and (in our Case)

of *Frugality* too. — *Others* besides our Author have suggested, That *those who have no Right to it, are the Men who call out for it most*. But can it be supposed that *such* will have any *lent* them? Are not the *Arts* of lending Money as well *known* here, and as much *refined* among us of late, as any where? So that there is no Danger from that Quarter, even tho' we had a Sufficiency of Bills.

Page 29. "*Long Credit is not one of the least of the bad Effects of Paper-Money*. Ibid.. *With ready Money, Business go's on brisk and easy*".— Can any Man rationally ascribe *long Credit* to any other Cause, but *Scarcity* of Money? Does not the Rate of *Interest* and the length of *Credit* depend upon the *Quantity* of Money in Proportion to *Demand*, as the Shadow upon the Body? The Practice of *Holland* and *England*, and all other Countries that have *low Interest*, sufficiently demonstrates this. Their Discounts or Abatements for prompt Payment are but trifling, to what they are here. Indeed some particular Commodities are so abundant in Proportion to Demand, that if Money were never so plenty, the Seller might be glad to part with them on long Credit. Therefore the one and only Remedy in our Case, is a sufficient Currency, and [**73**] the Advantages upon that Account would be vastly great, and in particular to the Mother-Country.

Page 35. "*The goodly Appearance we make in fine Houses, Equipage and Dress, is owing to Paper*." This and many other Speeches said to be made by the Populace, are dragg'd in to gloss his Cause, both in the Essay and Discourse. I affirm he is the first Person that pretends to Reason and Modesty, that ever I knew set the Matter in the Light he has done. His *Vulgar great and small*, the noble and ignoble, even the extravagant themselves, complain of our surprizing Excess in those Particulars, own the Cause, and the Necessity of a Reformation. However, all must confess, the goodly Appearance of the Province in necessary Supplies and Accommodations for Life, Trade, Fishery, and the vast additional Value of our real Estates, &c. are (next to a kind Providence) owing to our Bills.

He frequently expresses a compassionate Concern for *Posterity*, lest they should be overburthened with *Taxes*, and tempted to *Mutiny*. Not considering, that the *Funds* ever since the Year 1712 have been *kept out*, chiefly to fulfil the *Engagements* the Government then virtually took upon themselves to *supply* the Province with *Bills*, to serve as *Money*, and that in this Regard, there never ought to be *more* called in than what is absolutely necessary to defray the Charges of the *current Year*, which is no Inconvenience; nor that the Government might emit still upon *Loan*, for the Bulk of the running Cash, and upon *Funds* only for the Service of the Government, which might be punctually call'd in without the Hazard he mentions. Neither does he consider the vast *Damage* the rising Generation have already sustained in the *depreciating* of their *real Estates* by Means of the *Scarcity of Money*: For I suppose they will not fetch so much Money upon Sale now (additional Improvements necessarily excepted) as when Silver was at 20 s. per Ounce. Nor finally that they are upon the Brink of being further reduced by the same Causes, and Posterity in Danger of being under the Necessity of paying their Debts, contracted when Silver was at 20 to 29 s per Ounce, not under the Rate of Silver at 6 s. 10 d. per Ounce.

Page 39. He hints at several *Schemes*. The 1st is *palliative, to prevent our Currency's growing worse by bringing it to a Standard* &c. All Men are now and have been all along left to their absolute Liberty to make *Contracts* according to the current Rate of *Silver* every Day, and the [74] Law has always supported them in so doing; which is more equitable than a Settlement of once in 6 or 12 Months as propos'd. Some few have taken that Method in their Loans (others have gone beyond it) and that it has not been the general Practice, is by no Means the Fault of the Government, nor of the Borrower, but chiefly the *Lenders* who instead of taking their Bonds at a fixed Rate of *Silver* and 6 (or more) per Cent. Interest, have taken them conditioned to pay in *Bills*, from an avowed Expectation of the *Fall* of Silver, as an additional Profit. — Some such Act of Government however I am not against. Only I'm persuaded, it could never take full Effect under our present unhappy Circumstances, nor have the least Tendency to fix the Rate of Silver in the Market: For Silver, whether sold for Bills or exchanged in Barter, will always be rated according to the Course of Trade, at 20, 40 or any greater or lesser Number of Shillings per Ounce, variable till our Trade takes a new and more favourable Turn.

The Sum of what he says as to *Bills* emitted on a *Silver Bottom*, may be collected from *Pages* 43, 44, *viz.* "That however well *regulated* they might be as to *Periods* and *Discounts*, yet such Notes could never answer the Ends of a *Currency*; Nay in that Regard would be *worse than common Bills*, in Case there be any bad *concomitant* Currency, as *Rhode-Island Bills* &c. or unless a *Discount* be forced on those Emissions at least for the future." — I have already been large on this Subject, and made it appear, that *no Scheme* for emitting Bills on a *Silver-Fund*, and distant Period, whether publick or private, bearing more or less or no Interest, can effectually circulate as *Money* in our present Condition, and this whether we have other *concomitant* Bills or not : And the Way to put this Affair to the Test may be this; Let the Government give a Sanction to those Gentlemen's Scheme of a private Bank (which I agree with him is on some Accounts better than publick Emissions) who are for a Silver-Bottom, allowing them to emit Bills in any reasonable Shape, with this *Proviso*, That they shall undertake at all Times to *lend them out on such Security* as the Bank of *England* would gladly accept of, at an assigned *moderate Interest*, and further at all Times to *supply the Trade with Silver* at 29 *s.* per *Ounce*, or Bills of Exchange to *London* at — per Cent. as Returns to the Mother Country, and no other Place whatever. —— Now if they will enter into and execute any such reasonable Engagements, they may attain to fix the Rate of Silver; otherwise not.

[75] As to a *Discount* on *Rhode-Island* Bills &c. there's no doubt, common Consent might effect that, or might even destroy their Credit in this Province, by refusing them any Acceptance at all; But then it must be consider'd, the same might at least as easily be done on their Side by Way of Reprisal : And probably we should be no great Gainers. — Neither of these are likely to happen at present.

Page 42. "*Land Banks*: *The famous Mr.* Law" &c. Here he begins with a strange Excursion to attack that Gentleman's moral Character, doubtless with a View to prejudice the Reader against a *Land Bank*. But it's enough to my present Purpose, that he is allowed by very good Judges, to have wrote judiciously on Money and Trade, and concurring in his general Principles with the great Mr. *Lock*. Our Author here would palm an Absurdity upon Mr. *Law*, insinuating that in a Passage quoted from him, he meant, that *Land* (simply consider'd) could be negotiated as effective Money in the Market, and makes this wonderful Observation upon it, back'd with Reasons, viz. *It's ridiculous to imagine that it can serve as a Medium for foreign Commerce; because it cannot be ship'd off* &c Whereas Mr. *Law* through the whole Tenor of his Discourse only says, that *Land* is the best Security or Fund for a Bank (losing none of it's other Uses at the same Time) which Fund may be negotiated by *Bills* or *Transfers*. In all Countries even a common *Mortgage* may be used in some Measure as *Money*, being reducible to Silver or any other Commodity, for domestick or foreign Occasions. The Bank of *Scotland* (one of the best in the World of it's Bigness) is founded on *Land-Security*; and when it has happened to be shut up on some very extraordinary Occasions (as *Anno* 1715.) yet their Bills have nevertheless passed current, chiefly from the Reputation of its Security.

I have already observed, that we in *New-England* have not one Material that can be negotiated, as *Silver* is, in the Way of a *Bank*; and all that I understand by *Land Security* is only a Security to the Possessor, that the Bills emitted by the Bank shall have ready *Acceptance* at all Times by the *Bankers* themselves; to which if *common Consent* be added (for without that no Bills nor Commodity would answer the End of *Money*) such Bills would be upon as good a Bottom as any at all.

[**76**] Page 44. "*If the Scheme for emitting Company-Notes to be paid after fifteen Years*" &c. — It is to a Degree surprizing to find our Author patronizing a Scheme for Bills promising Silver at 20 s. per Ounce, at so long a Period, and without Interest, after he had been (in the Paragraph immediately before) inveighing against the *Merchants-Notes*, as a *Snare to many*, tho' upon a much better Foot than the Bills upon this Scheme; and after he had been condemning the *Maryland* Bills, and above all after he had through his whole Discourse declared in the strongest Terms against all such Bills; more particularly mentioning the Case of *Barbadoes* twice, and yet their Emission was no Ways to be compared to this now projected, being only liable to a Discount of l. 41 upon l. 141, whereas these now proposed ought not to be received any otherwise than l. 238 in Bills for l. 100 in Silver at 20 s. per Ounce prompt Payment, or in other Words, these Bills promising on the Face of them 100 Ounces of Silver, only equal to 42 Ounces on the Day of their first Emission. There were no *concomitant bad Bills* (as he calls them) in *Barbadoes*, nor *Maryland*; the Discounts were owing wholly to their distant Periods and short Allowances of Interest or Premium. And whatever he may propose and inculcate upon these Gentlemen as to their forcing a Discount on *Rhode-Island* Bills, or periodically raising the Value of their own Bills, *i e.* bringing them by certain Degrees in an arbitrary Manner up to their Promise of Silver 20 s. per Ounce, I am persuaded it will have no Influence at all to lower the natural Rate of Silver in the Market, will be hurtful to Trade, and unavoidably will open a Door for great Oppression to Debtors of all Sorts, who shall unhappily by their Contracts be made liable to

pay in these Bills, and so will become a *Snare* indeed to the People, as he often insinuates *Banks* in general will certainly prove. — I spare all Reflections here upon the Gentlemen so zealous for a *Silver-Fund,* as to the *Views* they may have, tho' our Author is very satyrical upon those who desire a *Land-Bank,* in his Reflection *Page* 42. which perhaps might be retorted; but I take no Pleasure in such kind of Censures; and shall return to his *Discourse* touching a Projection upon another Foot.

Page 42. "*A Credit or Bank of Produce and Manufacture*" &c. To pass over his indecent and unjust Censure upon the Country in general, and keeping to the Point, I shall observe, that although this Bank, I apprehend, is [77] not yet so well regulated, as it might be, yet I am persuaded the chief Managers are willing and desirous to remove all Objections, and to make all reasonable Alterations. I am not without Hopes therefore, it may turn out a seasonable Relief for our present distressing Circumstances.

Their *Design* is highly laudable, and I have no Reason to doubt that they have an *honest* View to the publick Good: Their *Foundation,* Land-Security, vastly preferable to any other: The *Subscribers* numerous, and principally Men of clear real Estate.

The general Promise of their Bill, viz. "*to receive this Twenty Shilling Bill as so much Money in all Payments,* is unexceptionable. Only I am of Opinion, that the Limitation to *lawful* Money might better be left out; it appearing to me utterly impracticable under the present unhappy Circumstances of our Trade, to negotiate the Bill in an exact Conformity to such *special* Promise (and so far it's liable to the same Objection as Bills upon a Silver-Bottom) for after all it will pass only equal to the current Rate of Silver, and other Things in the Market.

The allowing their Undertakers to pay Principal and Interest in *Produce* at certain regulated Prices, may have a Tendency to promote Industry, and so far be of the Nature of a Bounty. —

As to the Majority of the *Directors*, and the Majority of the *Partners*, being obliged to act in *Concurrence* in some Particulars of the Management, which our Author exclaims so much against, where is the prodigious *Inconsistency* of it? any more than in the several Branches of our Legislature having a Negative upon each other in the Management of the publick Funds and Loans &c. The Directors are to be first chosen, and future Vacancies supply'd by the Majority of the whole Society; also to be under Oath, and give Security: And I cannot conceive then how it can hurt the Possessor of the Bill, but rather think it may be a Benefit to him: However, that might easily be altered, if it should be thought requisite. — The whole Company are obliged to receive the Bill in all their Dealings: But the grand Point, as to general Currency, will be *common Consent*, without which no Bills can circulate.

Upon the whole, as this Scheme is built upon the best and only good Foundation we have, and has already met with some considerable Encouragement from Men of [**78**] Judgment, of Integrity, and sufficient Estates, I think it would be more generous in our Author, and others, who profess themselves Friends to the Province, to make experiment of what may be effected on the Foot of this Projection, than to raise Cavils at it without advancing a better.

He has offered every Thing to *perplex* the Affair, and

distress the Province, and nothing for it's *Relief* but what is either *impracticable*, or has a *ruinous* Tendency, by leaving us to the miserable Shifts of a *Trucking-Trade*, or *Shop-Notes*, which no Country of so large a trading Interest as this can long subsist under.

The Gentleman often shakes his Rod over us by threatning us with a *Parliamentary Inquiry;* but I have such an Opinion of the Wisdom and Justice of the Parliament of *Great Britain*, that I am in no Apprehension of any Severities from Home. It appears they are not insensible of the absolute Necessity this Province is in of having *Bills*, to pass as Money under our present Circumstances; since *Silver* will always be ship'd off, and none of it be kept here, till we have a Balance of Trade in our Favour.

To conclude,

Our *Author* makes a Random-Charge, that many will think unhappily recoils upon himself (Page 45) "*Some audaciously question the Power — Others impudently impeach the Integrity of the Majority of our Legislature*" &c. This would naturally lead me to take some Notice of his own numerous and gross Reflections upon the *civil Administration*, more particularly level'd at the *democratick Part of our Constitution* (as he calls it) or our House of *Representatives;* But they must be sufficiently obvious to his Readers, nor need any Comments to aggravate them; and having no Pertinence to the Business in Hand, I shall wave all Consideration of them.

FINIS

NOTE TO "AN INQUIRY INTO THE NATURE AND USES OF MONEY," ETC.

On the 15th of April, 1740, there appeared in the New England Weekly Journal the following advertisement:

This Afternoon will be Published, Sold by Kneeland & Green *in Queen-Street,*

A N Inquiry into the Nature & Uses of Money, more especially of the Bills of Publick Credit, old Tenor. Together with Proposals of some proper Relief in the present Exigence. To which is added a Reply to a former Essay on Silver and Paper Currences. As also a Postscript containing Remarks on a late Discourse concerning the Currencies.

The same advertisement was repeated in the Weekly Journal of the 22d. "Some Observations on the Scheme for £60.000," etc., was dated February 1, 1737–8. From internal evidence it is plain that the "Inquiry," etc., was written in the latter part of 1739 and in the beginning of 1740. Its apparent purpose was to meet the arguments put forth by Douglass in his "Essay concerning silver and paper currencies," etc. In this pamphlet Douglass prefaced an attack on "Some observations," etc., with a preliminary discussion of money, exchange, and of the laws affecting circulation so far as they were then known. In a similar way the author of this pamphlet introduced his main purpose, a reply to the "Essay," by a treatise on value, prices, money and banks, concluding the pamphlet as originally constructed with his reply to the "Essay." The preliminary discussion was essential for the comprehension of the argument, since the author differed materially from his antagonist both as to the meaning of the technical terms used in their pamphlets and as to the interpretation of historical events. While the "Inquiry," etc., was in press, Douglass's "Discourse" was published. A postscript was promptly added to the "Inquiry," etc., and in this form the publication was put forth.

The writer is not an ardent advocate of the "Land Bank." He believes abstractly in the principles on which this company was founded but does not approve of the scheme in detail. He suggests several methods of relieving the situation. The first of these was that a fund of £100,000 sterling should be established in London, by borrowing from the Bank of England on land security. With this fund as a basis, notes running for three or six months, payable in sterling drafts, might be emitted. These notes could be loaned to borrowers who should be required to pay the loans in notes of a similar character.

A second suggestion was to emit bills which should be loaned on good security at four per cent interest to borrowers who would pay their loans in silver at 29 s. an ounce. Differences in payments of principal and interest due to variation in the market price of silver to be adjusted "on the same Foot that the *Bankers* allow to the *Possessors*."

He describes the Bank of Venice, the depositors in which, he says, had given them on the books of the Bank, credit which could be disposed of by transfer in payments of debts, without using gold or silver. He doubts the statement that the bank had emitted bills. The Bank of Amsterdam he defines to be "a Bank of *pure credit;* founded upon common Consent; *no Silver* taken out, nor will it probably ever be the Interest of any Man to demand it." He submits a scheme for extricating the province from its present difficulties. A number of men were to associate themselves together and emit bills which in terms would express that the subscribers to the association would receive them on the basis of old tenor. Those who entered into the undertaking were to give security that they would carry out their agreement. They were to take out only ten per cent of their subscriptions. The association was to loan these bills and to discount commercial paper, but was to receive over its counters only its own bills and silver and gold.

Following this came the review of the "Essay concerning silver and paper currencies," etc., in which attempts are made to refute specific statements, to correct erroneous assertions, and to defend the language used in " Some observations," etc., from the aspersions of Douglass. The statement made in the " Essay," that " *Baron* Gortz *about twenty Years ago had reduced* Sweeden *to extream Misery by imposing Government-Notes instead of Specie*," is, for instance, specifically replied to as follows: "I was in *Stockholm*, the Capital, in the Year 1718, being the last of *Charles* XII and never then nor since heard of any *State-Bills* passing about that Time . . ."

The "Inquiry," etc., with its reply to the "Essay" filled sixty-three pages of the pamphlet and was evidently made up by the compositors with intent to issue it in that form. It was, however, held back by the author long enough for him to add to it a postscript of fifteen pages in length, devoted to the purpose of refuting Douglass's assertions and answering his arguments.

The "Inquiry," etc., is to be found in the Library of the American Antiquarian Society, the Boston Athenæum, the Boston Public Library, the Library of Harvard College, the John Carter Brown Library, the Library of Congress, and the New York Public Library. Professor F. B. Dexter informs me that there is also a copy in the Library of Yale University. The leaves measure 7⅞ by 4⅝ inches.

The "Inquiry," was anonymously published, although the writer gave one hint as to the authorship which may perhaps have served to help contemporaries penetrate behind the curtain of anonymity when he acknowledged, as he did on page 45 of the pamphlet, that he was also the author of "Some observations." There is nothing to indicate that he knew who wrote the "Discourse" although he recognized the fact that the "Discourse" and "Essay" were from the same pen and so stated in the opening sentence of his postscript. The writings of Douglass were easily to be identified by their style. He was a prolific author with whose publications readers of many types were familiar. Furthermore he continued, so long as there was any chance for participating in the polemics of the currency controversy, to publish from time to time new pamphlets on the subject; hence, it was impossible for the authorship of the "Essay" and the "Discourse" to remain unknown. Such was not the case with the author of "Some observations" and the "Inquiry." These two pamphlets stood by themselves, did not attract much attention outside the disciples of the doctrines of the Land Bank, and the author did not, so far as we know, follow them up by later contributions to the controversy. His name was first made known in recent publications through the following entry made on page 394 of the sixth number of the twelfth volume of the Bulletin of the New York Public Library: "'By Mr. Hugh Vance, Mercht.' is written on the title-page in an eighteenth-century hand." The Boston Athenæum possesses a copy of the pamphlet which also carries an inscription which apparently corroborates this statement as to the authorship. The edges of this copy have been trimmed off in the process of binding, and the inscription has thereby suffered. In addition some indiscreet person has superimposed a number, perhaps a shelf-mark, directly over the last name of the author. Enough remains, however, to enable us to make out the following legend: "The Gift of the Author Mr Hugh Vans Me[   ] in Boston, to —— J. Lowell." Through the courtesy of the Athenæum the facsimile of the title-page of the pamphlet was procured from that copy. A glance at this will show that without the suggestion derived from the New York inscription, the last name of the author could not have been easily deciphered.

The name, which is thought originally to have been De Vans and finally to have become Vance, suggests the idea that the family were Huguenots. A grandson of the author of the "Inquiry," a hundred years later, advanced this theory in a publication which he put forth as a disappointed litigant.[1] Hugh Vance left behind him enough traces of his career to enable us to classify him among the respectable merchants of Boston of that day. Such items concerning his connection with current events as could be found in our records have been collated and published in a paper entitled "Two Forgotten Pamphleteers in the Massachusetts Currency Controversy, 1720–1740," which was reprinted from the Proceedings of the Massachusetts Historical Society for March, 1910. From this paper the following deductions from these items are quoted:[2]

"He appears before us as an honored citizen of Boston, whom his fellow citizens made use of from year to year upon important committees. He published pamphlets which contain within their pages marks of study and of intellectual capacity for independent

---

[1] A new edition of the demand of William Vans on Stephen Codman. Boston, 1824.

[2] Two Forgotten Pamphleteers, etc., p. 21.

analysis. His whimsical theories must not be judged by the stand-
ards of to-day. The paper-money men of that time were the
pioneers in the promulgation of the doctrines of credit which have
resulted in the wonderful development of the use of money in our
day, through bank-bills, checks and drafts. The doctrines of the
hard-money men applied to their full extent would 'have held the
world back in its progress. Neither side in the discussion appre-
ciated fully what they were talking about. It is for us to-day to
recognize merit where we can see it, whether on the one side or
the other."

The copy made use of in this reprint was made from a copy of the
pamphlet in my own possession. The true chronological sequence
of the publication is violated by the introduction of the " Inquiry "
immediately after the " Discourse." In the polemical discussion, however, this is its true place, and as its relegation to the next volume
would reduce this volume below the size of the others and on the
other hand disproportionately swell the fourth volume, it has been
thought best to violate the chronological sequence of the pamphlets
in behalf of uniformity of size in the volumes.

It may be added, moreover, that the " Letter from a country
gentleman at Boston," etc., which precedes the " Inquiry" in the
chronological list in Volume I, should by rights have followed it.

INDEX

INDEX

Council of the Prince Society

1911